FREEDOM'S DAUGHTER

FREEDOM'S DAUGHTER

LETTERS
BETWEEN
INDIRA GANDHI
AND
JAWAHARLAL
NEHRU

1922-39

Edited by

Sonia Gandhi

Hodder & Stoughton
LONDON SYDNEY AUCKLAND TORONTO

British Library Cataloguing in Publication Data

Freedom's daughter: letters between Indira Gandhi and
    Jawaharlal Nehru, 1922–39
    1. India (Republic). Gandhi, Indira, 1917–1984.
    Correspondence with Nehru, Jawaharlal, 1889–1964
    I. Gandhi, Sonia
    954.04'092'4

ISBN 0-340-43042-7

First published in Great Britain 1989

Published by Hodder and Stoughton,
a division of Hodder and Stoughton Ltd,
Mill Road, Dunton Green, Sevenoaks, Kent TN13 2YE
Editorial Office: 47 Bedford Square, London WC1B 3DP

Photoset by Rowland Phototypesetting Ltd,
Bury St Edmunds, Suffolk

Printed in Great Britain by St Edmundsbury Press Ltd,
Bury St Edmunds, Suffolk

CONTENTS

ILLUSTRATIONS

(between pages 246 and 247)

Indira at six months old
Indira, one year old, with her father and mother
The old Anand Bhawan, where Indira was born
Indira with her grandmother and other members of the family
Family group in Geneva in 1926
Indira in a school performance
Geneva studio portraits of Indira
With two school friends in Switzerland
A letter to her parents
Jawaharlal Nehru at the Lahore session of the Congress
Indira with her parents in 1931
Pupils' Own school group
A holiday in Kashmir, 1934
Indira and Kamala in the porch at Anand Bhawan
Kamala and Indira at Panchagani, 1932
Indira with Mahatma Gandhi in Bombay
With Rabindranath Tagore in Santiniketan
Indira and two friends in Santiniketan
Excursion to Italy, 1936
Indira with Feroze and Madan Atal in Switzerland
Group photograph, Somerville College, Oxford
With her father during a visit to Malaya, 1937
Skiing holiday in 1939
Portrait of Indira taken by Feroze Gandhi
At a sanatorium in Switzerland, 1939

ACKNOWLEDGEMENTS

The poem 'Why do you walk through the field in gloves' by Frances Cornford is quoted by kind permission of the Trustees of the late Frances Cornford.

All the illustrations appear through the kind offices of the Indira Gandhi Memorial Trust, New Delhi.

INTRODUCTION

Indira Gandhi occupies a very special place in twentieth century history. She presided over the destiny of India for sixteen years as Prime Minister. One of her distinguishing attributes was a special concern for the very poor. She possessed great intellect, a rational perception and an acute understanding of peoples and problems. Above all, Indira Gandhi was gifted with a great sensitivity to Nature and the arts. These qualities went together with a formidable will and a physical and moral courage of rare quality. Yet, in spite of her innumerable achievements and her place in history, she was a very private person and, perhaps because of this, much misunderstood. To the very few who were close to her she was a most concerned and loving human being.

This first volume of the correspondence between Indira Gandhi and Jawaharlal Nehru covers the years 1922 to 1939 and shows us the changing relationship between father and daughter. The letters throw new light on Indira Gandhi's character and personality and on how these developed from a very early stage.

In order to fully understand these letters, it is necessary to say a few words about the family into which she was born. The Nehrus had migrated from Kashmir to the city of Delhi in the eighteenth century to serve in the Mughal court. Their fortunes were adversely affected during the Uprising of 1857, also known as the Indian Mutiny. They were obliged to take shelter in Agra, then moved to Kanpur and ultimately to Allahabad. Motilal Nehru, grandfather of Indira Gandhi, earned for himself a position of eminence as a lawyer as well as a nationalist. His son, Jawaharlal Nehru, went to Harrow and Cambridge and was called to the Bar from the Inner Temple. On his return, a legal career did not seem to absorb him. The stormy happenings of the time fascinated him much more. He participated in political gatherings. When a local chapter of the Home Rule League launched by Annie Besant opened in Allahabad during the First World War, he was immediately drawn into what was then the most militant manifestation of nationalism within India.

In 1916 Jawaharlal Nehru married Kamala Kaul. The Kauls, like the Nehrus, were Kashmiris. Though they lacked the social prominence which Motilal's successes had brought to his family, they were greatly respected in their community. Kamala Nehru was seventeen when she came to Anand Bhawan. The cultural environment of her family home had been much less westernised than that of her in-laws. This called for a good measure of adjustment by the young bride. However, Kamala possessed great inner strength and resilience. Between Kamala and her husband there gradually grew deep affection and understanding. She was to die young. Nehru's feelings for her were expressed in his autobiography which was dedicated 'To Kamala who is no more'.

No account of the family would be complete if it did not dwell upon Motilal Nehru. To outsiders, Motilal Nehru was the heroic public figure whose standing in the legal profession and in the nationalist struggle had earned for him a place among a select few in India. To the members of his family, he was a loving husband and a father who doted on his son, Jawaharlal, as well as his daughters, Vijaya Lakshmi and Krishna.

The birth of his first grandchild in 1917 filled Motilal with joy. 'This girl is going to be worth more than a thousand grandsons,' he observed with pride. Throughout the remaining years of his life, young Indira had a special place in his heart. Swarup Rani, Motilal Nehru's wife, who was 'Dol Amma' to Indira, completed, along with Jawaharlal's two sisters, the inner circle of the large household.

While Indira Priyadarshini (as she was called by her father), was still very young the family came under the influence of Mahatma Gandhi. This changed their lives dramatically. Sensitive and observant Indira, who was an only child, grew up in an environment from which her father, grandfather and mother could be suddenly taken away for long periods to 'the other home' – prison. Fortunately for her, even in the midst of such happenings there was time for the tender written dialogue which so powerfully shaped her personality. This exchange flowed from the bonds of affection which are such a distinctive feature of relationships within families in India.

Jawaharlal Nehru strongly believed that his daughter should grow up in a milieu which would increase her critical faculties and widen the range of her intellectual interests. He held the view that a liberal education through formal and informal channels was the best possible basis for shaping young minds. It is this belief and his concern for his daughter which prompted him to write to her a series of letters on the history of the world. These were later published as a book entitled *Glimpses of World History*.

The fact that Indira Gandhi grew up in an intensely political family where participation in public life was taken as a natural order of things, instilled in her a strong sense of commitment to the struggle for freedom. In the early 1920s, Mahatma Gandhi launched a Satyagraha, or non-cooperation movement, against the British Government. It was at this time that the first arrests, already referred to, were carried out in Anand Bhawan. The policy of the Congress was not to pay the fines imposed by the British Government. As a result, the police would often visit the house to realise the fines by taking away valuables and attaching properties.

Indira observed with great interest the stir around her. Her receptive young mind took stock of everything and she was much affected by the manner in which her family sacrificed its possessions and comforts for the country's liberty. A glimpse of how determined she was not to be left out of any activity connected with the fight for freedom comes through to us in an incident which took place when she was five years old. As a part of the boycott of foreign textiles, Motilal and Jawaharlal decided to have a huge fire of imported clothes and materials in Anand Bhawan. Indira asked her father for permission to be present. Jawaharlal did not give his consent since the bonfire was to be lit very late at night, when it was time for children to be asleep. However, she had decided to have her way. 'I did not take it lying down and went to my grandfather,' she later recalled. 'I told him that whatever the circumstances, I would go to the bonfire.' He promised to take her with him. Perhaps Motilal Nehru discerned in his grandchild's temperament a reflection of his own firmness and willpower.

In 1926 Jawaharlal, Kamala and other members of the family journeyed to Europe with Indira. After a period of travelling, Jawaharlal thought it appropriate to enrol his daughter, who was nine years old, as a pupil in the International School in Geneva and then in Ecole Nouvelle in nearby Bex. The latter was run by Mlle L. Hemmerlin. Later in life, while reminiscing about her student, Mlle Hemmerlin touched upon the extent to which the movement for liberating India had left a mark upon the young child:

> She greeted everybody with a winning smile and was very popular among her companions . . . Indira had a clear outlook about her country and a firm will to free it from foreign power . . .
> She often pronounced the name of Gandhi . . . She told us why he had fasted with risk to his life and how non-violent resistance was more powerful than hatred or weapons . . . The link between Gandhi and the whole world was created by Indira Nehru and lasts for ever.[1]

The political education which Indira received in the first few years of her life was reinforced by her experience of the next phase of the nationalist agitation in India in the 1930s. This was triggered off by the adoption of a resolution in 1929 by the Indian National Congress under the presidentship of Jawaharlal Nehru. The objective of the freedom struggle was defined as Purna Swaraj – complete independence as opposed to Dominion Status, favoured by a section of the Congress. She, in later years, was to recount with pride how she had been asked by her father to read out to him the 'Pledge of Independence' which he had drafted and how deeply moved she had been by this experience.

1. From *The Spirit of India*, Vol. I, Bombay, 1975.

Indira's early education had been unconventional. Jawaharlal Nehru in 1931 decided to send her to the Pupils' Own School at Poona, near Bombay. The school had been opened by a young couple, the Vakils, with a view to creating in children an awareness of their cultural heritage. Indira spent three years there. As in the school at Bex, both her teachers and schoolmates were struck by her quiet air of confidence and her eagerness to help those around her. Her flair for leadership became evident during her time at school. Indira was the President of the Sahitya Sabha, a literary society; she was editor of the school magazine and 'chief justice' of the school committee. Her letters from Poona during the early thirties were full of accounts of contemporary events, revealing the deep impression they made on her. In September 1932, Mahatma Gandhi, who had earlier been imprisoned in Yeravda Jail, near Poona, embarked upon a fast unto death in protest against the British attempt to create a separate electoral identity for the untouchable community. Indira wrote to her father:

> On 20th September when Bapu began his fast we all fasted here and had prayers. We also entered a new pupil. Of course pupils are entered nearly every week but this was a new kind – one, like whom we have never had before. Can you guess who she was? She was the daughter of our *mehatrani* – an untouchable. Of course she is to be taught free of charge . . . She is five years old and her name was Ura, but we had changed it to Urvashi . . .

In her letter dated 27th September we can see how intensely she shared Gandhiji's ordeal during his epic fast of September 1932. She sent her father a daily account of it.

> Bapu was looking very cheerful and certainly much better than yesterday. Yesterday he was very bad and the doctors were very anxious.

She also wrote to her father about the manner in which the fast was broken:

> At noon the Superintendent gave the good news that the telegram was on its way to Poona. Padmaja, Mummy and I rushed to the market and got the best oranges and other fruit that we could get. When we got back, we found that there was yet some time for the telegram to come, so we waited and each minute seemed an hour. When at last the telegram came Bapu said that he would not break his fast, till Dr Ambedkar had heard the contents of the telegram and agreed to them.

Dr Ambedkar was in Bombay, and it would have taken quite a lot of time for him to come. And it was nearly five o'clock and Bapu does not eat anything after six. So everybody, including Dr Tagore and the jail authorities, persuaded him not to wait for Dr Ambedkar. So immediately I prepared the juice of two oranges for him. Then Dr Tagore sang a Bengali hymn and the Ashram people sang Bapu's favourite *bhajan* 'Vaishnav Jan'. Then Bapu drank the juice and everybody was given fruit and sweets as prasad. Then we all went home happy after an anxious day.

Today I am in an extra good mood, for I think that it is the happiest day we have had for a very long time. It is Bapu's sixty-fourth birthday and he has begun eating fruit and he is much better than before.

After Indira's schooling in Poona was completed, Jawaharlal Nehru decided to send her to Santiniketan in Bengal. The poet Rabindranath Tagore had started a unique centre of learning, where gifted scholars and artists were gathered to teach. They encouraged the students to explore the intellectual and artistic world around them. The presence of Rabindranath Tagore was a source of inspiration to Indira and it made an indelible impact on her.

Soon after her arrival there she wrote:

I had better give you my opinion of the place. As yet I have only seen the girls' hostel and the office and have had a glimpse of the Library and Kala Bhavan. Everything is so artistic and beautiful and wild.

Indira's stay at Santiniketan was indeed an experience which enriched and transformed her. In a letter which she wrote to her father some time later she said:

I was glad of my stay in Santiniketan – chiefly because of Gurudev. In the very atmosphere there, his spirit seemed to roam and hover over one and follow one with a loving though deep watchfulness. And this spirit, I feel, has greatly influenced my life and thought . . .

Jawaharlal Nehru spent about a decade in various prisons in nine spells between 1921 and 1945. While in jail, the pain of isolation and separation from those he loved imposed on him a deep moral and psychological strain. 'Priyadarshini, dear to the sight,' he wrote to Indira from prison in 1933, 'but dearer still when sight is denied.'

Equally touching were the letters which Indira wrote to her father while he was away:

Ever since early this morning we were all waiting impatiently for your letter . . . But when the postman came we were very much disappointed. Anyhow I hope it will come soon – perhaps tomorrow . . .

It will soon be your birthday – on the 14th . . . All day we will be thinking of you. Of course I always am – but that day you will be more in my mind . . .

In 1934, Kamala's health suddenly deteriorated. Indira was therefore obliged to cut short her studies in Santiniketan. Kamala had been unwell earlier, in the twenties, but a course of treatment in Europe in 1926 had helped her considerably. Since Jawaharlal Nehru was in jail, Indira accompanied her mother to a sanatorium in Bhowali in the Himalayas. Later, she travelled with Kamala to Badenweiler in Germany, where the doctors had advised treatment. At Badenweiler Kamala's condition became so serious that Jawaharlal Nehru, too, was released from jail to enable him to be by her side. We have a moving account of Indira looking after her mother during her last illness:

Indira used to look stunned watching her mother struggling between life and death. There seemed a very close bond between mother and daughter and their eyes spoke the same language, a language of courage and sadness.

Kamala's death shortly afterwards in February 1936 was a great tragedy for Indira and Jawaharlal. Leaving his daughter behind in Europe to pursue her studies, Jawaharlal travelled back to India with the ashes of his wife in order to immerse them in the river Ganges. The letters, as if by tacit agreement, make no mention of Kamala, but they speak of the true loneliness which now descended upon him:

I have been living here in Anand Bhawan, a solitary individual . . . working alone except when I am in [the] office. I sit here in my room and the door connecting it with your room is usually open. And at night, and sometimes in the day-time too, I go to your room and have a look round and say good night to it. Your presence seems to hover around the room and I have not liked the idea of disturbing anything in it. Various oddments lie about, as you left them, and one has the feeling that the room has been recently occupied . . .

I rejoice in your letters which tell me of your life full of activity and work and joy. Your written word brings innumerable pictures to my mind, a crowd of memories and visions of days gone by, and the sense of emptiness in this silent deserted house goes from me. For otherwise it is

a lone house filled
with the cricket's call;
and the scampering mouse
in the hollow wall.

In 1937, Indira was to return from Europe to Anand Bhawan for the first time after her mother's death. She was now a young woman with intellectual interests and emotional attachments of her own, reflecting a new stage in the development of her personality. Feroze Gandhi, a young political activist from her home town, had grown very fond of Indira. She reciprocated his feelings. He had been known to the family, particularly to Kamala whose simplicity and sincerity of purpose he had greatly admired. After a few months in India, Indira was anxious to return to Great Britain to pursue her studies. Feroze, too, was a student in London. A contemporary at Oxford who travelled with her from Bombay has left us a telling portrait of Indira. As they embarked the ship, the *Viceroy of India*, Kamila Tyabji observes:

I wept bitterly . . . Indira, on the other hand, was calm, unruffled. It was the first glimpse I had of that intrepid training from her father she had had from her earliest years; the suffering, and the inevitable hardening that her family's intense involvement in the independence struggle had caused her. She was already a veteran at parting. We stood side by side, waving, as the ship sailed away; she, perfectly controlled, whilst I just did not know what to do with my tears . . .

Indira's brief stay at Oxford in 1937–9 was a period of great intellectual stimulus for her. In a very different way from Santiniketan, where she had gained an understanding of the cultural traditions of India at the feet of Rabindranath Tagore, Oxford greatly extended her horizons. She established rapport with people of radical and left-wing opinion in Great Britain. Indian students in Oxford were completely immersed in politics in the late 1930s, especially through the Indian Majlis, which provided a platform for debate on the great political issues of the day. Yet Indira's circle was wider than that of most students. The radical nationalist, V. K. Krishna Menon, who was a great admirer of Jawaharlal Nehru, took a special interest in her and drew her into socialist and anti-imperialist work in London.

From Oxford she wrote to her father:

. . . [I] went to tea with H. A. L. Fisher. He is awfully nice and his wife is perfectly charming – I wonder if you have met her. There were a number of New College freshers there . . . I had a marvellous time.

Then I had dinner with Mrs Rhys Davis and the Majlis Executive – afterwards was the Majlis meeting at which Mrs Rhys Davis spoke. By the way, I do not remember whether in my last letter I told you that I have become the Women's Secretary of the Majlis . . .

. . . I think I have told you that I have joined only two societies in Oxford – the Indian Majlis and the University Labour Club. There are all shades of opinion in the Labour Club and it is not affiliated to the Labour Party. But in two days is the County Council election and we want the Labour candidate to get in. I went out canvassing one night and spent a good hour yesterday folding and filling in blanks in election addresses.

In December 1939 Indira's health, which had been delicate, began to deteriorate, forcing her to interrupt her studies again. She was sent to a sanatorium in Leysin in Switzerland to recover from a bout of pleurisy. Away from her friends and from College, a strong feeling of depression came over her. However, she fought her illness with determination. With the worsening of the political situation in Europe, Indira decided to return to India. She began to plan her return journey in an atmosphere full of insecurity about her own future, as well as that of the world. Even in this moment of crisis, however, her poise and strength did not desert her. She wrote to her father:

So I left the money – just in case I needed it on my journey to India, when taking money out of England would be difficult. I am telling you this so that you may claim this money – just in case (this is highly improbable, but still) anything should happen to me. There is no point in making a present of it to Cook's.

While studying in England, Indira Nehru took an interest in the world political situation. She belonged to a young group of people who at Oxford followed closely the struggle between two opposite political and social currents: fascism and socialism. Indira's radical perspective from which she viewed world politics led her to differ from her father. This is obvious in her comment to Jawaharlal Nehru on his article on the Soviet Union which he wrote in 1940:

I have just been reading in the *National Herald* your article on Russia and the Finnish war . . . You seemed to be shocked equally by the Russo-German Pact and the war on Finland. And yet, doesn't the responsibility of both rest heavily on these eight years of British foreign policy? At Munich, England and France proved definitely on which side they stood. Russia's policy of collective security having failed, she retired into her pre-Litvinov isolation and her chief preoccupation was bound to be how to keep herself out of the impending European war. (Hence the advance into the Baltic.) The Russo-German Pact was certainly not a change of front, since Germany primarily asked no more of Russia than that this isolation should continue. And the pact has not made any difference to the Soviet Union's condemnation of Nazism and Imperialism – viz. Molotov's speech in November or the Manifesto of the Communist International on the present war. As to Finland, you agree that the Soviet Union's demands were justified. Why, then, did the war come as such a shock to you? Did you expect the Soviet Union, after her demands had been rejected at the instigation of the Allies, to sit back and say no more about it until the whole war should be directed against her? For such was – is still – the intention of the Allies, as the British press is at no pains to conceal . . .

It took months for Indira to reach London from Switzerland and months more to find a passage back to India round the Cape of Good Hope. It was April 1941 by the time she reached Allahabad. She was now in her early twenties. Feroze Gandhi and Indira had decided to marry. Because of different backgrounds the thought of such an unconventional union worried Jawaharlal Nehru. He initially reacted negatively to the proposal. However, as soon as he realised the depth of the feelings which existed between the two young people, he gave his consent. Indira Nehru married Feroze Gandhi on 26th March, 1942 in Allahabad. Indira's aunt, Mrs Krishna Hutheesing, has left a moving account of the wedding:

Lovely to look at, on this special occasion she looked lovelier than ever, frail and almost ethereal. She laughed and talked to those around her but sometimes her big black eyes would darken and hold a distant and sorrowful look. What dark cloud could mar the joy of this happy day? Was it due to a longing for the young mother who was no more, by whose absence a void had been created which even on this day remained unfilled? Or was it the thought of parting from the father, a father whose very life she had been?

Soon after their marriage the couple travelled to Kashmir, but the intensification of the political struggle made them return to Allahabad. The British Government had made it clear that it would not grant autonomy to India during the war. In August 1942, after the adoption of the 'Quit India' Resolution, Jawaharlal Nehru was imprisoned together with all the prominent political leaders of India. Indira Gandhi too was arrested in September 1942. In Naini Central Jail she involved herself in extensive reading and in looking after her fellow prisoners, amongst them a little child, the daughter of one of the jail inmates. Life in prison also gave her the rare opportunity to spend many delightful hours observing plants, trees and birds within the prison compound:

> Whatever differences stone walls and iron bars may make to the human soul, let us be thankful that they offer no obstacle to the vegetable kingdom, which follows the cycle of the seasons, year in and year out, come war or peace. We have a Peepal in our yard – a tree which, had it depended upon human praise and approbation, would have withered away long since. However, it ignored our derision and went on its lordly way. And now that Phalgun is come again, the few remaining shreds of last year's garment, yellow with age are being shed off and its bare limbs are being clothed in glorious sunset pink. It looks as if a deep blush were spreading along the branches which gives it rather a coy look. Amazingly beautiful it is. But spring doesn't last long and soon summer will transform this flimsy pinky garment into the thicker and more service-able green one.

Indira Gandhi was released from prison in 1943 while her father was to remain in jail for three long years. After her release, she wrote to her father frequently, keeping him informed on what was happening outside. She was soon to speak to him about the joys of becoming a mother. She went to Bombay to stay with her aunt for the coming event. The month of May found her in Matheran from where she wrote to her father:

> I have collected from Chhoti Puphi all the books on children and babies that she possessed and have brought them here. I am rather awed by the responsibility of bringing a new person into the world and of having complete control over his life . . .

Indira gave birth to her son Rajiv on 20th August, 1944. Her letters to her father, still imprisoned, are now full of the excitement and fulfilment of a mother observing the rapid growth of her little one and his increasing awareness of the world around him. On 26th January, 1945 she wrote to Jawaharlal Nehru:

> Independence day – we have had the usual flag ceremony at home. Rajiva helped me to hoist the flag! He also made weird accompani-ments to the flag song . . .

The correspondence between Indira and Jawaharlal Nehru while her father was still in jail continues to reflect upon private and public matters. Jawaharlal Nehru was released in 1945. Soon after, he played a crucial role in the negotiations which the British Government conducted with the leaders of India. In 1946 the British constituted an Interim Government which had Jawaharlal Nehru as the *de facto* First Executive of independent India. At this stage Indira Gandhi divided her time between her home in Lucknow and her father's in New Delhi. In December the same year, she gave birth to her second son, Sanjay.

For the next seventeen years Indira Gandhi carried out the duties of official hostess for her father. The exchange between father and daughter now became more that of the spoken word, with the exception of occasions when Indira left Delhi for short holidays or was on tour in India or abroad. Here again, between 1946 and 1964, we have some letters which give us an insight into the role which Indira Gandhi played in political affairs. Whether vacationing in Kashmir or working with ordinary citizens or with organisations (mostly connected with the welfare of children), she conveyed to her father with great sensitivity the temper of politics in the country and the climate of opinion among people of different social backgrounds.

Letters are conversation on paper – but more revealing. Indira Gandhi's shyness and sense of privacy made her express herself more freely on paper than in person. Therefore her writings, particularly the later ones, carry a greater charge of poignancy and revelation.

These letters, exchanged between a renowned statesman and writer and a reluctant, developing one, may lead to a fuller understanding of two individuals who left such a mark on India and the world of our time.

SONIA GANDHI

The Language of the Letters

Jawaharlal Nehru and Indira Gandhi wrote to each other in English except when Indira was a young child. All the letters in this collection are in English unless otherwise indicated. At home, the Nehrus spoke Hindi with a liberal sprinkling of Urdu. But, like most Indians who have had the benefit of higher education, they were fluent in English and corresponded in English – except for Swarup Rani and Kamala Nehru.

The Nehrus were prolific letter-writers, Jawaharlal particularly. Letters with biographical and historical interest have been included in this book. Those of a routine nature have been deleted. Within the letters, to save space, passing references to relations and minor events have been omitted. It could be said that over three-quarters of the correspondence between father and daughter is included in the selection. The style of indicating dates and the spelling of names have been standardised as far as possible.

Note about Names
It is customary in Hindi and in other Indian languages to add the suffix -ji (sometimes written as -jee) to personal names, especially to the given names; it denotes respect or affection, as the case may be. In the case of men, the word 'Bhai' (which means 'brother') is often used (e.g. Madan Bhai). With women, the suffix commonly used is 'behn' or 'ben' in the North; or 'bai' in the South. Discrepancies in the form of names arise from the use of Hindi adaptations of Sanskrit names (e.g. Shri Shridhara Nehru, the original Sanskrit form, becoming Shri Shridhar, the Hindi version dropping the final 'a'). This practice has been given further currency due to westernisation. Another example of this is found in the suffix -pur (from the Sanskrit *pura*, town) anglicised to -pore, as in Alipore.

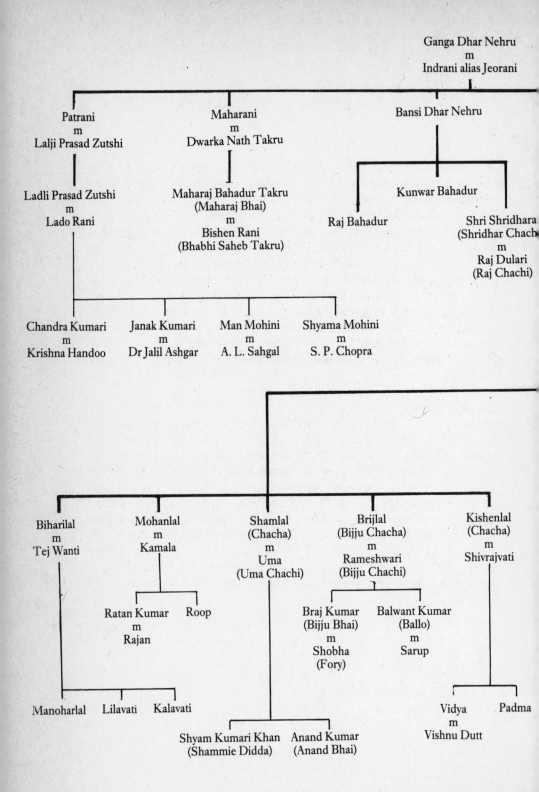

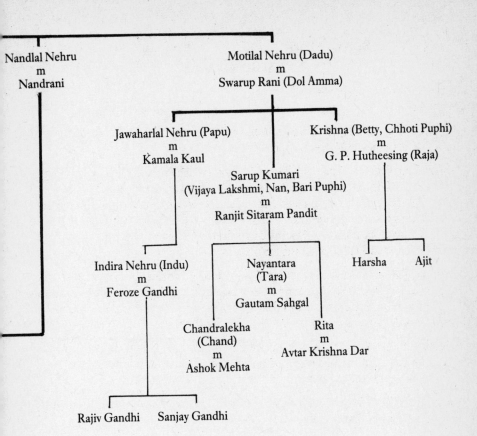

Nandlal Nehru
m
Nandrani

Motilal Nehru (Dadu)
m
Swarup Rani (Dol Amma)

Jawaharlal Nehru (Papu)
m
Kamala Kaul

Krishna (Betty, Chhoti Puphi)
m
G. P. Hutheesing (Raja)

Sarup Kumari
(Vijaya Lakshmi, Nan, Bari Puphi)
m
Ranjit Sitaram Pandit

Indira Nehru (Indu)
m
Feroze Gandhi

Nayantara
(Tara)
m
Gautam Sahgal

Harsha   Ajit

Chandralekha
(Chand)
m
Ashok Mehta

Rita
m
Avtar Krishna Dar

Rajiv Gandhi   Sanjay Gandhi

KAUL FAMILY

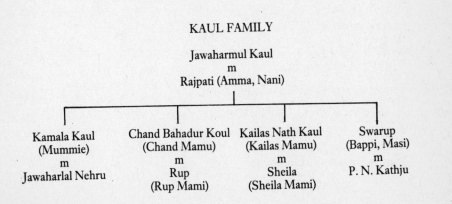

Jawaharmul Kaul
m
Rajpati (Amma, Nani)

Kamala Kaul
(Mummie)
m
Jawaharlal Nehru

Chand Bahadur Koul
(Chand Mamu)
m
Rup
(Rup Mami)

Kailas Nath Kaul
(Kailas Mamu)
m
Sheila
(Sheila Mami)

Swarup
(Bappi, Masi)
m
P. N. Kathju

JAWAHARLAL NEHRU, INDIRA GANDHI AND THEIR KINSHIP CIRCLE

GANGA DHAR NEHRU: grandfather of Jawaharlal Nehru, he was a police officer in Delhi, from where he fled in 1857.

MOTILAL NEHRU: lawyer, father of Jawaharlal Nehru, Vijaya Lakshmi Pandit and Krishna Hutheesing. Bought the house Anand Bhawan, Allahabad, in 1900. President of the sessions of the Indian National Congress in 1919 and 1928. Leader of the Swaraj Party in the Central Legislative Assembly. Indira called him Dadu, the Kashmiri variant of Dada meaning grandfather.

SWARUP RANI NEHRU: mother of Jawaharlal Nehru. Indira as a young child called her Dol Amma because she used to give her sweets from a *doli* or a cabinet with doors of wire-mesh used for storing food which needed ventilation (Amma = mother).

KAMALA NEHRU, NÉE KAUL: married Jawaharlal Nehru in 1916. Gave birth to Indira in 1917. Active in the national movement. Suffered from pulmonary ailment and died in 1936 at Lausanne.

BIBI AMMA: widowed sister of Swarup Rani Nehru, who lived with the Nehrus in Anand Bhawan.

FEROZE GANDHI: political activist from Allahabad. Studied at the London School of Economics. Married Indira in 1942. Member of the Constituent Assembly. Elected to the House of the People of the Indian Parliament in 1952 and 1957. Died in 1960 at the age of forty-eight.

RAJPATI KAUL (Amma or Nani): mother of Kamala Nehru, she was actively involved in the freedom movement and was imprisoned more than once.

CHAND BAHADUR KOUL: brother of Kamala Nehru. He served in the State Bank of India.

RUP KOUL: wife of Chand Bahadur Koul.

KAILAS NATH KAUL: brother of Kamala Nehru. Indira refers to him as Mamu (maternal uncle). A botanist, he was Director of the National Botanical Garden and Vice-Chancellor of the Chandrashekhar Azad Agricultural University.

SHEILA KAUL: wife of Kailas Nath Kaul. She was Minister of State for Education and Culture (1980–4) and is a General Secretary of the Indian National Congress.

SWARUP KATHJU, NÉE KAUL (Bappi): younger sister of Kamala Nehru.

MADAN ATAL: cousin of Kamala Nehru. A physician, he went to Spain in 1937 on a medical mission. He led the medical mission sent by the Indian National Congress to China in 1938. Accompanied Kamala Nehru to Europe during her last illness.

BRIJLAL NEHRU (Bijju or Bijji Chacha): a nephew of Motilal Nehru, he grew up in Anand Bhawan and rose to be a senior official of the Indian Finance Department.

RAMESHWARI NEHRU (Bijju or Bijji Chachi): wife of Brijlal Nehru. Active in politics, she was one of the founders of the All-India Women's Conference.

BRAJ KUMAR NEHRU: referred to as Bijju, son of Brijlal and Rameshwari Nehru. A member of the Indian Civil Service, he was Indian Ambassador to the United States, 1961–8, Indian High Commissioner in London, 1973–7. Later he was Governor of Assam and of Jammu & Kashmir.

SHOBHA NEHRU, also called Fory: Hungarian-born wife of Braj Kumar Nehru.

BALWANT KUMAR NEHRU: referred to as Ballo, younger son of Brijlal and Rameshwari Nehru. Engineer and business executive. Now Secretary of the Jawaharlal Nehru Memorial Fund.

VIJAYA LAKSHMI PANDIT, NÉE SARUP NEHRU: sister of Jawaharlal Nehru, born 1900. Married Ranjit S. Pandit. Called Nan, shortened form of Nanni or young girl. Indira Gandhi refers to her as Bari Puphi or Senior Aunt. Was Minister in the United Provinces. After Independence, represented India in London, Moscow and Washington. President of the United Nations General Assembly. Governor of Maharashtra, 1962–4. Member of the Indian Parliament, 1964–8.

RANJIT SITARAM PANDIT: husband of Vijaya Lakshmi Pandit. Participated in the freedom movement. Imprisoned along with Jawaharlal Nehru.

CHANDRALEKHA MEHTA, NÉE PANDIT: eldest of Vijaya Lakshmi Pandit's three daughters. Referred to as Chand by Indira Gandhi.

NAYANTARA SAHGAL, NÉE PANDIT: daughter of Vijaya Lakshmi Pandit. Author and novelist. Referred to as Tara.

RITA DAR, NÉE PANDIT: youngest daughter of Vijaya Lakshmi Pandit.

KRISHNA HUTHEESING NÉE NEHRU: sister of Jawaharlal Nehru. Born 1907. Died 1967. Called Betty, the anglicised form of Beti or daughter. Indira Gandhi refers to her as Chhoti Puphi or Junior Aunt.

G. P. HUTHEESING: husband of Krishna Hutheesing and known in the family as Raja. A member of the Socialist Party.

HARSHA HUTHEESING: son of Krishna and G. P. Hutheesing.

AJIT HUTHEESING: son of Krishna and G. P. Hutheesing.

SHRI SHRIDHARA NEHRU: a cousin of Jawaharlal Nehru. Mathematician and civil servant. Indira Gandhi refers to him as Shridhar Chacha. Chacha means paternal uncle.

RAJ DULARI NEHRU: wife of Shri Shridhara Nehru. Indira Gandhi refers to her as Raj Chachi.

RATAN KUMAR NEHRU: a second cousin of Indira Gandhi. Was a member of the Indian Civil Service. Retired as head of the Foreign Office.

RAJAN NEHRU: wife of Ratan Kumar Nehru and a social worker.

SHAMLAL NEHRU: a cousin of Jawaharlal Nehru; journalist and politician.

UMA NEHRU: wife of Shamlal Nehru who was active in nationalist politics.

ANAND KUMAR NEHRU: a cousin of Indira Gandhi.

SHYAM KUMARI KHAN: a niece of Jawaharlal Nehru. Active in politics and social work. Indira Gandhi called her Shammie Didda (Didda = elder sister).

LADLI PRASAD ZUTSHI: an uncle of Indira Gandhi and a lawyer.

SHYAMA ZUTSHI: a cousin of Indira Gandhi who participated in political activities.

JANAK ZUTSHI: a cousin of Indira Gandhi who was an educationalist and a nationalist.

VIDYAVATI DUTT, NÉE NEHRU: a niece of Jawaharlal Nehru.

KANWARLAL KATHJU (Nikku): a cousin of Jawaharlal Nehru.

MAHARAJ BAHADUR TAKRU: a cousin of Jawaharlal Nehru.

BISHEN RANI TAKRU: wife of Maharaj Bahadur Takru; Jawaharlal Nehru refers to her as Bhabhi Saheb Takru (Bhabhi = sister-in-law).

Anand Bhawan: Motilal Nehru bought a large house which stood in groves measuring more than ten acres in 1900. It had been built some years earlier by a Judge of the Allahabad High Court. Motilal remodelled it to suit his needs and named it Anand Bhawan (Anand means joy or bliss and Bhawan means abode). In the late 1920s, Motilal built a smaller house on the same grounds, on which also he conferred the name Anand Bhawan, giving away the original house to the nation. The 'old' house, which was renamed Swaraj Bhawan (or Freedom House), was the headquarters of the Congress until India attained independence.

POLITICAL CIRCLE

AMRIT KAUR (1889–1964): disciple of Mahatma Gandhi; participated in the freedom struggle; Minister for Health, 1947–57.

ANSARI, M. A. (1880–1936): prominent physician; nationalist Muslim; President, Muslim League in 1920; actively participated in the Khilafat and non-cooperation movements; President, Indian National Congress in 1927.

AZAD, MAULANA ABUL KALAM (1888–1958): scholar, theologian, journalist and nationalist; entered politics and started the Urdu weeklies *Al-Hilal* and *Al-Balagh*; came into close contact with Mahatma Gandhi during the non-cooperation movement; President, Indian National Congress, 1923 and 1940–6; served as Education Minister, 1947–58.

BAJAJ, JAMNALAL (1889–1942): businessman and philanthropist who participated in India's struggle for freedom; took keen interest in Mahatma Gandhi's constructive work.

BOSE, SUBHAS CHANDRA (1897–1945): was selected for the I.C.S. in 1920 and resigned in 1921; joined the freedom struggle in 1921 and suffered imprisonment on many occasions; elected to the Bengal Legislative Council; President, Bengal Congress Committee for several years; President, Indian National Congress, 1938, re-elected, 1939; founded the Forward Bloc, 1939; escaped to Europe during the Second World War; organised the Indian National Army; died in a plane crash in 1945.

CHATTOPADHYAYA, KAMALADEVI (1903–88): political activist, social worker and author connected with the theatre and handicrafts movements in India; associate of Mahatma Gandhi and Jawaharlal Nehru; Secretary, All-India Women's Conference; one of the founders of Congress Socialist Party; presided over its Meerut session, 1936; member, Congress Working Committee, 1946.

DOULATRAM, JAIRAMDAS (1892–1979): lawyer who participated in the national movement; General Secretary, Indian National Congress, 1931–4; Minister of Food and Agriculture, Government of India, 1948–50; Governor of Assam, 1950–6.

JINNAH, MOHAMED ALI (1876–1948): barrister of Bombay; President of the Muslim League, 1916, 1920 and from 1934 till his death; a nationalist who later agitated for and presided over the creation of Pakistan.

KATJU, KAILASH NATH (1887–1968): Advocate of the Allahabad High Court; took part in India's freedom movement; member, Constituent Assembly, 1946–7; Governor of Orissa, 1947–8 and of West Bengal, 1948–51; Union Minister for Law, Home Affairs and Defence, 1952–7; Chief Minister of Madhya Pradesh, 1957–62.

KHAN, ABDUL GHAFFAR (1890–1988): Congress leader of the North-West Frontier Provinces, popularly known as Frontier Gandhi; before 1947 suffered imprisonment for his participation in the nationalist struggle; was later arrested by the Pakistan Government and held in prison for many years; awarded Bharat Ratna, 1987.

KIDWAI, RAFI AHMED (1894–1954): nationalist Muslim leader from U.P.; member, Indian Legislative Assembly, 1926–9; member, Congress Working Committee, 1947–51; Union Minister for Food and Agriculture, 1952–4.

KRIPALANI, J. B. (1888–1982): General Secretary of the Congress, 1934–46 and President, 1946; later resigned from the Congress; Chairman of the Praja Socialist Party and member, Lok Sabha, 1952–7, 1957–62 and 1963–70.

MALAVIYA, PANDIT MADAN MOHAN (1861–1946): educationalist and nationalist; President, Indian National Congress, in 1909 and 1918; member of the Imperial Legislative Council; member, Swaraj Party and later organised the Nationalist Party; Founder of the Banaras Hindu University.

MEHTA, JIVRAJ (1887–1978): physician and nationalist; Chief Minister, Gujarat, 1960–3; Indian High Commissioner, U.K., 1963–6; member, Lok Sabha 1971–6.

MENON, V. K. KRISHNA (1896–1974): Secretary of the India League in London, 1929–47; High Commissioner in London, 1947–52; member, Indian delegation to the United Nations, 1952–62; Minister without Portfolio, 1956–7, and for Defence, 1957–62.

NAIDU, SAROJINI (1879–1949): poetess and nationalist; President, Indian National Congress in 1925; attended the second Round Table Conference in 1931; Governor, U.P., 1947–9.

PANT, GOVIND BALLABH (1887–1961): Advocate and leader of the Swaraj Party in U.P. Council, 1923–30; suffered many terms of imprisonment; Premier, U.P., 1937–9 and Chief Minister, U.P., 1946–55; Home Minister, Government of India, 1955–61.

PATEL, SARDAR VALLABHBHAI (1875–1950): lawyer who became associated with Gandhi in 1918 and participated in the nationalist struggle; organised a no-tax campaign in Bardoli, 1928, and thereafter came to be known as the *Sardar* (leader); President, Gujarat Congress Committee for many years; President, Indian National Congress, in 1931; member, Interim Government, 1946–7; Deputy Prime Minister and Minister for Home, States, Information and Broadcasting, 1947–50.

PRASAD, RAJENDRA (1884–1963): lawyer who joined Mahatma Gandhi in 1917 and participated in the non-cooperation movement; President, Indian National Congress, 1934, 1939 and 1946–7; Minister, Food and Agriculture, Government of India, 1946–8; President, Constituent Assembly, 1946–50; President of India, 1950–62.

ROY, BIDHAN CHANDRA (1882–1962): physician and nationalist; elected to the Bengal Legislative Council in 1923; President, All India Medical Council, 1939–45; Chief Minister, West Bengal, 1948–62.

TAGORE, RABINDRANATH (1861–1941): poet, novelist, essayist and dramatist; recipient of the Nobel Prize for literature in 1913; was deeply involved in the social and political regeneration of India; founded the Visva-Bharati University of Santiniketan in West Bengal.

CIRCLE OF FRIENDS

BAKER, MISS BEATRICE MAY: Principal of Badminton School, where Indira Gandhi spent some time in 1936–7.

BEY, FOUAD SELIM: friend of Jawaharlal Nehru from Cairo (Egypt).

BHANDARI, P. C.: physician who was associated with the India League, London; friend of the Nehru family.

BOSE, NANDALAL (1883–1966): distinguished artist on the faculty of Visva-Bharati; Padma Vibhushan, 1955.

CAPTAIN, GOSHIBEN: grand-daughter of Dadabhai Naoroji, a founder of the Indian National Congress.

CAPTAIN, PERIN (1888–1958): grand-daughter of Dadabhai Naoroji; took part in the freedom struggle and suffered imprisonment on several occasions.

CHAKRAVARTY, AMIYA (1901–86): taught philosophy at Visva-Bharati and at various universities in U.S.A. and Australia; Secretary to Tagore; joined Mahatma Gandhi in peace marches during communal disturbances, 1946–8.

CHANDA, ANIL KUMAR (1906–76): Secretary to Rabindranath Tagore (1933–41); member, Lok Sabha, 1952–62 and 1967–70; Deputy Minister, Ministry of External Affairs, 1952–7, and Minister, Works and Housing, 1957–62.

DARBYSHIRE, HELEN: Principal of Somerville College, Oxford, when Indira Gandhi was a student there.

DESAI, MAHADEV (1892–1942): Secretary to Mahatma Gandhi, 1917–42; participated in the freedom struggle; died a prisoner in the Aga Khan's Palace, Poona, in 1942.

DUFF, SHIELA GRANT: journalist friend of the Nehrus.

GANDHI, SHANTA: classmate and friend of Indira Gandhi.

GEISSLER, LOUISE: German national who helped Indians during the pre-Hitler period.

HARI: valet to Motilal Nehru; after his death attached himself to Jawaharlal Nehru; elected to the U.P. Legislative Assembly, 1937; died in 1961.

HARRISON, AGATHA (1885–1954): friend of Mahatma Gandhi and of the Nehru family, she was a Quaker who worked for India's freedom.

HEMMERLIN, L.: Principal of L'Ecole Nouvelle, Bex, Switzerland, which Indira Gandhi attended in 1926; she was again under Mlle Hemmerlin's care in 1935–6.

KATIAL, C. L. (1898–1978): practising physician in London, 1927–43; Director-General, Employees' State Insurance Corporation of India, 1948–53.

KRIPALANI, KRISHNA RAMCHAND (1907): scholar and author who taught at Visva-Bharati; Secretary, Sahitya Akademi, 1954–71; Padma Bhushan, 1969; nominated member, Rajya Sabha in 1974.

LASKI, HAROLD J. (1893–1950): Professor of Political Science at the London School of Economics, 1926–50; active in the socialist movement and Chairman, Labour Party, 1945–6.

MIRABEN (Madeleine Slade) (1892–1982): disciple of Mahatma Gandhi, she lived at Sabarmati Ashram for many years and participated in the freedom struggle.

MORIN, LOUISE (1883–1970): French journalist and friend of India who was in charge of the French unit of the All-India Radio, 1952–65.

NAHAS PASHA (Mustafa Nahas Pasha) (1876–1965): Egyptian statesman and leader of Wafd Party.

NAIDU, LEILAMANI (1903–1959): daughter of Sarojini Naidu; served in the Indian Foreign Service, 1948–58.

NAIDU, PADMAJA (1900–1975): daughter of Sarojini Naidu; Governor of West Bengal, 1956–66. She was called Bebee by kinsmen and close friends.

NAMBIAR, A. C. N. (Nanu) (1896–1986): worked for Indian freedom in Europe and lived in exile in Germany till 1947; Indian Ambassador to the Federal Republic of Germany, 1955–8.

NAOROJI, JAL: grandson of Dadabhai Naoroji and a close friend of the Nehru family; died 1938.

NAOROJI, KHURSHEDBEN (1894–1966): grand-daughter of Dadabhai Naoroji who was associated with Gandhian institutions.

PATEL, MANIBEN (1902): daughter of Vallabhbhai Patel; jailed for participation in freedom struggle; member, All-India Congress Committee, since 1951; member, Lok Sabha, 1952–62 and 1973–9, and Rajya Sabha, 1964–70.

SARABHAI FAMILY: the Sarabhais are a notable family of Gujarat, prominent in industry and in culture. Ambalal Sarabhai, a mill-owner of Ahmedabad, his wife and his sister came under Mahatma Gandhi's influence. Among Ambalal's children, Mridula Sarabhai was prominent in politics and social work. Vikram, a scientist, rose to be chairman of the Atomic Energy Commission. Bharati was a poet and writer. Leena founded a school which undertook educational experiments. Suhrid was another brother who died young. Vikram's wife Mrinalini is one of the country's foremost dancers.

SHERWANI, TASADDUQ AHMAD KHAN (1885–1935): Barrister-at-law; practised at Aligarh; arrested during the non-cooperation movement, 1921; President, U.P. Provincial Congress Committee, 1930; member, Congress Working Committee; member, Indian Legislative Assembly, 1926–30, re-elected to the Assembly in 1934.

SRI PRAKASA (1890–1971): contemporary of Jawaharlal Nehru at Cambridge; Secretary, U.P. Provincial Congress Committee, 1928–34; Secretary of the Congress 1927 and 1931; after 1947 served as Indian High Commissioner in Pakistan; Union Minister; Governor of Assam, Madras and Maharashtra.

THOMPSON, EDWARD (1886–1946): author and friend of Jawaharlal Nehru; supported the cause of Indian freedom.

UPADHYAYA, S. D. (1899–1984): served as personal secretary to Motilal Nehru, 1923–31, and to Jawaharlal Nehru, 1931–46; imprisoned several times; member, Lok Sabha, 1952–67 and Rajya Sabha, 1967–70.

THE VAKILS: Jehangir Jivaji Vakil and his wife Coonverbai; J. J. Vakil was teacher at Santiniketan; they opened a similar institution at Poona known as Pupils' Own School; Indira Gandhi was admitted to the Pupils' Own School in May 1931.

JOURNEYS UNDERTAKEN BY JAWAHARLAL NEHRU AND INDIRA GANDHI BETWEEN 1922 AND 1941

1. In March 1926 Jawaharlal Nehru, Kamala and Indira travelled to Europe where Kamala underwent medical treatment. They stayed for a few months in Geneva. During this period Indira joined L'Ecole Nouvelle in Bex. She visited Paris and London with her parents in 1927. Jawaharlal Nehru attended the International Congress Against Imperialism at Brussels in February 1927 as a representative of the Indian National Congress. Motilal Nehru joined them in Europe in September 1927. In November 1927 Motilal, Jawaharlal and Kamala visited Moscow to attend the celebrations of the tenth anniversary of the Russian Revolution. Jawaharlal, along with Kamala and Indira, returned to India later in December 1927.

2. After Motilal Nehru's death in 1931 Jawaharlal, accompanied by Kamala and Indira, visited Ceylon for a brief while.

3. Indira studied in the Pupils' Own School in Pune (Poona) from May 1931 to April 1934. She passed her Matriculation examination in April 1934 and in July 1934 joined Visva-Bharati University at Santiniketan, Bengal.

4. In July 1934 Kamala became ill again and Jawaharlal (then in prison) was released on parole for a few days to visit his wife. Indira also came over from Santiniketan. In October 1934 Kamala was admitted to a sanatorium in Bhowali in the Himalayan foothills and Indira accompanied her mother to this resort.

5. In May 1935 Kamala and Indira, accompanied by Dr Madan Atal, travelled to Badenweiler in Bavaria where Kamala was admitted to a sanatorium. Indira spent some time in Vienna and Berlin before joining her mother in Badenweiler. Jawaharlal Nehru was released from prison in September 1935 to join his wife in Badenweiler. While in Europe, Indira rejoined her old school at Bex. At the end of January 1936 Kamala was moved to Lausanne in Switzerland. She died there on 28th February 1936. After her cremation at Lausanne, Jawaharlal and Indira spent a few days at Montreux. Thereafter, Jawaharlal returned to India carrying Kamala's ashes for immersion, according to custom, in the *Sangam* (the junction of the Ganga and the Yamuna) at Allahabad.

6.   Indira joined the Badminton School at Bristol, Great Britain, in October 1936 to prepare herself for entry into Somerville College, Oxford.

7.   In the spring of 1937 Indira returned to India for a few months. In the months of May and June she visited Burma, Malaya and Singapore along with Jawaharlal Nehru. Thereafter, she went by herself to Mussoorie and Lucknow before returning to Anand Bhawan, Allahabad. In September, she sailed for Europe from Bombay. She joined Somerville College, Oxford, in October 1937.

8.   In the summer of 1938 Jawaharlal travelled to Great Britain and Europe. On his way to London he visited Barcelona, Spain, in the month of June. Indira was in London to receive her father when he arrived, and they were together in Great Britain from the end of June till the third week of July. Thereafter, father and daughter travelled to Paris, Prague and then to Budapest. They reached Budapest in the third week of August. Indira fell ill while in Budapest, and returned to Great Britain early in September and was admitted to Brentford Hospital, Middlesex. She returned to India with her father in November 1938. On their way, they broke their journey in Cairo and visited the pyramids. Indira spent five months in her country, most of which period was spent with her aunt, Krishna Hutheesing, in Almora.

9.   In April 1939 Indira returned to Oxford. In the summer of 1939 she spent a vacation in Switzerland. Later, she became ill and was first hospitalised in Brentford, Middlesex, and thereafter, in December 1939, she was admitted to a sanatorium in Leysin, Switzerland.

10.   Jawaharlal visited Ceylon in July 1939 and China in August 1939.

11.   From Switzerland, Indira returned to Great Britain via Portugal in January 1941. Accompanied by Feroze Gandhi, she sailed for India via the Cape of Good Hope, and reached Bombay on 17th April, 1941.

LIST OF PRISON TERMS

*Prison terms served by Motilal Nehru, Jawaharlal Nehru,
Kamala Nehru and Indira Gandhi*

Motilal Nehru

6th December, 1921 – 6th June, 1922	Lucknow District Jail (transferred to Nainital Jail in May 1922)
30th June, 1930 – 8th September, 1930	Naini Central Prison

Jawaharlal Nehru

First imprisonment
6th December, 1921 – 3rd March, 1922	Lucknow District Jail

Second imprisonment
11th May, 1922 – 20th May, 1922	Allahabad District Jail
21st May, 1922 – 31st January, 1923	Lucknow District Jail

Third imprisonment
22nd September, 1923 – 4th October, 1923	Nabha Jail

Fourth imprisonment
14th April, 1930 – 11th October, 1930	Naini Central Prison, Allahabad

Fifth imprisonment
19th October, 1930 – 26th January, 1931	Naini Central Prison, Allahabad

Sixth imprisonment
26th December, 1931 – 5th February, 1932	Naini Central Prison, Allahabad
6th February, 1932 – 6th June, 1932	Bareilly District Jail
6th June, 1932 – 23rd August, 1933	Dehra Dun Jail
24th August, 1933 – 30th August, 1933	Naini Central Prison, Allahabad

Seventh imprisonment

12th February, 1934 – 7th May, 1934   Alipur Central Jail, Calcutta

8th May, 1934 – 11th August, 1934   Dehra Dun Jail
(On parole for twelve days – 12th
   August, 1934 – 23rd August, 1934)
23rd August, 1934 – 27th October, 1934   Naini Central Prison, Allahabad

28th October, 1934 – 3rd September,
   1935   Almora Jail

Eighth imprisonment

31st October, 1940 – 16th November,
   1940   Gorakhpur Jail
17th November, 1940 – 28th February,
   1941   Dehra Dun Jail
1st March, 1941 – 18th April, 1941   Lucknow District Jail
19th April, 1941 – 3rd December, 1941   Dehra Dun Jail

Ninth imprisonment

9th August, 1942 – 28th March, 1945   Ahmadnagar Fort Prison
30th March, 1945 – 9th June, 1945   Bareilly Central Prison
10th June, 1945 – 15th June, 1945   Almora Jail

Kamala Nehru

1st January, 1931 – 26th January, 1931   Lucknow District Jail

Indira Gandhi

11th September, 1942 – 13th May, 1943   Naini Central Prison, Allahabad

PART I

Indira as a Child
(1922–9)

1.   [Original in Hindi]   17th October, 1922

Lots of love to dear daughter Indu from her Papu.[1] Get well soon and
write a letter to Papu. And come and meet me in jail. I am longing to see
you. Did you try the new spinning wheel which Dadu[2] has brought for
you? Send me some of the yarn which you have spun yourself. Do you join
your mother in prayers everyday?

Your,
Papu

2.   [Original in Hindi]   8th October, 1923

Induji,
Dadu says you and Mummie should go to Simla.[3] Return from there with
healthy and rosy cheeks. I am also sending you a balloon along with this
letter.

Love from,
Papu

3.   [Postcard: Original in Hindi]   [Allahabad]
                                                         [October 1923]

Dear Induji,
Received your letter. But write a letter yourself and send it to me.[4]

Papu

---

1. This is the first extant letter from Jawaharlal Nehru to Indira Nehru. It was written
from District Jail, Lucknow, in the form of a postscript to a letter addressed to Motilal
Nehru.

2. Indira's grandfather, Motilal Nehru.

3. A hill station in North India. It was an old practice in the plains of North India, where
summer temperatures soar well over 40°C, to spend the months of May, June and July,
until the outbreak of the monsoon, in resorts on the slopes of the Himalayas or in Kashmir.
Among the popular hill stations were Mussoorie, Nainital and Almora in the United
Provinces and Simla and Dalhousie in the Punjab.

4. Presumably Indira, who was then six, was sending letters to her father which were
written for her by someone else. Jawaharlal is asking her to write in her own hand.

4.   [Original in Hindi]   13th June, 1924

Love to dear Indu. I am sending you two books. You should read them. I am bathing in a pond. Ballo[1] is learning to swim in Gangaji.[2]

Yours,
Papu

———————————◄■►———————————

5.   Anand Bhawan,
                                                               Allahabad,
                                                              17th May, 1925

Indu darling,
I am waiting to get your letter from Dalhousie. Did you have a nice time in the train? Chandralekha[3] sends you her love.

Your loving,
Papu

———————————◄■►———————————

6.   [30th June, 1925]

Love to Papu,

from,
Indu[4]

———————————◄■►———————————

7.   [Original in Hindi]   Ashram,
                                                               Sabarmati,
                                                              11th November, 1925

Dear Indu,
I stayed in Rajkot for two days. Chandralekha remembered her *didda*.[5] She was very happy to see the motor-car you sent her.
    I am now in Bapuji's[6] Ashram. I met Manu Behn.[7] Do you remember her?

1. Balwant Kumar Nehru: son of Jawaharlal's first cousin, Brijlal Nehru.
2. The suffix -ji is used as a mark of respect, in this case for the river Ganges.
3. Chandralekha Mehta (née Pandit): the Pandits' eldest daughter.
4. This is the first extant letter from Indira Nehru to Jawaharlal Nehru.
5. The Kashmiri term for an elder sister. Indira was older than her cousin, Chandralekha.
6. Mahatma Gandhi was affectionately called Bapu (father) or Bapuji by the Nehrus as well as the people of India.
7. Manu Mashruwala (née Gandhi): a granddaughter of Mahatma Gandhi. Indira had visited Gandhi at Sabarmati with her mother and grandmother in 1922.

I bathe every morning in the Sabarmati river. The water is not very deep. You could also have bathed and swum.

There are a great many *langurs*[1] here. But they do not bother anyone.

Lots and lots of love.

Your loving,
Papu

8.　　　　[Postcard: Original in Hindi]　　　13th November, 1925

Love to dear Papu,

Received your letter.

Your daughter,
Indu

9.　　　　　　　　　　　　　　　　　　Geneva,
6th June, 1926

My dear Mummie and Papu,

I am sorry that I wasn't good. But from today I am going to be good. And if I am not good do not speak to me. And I will try my best to be good. And I will do what ever you tell me to do.

Love from your,
Indu

10.　　　　　　　　　　　　　　　　　Chesières,
27th July, 1926

My dear Papu and Mummie,

Did you give me a new toothbrush? Ask Mummie if my skipping rope is there, I cannot find it. Thank you for your letter.

I am sending a photo of you and me at Bretaye in the boat on the lake.

Yesterday all the children had a swimming bath and gymnastics.

Tell me all about Geneva. I will write a bigger letter next time. Give Puphi[2] her letter.

Love from your loving little daughter,
Indu

---

1. Baboons.
2. Aunt; refers to Krishna Hutheesing (née Nehru), sister of Jawaharlal Nehru.

11.   [Postcard: Original in Hindi]   Geneva,
                                                                   27th July, 1926

Dear daughter,
There has been no letter from you. Have you forgotten Mummie and
Papu? You had promised that you would write to us daily. You might get
the stamps there.

                              Love,
                              Yours,
                              Papu

                         ———————— ■ ————————

12.   Chesières,
                                                            2nd August, 1926

My dear Mummie and Papu,
Thank you for your letter. Ask Mummie what number is my new
toothbrush. Where is Rochers de Naye? We had a lot of fun yesterday. I
didn't send you the photo of you and me, I am sending it now. How are
you. Please let Mummie read your letter.
                         Love from your loving,
                              Indu

                         ———————— ■ ————————

13.   [Original in French]   Chesières,
                                                          28th February [1927]

Dear Papa,
Thank you very much for your letter. These past few days the weather was
bad; yesterday and today again it is nice. How is Mummie? The snow is
melting fast. It's not good for skiing but it is fine for sledging. The
mountains are very pretty. Yesterday a big piece of ice half the size of the
roof fell, more is going to fall. We are enjoying ourselves. This morning I
went on the sledge. There is no more snow on the trees.
    I send you my kisses.
                              Yours,
                              Indira

                         ———————— ■ ————————

14.
Geneva,
25th September, 1927

Indu darling,

Dadu and I have been in Geneva for the last three days. We shall remain here for another two days and shall then go to Lausanne to see M. Fouad Bey.[1] Afterwards we shall return to Montana.[2]

I hope you are enjoying yourself at the school. Write to me and tell me what you do. Send your letter to Montana.

I shall send you some underclothing from here.

Love from your loving,
Papu

15.
Montana,
3rd October, 1927

Indu darling,

I was very pleased to read your letter to Mummie. I am looking forward to getting a letter from you myself.

Mummie has already sent you some Indian stamps. I am sending you some more with this letter.

We all went for a motor drive to the Simplon Pass on Saturday. This pass leads from Switzerland to Italy. We have to climb up to it and then go down to Italy on the other side. The railway line does not climb up. It goes through a long tunnel called the Simplon Tunnel. Perhaps you remember this tunnel. We passed it when coming from Venice last year.

A friend of mine has sent a beautiful model of an aeroplane for you. I shall bring it with me when I come to see you next.

We hope to visit you on Sunday next. Please inform Mademoiselle Hemmerlin.

Hope you are well and happy.

Your loving,
Papu

---

1. Fouad Selim Bey: an Egyptian friend of the Nehrus.
2. The Nehrus had moved from Geneva to the small mountain resort of Montana during the summer.

16.   [Postcard]   Moscow,
                                                  10th November, 1927

[Dear Indu]
We are in Moscow in Russia.[1] I shall come for you soon. Hope you are
quite well.

Love from,
Papu

---

17.   Savoy Hotel,
                                                       Mussoorie,
                                                  16th May, 1928

Papu darling,
We arrived here at twelve o'clock. We travelled in the train till Dehra Dun,
we got down at Dehra Dun and went in a car to Mrs Chapman; here we
changed our clothes and made ourselves clean. Then Pupha and Puphi[2]
rode on horseback while Mummie, Chand and I came on *dandis*.[3] I
wanted to ride very much but Puphi said that it would be better if I didn't
because I did not have riding clothes.

I have just had my lunch. How are you? I have given the little piece of
paper on which you wrote something for Munshiji. Write soon, and tell
me when you are coming.

With love from your loving daughter,
Indira

---

18.   [Anand Bhawan]
                                                       Allahabad,
                                                  8th June, 1928

Darling Indu,
Thank you for your cards. If you want me to come to Mussoorie of course
I shall come soon. I shall try to finish my work in a very short time, say
three or four days, and shall then come to you. But when I come I wish to
find you looking well. I hope you go into the garden of the hotel every day
and play there.

I sent you yesterday two copies of the *Bal Sakha*.[4] One of these you can

---

1. For the tenth anniversary celebrations of the Russian Revolution.
2. Uncle and Aunt; refers to Vijaya Lakshmi Pandit (née Nehru), sister of Jawaharlal
Nehru, and her husband Ranjit Pandit.
3. A chair conveyance used on hills.
4. *Bal Sakha: The Children's Friend*, a popular magazine for children.

give to Chand. You will find an article by me on winter sports in it. There is also your silhouette.

I am trying to find some books for you.

Love and kisses.

Your loving,
Papu

---

19.   [Postcard: Original in Hindi]   23rd August, 1928

Indu,

Do you know this story? Napoleon was strolling about one night. He found a sentry fast asleep. According to Army rules this was a serious offence. A soldier on duty should not sleep. But Napoleon did not wake up the soldier. Instead, he took his gun and started keeping watch in his place.

Love,
Papu

20.

Anand Bhawan,
[Allahabad]
15th May, 1929
5.45 a.m.

Dearest Mummie and Papu,

Did you receive my two letters? Thanks for the two letters which I got yesterday evening.

Puphi could not find the x-ray anywhere. I know where the belt is so I will take it out today. It is only a quarter to six now and I am ready.

Our exam finished yesterday and as there will be nothing to do at school today and tomorrow I have taken a holiday.

How are you all?

Yesterday was Tara's[1] birthday and Bibi[2] had a *puja*[3] and Puphi, Chand and Tara had their food here.

Pupha went to the *kachahri*[4] and so he could not have his lunch here.

I sent Mummie two letters one typed, and one like this one.

Love and kisses to all.

From your loving daughter,
Indira

Please try and write some letters to me.

---

1. Nayantara Sahgal (née Pandit): the Pandits' second daughter, Chand's younger sister.   2. Bibi Amma: Indira's great-aunt, Dol Amma's sister.

3. Prayer service.   4. A court of justice.

PART II

Growing Up
(1930–6)

21.   [Allahabad]
                                        [No date][1]

Papu darling,

I am going to tell you something about what happened yesterday. Well, we were sitting in the verandah in front of Puphi's room at about four p.m. yesterday, when two men came and said a girl from their house had run away from home and had come to Allahabad to become a volunteer.[2]

I told them to go to the Congress Office[3] as perhaps she might have gone there.

At quarter to eight in the evening a man from the Khaddar Bhandar[4] brought her here and said that she was there since morning and that she had had nothing to eat.

On asking her questions I found that she was thirteen years old and that on coming she had left a letter for her brother, who was smaller than herself, saying that she was going to visit Pandit Jawaharlal [Nehru] and that she had taken two rupees for her fare to come here and that they were not to worry about her as she would become a volunteer and stay in Allahabad. After writing the letter she took the money and went to the station, took a ticket for Allahabad and when she arrived here she took an *ecka*[5] and told the driver that she wanted to be volunteer so the man went to the Khaddar Bhandar and left her there. She had her food here and at ten p.m. the two men came and took her away, because they said that her mother was crying for her. She lived in Babhni.

Now it is nearly time for this letter to go to you. So with heaps and heaps of love to Dadu and you.

                         Yours,
                         Indu

---

1. From external and internal evidence it appears that this letter was written sometime between 30th June and 8th September, 1930, when both Motilal and Jawaharlal were in Naini Prison.
2. An unpaid political worker of the Congress Party.
3. Local office of the Indian National Congress.
4. Under Mahatma Gandhi members of the Congress were expected to wear khadi (or khaddar) – hand-spun, hand-woven cloth – which became a symbol of the nationalist resurgence and anti-imperialist spirit. Imported cloth was boycotted and burned by nationalists. Bhandar means a store.
5. A two-wheeled vehicle drawn by a horse.

22.   Anand Bhawan,
                                              [Allahabad]
                                        11th November, 1930

Papu darling,
I do not know when Dadu is going to write to you and so I am writing now
so that my letter may be ready to go to Naini as soon as Dadu wishes.

Dadu has decided to start for Calcutta on the 16th. He is taking Chhoti
Puphi[1] with him and has also written to Madan Bhai[2] to come. From
Calcutta Dadu will sail for Singapore. The house will be so deserted when
he is gone. There will only be Mummie and I upstairs and Dol Amma and
Bibi downstairs.

On your last interview day[3] you told me to ask you any question I like, in
my letter to you, as we cannot have our evening talks now. Here is a
question I once asked someone when I was in Nainital, but I didn't get any
reply. Why do the toes bend downwards when we are walking? I have very
often noticed this while walking with *chappals*[4] on, and try as I would to
keep them straight they somehow bend.

Vallabhbhai[5] and Mahadeo Bhai[6] started for Bombay this morning at
seven thirty.

It is one thirty now, and I am going to Sundarlalji's[7], Manna Bhai and
the others' trial which will take place in the Malaka jail.

I have just come back and am going to tell you what happened while we
were there. We were all sitting in the court room. Shammie Didda[8] and
Uma Bhabhi[9] were also there. A police inspector came and put down two
warrants in front of Mr Sucha Singh, who was trying Mannabhai, etc. The
warrants were for Shammie Didda and Chhoti Puphi and they were
arrested and tried there and then with the others. They were arrested in
Act 188 and got Rs.50 fine, in default 1 month's simple imprisonment 'A'

1. Junior Aunt (Krishna Hutheesing).
2. Madan Atal: cousin of Kamala Nehru, a physician ('Bhai' means 'brother').
3. Prisoners who were convicted on political grounds were normally allowed to meet
one or two close relations once a fortnight. However, on some occasions even such
fortnightly interviews were not permitted.
4. Leather thongs, exclusively used in India.
5. Sardar Vallabhbhai Patel: campaigner in the nationalist struggle, President of the
Indian National Congress, 1931.
6. Mahadev Desai: a close associate of Mahatma Gandhi who also served as his private
secretary from 1917 till his death in 1942.
7. Pandit Sundarlal: a revolutionary nationalist who later became a follower of
Mahatma Gandhi.
8. Shyam Kumari Khan: Jawaharlal Nehru's niece.
9. Uma Nehru: wife of Jawaharlal's cousin, Shamlal Nehru. ('Bhabhi' means 'sister-
in-law'.)

class. Then we came home and packed Puphi's things and bedding and sent them to her.

In this letter I am enclosing my report of the work I did with my professor.

Now I must close up because after this excitement I am quite tired out and my brain is not working at all. I hope to write a longer letter next time.

Give my love to Pupha & yourself.

Your loving,
Indu

---

23. Calcutta,
[December 1930]

Papu darling,

I was coming to Allahabad with Mummie tonight, but as I had a teeny wish to remain here Dadu told me to stay on and that I would have the opportunity of seeing [you] in another fortnight. This is a long time to wait, but Dadu called me last night and talked to me for quite a long time. By his talk I gathered that he wanted me to stay. So although I wanted very much to see you I had to make up my mind to do otherwise.

I think Dadu has also written to you and you may find the cause why he wants me to stay in his letter.

I have finished reading *The Life of the Bee*[1]. I enjoyed it very much.

I have also begun *The Life of the Ant*[2]. But as I have only read a few pages I have not yet formed my opinion about it.

After finishing this I will read the book about Garibaldi that you gave me. At the present Dadu and Chhoti [Puphi] have both begun it and none of them has read the whole of it.

I will also read the other two books about Garibaldi. Puphi has got them here.

Au revoir, Papu darling, with lots and lots of love and kisses.

From your loving,
Indu-boy

My shorts have been made.

---

24. [Anand Bhawan, Allahabad]
25th December, 1930

Papu darling,

I came here with Puphi on the 22nd. Dadu wanted me to stay on [in

---

1 & 2. Both books are by Maurice Maeterlinck.

Calcutta] for a few days more but as he did [not] want me to come alone and there was nobody to take me [later] I came.

Chhoti Puphi phoned the day before yesterday and said that Dadu was much better than [when] we left him. Madan Bhai is going back to Lucknow as Dadu no longer needs him. Dadu is under the Kaviraj's[1] treatment now. The Kaviraj himself comes to see Dadu only once or twice a week as he is very old. But a pupil of his is staying with Dadu to make the medicines and his son comes to see him (Dadu) every day. As soon as Dadu is fit for travelling he will come to Allahabad. The Kaviraj said that he will be well enough for a journey in about ten days.[2]

I have read three books of Maeterlinck. *The Life of the Bee*, and *The White Ant*. I do not think you have read the *Ant*, I will therefore bring it at the interview together with the *Story of Youth*.

Everybody in Dakshineshwar send you their love.

Puphi wanted to go to the Educational Conference at Benares, but she suddenly changed her mind and went to Calcutta yesterday in the three o'clock train. She had a second-class ticket but could not get a seat in any second-class compartment, so she had to go first class. I am going to the Educational Conference with Mummie. We will probably stay in Benares for two or three days only. As there is nothing interesting on the first day we will stay at Mr Sri Prakasa's[3] house. We will go after your interview.

With heaps of love and kisses from your loving,

Indu

———— ▬▬ ————

25.   Poona,
                                                          20th June [1931]

Papu darling,
Thank you very very much for your letter[4] from the train. I am sorry I could not reply immediately. During school days there is very little time left for anything. Today being Saturday, a holiday, I am trying to reply to various letters I have received.

1. Kaviraj Shyamdas Vachaspati: a prominent Ayurvedic physician practising in Calcutta. Kaviraj is a title given to practitioners of traditional Indian medicine, the Ayurveda.
2. Motilal Nehru died on 6th February, 1931. See letter No. 5, Appendix A.
3. Sri Prakasa: a leader of the Congress Party in Uttar Pradesh and a close colleague of Jawaharlal Nehru; he became a minister in the Central Government after independence. His father, Bhagwandas, was a renowned philosopher.
4. Letter not traceable.

Tell Mummie that I have received the hair pins just now. Thanks for them. I have also written to Psyche[1] thanking her.

I do not know whether you will find me looking fatter or not. But I have certainly become much fresher. For we have already had the rains and it has become very cool and pleasant.

I am getting the *Bombay Chronicle*. But I do not know what address you gave the editor, as he addresses it as 55 Staveley Road. And there is some difficulty in its reaching me. Please write to him about it. I have written to Psyche asking her to tell him when she meets him.

Mrs Vakil[2] gives me all the fattening things she possibly can to eat.

Please send my books as Mr Vakil does not know what to teach me. You might also send my big & small skipping ropes. If you can't find the small one never mind. Mummie wanted some blouses from the Swadeshi[3] here. Tell her that Mrs Vakil says they are not nice. She (Mrs Vakil) will soon get some better ones. I will send them as soon as I can.

Write to me all about Mummie & yourself. With all my love to both of you.

Your ever loving,
Indu

---

26.   [Poona]
6th July, 1931

My dear Papu,
Thank you for the letter[4] and the parcel. The letter came early morning and parcel followed in the afternoon.

Please write before coming here. So that perhaps I may be able to come to the station & also Mrs Vakil will be able to make all arrangements she wants to make.

Now you must be in the train, or are you in Bombay?

I have written to Mummie and also to Chhoti Puphi. Chhoti Puphi must be thinking of coming down to A'bad – she said she would, in about a week or so, to become your secretary. But she need not come down while you are still down here.

1. Goshiben Captain (Psyche): a granddaughter of Dadabhai Naoroji, who was a pioneering leader of the national movement in India.
2. Coonverbai J. Vakil: wife of Jehangir Vakil, who along with her husband ran the Pupils' Own School at Poona (and later in Bombay). Indira Nehru studied in this school from 1931 to 1934.
3. Buying goods manufactured within India was part of the code of conduct of Congressmen. The reference here is to a store selling khadi cloth. The word *swadeshi* means 'belonging to one's own land'.
4. Letter not traceable.

You say you will come about the 10th or 11th. Tenth, I hope, as it will be a school day and you will be able to see the work done here.

Give my love to Mummie.

Lots of [love] to you.

Ever loving yours,
Indu

---

27.   [Poona]
2nd October, 1931

Dearest Papu,

In my last letter[1] I wrote that I would reach home on the 18th or so. But I am afraid that I will not be able to reach Allahabad till the 20th as I will have to come back here & then go through Bombay. First of all I won't be able to take my luggage to Ajanta & Ellora. And as I have got rather a lot of it, I want to bring it to Allahabad and then leave it there.

We had our entertainment on the 30th. It was a grand success. I am enclosing a programme. Please show it to Mummie.

We are going to have a sort of social gathering of the members of our Sahitya Sabha.[2] All arrangements for it are going to be made by me (helped by three other children). No teacher is to interfere.

Lots of love.

Your loving,
Indu

---

28.   Poona,
10th November, 1931

My darlingest Papu,

We have just come back from Sinhgarh. Your two letters & the telegram[3] was given to me. There isn't any post office at Sinhgarh, so the letters couldn't be sent there. Now I am feeling very hungry and very sleepy. So goodnight.

11th November, 1931

Good morning,

Now I am going to tell you all about Sinhgarh. We went by bus till the

---

1. Letter not traceable.
2. Literary Society.
3. Letters and the telegram not traceable.

bottom of the hill. It was nine thirty a.m. then. Then we started climbing. The whole way was very steep and parts of it were rather narrow. I walked up all the way. We had two *dandis*. The children sat in them by turns. Both Mr & Mrs Vakil wanted me to sit, at least for some time, but I would not agree. It's fun – climbing. When we arrived on top we found that [the] house in which we were to stay was locked. It was nearly eleven then and we were feeling exceedingly hungry so while we were waiting for the *mali*[1] to come & open the house we had food (we had brought some from Poona). By that time the *mali* arrived & opened the house. We explored everything and cleaned the place. We had tea & then our baths. Then we went round Sinhgarh. We saw many things, among them were Tanaji Malusere's[2] tomb & the place where his hand was cut off.

We used to go out everyday after breakfast, come back, have our baths – then lunch. Again we went out after tea and returned at seven o'clock. Poona seems quite hot after Sinhgarh. How is Allahabad?

It is past seven now and I must go for my bath.

Lots & lots of love.

Your loving,
Indu

Love to Mummie.

———————

29.   [Poona]
                                        12th November, 1931

Papu darling,

This is just to wish you many many happy returns of the day. I only hope this will reach you in time. This year my birthday also falls on the 14th.[3]

1. Gardener.
2. Tanaji Malusere was one of the generals of the seventeenth century Maratha ruler Shivaji, who defied the Mughal Empire and founded an autonomous state in Western India. Sinhgarh is a fort associated with Shivaji.
3. Birthdays and other events in India are celebrated on the basis of either the Christian Era (reckoned by the Gregorian Calendar) or the Samvat Era or other traditional eras. To convert a date in the Samvat Era into a date in the Christian Era, 57 years have to be deducted.
The Gregorian Calendar is a solar calendar based on the relative positions of the sun and earth, whereas the Samvat Calendar is based on the relative positions of the sun, the earth and the moon. As a result, events computed on the basis of the Samvat Calendar fall on different dates of the Gregorian Calendar in different years. The Nehrus generally observed the Samvat Calendar in their household so far as birthdays, etc., were concerned. But Jawaharlal Nehru apparently preferred the Gregorian Calendar. In 1931, as Indira Nehru points out in this letter, her birthday as well as her father's birthday fell on 14th November.

We have our December holidays from the 21st December to the 5th January, 1932. However the dates are not quite settled so don't make any plans.

Hope you have a happy birthday.

With tons of love & kisses.

Yours eternally,
Indu

———————

30.
Poona,
23rd November, 1931

Papu darlingest,

Thank you ever so much for the lovely things. I received them this afternoon. I did not know they could make such nice soup pots in India. I have begun reading the book. It is very interesting.

Puphi came here with Chand on Saturday evening.[1] She went away on Sunday morning. Chand was a little lonely on Sunday night but now she has made friends with the children and seems to be quite happy.

Thank Mummie for me & give her my love.

With lots of love & kisses.

Ever your loving,
Indira

———————

31.
Bombay,
27th December, 1931

Papu darling,

Yesterday morning at about nine o'clock Vallabhbhai came with Maniben[2] to see Mummie. We began talking about your arrest.[3] Vallabhbhai was perfectly sure that you would not be sent to your old home. After great arguments he went home and half an hour afterwards we received a phone message from him saying that you & Sherwani[4] were guests of our Christian Rulers. That very morning we had had news of

---

1. Chand had been enrolled at Indira's school.
2. Maniben Patel: daughter of Vallabhbhai Patel, she was jailed for her part in the independence movement.
3. Jawaharlal Nehru was arrested on 26th December, 1931.
4. T. A. K. Sherwani: lawyer, President of the U.P. Provincial Congress Committee, 1930.

Ghaffar Khan's[1] arrest and most of the arrangements for meeting and *Hartal*[2] had been made. We had a huge public meeting at Azad Maidan. Vallabhbhai was not well so he did not attend.

Thank you for your wire & letter.[3] Upadhyaya[4] brought the letter this morning. We received the wire last night. It came together with another telegram which said that Punthji[5] had left for Bombay. In our excitement we read Punditji instead of Punthji. Of course we could not make head or tail out of it. At last we phoned to Vallabhbhai. He told us that he had also had a wire, but that it said Punthji not Punditji. Then when we looked at our wire carefully we found our mistake. There is a strong rumour that you have been released. Even Jairamdas Doulatram[6] phoned saying you had left Allahabad.

Mummie is much better. She had been having a little fever in the evening but since yesterday she [her temperature] has been sub-normal.

28th [December]

I am going to the meeting just now so I must hurry. I could not write earlier in the day as I went to meet Bapuji at the Ballard Pier. I will tell you of the reception in my next letter.

Lots & lots of love & kisses.

Your loving,
Indu

———————

32.   Bombay,
                                    1st January, 1932

Papu darling,

Dr Mahmud[7] is going to Allahabad tonight. He has just come here to say goodbye. Mummie wrote to you this morning so I thought I would scribble a few lines also.

A few days ago I went to see a film of Bapu's reception. To my astonishment I found that I had become a film-star without knowing it. I was seen handing your letter to him. I look very funny. Yesterday I saw you

1. Khan Abdul Ghaffar Khan: Pathan leader who was a close associate of Mahatma Gandhi.
2. A general closure of shops as a mark of protest.
3. Letter not traceable.
4. S. D. Upadhyaya: personal secretary to Motilal Nehru and later to Jawaharlal Nehru.
5. Govind Ballabh Pant: nationalist leader from the United Provinces (now the State of Uttar Pradesh).
6. Jairamdas Doulatram: General Secretary of the Indian National Congress, 1931–4.
7. Dr Syed Mahmud: barrister and nationalist who held high office after 1947.

& Mummie also, in a show arranged by the Congress. You were asking Mummie to smile. Both of you looked adorable.

The Working Committee[1] sat till two thirty a.m. yesterday and made all their plans for the next fight. Bapu thinks he will be arrested very soon. He might come to see Mummie tonight.

Dr Ansari examined Mummie today in the presence of Dr Bharucha. Both were of opinion that she should take two or three injections & should stay in bed till her temperature would stay normal for at least three days. After that she can move about in the room. Then in a fortnight she can go to the hill station 'Panchgani'. He does not want her to go to Juhu. He says the weather there is too changeable. Mummie's weight is 78 lbs. But she looks much better than she was.

Dr Mahmud is going, so I must close up.

With lots & lots of kisses & cargoes of love.

Ever your loving,
Indu

———————— ◆ ————————

33.   Poona,
                                    26th January, 1932

Papu darling,

I received a postcard from Mummie day before yesterday saying that it was time to write to you, so I must hurry up.

Mummie is much better now. She has been going for drives for the last few days. I have been writing fairly frequently to her but she says she has not received anything.

On Saturday the 23rd we went to see a glass factory in Talegaon. Talegaon is a village on the way to Bombay. It takes about twenty minutes to get there from Poona. Our train was at seven fifty a.m. We put on the alarm at five thirty, but we were so lazy that we did not get up till after six. We walked to the station. We filled up nearly the whole of the third-class compartment. All the way we sang songs, shouted out *jais*[2] and made a great deal of noise. When at last we reached Talegaon we walked to the factory (we had not taken the smaller children with us). We were shown how when soda, lime & refined sand are mixed a paste is made. Glass is made out of this paste. The paste is put in a pot which goes round and round. Thick iron rods are dipped in the pot. By the rotation of the pot, the paste forms a bubble on the rod. The rod is then dipped in some acid.

---

1. The National Executive of the Congress Party.
2. Victory, a word widely used in slogans.

This rod is hollow and then a man blows through it till the bubble becomes long and thicker. It is then placed in a mould & then the vase or whatever it is, is nearly ready. But as yet it is still hot, so to make it cool it is put in a light fire. Now the ends of the vase are still uneven so it is rubbed on a big board. And then it is ready. Auntie [Mrs Vakil] bought a few jars. Then we returned to the station, only to find that we had just missed the train. Anyhow the next one was coming in half an hour, so while we were waiting for it we had our lunch. Then we caught our train & came back home.

Pupha's term[1] must be nearly over by now.
Ira[2] and Chand send their love and kisses.
With lots of love and kisses.

> Ever your loving,
> Indu

━━━━━ ▬▬ ▬▬

34.   Panchgani,
                                                         3.10.32[3]

Papu dearest,
After our interview, I went with Dol Amma to A'bad. On the 27th we went to Lucknow to see the Puphis. From there I came away straight to Bombay. I travelled in third, in spite of the protests of many people, including Dol Amma. I was quite comfortable & everything was all right except the people – ladies were frightfully dirty, they ate *pan*[4] all the time & spat all over the compartment. Most of my time was spent by giving them lectures on cleanliness, of which they soon got tired so they tried to be as clean as possible, which was a great relief.

On my arrival at Bombay I found that Mummie had already gone to Panchgani. I stayed for a day in Bombay, as I had to do some work for the Puphis.

It had been decided that Tara would come with me to Poona. But she got 102.4 fever on account of her injection & so was unable to travel.

When I came here I found your two letters[5] waiting for me. The one written on arrival at Bareilly and the other just after our *mulaqat*.[6] I was not expecting them, so it was a v. pleasant surprise.

The parcel of books, which you ordered for me from London has

1. Ranjit Pandit, imprisoned with Jawaharlal Nehru.
2. Ira Vakil: daughter of the Vakils.
3. Contrary to her usual practice, Indira is writing the date in the American mode. See paragraph seven of this letter.
4. Betel leaf.
5. Letters not traceable.
6. Meeting.

arrived. As I did not stop in Poona I could not see them. But as you have selected them, they are sure to be interesting.

How is your German getting on?[1] Mummie is learning French here. We have got a series of French lessons on gramophone records. They are rather good and Mummie is progressing well. It is also good for me, for if I do not keep it up I will soon forget my French.

You will perhaps be wondering about the funny way I have written the date in this letter. This is how the Americans write it. Pupha showed it to me in some book. The month is written first.

You asked for some snaps of Mums & myself. We have had some taken. I hope you will like them. They are fairly good, specially Mummie's.

Every morning & every evening Mummie goes for long drives. She also walks a little every day.

The mud in Panchgani & also Mahableshwar is red and so all the houses & the barks of the trees also become red. If you wear white clothes or shoes & go walking, they will soon be of the same red colour.

Panchgani is a small place & although it takes only two & a half hours to run up here from Poona, it is very much cut off from the rest of the world. It is quite dull compared with any other hill stations I know.

When I came here Pilloo & Mummie were the only occupants of this house. But Mrs Bahadurji came three days ago – this house belongs to Mr Bahadurji. And Murree[2] arrived this morning. That means that there are six of us now & of course the servants.

Before I came away from Allahabad, after I came back from Bareilly, Pupha took me for a picnic on the Jumna & of course on the *Nag Kanya*.[3] We also invited Mrs Higginbottom's children & had heaps of fun. We set off at about eleven o'clock and stopped on sandbank in midstream. Here we had a nice long swim in the river, then we had lunch on the sands under Pupha's big garden sunshade. Then we set off again to a huge rock island – called 'Singhaven Devta'. We explored the place till Tara, Rita[4] & Robert (Mrs Higginbottom's one and a half year old grandchild) joined us. These three had not come with us in the morning & had motored from Allahabad at three o'clock [and] reached us in about half an hour. Next we played the gramophone & had tea – we then played about & packed to go home. The kids were sent off again in the car, while we came in the boat. The sunset on the river is really wonderful. There are beautiful colours on the water as the fiery red ball gradually disappears.

1. While serving his prison sentence in Bareilly Jawaharlal Nehru was studying German.
2. Pilloo and Murree: the children of Mr and Mrs D. N. Bahadurji, with whom Indira stayed in Panchgani. A friend of the Nehru family, D. N. Bahadurji was a lawyer and played an active part in the national movement.
3. Ranjit Pandit's boat.
4. Rita Dar (née Pandit): the Pandits' youngest daughter.

You must have had your interview with Dol Amma on the 7th or 8th. Was it the same as the interview I had? – *Auf Weidenschauen* [sic].[1]

Oceans of love & tons of kisses.

From your loving,
Indu

I have written to Padmaja[2] and given her your message.

Chand has become very pink & sweet. It was her birthday on the 3rd & she was very excited about it. Our school is giving a grand concert on the 26th. I do wish you were here to see it. Do you know, I have been using a Spanish word for over ten years and only realised it a fortnight ago. In fact I had thought it was my own invention and I was a little annoyed at finding that in Spain it has been used for centuries. Can you guess the word? It's just 'Papu'. I got this knowledge from Mrs Wallace – Mrs Higginbottom's daughter, who has been in Spain. 'Papu' is father & 'Mamu' is mother.

Pilloo & others have already decided my future profession. That is of course after we have got Swaraj [Independence] – till then every one has just one job – fighting. Pilloo saw me helping Mummie with the French exercises & decided on the spot that I would make an excellent teacher. She told me that I should be a teacher of small children, as I adore them & my hobby should be designing rooms, clothes & jewellery, etc.

The other day we went to old Mahableshwar and saw the place where the five rivers – Krishna, Savitri, Gayetri, Koyna & Yenna rise. The people have built a temple on top of the place & have made a cow (which looks like anything except a cow) out of whose mouth the water of the five rivers falls. We also went to various points there, from which we could have lovely views.

We all expected your letter today and were waiting eagerly for the post. It duly arrived and much to the happiness of us all brought your letter.

Could you suggest any good French books for me? I tried the novels in our library but couldn't manage – it was a little bit too hard.

I would like something easy & interesting. Have you begun my letters[3] yet? Of course I will not be able to see them till – I do not know when. But still it is nice to look forward to reading them, it does not matter after what period of time.

If you were here you would be very pleased with our food. We have the usual things: vegetable, fish, eggs, etc., but our salad is extra good. We get fresh leaves every day & everybody eats more of it than anything else.

1. See letter No. 58.

2. Padmaja Naidu (Bebee): daughter of Sarojini Naidu, active in politics and social service. Governor of West Bengal (1956–66) and Chairman, Indian Red Cross (1971–2).

3. These are the 'letters' later published as *Glimpses of World History*; see Appendix A.

My eyes sometimes pain me whilst reading, so I will go to Bombay & show my eyes to the doctor. And if necessary get reading glasses.

The South Kensington Museum is one of the few places in London that I remember quite well. I also sometimes want to see it again.

Tons of love,
Indu

---

35.   Bareilly District Jail,
                                                              23rd March, 1932

Indu darling,

It was good to have your nice long letter[1] and to read of your doings. And it was delightful to see you, even in a snapshot. I am reminded of some lines of an old English poet when I get your letter and think of you:

> When, dearest, I but think of thee,
> Methinks all things that lovely be
> Are present, and my soul delighted . . .

So write to me long letters and tell me all about yourself and you will give me pleasure and delight and the fortnight of waiting will be amply rewarded.

I saw Mummie after just three months. She looked well and I rejoiced. But she told me that you were not as cheerful as you might have been, and sometimes you feel a bit depressed. Have you forgotten the sovereign virtue of 'plum pudding'? None of us, least of all you, has any business to be depressed and to look it. Sometimes you will feel a little lonely – we all do that – but we have to keep smiling through it. It is easy enough to smile when everything is right. But when everything is not alright? So, *cara mia*,[2] you must not misbehave.

Ranjit Pupha told me at the interview that he was going to Bombay and from there to the Konkan for a few days. He wanted to know if you could accompany him. Of course you can. I hope you will go with him and enjoy your little trip and then write to me all about it.

I cannot accompany you on your trips and excursions but I journey none the less in my own way. I have been reading travel books and with their help I have crossed great deserts and vast glaciers and visited strange cities cut off from the outside world. With Sven Hedin[3] I have been across the

1. Refers to letter No. 34.
2. My dear.
3. Sven Hedin: Swedish explorer. His chief field was Central Asia and his book, *The Gobi Desert*, was published in England in 1929.

Gobi Desert – 'mother of pearl and opal and above, dull sapphire' – and joined a caravan which took me right into the heart of Asia. With others I went to Kashmir and then to Ladakh and on over the Karakorum Pass to Chinese Turkestan. And as I made this mighty journey, I remembered vividly a little journey I had made, in the same direction, long ago, even before you had come to us to delight our hearts. It was in 1916 when I went Ladakh way and we crossed the Zoji-La, the pass which takes one from Kashmir proper to the high tableland which leads ultimately to Tibet. It was a wonderful sight from the top of the Zoji-La: on one side thickly wooded Kashmir, on the other bare rock with an occasional birch or juniper. From the other side of the Zoji-La – La means pass – I made a little excursion over the glaciers which had quite an exciting ending. We mounted up to about 17,000 or 18,000 feet and in crossing a huge ice-field I slipped and fell into a crevasse. Nothing much happened as I was roped up and was pulled out. But I had a delightful minute of suspense!

So I journey over mountain and desert and thus I satisfy the '*Wanderlust*' – as the Germans say – that I have. And I make wonderful plans in my head of the many journeys we shall make in the future. Will you not come with me? And we shall go to our land of Kashmir and explore many a beautiful but little-known valley where the tourist does not go. We shall journey on to Sonemarg and follow the old caravan road to the heart of Asia. We shall go to Baltistan and Skardu, where the snow leopard dwells, and cross many a little river by a rope bridge, swinging us high and low over the rushing torrent, till our heads feel giddy and our legs become just a wee bit unsteady. We shall reach the mighty Indus, mighty even near its mountain home, and even that we shall cross by a bridge of ropes. And so to Leh in Ladakh and the Karakorum and away from civilisation and newspapers and radio and cinema. And, if we so will it, we can follow the paths trod of old by Chengiz Khan and Timur and many a person famous in old story. The great desert routes will try us and test our strength and perhaps, just when we are feeling exhausted, we shall reach an oasis and know the joy that fresh cool water can give, and later delight in the fruits of the desert – melons and watermelons and maybe pomegranate!

Or, if you prefer, we can go another way and cross the Himalayas into Tibet and go to Kailas and Mansarovar the beautiful. There is no lack of places we can go to. The world is wide enough. Meanwhile the world we live in is a bit narrow! But it is the best of trainings and makes us appreciate many a thing which we considered too common to think about.

I have been reading a life of the poet Byron in French. There is a good description in it of his stay in Switzerland. As I read it the Castle of Chillon came before my eyes and the Dents du Midi seemed to glisten in the sunshine. A little beyond was Bex, was it not? And then Sierre, over which lies Montana!

You have asked me for French books – I am afraid it is difficult to get them here and then I am no judge. Pupha might give you some. But I have thought of a good way – I am writing to Mlle Hemmerlin and asking her to send you books and French periodicals. I wish you would write to her also. She would like to hear from you. You know her address: École Nouvelle, La Pelouse, Bex, Suisse.

I am also asking the Times Book Club in London to send you some books. These are really not specially meant for you. They are for myself. But you can keep them in Poona and send some at a time to me. And of course you will read any that you want to.

I have stuck to my German and have worked quite hard at it for the last six weeks. I have made some progress but it is not easy to pick up new languages when one is grey and old like me! That is why I should like you to keep up your French.

Mummie has left with me her book – *The Art of the Body* by Agniel – you told me that you had read it. Do you do any of the exercises? How I love the panther crawl! I wish I could do it with you and Chand. Keep up some of these stretching exercises so that your body may remain straight and flexible and healthy. I should like you to be like the deodars of the Himalayan forests – tall and straight and slender and graceful and at the same time strong!

We have many companions here – squirrels and monkeys and pigeons and bats – not to mention the smaller animals – bugs & beetles, etc. The monkeys sometimes come in the daytime and make faces at us. The bats of course come at dusk. We are not friends with them. Nor are we friendly with a cat that comes at night in search of food. The pigeons are pleasant to see and the squirrels are over bold. I watch for many minutes at a time a little squirrel and if I do not move it comes right up to me. How daintily it nibbles its food, sitting on its hind legs! Sometimes we look at each other and I smile at it. Suddenly a realisation comes upon it that it is very near a big mountain of a man and it drops its food in dismay. It looks almost hypnotised and then hops away.

I am sorry to say that I have not yet properly begun the series of letters to you. I have tried without great success. It is a question of mood. I have in a way to take hold of myself and twist myself round and look at the past and not the present and the future. Once this is done it is not difficult to write. I shall try the twisting process and I hope to succeed.

So 'Papu' is Spanish! This is indeed interesting. I did not know it. As you have been unconsciously using a Spanish word perhaps you may find Spanish an easy language to learn.

I am sorry I cannot be present at your great school concert on the 26th.

But I shall think of you all that day and await your description of it and specially of the part you and Chand played in it.

So you have decided your future profession. It is a very good one and of course one must have a profession. One cannot simply loll through life, specially when there is so much work to be done. For the present anyway each one of us has got his or her work cut out.

I have written you a long enough letter. I could go on of course, but I must not presume too much on the good nature of the jail officials.[1] I am told that your holidays begin in about a month's time. If you like you can come up then and pay a visit to your old Papu. But you must not forget that Papu can stand much but he cannot stand one thing – depression and a long face in Indu. So away with melancholy and its brood and remember that your job is to keep smiling! Laugh and grow fat and when I have news of this I shall rejoice.

Soon we shall have Nauroz[2] and a new year will begin. My love and best wishes for you, my dear, and Chand for this year that is coming and for many and many a new year.

Your loving,
Papu

Here is pretty little French poem for you. It was written by a man called Arnault over a hundred years ago. It is about a leaf blown hither & thither:

La Feuille[3]
De la tige détachée
Pauvre feuille desséchée,
Où vas-tu? – Je n'en sais rien.
L'orage a brisé le chêne
Qui seul était mon soutien;
De son inconstante haleine,
Le zéphyr ou l'aquilon
Depuis ce jour me promène
De la forêt à la plaine,
De la montagne au vallon.
Je vais où le vent me mène,
Sans résister, sans crier;

1. Nehru was allowed to write one letter a week to one member of his family. He wrote letters to other relations as enclosures to the main letter, a practice permitted by the jail officials at their discretion.

2. The various religions and regions of India have their own New Year Day. Nauroz (also Navroz, Nawroz and Naoroz) is the New Year Day of the Kashmiris. The exchange of gifts is a common practice of such festivals.

3. For English translation see Appendix C, I.

Je vais où va toute chose,
Où va la feuille de rose
Et la feuille de laurier.

C'est joli, n'est-ce pas? Au revoir – bien aimée.[1] Send Mlle Hemmerlin a snapshot of yourself.

---

36.   Poona,
                                                               [April, 1932]

Papu darlingest,

I am sorry I could not write in time for the last letter. But I got practically no time – because of our 'Variety Entertainment'.

Our show was quite a success. It was a joint affair of our school and the Physical Institute. The first item was a play called 'Vasant' – by us. In it there was singing, dancing – it is hardly possible for us to have anything which does not include one of these. I wanted to send you a booklet of it, but it is in Gujarati and you may not be able to read it. I could not take much part because I only came to Poona three or four days before the show. I was 'Mallika' (a flower) and had to take part in most of the singing & dancing. Chand recited a funny Hindi poem called *Ek thā Adhela* & also took part in an English playlet 'Why?'

Pupha came here sometime ago and left Tara & Rita. They are both very happy & have improved in health – Rita has gained 1½ lbs already. They have made friends with the boarders and play about all day.

Last time when I came to Allahabad in October I told you all about our Sahitya Sabha [Literary Society], etc. When I came here after seeing Mummie off [at] the station I found that our old working committee had been changed – all except myself and two others. Formerly our president was one of the teachers. He resigned, saying that we should have a president among the students. So a new one was elected. This boy used to boss over us and got on our nerves. When I came from Bombay he began straight away with 'Have you done this & have you done that?' Also at our meetings he used to say all sorts of things. So I resigned & afterwards many others also. So yesterday we had new elections. I am now president!

Yes, both of those journeys are inviting enough – but, as you say, at present we can only think & wish for them.

I heard from Pupha that you want Mummie to come back here for the summer. My holidays are from 22nd April to 7th June. I would like to be in Allahabad for at least a fortnight. During this period I will see you & the Puphis and after that I will decide with you & Mummie what to do.

---

1. Isn't it pretty? Goodbye – Loved one.

I bought some French plays & other books in Bombay – I have read some already. They are quite good.

It is very hot here, specially between two and four in the afternoon. The nights and evenings are pleasant as yet, but are gradually getting warmer.

Can you play Chueti?[1] It is a very interesting game. It is very popular here & I like it very much. It has a lot of running but requires more understanding of the game. We play this every evening here, as many of the day scholars & other children also come. The new name for Chueti is 'Kho', I prefer 'Chueti'.

My Gujarati is steadily improving and I hope to be able to speak fairly well by the end of two months. The Vakils, Chand, Tara, Rita & some other children are going to a seaside town – Dumas for the holidays. When I go to Allahabad I will send Chand her bathing suit.

About two weeks ago a photographer took photographs of the school at work and play, but as it got rather late that day, he is coming again today to take a group of all the children.

We have now got nearly forty children – boys & girls in our school.

We have school from eight thirty a.m. to eleven thirty. Then from eleven forty-five to twelve fifteen we have our singing class – the extra one. That is all the lessons we do except that I have one hour of Sanskrit every alternate day. You will be pleased to know that I like Sanskrit much better than I used to.

I have read all except one of the books you sent for from London. I liked them immensely.

12th [April]

Yesterday, we went to the wedding of Mr Vakil's sister. I was interested, as I had never seen a Parsi wedding before. I will tell you all about it. The wedding always takes place in the girl's house. First the girl's sister-in-law garlands both of them & puts the *tika*.[2] Then the pair go & sit on a new pair of chairs & the 'Dusturji' – that is a priest – says a long prayer & throws rice on them all that time. This lasts for about forty-five mins. Then the man puts the ring on the woman's finger & they're married. We spent the whole day there & enjoyed ourselves immensely. We played lots of games & when we returned here – after having dinner – we were dead tired. We were also late for school this morning, as we could not wake up early enough.

Mr Vakil-*Kaka*[3] is an examiner, so he went to Bombay this morning for

1. Chueti or Kho-Kho: (also called Kabaddi and Hu-Tu Tu) a traditional Indian game in which members of a team invade a place occupied by the opposing team, uttering an agreed sound and, in the same breath, return to base without being touched. 'Chueti' means 'being touched'.

2. Vermilion mark on the forehead.

3. Uncle.

the exams. We have decided to hold a sort of 'Purnima Samelan'[1] – we will give some entertainments in the moonlight, on the 20th, that being a full moon day. There are only ten days left before the holidays. I am looking forward to them and specially as I will be able to see you.

We are learning two very nice Gujarati songs for the 'Samelan', one is for the Garba[2] we are going to do – it is all about the joy of the moonlight. The other is a translation from the Bengali, which was written by Rabindranath Tagore. The translation is by Mahadeo Bhai Desai.

Lots of love and kisses from your ever loving,

Indu-boy

37.

[Anand Bhawan]
Allahabad,
25th April, 1932

Papu darlingest,

I arrived here day before yesterday night by the Calcutta mail. Mummie came with Shama Chacha[3] at Chheoki station – by car, in spite of my asking her not to bother to come even at A'bad station.

The mornings are very pleasant, but – afterwards it is just a little bit too hot. Mummie does not feel the heat at all. Perhaps this is because she has been staying here since March. But I have just come from Poona, where the days are very cool & pleasant – at night a warm blanket is needed.

I have only got two books here, out of the four that came from London. I am afraid the one about China – *Roar China* – is in Poona. I will bring the two I have got here at the next interview. The other ones I will send from Poona, when I go there. I will also bring *Alice's Adventures in Wonderland.* I am afraid that I have not got the other book. Just after our return from Europe, Chhoti Puphi lent it to some friend of hers. Since then I have not had it back.

I am afraid I do not use your old book in Sanskrit. My book has all sorts of short stories. These stories help me a lot in grammar – otherwise I find the grammar book very tedious.

I know Dumas is a quiet place, but Mrs Vakil has gone with ten children and I doubt whether it will [be] quiet for her.

We have weekly meetings of the Sabha in which we make small programmes, consisting of essays, stories, songs & recitations. For these meetings, we have a new president each week. There is a small school in

1. A meeting held on a night of the full moon.
2. A folk dance from the Gujarat region.
3. Shamlal Nehru: a cousin of Jawaharlal Nehru. ('Chacha' means 'uncle'.)

Poona, which takes great interest in our Sahitya [Sabha]. The children of that school often come to our meetings. We often choose our president [from] among [them]. The only difficulty is that they are much too shy. And when any of them are presiding we have to cancel the last item, which is *Pramukh ka bhāshan*.[1]

Since I have come to Poona I have learnt many Indian games. Before that I had not even heard of them.

I am sorry I forgot to write to Mademoiselle H. But I will write as soon as possible.

I am looking forward to seeing you in a few days. Till then all my love. *Au revoir*.

Ever your loving,
Indu

38.   [Allahabad]
                                            [10th May, 1932]

Papu darling,

I received your letter[2] [the] day before yesterday. I got a letter from Mlle Hemmerlin yesterday. She has mentioned the following books:

> *Romain Rolland* by Stefan Zweig
> *Goethe* by Ludwig
> *Michel Ange* by Rolland
> *Les Paroles d'un Croyant* by Lamermain
> *Le Prisonnier qui Chantait* by Bojer.

She says that these books are good & if you approve of them she will send them. She also thinks that I should read Romain Rolland's books on India.

The parcel of books from the Times Book Club also came yesterday. It contained twenty-one books.[3] All evening I sat with one & finished it this morning. I have begun another, which is so good that some newspaper has printed: 'Give this book to your child & if after reading 50 pages, he does not want to read more – send for the doctor.'

Every day I have a long swim in our swimming-bath. My dive is much better than before but as yet I cannot dive standing erect. But I am practising hard at it and I hope that by the time I go away I will be able to do it. I also practise under-water swimming – I [am] terrible at it.

1. Speech by the president.
2. Letter not traceable.
3. See Appendix B, I.

Today is Puphi's wedding anniversary; so we had *mētha bhattā*.[1] It is ten years since she was married. All I remember of the wedding is that someone put *mehndi*[2] on every ones feet & hands. I also remember something of the ceremony. At that time I was four years old.

Hills of love.

Ever your loving,
Indu

39.

[Anand Bhawan]
[Allahabad]
21st May, 1932

Papu darlingest,

Ever since early this morning we were all waiting impatiently for your letter (generally it comes on Saturday morning). But when the postman came we were very much disappointed. Anyhow I hope it will come soon – perhaps tomorrow . . .

Now at night we sleep on the verandah which is on top of the portico. It is quite cool there and we don't need a fan. All night 'Chanda Mama'[3] smiles down at us and keeps away the warmth. But I am afraid it will become warmer on the dark nights. For the last four nights I got no sleep till twelve & sometimes one o'clock. I lie in my bed and watch the curious shapes the clouds make – such funny faces and animals. [The] night before last there was a black, black cloud in the shape of a face. There were two round holes for the eyes and one oblongish one for the mouth and the moon was peeping through one of the eye holes. It looked just as if 'Kali Devi'[4] was looking at the world from Heaven! It is very interesting to watch the shapes change suddenly and form other things. You can watch for hours without getting the least bit tired.

Some days ago – I think on Wednesday or Tuesday – my parcel of French books came from Mlle Hemmerlin. There are forty books and all look interesting. I don't know if they are or not. There are two books on 'La Suisse'. They have got the most magnificent pictures of the mountains and towns of 'La Belle Suisse'.

Bibi Amma is still in Lucknow. I don't think she will come back as yet. Dol Amma (I've decided to call her Diddajee from now onwards) –

1. Sweet rice, served in Kashmiri families on auspicious occasions.
2. Henna.
3. Uncle Moon, a common appellation for the moon by children in India.
4. The Goddess of Retribution.

intends to write to her to stay on in Lucknow till we come, so that she will be able to take the next interview also . . .

23rd May

Your letter[1] was very welcome when it arrived this afternoon. As I have already written, I had not been swimming till today. This morning I went in for fifteen minutes.

Yes, Mlle met Bapu at Villeneuve and later, when Bapu was passing Bex she took all the schoolchildren to the station and they sang a farewell song in French. Some of my old friends sent me presents through Bapu. Mademoiselle sent a box of Swiss iced fruit – which shows that she still remembers what I like.

I am enclosing a list of the books.[2]

I have read all the new English books except six or seven. Yesterday I received a small booklet, *Labour's Song Book* from London.

Mountains of love.

Ever your loving,
Indu

40.   Poona,
16th [June, 1932]

Darlingest Papu,

I am very sorry not to have written last time, specially as Mummie didn't write either. Mummie must have told why I did not write. It was so hot in Allahabad and my brain refused to work. I tried to write three or four times but had to give it up as hopeless.

I was to leave Allahabad on the 8th morning, as was arranged with you. But Shama Chacha & many other people said that it was not safe to go alone, because of the riots – there was also some trouble at Kalyan.[3] It was decided that Jessie should accompany me. And as the old lady had to attend a wedding or something, she could not leave A'bad earlier than Saturday. So we started from Allahabad on Saturday morning. Mummie, Nani,[4] Diddajee, Shami Didda & Nadir came up to Chheoki. There was no room in a ladies' compartment so I came in the other second-class compartment. There was an Anglo-Indian gentleman & his wife with me.

1. Letter not traceable.
2. See Appendix B, II.
3. There was an outbreak of riots in Bombay in 1932. Kalyan is a suburb of Bombay which was affected by these riots. Since Indira, who was at Allahabad, could only proceed to Poona through Kalyan, she was advised not to travel alone.
4. Maternal grandmother; refers to Rajpati Kaul, Kamala Nehru's mother.

The journey was quite pleasant and it was not at all hot. The night was fairly cold. The weather here is very nice. It is so cool and pleasant – there is a cold breeze blowing all the time.

The school timetable has changed a lot. School now begins at ten o'clock. Our recess is at one o'clock to two. Then study till four. From four to half past a man from the *vyayam shala* comes to teach us drill & afterwards he will also teach *lathi*[1] & the rest of it. From nine to ten in the morning we have our music class, before that we do gardening, exercises, running and our homework. In the evening we either play or go for a walk.

We got a wire from Lucknow to send back Sarah with Jessie and get a new ayah for Rita. So the two of them left Poona on the 14th night. A Christian ayah called Mary looks after Rita now. She has been with us for sometime and Rita likes her very much.

It is very cloudy today and I think it is going to rain.

With all my love and heaps of kisses.

Ever your loving,
Indira

---

41.   [Poona]
                                                           1st July [1932]

Papu dearest,

You might or might not have received my letter,[2] by the time this reaches you.

I hear that your interviews have been stopped for a month. Although I am not there to see you I'm feeling pretty bad that you won't be able to see anyone from home for thirty days.

I'm flourishing except for a bad cold & cough. Chand, Tara & Rita are quite well & happy. Rita talks a great deal and has learnt quite a lot of Gujarati songs. There is no peace for any one when she is in a mood to sing.

The Pupils' Own School is gradually getting larger. We have four wholetime teachers, including Mr & Mrs Vakil, and five who come for an hour each. We learn *lathi* & *laziume*[3] after school & by the time we meet again I shall be quite an expert with them.

---

1. A long stick used by policemen. The Congress volunteers practised keep-fit exercises using the *lathi*. *Vyayam shala* is a gymnasium.

2. Refers to letter No. 40.

3. The correct spelling is *lezim*. The *lezim* is an instrument to which jingling metal pieces are attached. It is used in drill and marching and is especially popular in Western India.

2nd [July]

I would have written more but for the last few days I am not very well. This morning I suddenly felt very giddy & fell down. Mrs Vakil sent for a doctor, who said that my tonsils were very much inflamed & I was developing adenoids. He gave me a medicine, to be taken four times a day. At present I have 101.4 temp. but it is nothing to worry about, I will soon be all right. So I finish.

Lots & lots of love & kisses.

Ever your loving,
Indira

Excuse pencil.

———————————◄►———————————

42.   [Dehra Dun Jail]
                                           26th July, 1932

Indu darling,

Your letter of 1st July[1] reached me three weeks after it was written! But Mummie sent me your card to her and this gave me some more and later information. I do not know how you are now, and what is going to happen to your tonsils. Of course cutting off the tonsils is quite a small operation. Nothing to worry about. If it is quite clear that they must be cut, let them go. I have suggested to Mr Vakil that if it is necessary you can consult doctors in Bombay and also have the operation there. If you like Mummie to be with you at the time, you can send for her.

The doctors tell me now that my insides are more or less right, and what is wrong with me is not the lungs. The teeth are supposed to be the root cause of trouble. I had one tooth taken out yesterday and perhaps more may come out soon. So I shall not grow in beauty as the days go by!

I had a nice little trip to Mussoorie to have my X-ray photograph taken. The motor road goes much further now – right up to Sunny View. We started from Dehra Dun after twelve noon and it took us just two hours to reach our destination in Mussoorie – one hour by car to Sunny View and then nearly an hour in a rickshaw, which took us to the Happy Valley, where the doctor lived. We spent three hours there and were back in Dehra Dun Jail by seven thirty in the evening. It has been raining here a lot but that day, fortunately, it kept clear.

Keep well, my dear. It is rather silly for anyone to fall ill. I am very

1. Refers to letter No. 41.

annoyed with myself for the trouble I have had myself, and have given others, over my health. But soon I hope to be quite fit.

Lots of love.

Your loving,
Papu

Give my love to Chand, Tara and Rita.

---

43.   [Poona]
                                                  27th [September, 1932]

Papu dearest,

Mummie gave me your letter[1] when she came from Bombay on Sunday.

I have just returned from Yeravda Prison.[2] Bapu was looking very cheerful and certainly much better than yesterday. Yesterday he was very bad and the doctors were very anxious. And specially when we read that the cabinet was going to meet on Wednesday, we did not know what was going to happen. I stayed the whole day with Bapu and it was terrible to wait for the telegram to arrive, when the old man was getting weaker & weaker. At noon the Superintendent gave the good news that the tele. was on its way to Poona. Padmaja, Mummie and I rushed to the market and got the best oranges & other fruit that we could get. When we got back, we found that there was yet some time for the telegram to come, so we waited and each minute seemed an hour. When at last the telegram came, Bapu said that he would not break his fast, till Dr Ambedkar[3] had heard the contents of the telegram and agreed to them. Dr Ambedkar was in Bombay, and it would have taken quite a lot of time for him to come. And it was already nearly five o'clock and Bapu does not eat anything after six. So everybody, including Dr Tagore and the jail authorities, persuaded him not to wait for Dr Ambedkar. So immediately I prepared the juice of two oranges for him. Then Dr Tagore sang a Bengali hymn and the Ashram people sang Bapu's favourite *bhajan*[4] 'Vaishnav Jan'. Then Bapu drank the juice and everybody was given fruit and sweets as the *parshad*.[5] Then we all went home – happy after an anxious day.

---

1. Letter not traceable.
2. Indira is describing the end of Mahatma Gandhi's 'fast unto death'. See also item 6 of Appendix A.
3. Dr B. R. Ambedkar: leader of the Depressed Classes, who played a significant role in drafting the Constitution of India.
4. Hymn.
5. Food offered to a deity and distributed among the devout. Also spelt *prasad*.

Today I am in an extra good mood, for I think that is the happiest day we have had for a very long time. It is Bapu's sixty-fourth birthday[1] and he has begun eating fruit and he is much better than before.

We have a holiday today, and we celebrated Bapu's 'Sal gira' [birthday] by having lots of singing. We invited many people & made the poet the president of the occasion. He read one of his poems of the Gitanjali. He did it very well & we all liked it immensely.

I think it is very wonderful, how one man can do such a lot. Up till now I had thought Bapu a great man, no doubt, but I had somehow never thought him capable of this. So this fast has made a great impression on me and has taught me a great lesson. These last seven days have been terrible. Till the 30th morning I had every hope that Bapu would be all right. But on that date, when I saw his condition, I thought he would not survive. And from eight o'clock to twelve were some of the worst hours I have spent in my life. But now I am perfectly assured that Bapu can do the most imaginary things.

I am sending some snaps of Mummie & myself. They were taken at Juhu, when I went to Bombay a fortnight ago – I am wearing Goshi's bathing costume – it is big enough for two people like me to get into at the same time. The dog in one of them is 'CoCo' and he belongs to Perin.[2] He swims very well & we had great fun with him on the shores of the Arabian Sea.

Dol Amma has also come here. She is looking better than what she was when I last saw her in Allahabad. Both she and Mummie are staying with some gentleman called 'Ram Narain Lal'. Bapu had the arrangements made for them there.

Everybody is quite well. How are you?

The last three days have been exceptionally hot. But the nights have been quite cool. Last night it rained a lot.

Lots of love and kisses,

> From ever your loving,
> Indu-boy

---

44.   [Dehra Dun Jail]   3rd October, 1932

Darling Indu,

Your letter[3] was very welcome. I liked reading your vivid account of

---

1. In 1932 according to the Samvat Calendar Mahatma Gandhi's birthday fell on 27th September.

2. Perin Captain: a social worker and freedom fighter. Like Psyche she was a granddaughter of Dadabhai Naoroji.

3. Refers to letter No. 43.

Bapu's last day of fast. You were very fortunate in being near him during these trying days, though it must have been a great trial for you and all others with him. You were present at his Delhi fast of twenty-one days also. Do you remember it? That was a much longer fast but it appears that Bapu suffered more this time during his week's fast. I am not surprised at the impression all this must have made on you. Bapu is an extraordinary man and it is very difficult to understand him. But then great men are always difficult to understand, and there can be no doubt that he is among the greatest of men. It is amazing how he conquers his opponents by his love and sacrifice. By his fast he has changed the face of India and killed untouchability at a blow.

You have met, probably for the first time, another great son of India – Rabindranath Tagore. He is very different from Bapu, but he is a great writer and artist and it is a privilege to meet him.

Poona was the centre of India for some days and all eyes were on it. You were in the middle of the excitement. Some little bit of the excitement came here too, as elsewhere, and we followed developments anxiously. I was so pleased to get a long telegram from Bapu. He took the trouble to tell me in it that he had seen you and Chand & her sisters and that you were looking well!

Well, the excitement is over now and Bapu leaves his mango tree and goes back to his cell,[1] and you go back to your school routine, and I, well, I remain where I was! And I read and write and spin and stand on my head. There is a new diversion. We have got baby squirrels. Two of them were picked up one day in our barrack and my companion here took charge of them and became their nurse. I named them Tit and Tat. They were very small and required a deal of care. My friend spent most of the day cleaning them and feeding them every two hours and sunning them and playing about with them – I joined in the last activity. Quite a cunning way was devised to feed them and a very serviceable feeding bottle was made out of a fountain pen filler and cotton wool. Cotton wool beddings were made for them, and altogether they got more care than the average baby boy or girl does. We grew quite fond of them and as they grew they became friendlier and used to run up to us. But the place they liked best was a pocket, where they would curl themselves up and rest quite content. But this was not to last long. Little Tit fell ill and began to behave in a strange way. One day it got stuck in a mousehole and in trying to pull it out, its tail came off! It did not long survive this tragedy, and that was the end of Tit. Curiously enough on that very day a third little squirrel dropped down from a branch in our barrack and was caught. So again we had two. I named the new one

1. Mahatma Gandhi had undertaken his fast in the open compound of the jail under a mango tree.

Twee. Tat and Twee soon made friends and are now on the best of terms.

Soon you will have your birthday and you will actually become fifteen – what a big girl you are now. I have been wondering what you would care to do when you grow up, what your special subject or business in life would be. Of course there is no hurry to decide this for many years, but if one wants to do anything it is as well to do it well, and to do it well one has to be trained for it. When one goes to the university one has to choose one's subjects accordingly. Some time or other you would naturally like to go to a university and study some subjects which you like. In India today we are placed in a great difficulty, for almost all the universities are official and neither you nor I would care to have anything to do with them. Besides they are not much good and I do not care for the way they teach. The few non-official universities in India are better in some ways but they are not much good either. No one can say what will happen in our country during the next few years and it is difficult enough to make plans for the future. It seems to me however that it would be a good thing if you went to a foreign university when the time for this comes. A foreign university might mean an English university or a Swiss or French. I would personally like you to spend a little time at both an English and a Continental university. But all these are castles in the air at present. I have merely mentioned them because I have been thinking about them and I wanted you to give some thought to the subject. There is just one question which arises now. If one has to go to a university some kind of entrance examination has to be passed for it. If one keeps this in view one can easily prepare for it. I do not like examinations as a rule but to some extent one has to put up with them. The only examination I can think of which is available in India, is the Cambridge Senior. Perhaps there are others which I do not know of. I should like to discuss this matter with Mr Vakil, as he might be able to make a helpful suggestion. Perhaps you might show him this part of the letter and have a talk with him on the subject. Then you can write to me what you and he think about it.

I do not like the snapshots Mummie has sent me. They are no good. Send me a better one of yours.

Love,

> Your loving,
> Papu

Tell Padmaja that I have got her letter and I shall write to her when I have the chance. How long will she stay in Poona?

45.   [Poona]
                                        4th October [1932]

Papu dearest,
This time there was no letter from you. But I think that you had written
and sent it to Mummie and it will arrive in due time.

Since the last week or two it has become very hot here. Clouds often
assemble, but after some time they also disappear and all hopes of rain
vanish. And now hardly anyone trusts them.

All of us here are quite well. Tara & Rita have some boils on their
bodies. Rita is much better now. But Tara has still got a good many. Both
of them are kept on fruits, fruit juice & sometimes milk. Chand is all right.
All three send their love. Also Ira [Vakil] sends her love to Jawaharlal. Ira
is now five years old & she feels very grown up. She is getting sweeter &
sweeter.

In my last letter[1] I forgot to tell you that on 20th September, when Bapu
began his fast we all fasted here & had prayers. We also entered a new
pupil. Of course pupils are entered nearly every week. But this was a new
kind – one, like whom we have never had before. Can you guess who she
was? She was the daughter of our *mehatrani*[2] – an untouchable. Of course
she is to be taught free of charge. Her clothes, books, etc., will also be
supplied by the school. She is five years old & her name was Ura, but we
had changed it to Urvashi. She is very sweet & also bright. The first day I
bathed her & so she is very friendly with me.

About two months ago on the Coconut Day & some big Akadashi[3]
holiday in August we all went to Bijapur and saw the palaces made by the
Mughal kings[4] at the time of Chand Bibi.[5] The first & last thing we saw,
was the best. It was the Gol Gumbaz.[6] The most marvellous thing about it
was the whispering gallery. We tested it by whispering, talking, shouting &
singing. Even the tick of a small wrist-watch could be heard distinctly by
people standing right at the other end. I do not know the exact distance,
but I can say that it was a great deal. Another we liked very much was the
Asar Mahal;[7] this had very fine old frescoes. First we had put up at the
travellers' bungalow. But the food was simply rotten. We could have stuck
to it, but it was also very expensive. So Mr Mirchandani invited us to stay

1. Refers to letter No. 43.
2. Cleaning woman.
3. Festivals in the Maharashtra region.
4. The palaces were actually built by the Bahmani Rulers of the region.
5. Queen of Bijapur in medieval times who fought against the Mughal Emperor Akbar.
6. Circular dome, a seventeenth century building in Bijapur. Its dome – 114 feet in
diameter – is one of the largest in the world.
7. A palace in Bijapur built at the same time as the Gol Gumbaz.

with him. Mr Mirchandani is the Asst. Collector of Bijapur.[1] He was very kind to us & we enjoyed ourselves immensely. When we were returning we shouted, '*Mirchandani Kaka ki Jai.*' He also presented our school library with an expensive set of *Children's Dictionary*, consisting of eight volumes. He told us about your visit to the place just before your arrest.

This year we have no holidays in October – only the four days of Diwali.[2] Instead of the fortnight in October we will have nearly a month in December. The Christmas holidays will be from 12th December to 5th of January.

In these holidays the Vakils intend going to Ajanta and Ellora.[3] And then they will probably pay a visit to Santiniketan.[4] Mummie says that it will be better if I accompany them, for I have seen her & also Dol Amma, and your interviews are stopped. I also think I would like to see the famous caves. What do you think about it?

Kaka, that is Mr Vakil, tells me that you want me to appear for some examination. For the Cambridge or Matric? In either the only difficulty lies in the second language. I am doing Sanskrit, but it is going very slowly. And I have forgotten my French. So for either of these will take some time. Though on the whole, I think French will be easier. Please write about it all.

Last month I had gained four lbs but this month I have lost one. I think this is due to the rushing about on account of Bapu's fast. However I hope I'll get it back again.

Dol Amma is still here & intends to stay on for some days. She comes to see us every evening. Generally Bebee comes with her. On Saturday Dr Mahmud also came.

Au revoir, Papu darling and with heaps & heaps of love & kisses, I close.

Ever your loving,
Indu-boy.

---

1. Assistant administrator of a district. The children shouted 'Victory to Mirchandani Uncle' because of his generosity to the school library.

2. Festival of Lights, one of the most important festivals in India.

3. Cave temples near Aurangabad in Maharashtra, decorated with Buddhist and Hindu paintings and sculpture.

4. The town in West Bengal where Rabindranath Tagore established his university, Visva-Bharati, which offered special facilities for education in the artistic and cultural heritage of India. Indira was a student here between 1934 and 1935.

46.　　　　　　　　　　　　　　　　　　　　　　　　[Poona]
　　　　　　　　　　　　　　　　　　　　21st October [1932]

My dearest Papu,
Thank you ever so much for your letter.[1] Now every time I see a squirrel, I
think of Tat and Twee. What a pity, poor little Tit died.

I showed the letter to Mr Vakil – the part about the universities. And he
said that I had better leave off Sanskrit and start learning French. For I
have forgotten most of it and he says it will take at least a year & a half for
me to be prepared for an exam. A lady called Miss Kohn, living near us, is
an expert in the language and teaches in a college; I might take tuition
from her. But she is rather expensive. Of course there are many other
people who could teach. I do wish we could meet and talk over all this. It's
very difficult to write all this, specially when we have to wait for a fortnight
for an answer.

Gov. [the Governor of Bombay] has not sent any reply to Bapu's letter
about Dol Amma. But Bapu has now given permission to her to go to
Allahabad if she wants. She is going to open some store in Bombay on the
26th, so she will probably go to Bombay tomorrow or the day after.

Yesterday was Rita's birthday. She is three years old. Dol Amma spent
the day with us. In the evening Bebee came to tea. Rita was very happy and
excited and looked very sweet. She got heaps of toys and is still playing
with them. Padmaja gave her a whole menagerie of Singapore-made
rubber toys – animals. Saraswati Bai[2] sent the birthday cake from
Bombay. Unfortunately Puphi's present has not yet arrived.

It will soon be your birthday – on the 14th. But as we will not be able to
write to you on that date, I wish you a happy birthday. All day we will be
thinking of you. Of course I always am – but that day you will be more in
my mind.

The Puphis were to be released on 25th November, but to the great
disappointment of all of us, they will not be able to come till the 8th
November [December?].

This letter is very untidy – I'm sorry. But it is due to my pen. My
fountain pen nib got spoilt and I began writing with this pen and I can't
manage it properly.

Mummie went back to Allahabad on the 11th. I hear she went to
Lucknow and Cawnpore also. She writes that it is quite cool in Allahabad
at night. How is it in Dehra? Here it rains regularly every night and is hot
in the day.

Last Sunday we all went to a picnic at the Lloyd Dam. I had been there

1. Refers to letter No. 44.
2. Saraswati Bai Pandit: Ranjit Pandit's sister-in-law.

twice or thrice before. But I like to see the water rushing out of the gates very much, so it is always a pleasure to go there. We had our lunch there. We went in two cars & a bus. Of course I went in the bus – it's much more fun. On the way we went to a place called Baneshwar. Here there was a temple, in front of it was a tank, nearly all of us knew swimming & jumped in . . . [incomplete]

———◆——■——

47.   Calcutta,
5th January [1933]

My darling Papu,
I arrived here yesterday morning with Puphi, Dol Amma & Tara . . .

Dol Amma has not made her plans yet, she might stay on for a fortnight or go with Puphi or go with me. I have to reach Poona by the 16th, as my Xmas concession ticket expires on that date. So I will probably stay here for a week.

At Allahabad I met Bijji Chacha[1] & Ballo. Ballo has grown very tall & well built. I almost didn't recognise him. But he is still three or four inches under Bijju Bhai[2] and hopes that he will soon catch up. He likes Fory[3] – my future *bhabi* [sister-in-law] – awfully and praises her no end. His college opened on the 4th, so he left A'bad on the 2nd for Lahore. On the same day Bijji Chacha left, to come here. He came to see us yesterday & took us out for a drive and afterwards to his flat. The flat is quite big – more than enough for two people, but he wants to get a larger one.

I will have some photographs taken here. Of course they'll be in a frock – I rarely wear anything else now, which, everybody says, is a great improvement.

I am very fit now. Fitter than I have ever been, with the exception of Europe.

I do wish I could see you – there are such heaps of things I want to say that are difficult to write.

I'm sorry about the letter[4] going to Dharwar. But I was sure something like it would happen. It nearly always does when Bebee addresses the envelope.

Mlle Hemmerlin has sent me some lovely photos of La Pelouse and a very sweet one of herself. They all remind me of the old friends and

1. Brijlal Nehru: a nephew of Motilal Nehru.
2. Braj Kumar Nehru: elder brother of Balwant Kumar Nehru.
3. Shobha Nehru (Fory): the Hungarian-born wife of Braj Kumar Nehru.
4. Letter not traceable.

everything I did there. And I also imagine I'm skiing or having a snow fight and then, all of a sudden, the snow & the happy rosy-cheeked Swiss children, with whom I'm chatting *en français*,[1] vanish and in their stead remain the hot rays of the sun, girls in five-yard saris, who can't imagine what is the attraction of snow and who would far rather sit & talk than make snowmen & play in the wonderful snow. Instead of French I find I'm speaking in a mixture of Hindi & Gujerati. It's nice to have some imagination, *n'est-ce pas?*[2] It's so wonderful to be able to fly anywhere you like in a second. But of course when somebody interrupts – I'm furious.

When Puphi reaches Allahabad, Chhoti Puphi will come here. She will probably return with me.

With tons & tons of love and a shipload of kisses.

Your ever loving,
Indu-boy

48.

Dehra Dun Jail,
23rd January, 1933

Indu darling,

Our interview after seven and a half months has come and gone, and you are again far away in Poona. It was good to see you looking healthy and well, but what is the good of having brief interviews and trying to rush through all one has to say with one eye on the watch all the time? Of all the many things I wanted to tell you and ask you, very few came to my mind at the time. I shall not see you again for many months.

I have written to Mr Vakil suggesting that you might prepare for the Cambridge Senior and not for the Matriculation. The Senior will probably fit in better with a future course of study in Europe. Where this future course is going to be I do not know. We shall have to consider this later on together. There is no hurry. Much will depend on what you want to be. Have you thought of this ever? Last year you wrote to me once that you wanted to be a teacher. To teach others is a very wonderful thing but of course one can only teach after one has learnt a lot oneself. There are many other fascinating kinds of work in the world but to do anything well a great deal of training is necessary. Boys or girls in India have not had many professions or lines of activity open to them. Large numbers of boys want to become lawyers or take [entrance examinations into the civil] services and even girls are trying to go the same way. But this is just a way to earn money. It is not good enough just to earn money, although in our present

1. In French.
2. Isn't it?

world some money has to be earned. What is far more important is to do something that is worthwhile and that does good to the larger society we live in. I dislike intensely my own old profession, that of a lawyer. I call it an unsocial profession, for society does not profit by it. It makes people selfish and just clever enough to exploit others. I would not therefore call the lawyer's profession a worthwhile one. He does not create anything or add to the good things of the world. He merely takes a part of other people's belongings.

There are other unsocial professions also like the lawyers. Indeed the most honoured people in India still are those who do nothing at all and merely live in luxury on what their parents have left them. We need not consider all these unsocial people.

What are the social and useful forms of activity? There are so many, I cannot even give a list of them. Our present day world is so complicated that thousands of kinds of activity are necessary to keep it going. As you grow and study and your circle of knowledge widens you will have some glimpse of these varied activities. Millions of people in different parts of the world producing goods – food, clothing and innumerable other things; millions of others carrying these goods to others and distributing them. You buy something in a shop. Behind the shop there are all manner of factories and machines and workers and engineers, and behind the factories are the fields and mines supplying materials. It is all very complicated and fascinating, and the worthwhile thing to do is for each one of us to help in this useful work.

We may be scientists, for science today is at the back of everything; or we may be engineers or those who apply science to man's everyday needs; or doctors who apply science to lessen human suffering and root out diseases by hygiene and sanitation and other preventive measures; or teachers and educationists training all ages from babies up to grown men and women; or up-to-date modern farmers on the land, increasing the yield of the land by new scientific devices and thus adding to the wealth of the country, and so on.

What I wanted to tell you was that we are all members of a huge living thing called society, which consists of all manner of men and women and children. We cannot ignore this and go our way doing just what we please. This would be as if one of our legs decided to walk away regardless of the rest of the body! So we have to fit in our work so as to help society in functioning. Being Indians we shall have to work in India. All manner of changes are going to take place in our country and no one can say what it will be like a few years hence. But a person who is trained to do something that is worthwhile is always a valued member of society.

I have written all this just to make you think on the subject. Of course I want you when you grow up to be strong and self-reliant and well trained for useful work. You do not want to depend on others. There is no hurry to decide.

If you go to Europe to carry on your studies you must know French well. I should have liked you to know German too as this is very useful in many things. But that can wait. The younger you are the easier it is to learn languages.

Do you know, you are just about the age now that I was when I first went to England with Dadu and was put in Harrow School. That was long long ago – twenty-eight years ago!

We had hail here today and all the mountains are covered again with snow. You were not lucky enough to see this fine sight.

All my love and kisses.

Your loving,
Papu

---

49.   [Poona]
                                                       28th January, 1933

Papu darling,

Yesterday I got Mummie's letter saying that this must be sent to you as soon as possible. There was very little time yesterday so I am writing now.

When I arrived here from Allahabad, I felt very hot, then it got colder but now it is again warm.

There are two more boarders now – both sisters. They are Parsis from Bombay. One is my age and the other is only a few months older than Tara, but she is nearly as tall as Chand. Jamnalalji's[1] son – Kamal Nayan – is also coming to study here. He will stay here, but his food will be cooked by his own cook in a separate room. He is about eighteen, but is very tall & broad. He will look like a giant amongst the rest of us. He will most probably come by this evening.

Auntie [Mrs Vakil] has now kept a matron to look after the house and the children, apart from school hours. She is also coming today. I haven't seen her yet – she is a Parsi. Some days ago we had the election of the working committee of our Vidyarthi Mandal[2] (we have it every term). Everybody wanted me to be the general secretary again, but I refused. It's such a lot of work and I'd been doing it till now and was quite tired of it. So now I'm the *nyāyadhish* – judge. I have to settle the quarrels of the children and see that everybody keeps our rules properly. This is the post in which one has to do the least work.

1. Jamnalal Bajaj: a businessman and industrialist who was prominent in the freedom struggle.
2. Students' Union.

Tomorrow our school is going to a picnic to a place called Vithalvadi. We will start in a bus at seven thirty and will return in the evening. The place is a very beautiful spot some miles from Poona. It is a stream on whose banks there are nice shady trees. It is the ideal place for a picnic.

In the evening after returning from Vithalvadi – if we can get away soon enough – we are going to hear some singing of a thirteen-year-old girl who has got a wonderful voice.

Puphi wrote to say that she would be leaving A'bad on the 28th – today. But we have no news yet.

With a huge big hug and a bagful of kisses.

Always your loving,
Indu

———————————

50.   Dehra Dun Jail,
7th February, 1933

Indu darling,

I have your letter.[1] You need not trouble to keep an accurate record of the dates when you have to write to me. Write to me roughly once a fortnight – say at the beginning of the month and the middle – and your letter will be delivered to me whenever it is due. Or you can answer my letters when you receive them.

You must have been not a little surprised to find from the postcard I sent to Mr Vakil that I had changed my mind about your appearing for the Matric. I must apologise to you for this quick change! When you came here we hardly talked on this subject. I dislike the Matric as an examination simply because it is meant to open the door to some of the universities here which I do not fancy. So I told you not to bother about it. I also wrote accordingly to Mr Vakil. Two days after writing to him I received a letter from him. In this letter he mentioned several things which made me change my mind. The first was that many of your fellow students were preparing for the Matric and it would make it pleasanter for you to study with them and have a common aim. To work singly and on one's own account is apt to get rather boring. The preparation for the Matric would not come in the way of your Senior later on but would be a help. And then exams are funny things. If one is not used to them, one gets worried and flustered at the time and is unable to put down even what one knows. This is just a question of getting used to it, as there is no reason why one should worry. Mr Vakil suggested, and I think rightly, that a simpler exam like the Matric would help you in getting used to exams and

---

1. Refers to letter No. 49.

then later when you appear for the Senior you would feel much more at home. These were the reasons which made me change my mind. I hope you agree. I gathered from Mr Vakil's letter that you were quite agreeable to take the Matric. So go ahead! By the way, when is this Matric?

I understand that you feel a little crowded and would like a little privacy for your study. I quite appreciate this. It is not easy to work in a crowd, and besides one likes to sit by oneself occasionally. I hope something will be arranged. I understand that your school is going into bigger quarters in July. But even before that some arrangement might be made. Now that Kamal Nayan also has joined your school as a boarder, you must be a tight fit. Where does he live? I suppose it would be easy to fit up tents if necessary. Anyway as Mummie is in Calcutta and I am in Dehra Dun, you might speak to Puphi of anything that you may want and she will try to fix it up.

Your school, as you know, is a private school. One might almost call it something between a home and a school. As such it has certain advantages which an ordinary school has not got and at the same time there are certain disadvantages. The advantages are that you get more care and attention and affection and a kind of home life. That is a very great thing and it has made me happy to know that you are with friends and are well looked after. If you had been at an ordinary school I would have been anxious about you. The disadvantages of a private school are that you have few companions. A big school is a world in itself and prepares one in a way for the wider world, or at any rate for the university. At present you may feel rather cooped up occasionally and wish to have more companions. But soon enough you will enter the wider sphere of a university or wherever you go to continue your studies and you will have crowds of companions there. You have a bare year more for your present school work. After the Senior you will naturally have to work in a wider sphere. A year is not a very long time. Employ it to fit yourself mentally and physically for the bigger world you may enter next year.

I presume you are carrying on your French lessons with the Mlle. How do you go to her? Do you go walking or by a conveyance? It depends how far she lives. If she lives some distance away it might be convenient for you to go by bicycle. If so we could easily arrange to get a bicycle for you in Poona or Bombay. You are not used to cycling but you can soon get with it. One should know it.

I am glad you have got a matron to look after the kids now. This will give more time to your Auntie to do other things.

I am interested to know that now you are the *Nyayadhish* of your school society. If this means less work for you, your school children must be very well-behaved.

I hope you enjoyed your picnic to Vithalvadi.
Love from your loving,
Papu

---

51.   Dehra Dun Jail,
21st February, 1933

Darling Indu,

Yesterday I sent you two books. One was a child's book, *Toolteoo*. I hope you will not think it beneath your grown-up dignity to receive a book for children! I sent for it as I had read somewhere that it was very good and comparable to *Alice in Wonderland*. Alice being an old favourite of mine, I could not resist the temptation of sending for a book which was thought good enough to be compared with immortal Alice. *Toolteoo* was of course quite different but I enjoyed it and could not help laughing at many of the pictures. I hope the book amused you and the other children.

The other book was Bernard Shaw's play *Saint Joan*. Do you remember seeing this play in French in Paris, when a little Russian woman made a charming Jeanne? We also saw the play in English later but I do not remember if you were with us then. It is a very fine play. Some parts of it may strike you as a bit dull. But the story is a great one and it bears reading and re-reading. As Jeanne is an old favourite and heroine of yours, you will like it. The book also contains another play which perhaps you may not like. The two long prefaces also might prove a bit dull for you.

You must be busy with your work and your preparation for the examination. Still I suppose you do have some time occasionally for other reading. That is why I sent you *Saint Joan*.

Mummie writes to me that someone from Austria came to see her accompanied by Bijju Bhai and he offered to take you away immediately to Vienna for schooling! Vienna is a very beautiful place; it is the home of music. The Viennese are delightful people but their country is having a terrible time at present. Puphi told me that a German lady, who stayed in Anand Bhawan recently, was keen on making arrangements for your education in Germany. Plenty of people seem to be interested in your future education besides your father and mother! Well, perhaps some day, before very long, you will go away to a far country to carry on your education, leaving us rather lonely here. We have trained ourselves for it by long spells in jail! Anyway, we shall put up with it of course, for it is more important that you should have good training and every opportunity to fit yourself for the work that may lie ahead of you, than that we should have the selfish joy of seeing you frequently and having you near us.

But all this is still a part of the future and we need not worry ourselves about it just yet. For the present you have to carry on with your present work and to do it well so that you may easily triumph over any examinations or anything else of the kind that may come your way. And for the present I have to carry on in Dehra Dun Jail!

But I should like you to write to me about your own ideas about your future. You will remember my asking you about this in one of my recent letters.[1] What you would like your job in after life to be? What subjects and what work interest you? Of course as we grow we change our opinions about this very much. The boy's ideal in life is to be an engine driver! But still, if you will write to me from time to time what ideas you have in your little head I should be so glad.

I gather that you were vaccinated again in Bombay. I dislike vaccination but I suppose it has to be done.

Dol Amma or Dadi – what do you call her now? – will probably go to Poona next month. Bapu wants her to stay there for a while near him.

Love from your loving,
Papu

52.   [Poona]
                                          17th [March, 1933]

Papu darlingest,

Since the 14th, we have been having morning school – that is, school begins at seven thirty a.m. and closes at eleven thirty. Up till now I had arranged to go for French at six thirty a.m. on Mondays & Wednesdays – but now the teacher says that this time does not suit her as she misses her morning walk. So, from next Monday I have to go at 11.30 o'clock. Now, after having our meal we are free for the whole day, which is very convenient as we all feel very hot and sleepy in the day-time. Of course I have to get up early (I get up at six), but I find it agrees with me.

Miss Kohn, my French teacher lives close by – It takes barely three minutes to walk over to her house. So there is no difficulty whatsoever in going.

We, meaning Kamal Nayan, Ramkrishna[2] (his brother), Chand & myself, go to see Bapu every week on Saturdays. We have just returned from the jail. Bapu was very cheerful and pulled my ear so hard that I thought it would come off. It's still a little red. Bapu asked us to bring Tara too, but she gets bored and prefers staying at home.

You asked Mr Vakil what science I learn. We do Physics and Chemis-

1. Refers to letter No. 48.
2. Ramkrishna Bajaj: son of Jamnalal Bajaj; active in the struggle for freedom, now prominent in business.

try. We just began Chemistry about a month ago. Physics we have been doing since some time. I find them very interesting.

It is very hot here in the daytime but at night a blanket is needed. We sleep right outside and it is very pleasant. We do not do any special exercises, except the Lathi, etc., in school-time – but we play in the evening, which makes up for it.

Mrs Vakil is not very well and she is at the Nature Cure Clinic with little Ira, who had also been keeping bad health lately. Instead of Auntie, Mrs Vakil's sister is staying here. Mrs Vakil went to the hospital on the 13th and as yet it is not decided when she will be back.

After all, the matron did not arrive. Something or the other happened to her. So again Mrs Vakil is hunting for another one.

Some days ago 'Kaka Saheb' (Kaka Kalelkar)[1] came to Poona. So we had a little programme for him on Sunday evening. It was not as good as it might have been, for we only decided to have it on Saturday and everything was in a terrific hurry.

Chand & I went to see Padmaja day before yesterday. She is better, but is still taking the injections.

The summer holidays begin somewhere in the middle of April. What am I to do? If Mummie is there, I might come to Dehra Dun. The Vakils are planning to go to Mahabaleshwar or Ootacamund. But if possible, I would much rather come to see you. I will also write to Mummie about it and see what she says.

Puphi is still in Bombay, she is having some eye treatment. Chhoti Puphi will also be coming here soon. She wrote to say that she would start from Allahabad on the 20th instant.

Padmaja got a wee little tent for me. It is as yet very dirty and I am thinking of having it dyed.

With heaps of love and many many kisses.

From your loving,
Indu

I enclose my last month's school report. I have lost a few lbs but am otherwise very well so don't be alarmed. How is your cat?

---

53.   Dehra Dun Jail,
                               20th March, 1933

Indu darling,

... I am writing to you today, specially as in a few days there will be Nauroz and the new year (according to the Samvat Calendar) will

1. Kaka Kalelkar: nationalist leader and educationalist.

begin, and I must send you my love and good wishes for this New Year.

I am sending you a book also as a Nauroz gift. This is Van Loon's *Geography*. The writing part of it is not up to much and is full of errors and wrong statements. Allahabad, you will be interested to know from it, is the holy city of the Musalmans, because of its name! Besides I do not like his style of writing, American or whatever it may be. But the pictures are really good. The outside cover happens to be a map of the world. Take it off and give it to Mr Vakil. He might like to hang it in school.

Some weeks ago I sent you a book by Bernard Shaw. I have had no receipt or intimation that you have received it.

Some time ago you wrote to me about the delights of having a good imagination and imagining all manner of things. Imagination is certainly an excellent thing so long as it helps us on to act in this world. But if imagination means just losing oneself in the air and losing contact with the world and what one has to do in it, then it is not much good, and it is apt to make one just a selfish little cloud of humanity thinking of oneself and of nothing else.

I do not know what you will do in after life. It is difficult, and not necessary, to decide so early. But whatever you do I have hoped that you will do it well and distinguish yourself in it. I have wanted you to play a worthy part in the world and to be full of life and intelligence and activity. I hope you will do so . . .

Love,

Your loving,
Papu

---

54.   Dehra Dun Jail,
                                                       3rd April, 1933

Indu *bien aimée*,

. . . Chand writes to me that your school closes up on the 20th but I gather from Mummie that the date is the 22nd. Whichever the date may be I think that you might come direct to Dehra Dun. My interview will fall due on 25th April. I should like you to be present then. If you are delayed in reaching here by a day I can postpone the interview for a day or so. But I should not like to postpone it for long as Mummie will be waiting for it here.

I do not know if you want to go to Allahabad or Bombay on your way up here. In any event you will go to Bombay for a day or two and take the train from there. Allahabad will hardly be worth a visit with no one else there in Anand Bhawan. If you want clothes made, probably you will find good tailors here. And then you must remember that Mussoorie is just two hours from here and you can always go when you want to.

I have an idea that a direct carriage runs between Bombay and Dehra Dun. If so you should get a berth reserved for yourself in it. Anyway you are an experienced traveller now.

Dehra Dun of course is not exactly a health resort in summer. Just now it is very pleasant. Next month it will be hot, but it is never so hot as in Allahabad.

Dol Amma – do you call her that still? Or what do you call her? – has managed to reach the place of rest also. I do not know how long she will stay there. I imagine it will not be long and that she will be in Poona this month.

I am glad you are doing Chemistry. Chemistry was one of my special subjects in which I took my degree at Cambridge. The other subjects were Geology and Botany. I am afraid I do not remember much that I learnt in those far-off days. And yet, the study of science makes a tremendous difference to a person and I am very grateful to science for the help it has given me in life. The help has been chiefly in the training it has given and the outlook of the mind. It was because of my early scientific training and outlook that I wrote those letters to you to Mussoorie, which were published later.

So I am glad you are doing some science. Almost all our modern life is based on science and a person who does not know something about science is rather lost in the modern world. Science really means experiment, the finding out of truth by experiment, and not merely accepting facts just because somebody has said so.

When you come here will you please bring the *Outline for Boys and Girls* with you? I should like Mummie to read it, and if you have not read it, you can also do so. I like the book so much that I have sent a copy to Ballo and another to Zohra (Dr Ansari's[1] adopted daughter).

You might also bring with you Van Loon's *Geography* to show Mummie, minus the cover, which you had better present to your school!

Please tell Mr Vakil that you will be spending most of your holidays, with us (or near me) in Dehra Dun. I hope both Mr & Mrs Vakil are well now and will have good rest after their strenuous term-time.

All my love, sweetheart. I am looking forward so much to seeing you.

Your loving,

Papu

---

1. Dr M. A. Ansari: prominent physician and leading member of the Congress, a close friend of the Nehrus, he treated Kamala Nehru from time to time.

4th April

I find from this morning's paper that Dol Amma has been discharged and has gone on to Calcutta. Perhaps she will go to Poona from there.

You say in your letter that the Dakshini New Year's Day[1] fell on the same day as Nauroz. Of course. They are the same day – the first day of the Vikrami Samvat Era which is about 57¾ years in advance of the Christian Era. Thus the Samvat Era which began last week on Nauroz is 1990. Most Indians do not observe the Nauroz day as a special day, but Kashmiris and Dakshinis do. It is curious what a lot of common customs there are between the people of Kashmir and those of Maharashtra.

Love,
Papu

---

55.   Dehra Dun Jail,
                                                 2nd May, 1933

Indu darling,
You were not looking the picture of health when I saw you that day! I hope you have got rid of your pain and fever. You must have caught a chill. The weather is so changeable here and one must be careful. If you have still any pain in the neck have it massaged with the almond oil I gave Mummie.

I am glad, you are corresponding with your old French school mate. Why not write to her in French and ask her to do so also? Is she still at Bex? And how is Bex getting on?

Don't read too much here – walk and run and generally live a physical life. Of course too much of the physical life is apt to be boring and the mind must be kept well oiled and functioning. But the holidays are not meant for hard mental work. Also I have often felt that you read rather fast. In doing so one is often liable to miss much in a book. Some light books of course have to be read fast; there is little in them. But a worthwhile book deserves a little more time and attention. Think of the pains and the great deal of thinking that the author has put behind what he has written, and when we just rush through it we miss his real meaning, and forget soon enough what we read.

A very good habit to develop is to keep a notebook in which we can jot down anything that pleases us or strikes us specially in a book we read. These notes of ours help us to remember much and we can always go back to them with interest. In jail I have specially developed this habit and I am now running my seventeenth notebook!

1. New Year's Day of the Maharashtra region. Dakshini means Southern.

I hope anyway that you will read my series of letters to you rather slowly and a bit at a time. Don't rush them; otherwise they will bore you tremendously. They are not very light reading.

I suppose you have enough books to read. If not just let me know and I can suggest or send some.

During our last interview I talked and talked and talked. Terrible, was it not? Like a tap left open! Next time you will have to do the talking and I shall listen; and if I try to talk too much, stop me. I keep bottled up for two weeks and then when I get a chance I am apt to rush away with it.

There are plenty of birds in Dehra Dun at present. I wish I knew all their names. I suppose your garden has many of them. There is the *koel* of course, and the 'brain fever bird', I think that is the name. Why this curious name has been given to it I don't quite know, unless it is because its persistence is likely to give people brain fever! I must say that it is very trying sometimes. Its four notes are pleasant enough but ceaseless repetition night and day – rain or sunshine – is too much of a good thing. It goes on hour after hour. I do not know its Hindustani name but it is referred to in a variety of ways. People here say its four notes mean *main sotā thā.*[1] Up in the hills they say the bird sings *Kakhal Pāko,*[2] *kakhal* being something grown in the fields. This is the time for it to ripen & so the bird announces it! You can imagine almost anything out of the four notes – *utho jago.*[3] A powerful noise it makes – it carries a good way.

Bapu has hurled another thunderbolt[4] at us and I do not know what is going to happen.

I have no news of the Puphis' other children. They ought to be in Mussoorie today.

Au revoir, bien aimée and love.

Your loving,
Papu

---

56. Dehra Dun Jail,
16th May, 1933

My darling Indu,

I was just thinking that you ought to pay a little visit to Mussoorie, and had decided to write to you about it, when news came that you were going to do so. I am glad you are going or perhaps have already gone. Dehra Dun is at

1. I was sleeping.
2. The crop is ready.
3. Rise awake.
4. A fast undertaken by Mahatma Gandhi in support of the untouchables, whom he called Harijans.

the best of times rather a quiet and dull place and I don't suppose you have many acquaintances here. A little change now and then will do you good and cheer you up.

That is as it should be. We are all sometimes rather apt to get hot and bothered. But it is rather silly, don't you think? And it makes us look a bit ridiculous to others. No one who is excited and worked up looks his best. Of course we can't always help getting a little excited but it is always a sign of a crack in our education or training. After all, what is the whole end and aim of education – from one point of view at least? It is: not to be hot and bothered whatever happens and to fit oneself to the people one comes across and try to cooperate with them. In India, I am afraid, one is always coming across people who are losing their tempers and generally making a nuisance of themselves. Perhaps they think that they cut a fine figure, not realising how silly they look. They shout and curse at servants, a thing you hardly ever see in the West. In England, among decent people, it is considered the limit of bad form to shout at a servant, for the poor servant is not in a position to answer back. It is like kicking a person who is down. And yet in India most people indulge in this degrading habit. If people only realised that they injured themselves more by such habits than they do others, probably they would behave better.

I did not know about Shama joining a film company till I read about it in your letter.[1] I agree with you. It would have been far better if she had joined a good company once she was about it. As a matter of fact it would have been an easy thing to arrange and, strange as it may seem, I might even have helped from here! I don't suppose Ladli Chacha is very happy about this.

You seem to have frightened Bebee about my health and she has sent me a letter full of worry and anxiety. How did you think, my dear, that I was languishing away? Perhaps the long stream of talk that I indulged in! I am keeping remarkably well and little things, like applying iodine for an old pain at the side, have nothing to do with it. In your letter you tell me that you had a terrible headache. Do you know that I hardly know – in spite of my forty-three years – what a bad headache is – or for the matter of that even a mild one?

We have had two interviews, you and I, and on both the occasions I have done most of the talking. A jail interview is not a natural way of meeting; one feels a little constrained and the time limit oppresses one. Still, I would like you next time to tell me something about yourself and your school and what you would like to do. If you do not tell me how you feel how can I help you? The secret of doing a thing well, whatever it may be, is

---

1. Letter not traceable. Shama is Shyama Zutshi, daughter of Indira's uncle, Ladli Prasad Zutshi.

to cooperate with others in the doing of it. Do you know that in school and in homes there are supposed to be two kinds of children who do not make good progress and who give a lot of trouble? They are called problem children. One is the spoilt child who has been used at home to getting everything he or she wants without working for it or any other trouble? The other is the neglected child whom people at home, usually in large families where there are many children, ignore and who is thus not properly looked after. Both the spoilt child on the one hand and the neglected one on the other get little chance of cooperating with others, of working together with others in a common undertaking. So they do not develop the habit of cooperation and all their subsequent troubles are said to be due to this. It is because of this that they become what one called problem children who offer special problems to their teachers as to how to deal with them. The spoilt child when he or she goes out into the world expects everyone to pat him on the back all the time as he was patted at home. Of course nobody does so and the spoilt child gets very angry and blames everybody when really the fault is his own and not other people's. The neglected child has been badly treated at home and is not used to meeting people. So when he goes out, he keeps apart from others and feels dissatisfied and angry and blames everybody.

This is not so with children only, but with grown-ups also. Most of us are either spoilt or neglected and so have grown up rather crooked and we are always blaming others for our own faults. The right thing of course is to be neither; to be something in between the two, healthy in mind, meeting others and always trying to cooperate with them and doing one's own share of the job without expecting others to do it.

Children, naturally, do not and cannot understand all these niceties. They behave as they have been taught to behave or as they have seen others behave. I am writing all this because you are a sensible girl and I can speak to you more as a friend than as a daughter of mine. I know you will understand. Your father was himself a bit of a spoilt child. For many years he was the only child, for his sisters came long afterwards, and only children are apt to be spoilt by their parents by too much affection. I suppose he still bears traces, and very evident traces, of having been spoilt not only by his parents but by so many other people! You are an only child also and a dearly loved one and perhaps unconsciously your parents and grandparents have spoilt you just a wee bit also and made you expect much in the world that you may not find there. I cannot judge, neither can you, for we are both partial and we are too near each other to have a good view. But I imagine that however much we may have erred, led away by our exceeding love for you, recent events or rather public happenings since your childhood upwards have strengthened you and stiffened you and pulled you up from the spoilt variety which always thinks of itself and little of others.

I do not know why I am writing on like this. It is more of a talk – as if you were sitting by me. What I began with was this – that I should like you during our next interview to have a talk with me about yourself and your school and your ideas in general about the future. As you know, your time in your present school will end before long. What is more important is the next step and we must have a talk about that and discuss it among ourselves and cooperate together to make this step a real good one. So, my dear, that must be the programme for 23rd May, nine a.m. But only if you are willing and will cooperate.

I hope Rust[1] will make some good pictures of you both in a frock & in a sari.

Love,

Your loving,
Papu

There is a delightful story about a lion cub in the *New Statesman* I am sending. It is at page 503 & is called 'The Lion that Lost its way'.

---

57.   28th May [1933]

Mon cher[2] Papu,
On the 6th we will have our last interview and then I will go back to Poona and will not be able to see you till after your release. That is of course if you do not return to jail before December or if you come to Poona before our holidays. Anyhow we will write every fortnight and think of each other every day. And this time I mean to write regularly – not like last time.

I'm sorry the photographs were so bad. But is it necessary to have them taken again? Quite lately I had those Calcutta ones taken and we can have other ones later. Though there is little chance of having one taken by Julian Rust if I don't go now. However I'll do as you say.

Yesterday it was very pleasant & cool because of the rain and hail. But again this afternoon it has been quite hot.

Suddenly about an hour or so ago my voice became quite hoarse and Mummie began grumbling that I must have caught a cold. But I had a good gargle with Listerine & hot water and now the voice is quite normal. Nineteen hours more and Bapu will be sipping orange juice. Every day we eagerly looked out for the newspapers to find out his condition but

1. Julian Rust: photographer.
2. My dear.

somehow from the very beginning we never expected to find that there were any complications. Indeed if there had been the slightest trouble I would have been surprised. Wonderful old man Bapu is.

Tomorrow at about the time Bapu breaks his fast Mummie has asked twenty Harijan children to come here. They will be bathed, dressed in khadi and given some food.

Anand Bhai[1] is coming here on the 2nd and will not be going to Mussoorie. Instead he will stay here till the 7th. So perhaps Mummie will not be able to go to Mussoorie with me. Though I don't see why she shouldn't – Anand Bhai is no stranger and besides he is in his office all day.

We got a note from the Puphis to say that everybody up there was quite fit.

And now I'll say – '*Auf Wiedersen*,[2] darlingest' with a big kiss, a huge hug and tons of love. (Hasn't something gone wrong in the spelling?)

Eternally your loving,
Indu

———————— ◄▬ ————————

58.　　　　　　　　　　　　　　　　　　　　Dehra Dun Jail,
　　　　　　　　　　　　　　　　　　　　30th May, 1933

Indu *bien aimée*,

Yes, a week today we shall have our interview, the last for a long while. It has been very delightful to have seen you so many times during these past weeks. Jail interviews are of all things perhaps the most unsatisfactory, and yet one must learn to be thankful for small mercies, and even these unsatisfactory meetings become like oases in a desert. Does your next school term last six months to December? That seems a long stretch. But I shall see you before that. If I can move I shall go to Poona of course. And if I am a fixture, as is quite possible, then you will have to cross the mountains and plains of India which will divide us. Do you know the story of the mountain and Mahomet? Well, neither of us are exactly mountains but, so far as I am concerned, I am becoming almost as immovable as a mountain. And so it will be for you to come to the mountain.

The photographs were really too bad. The one in profile is not so bad but I do not care for that very much either. I am surprised at Rust making a mess of the job. It is obvious that you are feeling uncomfortable and being made to pose and smile to order and that would spoil any photograph. It is absurd to try to smile in this forced way. A photographer should make the

1. Anand Kumar Nehru: a cousin of Indira.
2. See letter No. 58.

sitter feel as unself-conscious as possible. The sitter should really forget about the photograph.

I think you should give some more sittings to Rust. This is desirable as it would be a good thing to have some decent photographs. The Calcutta ones were mediocre. (Where are they? I have not seen them.) Besides, now that we are rejecting Rust's previous attempts it is up to us to give him another chance. Otherwise it would not be fair to him. In the fresh sittings you give tell Rust that I would like a close-up of the face, full or three-quarter. Something like one of your pictures taken at Geneva. I liked that very much.

You might go to Mussoorie as soon as you can. I would suggest your going not later than Friday. Go on the morning of 2nd June by yourself, informing Puphi by telephone previously. You can easily go by yourself. Ask Puphi to fix up with Rust. Two days later, Mummie might join you on the 4th morning. She will have some business with the dentist. On the 5th evening you can both return to Dehra, and if the Puphis intend coming down, they can also do so. The next morning I shall have the interview. I have suggested Mummie going up later as probably she would not like to leave Dol Amma or Anand for several days. Dol Amma must not go to Mussoorie as this might upset her health and she would be inconvenienced. There is no difficulty in Mummie going up for a day or two even though Dol Amma remains behind and Anand is staying here. If she likes she can even go for a longer period.

I hope your voice or your throat has not given any more trouble. Use a gargle daily. Why not use a gargle of hydrogen peroxide mixed with water? This is very good.

During our last interview, as usual, I held forth to you for a long time and gave you what I considered was good advice. But too much good advice is a nuisance, is it not? I hope I did not bore you too much. I am so anxious to be of some help to you if I can that I sometimes run away with my ideas. The world is not always a pleasant place to live in and all manner of problems arise. There are problems between nations, and national problems, and family problems, and each person's individual problems. You can see for yourself many of these problems surrounding us and giving us no peace. To some extent we can profit by other people's experiences, though in reality we have to solve most of our problems and difficulties ourselves. So, thinking that perhaps I can help you, I sometimes write to you or talk to you on these subjects.

It is a very foolish thing to shut our eyes to difficulties and problems. They do not vanish away by our following the example of the ostrich and burying our heads in the sand. There is conflict and trouble enough in the world. Let us face them and where necessary even take part in the conflict. But this does not mean that we should create conflict or imagine conflict or trouble where there is none. The world is troublesome enough. Why make it worse? Can anything be more foolish? And yet that is exactly what many of us do by picking out faults in others and imagining grievances. We get angry because someone does not pay sufficient attention to us or acts in a way we do not like. Everybody in the world is not going to pay attention to us, and we are sure to feel miserable in afterlife if we expect too much attention from others. We become like a beautiful china plate – fragile and delicate and easily cracked. It often happens that a parent or teacher deliberately acts in what seems a slightly hard way in order to strengthen a child, knowing that too much coddling may be harmful. With a small child one cannot explain these matters but a grown-up girl or boy can understand these things for herself or himself.

The thing to remember is that it is unworthy and undignified to run away from trouble. Real troubles have to be faced and if necessary fought; imaginary troubles are to be removed by frank talks. To mope and nurse a grievance secretly is a sign of weakness and folly. It is most undignified. Discuss the matter, have it out, try to understand the other party's viewpoint, and tell him or her your own. Probably our misconceptions will be removed by this and our anger will disappear even though we may not agree with the other party. If we accept the good faith of the other party, and we both work for the same object, it is usually possible to carry on easily together in spite of differences.

There are many things which deserve our anger; many things against which we have got to fight. Are we going to waste our energy and our strength and our righteous anger over the trivial things of life or the really big things? By getting excited over the trivial things we lose dignity, we look cheap. We must never make ourselves cheap to anybody or on any occasion, nor must we make ourselves ridiculous. If we are worthy of it, the world's attention and respect will come to us, whether we care for it or not. If it does not come there is something wrong in our own make-up and the sooner we put it right the better. Only foolish persons get angry at obstacles. Does one get angry at a stone against which one has stumbled, or shout out at the darkness because we cannot see? So also with the human beings we come across. It is no good shouting at them or getting angry at them. Try to understand them, try to cooperate with them and, if necessary, even fight them, but don't lose your temper or your self-control.

I write all this although the time is yet distant when you will have to face the big problems of the world. For the present you must not worry about these things. You must keep care and worry away from your youth and grow up healthy and strong in mind and body. But strange things are happening now-a-days and during times of trouble one cannot avoid thinking and growing rapidly.

There is a passage written by Bernard Shaw which appeals to me tremendously. It runs as follows:

This is the true joy in life, the being used for a purpose recognised by yourself as a mighty one; the being thoroughly worn out before you are thrown on the scrap heap; the being a force of nature, instead of a feverish, selfish little clod of ailments and grievances, complaining that the world will not devote itself to making you happy.

I hope you will have an enjoyable three or four days in Mussoorie and return freshened up with bright eyes and a bright heart and a touch of pink in your cheeks! And so, *carissima mia, auf wiedersehen*[1] (which is a silly mixture of Italian & German). I am using the German words to show you the right spelling. Yours was all wrong.

Love,

> Your loving,
> Papu

59.

Dehra Dun Jail,
13th June, 1933

Indu, *carissima mia*,

You must be in Poona town now in your new abode. The journey must have been trying but Poona during the monsoon is delightful, as you know by experience. I hope you like the new house and you have got your little corner to study there.

I had a visit from Bijji Chacha & Chachi and Ballo day before yesterday. I was amazed to see Ballo. I had heard that he had grown and expected to see a big boy but nearly six feet of him was more than I expected. I don't think I would have recognised him by himself.

I do not know how many photographs you have ordered from Rust. You will naturally want some for your friends. You had better let Mummie know how many you want and she will send them to you.

My next interview will be rather dull and empty without you. But I must not be too greedy. I had my full share during the last six or seven weeks.

I think you had better write to me direct to the jail as Mummie is likely to leave Dehra Dun soon.

Love,

> Your loving,
> Papu

---

1. My dearest, till we meet again.

60.   Poona,
20th June [1933]

Papu darling,

I was terribly sorry not to write to you last time and am sending this sooner than its time so that it does not miss you this time also.

I forgot to wire the Vakils of my arrival, but fortunately he had come to the Poona station to meet somebody else, who had come by the same train.

The new house is much more cheerful and attractive than the address sounds. It is certainly more spacious. Just opposite is the military shooting-practice ground and every morning we have the pleasure of hearing machine-gun shots. Fortunately for us the military do not practise during our school time. But this ground is a great advantage to us, for because of so much open ground we have plenty of breeze and we can go there to play any time we like. Change of surroundings has a great effect on our minds. And since we have come here everybody seems much more cheerful. My classroom is the largest and brightest in the house. And we are not at all disturbed whenever we want to study – so a private room will not be needed. We have changed our mode of living completely. We now eat no eggs, fish or meat and have vegetarian wholesome meals at ten thirty a.m. and seven forty-five p.m. At seven in the morning we have just a cup of hot milk and at two thirty, milk and fruits. This diet suits me very well and I'm quite fit.

The weather is perfectly delightful, especially after coming from the awful heat of Allahabad.

In the old house we were always afraid, lest the roof or walls collapse on our heads. Here at least we are spared this mental agony.

I am gradually getting more and more interested in Physics & Chemistry. Just a degree more everyday. At present these are my most looked forward to subjects, of course not including Literature, which has always been highest in my thoughts. Just now I have not got anything to read apart from the Matric course. I was very interested in Adler's[1] book about life and Mummie said she would send it as soon as she finished it. If there are any other suitable books – not very high reading – you might please ask Mummie to send them along too.

How are the dogs? I had a letter from Bebee some time ago. She seemed to be very excited about a 'perfectly swish Alsatian' – as she called it – that somebody is going to send her.

I have begun bathing with cold water and hope to keep it up all the year round. Of course hot water is much more soothing if you are tired but cold is best to freshen you up.

---

1. Alfred Adler: Viennese psychologist and psychiatrist.

We have a new boarder, a five-year-old Sindhi girl. As yet she does not know Hindi or Gujerati and goes on talking nineteen to the dozen in Sindhi, whether anyone is listening or not, whether anyone understands or not. So I have picked up a few Sindhi sentences.

Miss Kohn, my French teacher, lives near our old house, which is rather far from here. And to make the way shorter, I go through somebody's compound and climb over a wall and then I arrive in Miss Kohn's garden. I go at eight in the morning thrice a week. It is a nice walk and gives me an appetite for breakfast & I rather like it.

The Vakils & their children send their love.

Jamnalalji Bajaj came to see me when he was in Poona – he sent his *namaskars.*[1]

With heaps of love.

Always your loving,
Indu

———————

61.   Dehra Dun Jail,
                                                 27th June, 1933

Darling Indu,

I was very glad to get your letter[2] from Poona. You must not trouble about writing to me on appointed days and trying to remember them. Write to me once a fortnight on any free day you may have.

So the new school house has met with your approval. That is good. A cheerful house with bright and airy rooms and plenty of open space in front makes all the difference to one's school work. Have you any garden? Why should not the school children interest themselves in a little gardening? Poona is an ideal place for this. Perhaps you know that most of our flower and vegetable seeds come from Poona nurseries.

Physics and Chemistry are fascinating subjects – all science is. The more one learns about them the more they fascinate. All our modern world with its complicated machinery and railways and aeroplanes and wireless telegraphy and thousands of other things, is based on science. It is as well therefore to know something about science. But the importance of science really consists in teaching us the way of experiment, and training our minds so that we may apply this method to life's problems and difficulties. If more people had a scientific training there would be far less of unreason and bigotry and conflict in the world.

---

1. Salutations.
2. Refers to letter No. 60.

I wonder if you have read the chapters on science in the *Outline* I sent you. These are easy chapters and I found them interesting. There is not only something about physics and chemistry in them but also about biology and physiology and perhaps some other sciences too. The way to read this *Outline* is not to try to read it through from beginning to end, but to dip into it here and there. If any subject interests you read the chapter on it.

Mummie will send you Adler's book. Perhaps this might interest Mr Vakil also. You can give it to him after you have read it.

As for my recommending to you good books to read, I shall gladly do so. There is no lack of such books in English and French and mountains of new books continue to appear. As a rule new books should be avoided. Many of them look attractive and they are boomed up for a while and then forgotten. A book that has survived the test of time is likely to be good, to be literature. When there are so many of the really worthwhile books for us to read, it is rather silly to waste time on trash.

Why don't you read some of the famous old novels in English and French? They will be light reading and at the same time good reading. Dickens, Scott and Thackeray are all good in their way and each very different from the other. You may like one and not the other. Victor Hugo or Dumas are fascinating. Reading these classic French stories you will improve your knowledge of French. Mlle Kohn, your teacher, might be able to suggest books to you. Did you read all the books sent by Mlle Hemmerlin last year? About English books you can ask Mr Vakil for suggestions.

There is a strange magic about good literature which is wonderfully refreshing and soothing. This magic comes to us slowly as we make friends with good books, and when we have begun to feel it, we have found the key to the wonderland of books. They never fail us, these friends that neither age nor change. They have been dear companions to me, especially in prison, and I have got more pleasure from books than from almost anything. There is only one other thing which is, in its own way, more magical, more wonderful, and that is music. I have always regretted my ignorance of it. How much I have missed because of this! Literature, art, music, science – all make our life rich and deep and varied. They teach us how to live.

Did you find the book by Hans Kohn[1] in Anand Bhawan which I wanted you to take to Vallabhbhai Patel? And did you send it to him?

My dogs are flourishing. I am having more of them than I want to for they all crowd into my little place when it rains, and it rains a lot, night and

---

1. Hans Kohn: German historian of nationalism and national movements.

day. The problem of their future is already troubling me. What shall I do with them when I go from here?

Love,

Your loving,
Papu

---

62.   [Poona]
                                                   2nd July, 1933

Papu darling,

Your letter[1] arrived just a few minutes ago. And it being a Sunday, I had nothing else to do and so I sat down to write to you. I can never express myself well in letters. But there is a strange pleasure in writing to you – I feel I am in quite another and a very happy world.

If two or three flower-beds can be called a garden, we have one. There is no room for any more. We all miss the lovely trees of 3, Staveley Road.

Every morning we do a little digging – and are trying to make another long bed. When the flowers come there, it will look very pretty, but all flowers anywhere look beautiful, so that is not saying very much. We have now got two new boys in our class – the Matric class now has nine pupils and another one will soon be coming.

About a week ago Mrs Naidu[2] came to see me. I told her I would like to see Bapu and she took me there.[3] Bapu was not very pleased at my delay in coming to him and as soon as I told him my difficulty, he arranged for the car. So now we have decided that every Sunday he will have a car sent between ten and eleven. Today I will probably have my lunch at Parnakuti. Bapu is much better now and very cheerful. He cracks jokes in his usual old way.

5 o'clock

While I was writing this morning I was interrupted by Girdhari Kripalani,[4] who came to take me to Bapu's. I have just returned. Bapu started his *maun*[5] at eleven thirty and I could only talk to him for one and a half minutes, for when I arrived at Parnakuti a Harijan meeting was going on. Of course I spoke to Bapu even after he had begun his *maun*. He insisted on my having lunch at Parnakuti every Sunday. He sent you his love.

1. Refers to letter No. 61.
2. Sarojini Naidu: nationalist leader and poet.
3. Mahatma Gandhi was staying at Parnakuti, the residence of Premlila Lady Thackersey.
4. Girdhari Kripalani: nationalist and social worker.
5. Silence.

My eyes were troubling me since some time. Mr Vakil took me to a certain Dr Patvardhan to be examined, the result being that I will have to wear specs all day – whether I am reading or not. I do hope this will not be for long. But there is nothing to get alarmed at – my [lens] number is a very small one.

The weather here is perfectly delightful. It rains every day. The rain here is very slight and pleasant. I enjoy walking in it.

I walk over to Miss Kohn thrice a week. If I walk briskly it takes me eight and a half minutes to go there. I go at eight o'clock and enjoy myself thoroughly.

Two more boarders have come – Parsi twins. They have spent most of their lives in France and speak French fluently. This will help me a lot in my French conversation.

I do not remember if I wrote to you about our new routine. We have changed our style of eating altogether. We eat pure Gujerati food exactly in the Gujerati way. We have left off meat & fish. I like this food much better and find it agrees with me.

There is a strong rumour here that you are going to be released in time for the meeting on the 12th.[1] One can never rely on these rumours.

My fondest love,
Indu

Everybody sends love.

---

63.   Dehra Dun Jail,
                                            11th July, 1933

Darling Indu,

You wrote in your letter[2] that there was a rumour that I might be with you on the 12th. Rumour is a shameless thing – it has been called 'a lying jade' – and must never be taken seriously. You will have to wait for me for at least two more 12ths. Meanwhile Mummie has gone to you and that should be enough.

I am sorry to learn of the trouble you have had with your eyes. Of course if the eye doctor says so, you should wear glasses. The trouble will probably pass after a while if care is taken at an early stage. Danger comes from neglect. Big Puphi had to wear glasses for some time when she was your age but she has not done so for a long time now. My eyes have never

---

1. This was an informal conference of Congressmen, where proposals for the unconditional withdrawal of the Civil Disobedience Movement were rejected, but Mahatma Gandhi was authorised to meet the Viceroy in order to negotiate a settlement.
2. Refers to letter No. 62.

given me any trouble whatever and I have not had to wear glasses at any time, although I read a lot. Perhaps this is due to my general good health. Wash your eyes regularly with boric lotion. A little rose water added on makes it very refreshing in summer. Do you know how I wash my eyes every day? I use a *lotā*[1] for an eye-cup and fill it with fresh water! What I like doing is to have a basin full of fresh water into which I can put my face and, opening my eyes, roll them about in all directions. This rolling about from right to left and left to right and diagonally and in a circular way is good exercise for the eyes. When we read we keep them in one position for a long time and naturally they get tired. Rolling them in fresh water refreshes them greatly, just as stretching a tired arm. But if you start rolling your eyes before other people they might begin to suspect your sanity!

Mr Vakil writes to me that he has recommended some of Scott's books to you. Did you read the book by W. H. Hudson[2] which I sent you last year – *Far Away and Long Ago*? I found the book as delightful as its title would lead one to expect.

I am glad that you have got the French-speaking twins in your school. There is nothing like speaking a language to get to know it.

The Poona rain is very like English rain and very unlike Dehra Dun rain. Here in Dehra we have an inch or two everyday and it pours and pours till one wonders where so much water comes from. Sometimes, when it rains long and hard, one feels cooped up and bored. But generally it is pleasant to hear.

> *O doux bruit de la pluie,*
> *Par terre et sur les toits!*
>
> *Pour un coeur qui s'ennuie,*
> *Oh! le chant de la pluie!*[3]

So sings Paul Verlaine,[4] and I often remember his lines when the rain beats down on the *toits*. But the noise is not so *doux* and sweet always; sometimes it sounds angry and fierce as it tries to beat and batter down everything that comes in its way. Then it is a fit companion for Jove's thunder and lightning.

The frequent rain here interferes a little with my little walks, morning and evening, in front of the jail gate. One evening I decided to ignore it

---

1. A small metal pot.
2. William Henry Hudson: English author and naturalist.
3. For English translation see Appendix C, II.
4. Paul Verlaine: French poet of the nineteenth century.

and I sallied out in a mackintosh. It was one of the angry and fierce days and the rain beat down on me as if it wanted to flatten me out on the ground, and the wind shrieked and moaned. My poor mackintosh was in a bad way and I was soon soaked to the skin. But I carried on and faced the wind and the rain and defied them to do their worst! And then they seemed to become friendly to me and I almost thought that they were caressing me in all their wild fury. I shall remember that evening and how exhilarated I felt.

I am glad you visit Bapu regularly. He must be very busy just at present.

Love from your loving,
Papu

64.   [Poona]
15th July [1933]

Papu darling,

I have your letter.[1] Mummie told me it would arrive on the 12th or 13th and we looked out for every post. At last it arrived about half an hour ago and I jumped with joy.

I do not know what has happened to me and I'm quite fed up with myself. After my eye trouble, I hurt my leg. When that got all right on Saturday last, I got fever. This fever has continued till this morning. At present I have no temperature and have been allowed to walk about a little. This is a great relief as I am quite tired of lying in bed – seven days is long enough. The doctor said it was entirely due to my stomach and throat. I am quite all right now and if my temp. remains at normal, hope to go and see Bapu this evening.

Don't get alarmed.

I liked Verlaine's lines about the rain very much. They just suit the Poona rain – soft and cool and lovely. But sometimes one gets tired of this gentleness and longs for it to get noisier and fiercer. However this latter sort is not very good to walk in and it would not be a bad idea if you got a better mackintosh for yourself . . .

Have you decided anything about your dogs? I hear that Simbhir gave Mummie quite a lot of trouble in Dehra Dun after I left. I was sorry to hear this and I think it was better that she sent him to Allahabad.

In Poona we have some very lovely roses just now.

Puphi tells me that all three children have joined the Convent at Allahabad. Chand does not want to come here. But I do not think this will be very good for her. She should be separated from home and be sent to

---

1. Refers to letter No. 63.

some place like this. Though of course this is not for me to decide. I have stayed a great deal with Chand and have got to know her well. I feel that at home she will be quite spoilt . . .

With lots of love and heaps of kisses.

Ever your loving,
Indu

65.   [Vile Parle]
11th November, 1933

Papu darling,

This is just to wish you very many happy returns of the day. I had hoped that you would spend your birthday with me, here in Vile Parle. But now that your visit to Wardha has been cancelled there is no hope of seeing you in the near future.

I wanted to send you something but nothing is available in Vile Parle. And we don't go very often to Bombay. Kaka went yesterday, but it being a *hartal* day I did not like to buy anything. All I can give is my love. And this has always been yours and always will be.

Often I do and say things which I ought not to. And sometimes you get angry. Of course it is my fault – but will you please forgive and forget? I have not had much time to read anything except text books – so No. Ten is not yet finished. I will however send it as soon as possible. Mr Vakil would like to read the preceding numbers. Could you send them?

I work quite hard. But there is not much possibility of passing this year . . .

Ever your loving,
Indu

How old are you now?

This school is quite stylish now – we have bucked up a lot. We have got our own exercise & drawing books and catalogue of text books. And new teachers.

Please ask Puphi to send the bill to the Poona photographer. He has reminded Mr Vakil several times.

Love,
Indu

66.   [Anand Bhawan]
                                                      Allahabad,
                                             14th November, 1933

Indu sweetheart,
We returned from Benares last night after a very strenuous and tiring visit.
This morning I received your letter,[1] well timed to reach me on my
birthday. When one gets so old as I am birthdays are not quite so welcome
as they used to be. But a birthday letter from you is always very welcome
and your few lines made me happy.

But why did you suddenly think of apologising for something that I do
not know? 'Forgive and forget' – what am I to forgive and forget? There is
seldom any question of forgiving and forgetting between friends, and I
hope you and I are friends, though you happen at the same time to be a
dearly loved daughter. What is far more important is for people to
understand each other.

I sent you your books from Benares. There were two small French
dictionaries. You wanted an English-French one. I could not find a good
one here. The pocket one I have sent is not much good. I think you had
better get Cassell's French-English and English-French in one volume.
This is the best students' dictionary that I know of and it is not expensive. I
used it in Harrow! Of course since then there have been many later
editions. You can easily get a copy in Bombay.

I enclose some stamps, stamped envelopes and postcards. About the
torch – I can't find a decent one here. There is no point in my buying a new
one here and sending it to you. The postage will be nearly as much as the
cost of the torch and there is a possibility of its breaking on the way. I am
therefore asking Jal [Naoroji] to get a new torch for you. He will send it to
you or give it to you.

My age is becoming a delicate subject, not fit for public reference. I was
born on the 14th November, 1889 – so you can calculate it. The date is a
hundred years after the storming of the Bastille, which took place in 1789
and began the French Revolution. That is something to help you to
remember it by if you think it worth remembering.

Chhoti Puphi is apparently still in Ahmedabad. Her address there is:
Ghikanta Wadi, Ahmedabad. If she goes to Bombay she will of course let
you know. Raja's[2] address there is: 21, New Marine Lines, Fort.

I am glad you like your new school. Why do you say that there is little
possibility of your passing this year? Of course you will pass and pass well.

---

1. Refers to letter No. 65.
2. G. P. Hutheesing (Raja): Krishna Hutheesing's husband.

I am afraid there is little chance of my going to Bombay. Jal wires to ask me to come down but I doubt if I can go.

We have had a French couple here in Allahabad. They brought a letter of introduction from a certain Prof. Alba who wrote to say that he had come here last year, when I was in gaol and had met Miss Nehru who talked in French to him. Was it you who met him? I have had a chance of French conversation with the couple who came. It was a very halting affair but they were perfectly delighted to hear French and to talk it after a long interval. They did not know much English. Poor Madame got malaria and was laid up for a week. They have gone now to Benares and may go on to Bombay. Their names are M. and Mme. Deleplanque. Bari Puphi[1] has had the Poona photographs.

I learn that Chhoti Puphi has gone to Bombay.

I shall send you typed copies of the letters[2] for yourself and Mr Vakil after a few days. I want to revise them before sending them, to correct typing mistakes.

Love,

Your loving,
Papu

---

67.   [Vile Parle]
                                        18th November [1933]

My darling,

I'm glad you got my letter[3] in time. I was afraid it would be too late.

Puphi wrote and said she would come one day to pay me a visit and didn't turn up. This evening I got another letter from her, asking me to spend the day with her tomorrow, it being a Sunday & my birthday. If I am allowed I will go. Though of course I do not want to go often. Kaka just came in and has given me permission to go. Puphi will call at about nine in the morning.

Our number of pupils is increasing daily. We are now about ninety. Several children come from the other side of Parle and Khar (another suburb) so a bus has been arranged.

We have got very nice grounds here. There are lots of banana trees and also *chiku* trees. There are also guava [trees] and a sort of an almond tree

---

1. Senior Aunt; refers to Vijaya Lakshmi Pandit.

2. This refers to letters (see Appendix A) which were later published as a book entitled *Glimpses of World History* (Allahabad, 2 volumes, 1934).

3. Refers to letter No. 65.

(everybody here calls it *lal badam*). In taste the fruit are like almonds, only nicer.

Everyday I stay up till at least nine thirty but today I am already feeling very sleepy. So I'll close now.

I am quite well, even the cold is much better. By the way, you might mention to Bari Puphi that there is a substance (tablets) called 'Stanoxyl' which is simply wonderful for boils. At least it acts like magic on me. It might come in useful for the kiddies – they're always having something wrong with their skin.

Love to Mummie, Dol Amma and a big fat kiss for you.

Toujours la tienne,[1]
Indu

Ask Mummie to send the sari.

----

68.   Anand Bhawan,

Allahabad,
23rd November, 1933

Bien aimée,

I have your letter.[2] You must forgive me for not remembering your birthday according to the Gregorian calendar. The two dates for birthdays are rather confusing. I hope you enjoyed your outing to Bombay for the day. Chhoti Puphi has written about it. She liked your new school and friends. The change over to Vile Parle from Poona seems to have been good for the school. I hope it will be equally good for you.

You are working hard now. Hard work does not harm anyone, but two things are quite essential if one is to keep fit and bright – sufficient rest and exercise. I hope you will remember this and never give up some form of exercise. Swimming is an ideal exercise but you tell me that swimming is not allowed at present because somebody got drowned. Anyway you can run on the sands or walk, though walking is not very exciting and takes time.

You will remember that I bought a very large number of picture postcards from the museums in London showing all manner of animals, plants, stones, crystals, etc. These were educational cards for schools. They have been lying here in the library for years and I hate this kind of waste of a good thing. I have therefore sent most of them to you today by registered parcel post. You may like to look through them. It would

1. Ever yours.
2. Refers to letter No. 67.

perhaps be a good thing if you presented the lot to your school so that all the children can enjoy them.

I wonder if you have a good atlas. I find there is a small but good atlas here. If you like I can send it to you. There is . . . [incomplete]

---

69.   [Vile Parle]
                                              27th [November 1933]

Papu *chéri*,[1]
I went to Bombay with the Vakils on Saturday morning and returned today in time for school.

The Tagore week is in full swing. We saw their – Santiniketan Artists' – exhibition on Saturday morning. There were 140 pictures by the Poet himself.[2] Most of these were of course far above me, but fortunately I had read an article on them a few months ago and this enabled me to understand the quaint lines better than I would otherwise have been able to.

On the whole I liked the pictures very much especially one by Nandalal Bose.[3] It was a full length 'live' picture of a Buddhist monk. The face and hands were beautiful but the expression of the eyes was something indescribably marvellous.

After the exhibition I had to go to a party at the Tata Palace – that's where Tagore is staying – Mrs Naidu, Chhoti Puphi & Raja were also there. From here we went for a long drive and walked a while in the Hanging Gardens. Arriving home (Auntie's house in Bombay) we dressed and had food and then went to see the show by the students of Santiniketan – *Sap Mochan*. This was perfectly wonderful. It was full of songs and dances and the actors did not speak and I must say the acting was very good. It was the first thing of its kind that I had ever seen and I was charmed. *Sap Mochan* was done on Saturday & Sunday and the next two days there is to be a change of programme. All the seats have been booked and it's terribly difficult to get tickets of any price.

Tagore has grown much older and weaker ever since I saw him last in Poona. He is far from well and has come here in spite of the doctor's orders to stay at home.

The chief object of his coming with his party is money. They are very hard up and the boarding is becoming worse and worse. We are trying to

---

1. Darling.
2. The reference is to Rabindranath Tagore, the Nobel Laureate, who was the founder of Visva-Bharati University at Santiniketan.
3. Nandalal Bose: Bengali artist prominently associated with Santiniketan.

get a purse ready in Vile Parle but we have very little time at our disposal and so I do not know how far we will be successful. The party is leaving on the first. Yesterday I also went to hear the grand old poet on 'The Challenge of Judgment'. He spoke very well but was thoroughly exhausted at the end.

I have got your letter[1] and the postcards. I am quite well now though everybody says I looked low and pulled down.

Give my love to Dol Amma, Mummie, Bibi and 6, Cawnpore Rd. people.

Toujours la tienne,
Indu

---

70.   [Anand Bhawan]
                                           Allahabad,
                         16th December, 1933

Darling,
I have just come back from Delhi and Aligarh. I am sending you Rs. 20/- for your petty expenses. Of course you will want more for your travelling expenses to Allahabad – I shall send this soon.

Do come for a few days during Christmas or else you may have to visit me in Naini! Even now it is doubtful if you will find me here.

Love,
Papu

Jamnalalji is here and he sends you his love.

---

71.   Anand Bhawan,
                                           Allahabad,
                             1st January, 1934

Indu sweetheart,
Today is New Year's Day and my thoughts travel to you and I want to send you all my love and good wishes. We did not see very much of each other during your brief stay here but it was a delight to have you even for a few days. I am afraid we shall not meet for three or four months and even when we meet then it will be perhaps for a twenty-minute interview! But I shall feel happy in the thought that you are growing up in mind and body and fitting yourself for the great work you will have to do in afterlife.

1. Refers to letter No. 68.

There is some chance of Mummie and I going to Calcutta about the middle of this month. If we go there we shall certainly pay a visit to Santiniketan.

We are expecting Psyche and Perin here for a day or two on their way back from Lahore where they had gone to see Bul.[1] Padmaja may also come here on her way back from Calcutta.

Please remember to send me Vol. 10 of the Letters[2] which you have got. Mummie sends her love.

Love & kisses from your loving,
Papu

---

72.   'Uttarayan',

Santiniketan,
Bengal,
19th January, 1934

Darling Indu-boy,

We had three and a half very strenuous days in Calcutta and now we are at Santiniketan. We arrived here this evening and were welcomed by the Poet and all the students and staff who had gathered together. The Poet read out some lines in welcome which were very beautiful.

We have been put up in the Poet's own house. We have got delightful little rooms with fascinating furniture – low chairs and tables and little artistic knick-knacks. Art is of course the strong point of this place and everything has the artistic touch.

The electric lights have all gone out and I am writing this by the light of a hurricane lantern. It is nearly midnight and Mummie is asleep. Although I am tired I wanted to send you a few lines for I have not written to you for many days and I may not be able to write again soon. We shall be travelling for another three days before we reach Allahabad.

Tomorrow we shall go over [to] Santiniketan and Sriniketan, where the farm is. I shall have a talk with the Poet and later with the students and staff. And at night we shall again take to the train and journey on. Our next halt will be Patna. We are staying there for the day to see Rajendra Babu and confer with him about relief work for the earthquake areas. There has

---

1. Khurshedben Naoroji (Bul): A disciple of Mahatma Gandhi and a friend of the Nehrus. She, too, was a granddaughter of Dadabhai Naoroji.
2. Refers to *Glimpses of World History*.

been terrible destruction and loss of life and large numbers of children are homeless.[1]

We felt the earthquake distinctly in Allahabad on the 15th. I was standing at the time in the verandah speaking to a crowd of *kisans*.[2] Suddenly I started wobbling and when I discovered that it was an earthquake I was interested and greatly amused. Nothing much happened in Allahabad but in Bihar it has not been a matter for amusement. Whole cities have been destroyed. Did you feel the earthquake?

We hope to be back in Allahabad on the 22nd.

I have given the 'Last Letter' of the series I wrote to you in prison to the *Modern Review* to be published in the next number. A Hindi translation will also appear in February in the *Saraswati*.

I must go to bed now for we have to get up early to have tea with the Poet.

All my love (and Mummie's also, although she is asleep!).
Your loving,
Papu

73.
Anand Bhawan,
Allahabad,
25th January, 1934

Darling,

It is the eve of our Independence Day[3] and I am sitting down to write to you wondering when I shall write to you again from Anand Bhawan and from this library table where I have sat, surrounded by my books, for so many long hours, month after month. I love the company of books, even when I have no time to read them. They stand there, row after row, with the wisdom of ages looked up in them, serene and untroubled in a

---

1. The province of Bihar was rocked by a major earthquake on 15th January, 1934, which resulted in substantial loss of lives and destruction of property. The Congress set up a Relief Committee under the chairmanship of Dr Rajendra Prasad, a prominent nationalist leader from Bihar, to assist the people of Bihar in overcoming the after-effects of this earthquake.

2. Peasants.

3. As decided at the Lahore session of the Congress in 1929, a pledge to struggle for complete independence was first taken by people all over India on 26th January, 1930. Until 1947 this day was observed as Independence Day. The Republic of India was proclaimed on that day in 1952 and 26th January is thereafter celebrated as Republic Day. The present Independence Day in India is 15th August, the day on which transfer of power took place in 1947.

changing and distracted world, looking down silently on the mortals that come and go. I shall miss them for a while if I go away and I shall remember them. But it really does not matter either way, for I try to fit in with my surroundings wherever I may find myself.

I rather liked Santiniketan and so did Mummie. I think it will be a good thing if you spent a year or so there. You may not have comforts there but that is a little matter and one should get hardened a little. It is a remarkably peaceful place. There is a German there who is a Buddhist monk. He teaches both French and German. I do not know how good he is at his work but he had an attractive face, as Buddhist monks often have. The art section is of course very good. If you go there I think it would be a good thing if you took up painting. Nandalal Bose, the man in charge of the art section, is one of the leading Indian painters of today, and he is a good teacher. But all this is rather premature. We can discuss it later when the time comes.

One idea, however, appeals to me. I want you to get to know the various peoples of India and if you go to Santiniketan you will pick up Bengali and get to know the Bengalis a little better. You know some Gujarati now and perhaps a little Marathi.

And now I must say *au revoir* and end this letter with my love, which indeed you always have.

Yours loving,
Papu

74.

Anand Bhawan,
Allahabad,
29th January, 1934

Indu dear,

I have survived Independence Day although I did my best not to do so! What is to be done?

Your letter[1] came today. No, I am not at all superstitious about the 13th. I think it is as good or bad as any other day. You must be, of course, a little excited about your preliminary examination. But examinations are not worth getting excited over. They seem rather terrible at a distance but if one takes them coolly there is nothing exciting in them.

I have received Vol. 10 of the letters.[2] Thanks.

We are all busy collecting money for Bihar relief. Anand Bhawan is full of blankets and clothes which people are sending.

1. Letter not traceable.
2. Refers to *Glimpses of World History*.

Dol Amma is getting on well. Mummie is terribly busy, going from house to house and shop to shop collecting money.

Love,

Your loving,
Papu

75.

Anand Bhawan,
Allahabad,
1st February, 1934

Indu darling,
I am sending you some snapshots I took at Muzaffarpur on 22nd January. You will find a description at the back of each.

My foot is quite sound and well. The report that it had been hurt was wholly baseless.

Show the snaps to Puphi when you see her.

Love,
Papu

---

76.   [Telegram]

Allahabad,
12th February, 1934

To
Indira Nehru,
Ghorbunder Road,
Vile Parle
Am going back to my other home for a while all my love and good wishes cheerio.

Papu

77.

Presidency Jail,
Calcutta,
13th February, 1934

Indu *bien aimée*,
So I am back again to my other 'home', as I wired to you.[1] It was time I came, for I was very tired with the various activities I indulge in and badly wanted a respite. My nine days in Bihar, touring the earthquake areas,

---

1. Refers to letter No. 76.

were a tremendous strain and I reached Allahabad day before yesterday dead tired. I shall have plenty of rest now – perhaps too much of it!

I thought of you a great deal today. Today was the day of your examination and just before it began the news of my arrest must have reached you. I hope this did not worry you in the least. It should have acted as a fillip!

My trial has been fixed for day after tomorrow, the 15th. I do not know what will happen afterwards and whether I shall be kept in this jail or elsewhere. When you write to me send your letter to Mummie and she will forward it on.

You will be busy during the next two months or so with your examinations. I am sure you will do well in them. Take them easily without worrying at all. And then I hope to see you, wherever I may be at the time.

I have missed seeing Fory – just missed her. You met her. How did you like her?

All my love, *cara mia.*

Your loving,
Papu

---

78.   [February, 1934]

Papu darlingest,

I got your telegram[1] just as we were setting off for our exam – we had to come up to Bombay for it. But I have got accustomed to these surprises and have learnt not to be very astonished at whatever happens. Besides, I expected to hear of your arrest since quite a long time, so it was not so hard to bear up. But I'm glad you sent the telegram, it's much better to get the news that way than from the papers.

The night before we heard of your arrest, Goshibehn had a dream. She saw you playing with a sweet little child who was sitting on a wall and suddenly a man came and arrested you. The poor child was left alone and it began howling. Goshibehn woke up with a start and told her husband that you had been arrested; he wouldn't believe it then, but later they both saw it in the papers. She was so cut up that she sent me a basket full of lovely flowers.

My exam finished on Saturday. I did rottenly in Arithmetic but made up in Algebra and Geometry. On the whole I did quite well and think I will get the form for the Matric. Mr Vakil said I could take a rest for a few days, so I am here. I will return tomorrow morning.

We are giving a show on 10th March. It is Tagore's *The Cycle of Spring.*

1. Refers to letter No. 76.

The dialogue is to be in Gujerati but the songs are in Bengali. A boy from Santiniketan teaches dancing to the boys. Mrs Vakil and three of the girls go to Menaka's[1] dancing class to learn the technique of Indian dancing. Mrs Vakil teaches the schoolgirls dancing.

Now I suppose letters will have to be regulated. Do I send you my letters direct or through Mummie? Mummie and Puphi wrote very sweet letters, but because of the Prelim I could not reply as yet. It will be good for Mummie if you are kept in Calcutta for some time as she will be able to take her treatment, which she has been neglecting for so long.

The Matric will take place somewhere in the middle of April, and I will arrive home in the end of that month. So till then, *au revoir*.

With tons & tons of love and all my kisses.

Your loving,
Indu

79.

Alipur Central Jail,
Calcutta,
1st March, 1934

Indu *bien aimée*,

So you have had your first examination and must be feeling tremendously relieved. But then the other one hovers in the distance and perhaps worries you a little. These first examinations are troublesome little things, simply because one is not used to them. There is really nothing much in them but it is quite natural for one to feel a little nervous about them. I hope that after your first experience this nervous feeling has worn away to some extent and you do not worry. Take it quietly and you are bound to do well.

The line of work I have chosen for myself in life is such that I can never settle down safely into a rut. Always I have to face novel situations and I have frequently the sensation of appearing repeatedly at the examinations that life has a way of thrusting on us. They come suddenly and there is no course laid down which one can prepare! And life has become for me a long succession of tests. Sometimes I succeed and sometimes I am not so successful. But the curious thing is that the final and real judge of this success or failure is oneself. Others, of course, pass their opinions on it, and often they praise when there is little to praise, and often they condemn or are indifferent when a real victory has been won. But in one's heart one knows, or ought to know, the real measure of success or failure. What occurs on the surface is not so important, and those who have to face life's tests develop restraint in expression, for they do not wish to give themselves away. Indeed all our education and training teaches us some form

1. A well-known exponent of classical Indian dance.

or other of restraint. We can have little regard for those weaklings who get buffeted about hither and thither and have no control over themselves.

What a bad habit I have got into! I have allowed myself to muse and philosophise. That shows that at any rate I have not got much self-restraint! But the subject of examinations set me thinking and all life seemed to me an examination – a stiff one which few succeed in.

So now you must be preparing for your next effort, six weeks hence. And then you will come to see me, I hope, about the end of April, and have a good holiday (not with me!) which you will have earned. It is delightful to have rest after hard work. Where you will go for your holiday I do not know. Perhaps Mummie will have finished her treatment here by then. I have asked her to come here for it immediately and she may remain here for a month or two. You can then go off with Mummie to some odd corner. And afterwards? We shall talk of that when we meet.

I was interested to learn of Goshibehn's dream. Give her my love and tell her to dream of better and more useful things than my arrest.

Do not write to me direct. Send your letters to Mummie and she will enclose them with hers. If you write soon on getting this, you will be in time for the next lot.

Give my love to the Vakils.

Love & kisses from your loving,
Papu

Today is Holi![1]

———————————

80.

Alipore Central Jail,
Calcutta,
30th March, 1934

Darling Indu-boy,

I have not had a letter from you for about six weeks. I suppose you have been well occupied with your work and other things. Some news of you has come to me from other people and I am glad to know that you are keeping well. Soon you will have your examination and I am sure you will do well in it and deserve a good holiday. Will you let me know the dates of your examination and when it will be over? When does the result come out? Chhoti Puphi wrote to me that she wanted you to stay with her for a week after the exam. Of course you could do so if you liked. But there is

1. A spring festival marked by revelry and the throwing of coloured water and coloured powder.

another proposal which I want you to think over. Bari Puphi & Ranjit Pupha & the children are going to Kashmir at the beginning of May for six weeks and they suggest that you might accompany them.

Kashmir is a place well worth visiting and as you know it is our old homeland and has a special claim on us. Long, long ago we left it and since then the whole of India has been our home. But the little corner of India which is Kashmir draws us still both by its beauty and its old associations. We have not been there for seventeen years or more and you have not been there at all. It is worth visiting when you have the chance. I should have liked Mummie and you both to go there but I do not know if she will agree as this will mean leaving Dol Amma by herself. If you decide to go with Puphi, you had better come away from Bombay as soon as the exam is over. There will not be time for you to spend a week with Chhoti Puphi then. You will first go to Allahabad and have a look at your old room – I am told it has developed cracks in the ceiling – and meet people there. Especially you have to visit Ummi Chachi. Then you can come to Calcutta for a better peep at your old Papu. Mummie and Dol Amma are likely to be here then also and you should spend some days with them. We shall also have to fix up about the future.

I heard of your appearance at the show at the Royal Opera House.[1] Girdhari Lal has sent me a newspaper cutting containing a picture. I am told there was quite a lot about it in the press.

I had an interview a few days ago with Bari Puphi, Bijji Chachi & Fory. I liked Fory. She seemed to me a bright and lovable little girl.

Give my love to Chhoti Puphi & Raja when you see them.

All my love.

Your loving,
Papu

---

81.   [Srinagar]
                                       28th May [1934]

Darling Papu,

I haven't written to you for a long time and perhaps even this may not be delivered to you for sometime.

Mummie must have interviewed you since my departure, but there is no news of you as she has not written. We expect Pupha to arrive either this

---

1. The students of the Pupils' Own School staged Rabindranath Tagore's play, *Cycle of Spring* at the Royal Opera House, Bombay, on 10th March, 1934.

evening or tomorrow and he will be able to tell us something about you.

As yet we have not been out of Srinagar. Indeed we have not even seen anything of the place except round about our house and the post office. Yesterday we went to the Nishat Bagh[1] and Puphi agreed to go only because the Vakils insisted & persuaded so. By the way, I forgot to mention about the Vakils. Of course I knew in Vile Parle that they were spending the summer vacations in Kashmir & when I arrived here I made enquiries about them at the post office and was told that they were in Kashmir & came every few days for their letters. So day before yesterday I left a letter for them at the P.O. asking them to come over if they had time. Well, that very morning about an hour and a half since I had been at the P.O. I saw them at our gate. Apparently they had also made enquiries about me. I went back with them to their houseboat & spent the rest of the day there. It's quite a nice place.

I talked with Kaka about Santiniketan. It appears that Soniben – Raja Bhai's sister – has a cottage in Santiniketan, in which she stays whenever she goes there. Now that she is in Bombay it is not in use. Kaka suggested that as the boarding will not be a convenient place at all for me, specially the food, I might write to Soniben, asking her to let me use the cottage. I could take a servant from Allahabad who would cook for me & also do some of the other work. Of course I could help him. Kaka says that otherwise it is very probable that I should fall ill soon after my arrival. Do you think I should do this? I might at least try. But whatever is to be done should be done and settled before Santiniketan re-opens.

I love this place, even the little I have seen, and I'm glad I came. The sweet [children] are ever so sweet but very dirty. Puphi and I often make plans that years later we are coming back here and are going to open a 'Scrubbing Washing Home' for children!

The things made here are very beautiful & artistic. I had seen the embroidery before, as nearly every lady of our community has a shawl or two made here, but the papier-mâché & wood carving are wonderful.

As I mentioned before, we went to Nishat Bagh yesterday. It took us over two hours to reach the place in the Shikara and another fifteen minutes to find the Vakils, who were to meet us. The gardens were very nice and it being a Sunday all the fountains were playing. There were many people. We enjoyed ourselves, though the Vakils had brought a lot of food-stuffs and we nearly got a tummy-ache.

The climate is very English. When we arrived it was raining slightly &

---

1. A terraced garden created by the Mughal Emperor Jehangir in the seventeenth century near Srinagar, the capital of Kashmir. The garden is a popular picnic spot even today.

[was] very cold, then for a few days it cleared and we had bright long days and it was hot. Since last evening it is again raining. On our return journey from the gardens we were caught in the rain & had to stop several times as the wind would not let us proceed.

We met an old man who recognised Puphi and talked of you being as big as Chand. He sent his salaams.

With much love and kisses.

Ever yours,
Indu

---

82.   [Srinagar]
                                        11th June, 1934

Darling Papu,

It takes ages for letters to reach anywhere from here but I'm writing so that I don't miss Mummie's letter again.

By now I have seen quite a lot of Kashmir. A few days ago we went to Achhabal. It is a beautiful place and Puphi tells me it was even lovelier when she came in 1916 – before I was born. The present *mali* [gardener] is Samat Khan's son and he remembered you and said he still had a few old suits of yours which were given to him when you came here before going to Harrow! What a very long time ago that seems and yet he remembered everybody and enquired about Maharaj Bhai[1] & others. While we [were] in the gardens some local musicians entertained us. Their voices were awful but I liked the Kashmiri song very much; it was something about flowers and was just suited to the beautiful atmosphere of the place. Do you remember you all camped in these gardens in 1916? Naturally our brief stay revived old memories and Puphi was very sad.

On our way to Achhabal we stopped for some time at Verinag, that is the source of the Vitasta. The water here was as cold as ice and when I washed my hands & face they became quite red.

In this wonderful land, no matter where you are you get a lovely view of the snow-covered peaks which surround it and the beautiful springs. I don't think the waters of Kashmir can be compared with those of any other country. They have a standard of their own. All the gardens have fountains in them, which play every Sunday. And on this day those near Srinagar are crowded with people of all descriptions, caste & creeds, even the poorest Kashmiris sally forth with their samovars.

We went to see several temples which are now in ruins. They were built

1. Maharaj Bahadur Takru: a cousin of Jawaharlal Nehru.

on the most marvellous sites imaginable and are still magnificent . . .

The wood carving, papier-mâché and embroidery are lovely. It is such a pleasure just to watch the shops. One of the leading shop-men – he calls himself 'Ganemede' – invited us to tea. The tea contained soda, salt, butter & some spices & was a lovely pink in colour. I rather liked it but Puphi felt sick.

We have taken several snaps. If they are good I will send you some.

I have not gained in weight but feel very much fitter and look it too. The air here isn't as fresh as it is on other hill stations.

This letter isn't going for sometime yet so I might as well take advantage and add a few more lines.

Nora[1] is also here with her father-in-law. They stay in an old dirty houseboat and have not been anywhere except to two or three gardens and as far as I know they do not intend to either. Nora hasn't been to any shops and says that there isn't any use of looking at things as Pyarelalji[2] will not buy anything at all. There is a gentleman with them called Upadhayaji, who told Puphi the other day that you got no fruit in Kashmir. Then he saw the amazed look on Puphi's face and added, 'Oh! Yes cherries & strawberries are available, but I don't call them fruit. They are not worth eating.' Some people do have queer ideas. The other day Subhadu Didda came with her husband. We were talking about the flowers & trees of Kashmir and she said that she liked the poplars but didn't care for the *chenars* as they were just like the *peepals* of the rest of India! This was quite a blow to me. Ever since I first saw the *chenar*, I've been lost in admiration. It's a magnificent tree.

It is very interesting to watch Kashmiris quarrelling – especially the women. A few days ago we saw such a quarrel as we were drifting down the river. The parties were standing on opposite [banks].

The cherries and strawberries are almost finished. We used to eat them all day (I used to put on my shorts & climb up the cherry tree), but Nikku Chacha[3] says we did not do justice to them.

Pupha's car has a national flag on it. Now our flag as well as the Kashmir State flag has orange as the top colour, so whenever we go out in the car all the soldiers get a glimpse of the orange &, not bothering to look at the rest of the flag, give us the salute. When we pass in front of the Palace the guards are usually reposing and when they see the flag they rush for their guns & salute. Up to now Pupha used to take the salute in great style. But last evening he purposely slowed down & made the soldiers realise their

---

1. The name by which Purnima Banerji, a leading nationalist of Allahabad, was known to family and close friends.
2. Pyarelal Banerji: father-in-law of Purnima Banerji.
3. Kanwarlal Kathju (Nikku): a cousin of Jawaharlal Nehru.

mistake. Fortunately they had a sense of humour & began laughing at their own foolishness. But Chand was very disappointed & said, 'Now we'll never be saluted again'!

I met the Vakils here sometime ago. They returned on the 6th as the school's opening date is nearing.

I miss you very much. It's awful to be on holiday when those you love aren't with you.

With all my love and many kisses.
                    Always your loving,
                         Indu

———————◆———————

83.   Dehra Dun Jail,
                                       15th June, 1934

Indu darling,
I was glad to receive your letter[1] after a long time.

About Vakil's suggestion that you might take Soniben's cottage at Santiniketan and set up a separate establishment there with a cook, etc., I am afraid I do not agree at all. I dislike very much the idea of your keeping apart from the 'common herd' and requiring all manner of special attention, just as the Prince of Wales does when he goes to school or college. This seems to me to savour of vulgarity and snobbery. It is a bad beginning to make in any place to shout out to the people there that they are inferior beings and you are a superior person requiring special and particular treatment. Do you think any self-respecting boy or girl would care to make friends with you under these circumstances? And what would the teachers & professors, who run the college there, feel? Would they not feel that they had been insulted to some extent by our having made our own arrangements over their heads? No, this kind of thing will never do. Wherever we go we must keep on a level with our surroundings and not imagine that we are better or superior. It is better not to go to a place than to go as a superior person. If you even desire to work among village folk or poor factory workers, how do you think you would live with them or visit them? As a society lady with a scented handkerchief to keep off the bad smells, occasionally patronising them or doling out charity to them? That is not the way to meet your kind or to do human service. This method of charity and condescension irritates me exceedingly and I have no use for it.

I think I have told you that it has long been my desire that a part of your education – and every boy's and girl's education – should consist of real

———————

1. Refers to letter No. 81.

honest work in a factory or in the fields. Unfortunately this cannot be arranged in India under present conditions but this idea of mine will give you some notion of what I think of education. If you went to work in a factory do you think you could do so as a superior person living apart and in a much better way than the others? The idea is absurd. The very object of going there is to learn from the sufferings, discomforts and misery which surrounds and wraps up the great majority of people; to see the drama of real life; to become akin to a small extent at least with the masses; to understand their viewpoint; and to get to know how to work so as to raise them and get them out of their misery. This cannot be done by people who live in cotton wool but by those who can face the sun and the air and hard living. However all this does not arise at present and much will depend on what ideals in life you have. I cannot impose my ideals on you. If you want to make your life worthwhile you will have to decide for yourself what your life-philosophy should be.

There is no question of any such great decision before you go to Santiniketan. As a matter of fact that is a delightful place and I am sure you will have no physical discomfort there. I think you should stay wherever the college authorities put you. If it is the boarding house, certainly you should remain there. Why shouldn't you? Take the food also as it comes. If it does not agree with you you can say so to the matron or other friends there and get it changed or added to. There will be no difficulty about this. My fear is that you will be too much looked after there, not too little. That can't be helped because you happen to belong to a notorious family. But you must not put a barrier between yourself and the other students. Many of the girls there are very decent and you will soon be friends with them.

You seem to have an idea that you will have to spend a lot of time in washing clothes! I do not know but I think you are mistaken. A little washing is rather good for one.

Do you know what I had to put up with at Harrow? We never had a full meal at school unless we bought it for ourselves. As junior boys we had to wait on the seniors as fags, get their goods, clean their places up, sometimes clean their boots, carry messages for them, etc., and be continually sworn at by them and sometimes beaten.

So I think you had better go to Santiniketan without making any special arrangements. I have already written to them there and they will fix you up. Mummie can accompany you when you first go. There is a young girl there, Mrs Chanda, the wife of the Poet's secretary,[1] who is a bright little thing and is a good artist. She will help you in every way. There is no question of your falling ill. If anything disagrees with you, say so.

1. Anil Kumar Chanda: private secretary of Rabindranath Tagore, the poet. He later held high political office.

The college opens on 1st July but they have said that you can reach there by 7th July. You should try to do so. This means leaving Allahabad on July 6th at the latest. You should spend a few days in Allahabad before going. Yesterday I had an interview with Mummie and she suggested that you should leave Kashmir so as to reach Dehra Dun on 30th June (Saturday). On that day you can have an interview with me and leave for Allahabad the same night. The date for the interview must be definitely fixed as it is just possible that Chhoti Puphi might come on the same day. Or perhaps Fory. If Fory comes she could join you at Lahore.

Two weeks ago I wrote to Bari Puphi that you need not take the trouble to come to Dehra Dun on your way back as this would take an extra day and reduce your stay with Mummie at Allahabad. Mummie however wants you to come to Dehra and if you feel that way you can certainly do so.

I am sending you a prospectus of Santiniketan. This will give you a great deal of information. On p. 13 the subjects are given. Among the compulsory subjects I think you should choose Hindi (as an Indian language) and French (as a modern language).

There are several interesting optional subjects – the three sciences, Botany, Physics, Chemistry, and Music, Fine Arts, etc. You must choose two of these. I am rather partial to science as the modern world is based on science. At the same time the Fine Art department of Santiniketan is very good and if you have any inclination that way you should join it. You need not decide yet. Go there and see for yourself and then decide.

Do not be prejudiced before even you go to S.N. It has its faults but it has its good points also and I think the latter far outweigh the former. I am sure you can learn a great deal and develop rightly there. After three months there will be the long Puja vacations.[1] And remember that the place is easily accessible from Allahabad, at least compared to Poona or Vile Parle. It is practically a night's journey.

I am glad you are enjoying your visit to Kashmir and are growing fond of the place. You will be sorry to come away so soon leaving the others behind. What is a month in Kashmir? But look upon this month as an introduction to the place. Let us hope that later on you can renew the friendship and stay longer.

I hope you have been able to meet some good Kashmiri families – some people beside the *manjhis*,[2] etc. I am told that better class Kashmiri women have now all taken to the sari. Only a few years ago they wore the *phiran*.[3]

---

1. The autumn holidays in Bengal for the festival of the Goddess Durga.
2. Boatmen.
3. Woollen gown worn by Kashmiri women.

I enclose a picture taken from a paper. Is this how you people hike? With little Rita also carrying a rucksack on her back?

My love to all your party & to you.

> Your loving,
> Papu

84.

Santiniketan,
7th July, 1934

Darling Papu,

Santiniketan at last! I was never so excited as I was last night – at least before joining a boarding school. I had heard such a lot about this place, for and against, that I was longing to judge for myself. Many people came to see Mummie and told her not to send me here, describing all the various disadvantages & discomforts of the place. But I noticed that all these people who did not like S. had never been here and had only second or third hand information. Everyone who had stayed here said I would love the place. And now here I am! And I had better give you my opinion of the place. As yet I have only seen the girls' hostel & the office and have had a glimpse of the Library & Kala Bhavana.[1] Everything is so artistic & beautiful & wild. And to cap it all, we have come in the best season. It is during these months that S. is at its loveliest.

On our way here, something in our engine gave way and we had to lie miles away from any town for two & a half hours till another engine came to help us. So we missed our train at Burdwan and arrived here at about eight o'clock last evening. I spent the night with Mummie. I intend shifting to the hostel sometime this afternoon.

In spite of the strict rules in the prospectus, I find that most of the students haven't yet arrived so the classes are quite settled.

The only difficulty here will be the language. Bengali is a very sweet & nice language . . .

We went to see the Poet just now. I rather like his funny little house with every room on a different level. It must be fun to go up & down all the time. Gurudev [Tagore] suggested that I do some gardening in my free time. He seems to be very fond of it and was complaining that so few girls take it up.

From Srinagar, I took a seat in a taxi & came alone to Pindi. I was fated that the railway & I should be friends – I always seem to be travelling. And I'm quite fed up of it, especially when I am alone. These trains are so dirty & dusty & generally crowded and most of my journeys are long.

---

1. The College of Art at Visva-Bharati.

In my next letter I will be able to tell you about the 'real' Santiniketan – what it is like under the cover of beautiful surroundings & artists.

With lots of love,

Your loving,
Indu

---

85.   Santiniketan,
16th July, 1934

Darling Papu,

You must have had your interview on the day before yesterday. And all day I was thinking of you and that I might have had the chance of meeting you even though it may not be long, had I not been here. However we cannot meet before October so let us wait patiently.

Regular classes have begun. The History class is by far the most interesting and I look forward to it. You know my subjects are English, Hindi, History, Civics & Chemistry. Chemistry seems to be out of place, unless one takes the science course. The Principal suggested Logic instead, but as you wanted me to take it up and I also like it, I attend the Chemistry classes.

I have also joined the painting classes & dancing.

I can now understand a little Bengali & can also say a few sentences. But it is not enough to carry on conversation in the language. The older girls are not very social & won't mix at all. So we new ones have formed a group of our own. We get on very well together, and so life is not as miserable as it would otherwise have been.

Mrs Tagore.[1] the Poet's daughter-in-law, is the Superintendent of the girls' boarding school. She comes here twice a day and is very kind. The matron is a Danish lady, wife of Mr Chakravarty,[2] the Poet's former secretary who is now somewhere in Europe or America. She has been here for eight years and is thoroughly Bengali in all her ways. Her little daughter can express herself only in Bengali. But the lady is very good and takes great care of us all.

Bapu was to have visited Santiniketan, but apparently he is not coming now, so Gurudev & Mrs Chanda are going to Calcutta tomorrow to meet him.

If I do not post this letter immediately, it will probably not reach Mummie in time & you will not get it. I do not know how long it takes for letters to reach A'bad. I have not heard from Mummie since her arrival

1. Pratima Devi: daughter-in-law of Rabindranath Tagore.
2. Amiya C. Chakravarty: member of the academic faculty at Santiniketan, secretary to Rabindranath Tagore, 1926–33.

home or from anyone else, although I have been writing almost every day.
    Heaps of love & many kisses,
                          Always your loving,
                              Indu

---

86.   Burdwan,
                                     29th August, 1934

Papu darling,
I was very glad to have been able to see you before leaving Allahabad, even though we could not say much to each other.

I am writing this in the waiting room at Burdwan station, as I am not sure of getting enough time at Santiniketan.

You were rather irritated at my asking you about Manohar Bhai's staying at Anand Bhawan and at the interview I could not explain the necessity of so doing. But I would like you to know that it was absolutely necessary. Do you know anything about what happens at home when you are absent? Do you know that when Mummie was in a very bad condition the house was full of people, but not one of them even went to see her or sit a while with her, that when she was in agony there was no one to help her? It was only when Madan Bhai came that she got a little comfort and with your release everything was changed – people flocked from all directions, came to ask about her; sat with her. Now that you have again gone and Madan Bhai cannot come as often as before, there was some danger of Mummie being left to herself as previously, and so we thought of Mannu Bhai. But the latter is very sensitive and as several members of the family resent his presence, they are rude to him & have insulted him on several occasions, he says that although he is ready to bear everything for Mummie's sake, he would like to have your consent – so that at least he may not be regarded as an intruder in the house.

As soon as Mummie is strong enough she should be removed to any place outside Allahabad & she is sure to improve rapidly.

But please don't worry, she is much better now and will soon be well.

You were not looking too well yourself. But that I suppose was due to the strain & irregularity of sleep & meals, which you underwent during your brief stay outside jail[1] and I hope you will take exercise and get better and do take care of your food, etc.
                          Yours for ever,
                              Indu

---

    1. Jawaharlal was on parole for twelve days from 12th–23rd August to see his ailing wife.

87.   [Naini Central Prison]
30th August, 1934

Indu sweetheart,

I do not know if you have gone back or are still here. I fancy you must be back. Your visit here in the midst of term and stay for a fortnight must have broken the continuity of your work and come in the way of your settling down in Santiniketan. I know the feeling for, in another sphere, I had a similar experience and I am taking some time to adjust myself again to my new surroundings. But I was very glad indeed to have those eleven days in Anand Bhawan, to see Mummie and to have a chance of being with you for a brief while. That interlude refreshed me greatly and I have something to look back to when I feel a little stale and weary.

It won't be very long, I hope, before I see you again – six or seven weeks when your *Puja* holidays begin. I am hoping that by that time Mummie will be well enough to go to the hills.

I should like her to spend October and November, and if she likes, the whole winter, in the Almora hills. I shall not be able to see her for I shall be at Naini, but then I can't see her even when she is at Anand Bhawan.

You could be with her for some weeks in the hills but you will have to come back for your college. Perhaps Bul might agree to stay with her. However, we need not worry ourselves about this future programme yet.

I was not at all happy to find how weak physically you were when you could not do some simple exercises. I was quite surprised. I wish you would not allow yourself to grow limp and flabby. Not to be physically fit seems to me one of the major sins that a person can be guilty of.

Write to me and tell me of your experiences at college. I suppose you will begin your French afresh now as Kripalani[1] suggested.

Your loving,
Papu

———————

88.   Santiniketan,
16th September, 1934

Papu darling,

Need I say how glad I was to get your letter?[2] Those few days we were together in Anand Bhawan were just wonderful and I shall never forget them. It was like a beautiful dream to find you with us and to be near you for some days. But it was too good to last and suddenly I woke to find the

1. Krishna Kripalani: scholar and writer from Santiniketan. He later became Secretary of the Sahitya Academy and Chairman of the National Book Trust.
2. Refers to letter No. 87.

high walls of Naini separating us. We were so near and yet so far apart. And now that I have come to Santiniketan we are further apart. Most of the year you are in your 'other home' and even when you are out, we are not very much together, yet I miss you so much. Sometimes one feels so lonely. It is awful when surrounded by crowds & amidst all their chattering and playing, their rowdiness and noise, one has the feeling of being alone. Yesterday while reading one of Gurudev's novels I came across this line – 'How terribly lonely is he, who misses companionship in the midst of the multitudinousness of life' – (I am not sure whether these are the exact words). I liked it very much – it is so true.

Everything has been settled about my French. The lessons will begin from day after tomorrow. My teacher, Govinda Brahmachari, is a German monk. Probably he is the man you mentioned to me. He hesitated to take my class, at first, saying that he was out of practice. But he speaks very fluently & with quite a good accent. He seems to be a nice man.

When I returned from home, I could hardly bear the heat here – partly because I had got used to the fans of Anand Bhawan, but the main reason being that as it had not rained since my departure, the atmosphere was close & very hot. Yesterday & last night were simply awful; we couldn't do a stroke of work in the day and kept awake all night and this morning also it was impossible to do anything so we demanded a holiday & got it (the Professors being as fed up as we were). Just as we had dispersed it began raining and it poured for quite a long time. For two hours it was cool & pleasant & now again it is warm.

We are getting a month's holiday for the Puja in October – 9th October to the 12th November. I am looking forward to it as it means going to Mummie.

I get a p.c. daily from Allahabad informing me of Mummie's progress. This is a great relief, and as everyone here is anxious to know I have to learn the content of the card by heart & repeat it to almost every person I come across.

With all my love & kisses,

Always your loving,
Indu

———————— ▬ ▬ ————————

89.   Chandra Bhawan,
                                                       Bhowali,
                                                  [18] October, 1934

Papu darling,

I am ever so sorry for the delay in writing to you. I was under the impression that Bul would write & I would put in an enclosure, but it appears that Madan Bhai has sent you an account of the journey & Mummie's arrival here, and Bul is not writing.

Bul had a brainwave when she thought of Ammaji's[1] & my coming here a day earlier than the rest of the party. When we arrived here, the place was in confusion, the houses weren't quite ready and it was only after rushing about all day & getting dead tired that we could make the house fit for Mummie's arrival. Now however we are all comfortably settled.[2]

Bhowali is a nice place; on arrival I thought everything looked very familiar and now I remember I passed through in 1930, when we were going to Bhimtal from Nainital. I had also been here in 1921 when we were all going to Ghorakhal – but of course I don't remember anything about that. Both the cottages are neat & nice, though the rooms are queerly planned. We get quite lovely flowers and a very beautiful view of the Bhimtal Lake & another smaller one – I forget the name. On every side there are mountains. Behind the one just in front is 'Sattal'.[3] It is a beautiful place. There are seven lakes close together & reminds one of Switzerland.

I have not written anything about Mummie, as the doctor could give you a much more accurate report than I could manage. Since our arrival she is definitely more bucked up and looks brighter & more cheerful. I am writing this in her room, as the nurse has gone for her breakfast. Mummie sends you lots of love.

I hear that it is probable you might be transferred to Nainital or Almora, and in that case you will be allowed to see Mummie now & then. If you are, you will need plenty of warm clothes. (It is very chilly at night, but in the day the sun is quite hot.) Your *achkans*[4] are in a trunk in Mummie's dressing room and I have left a blanket or two with Upadhyaya. Ask him for anything in the line of clothes that you may need. I hope you have received the light blanket & the other things you had asked for.

All of us are quite well. I had a slight cold & felt rather low yesterday, but am all right now. Madan Bhai & Feroze[5] have made a plan of making Bul & me fat and make me consume enormous quantities of food-stuffs. I have begun taking meat again, I might mention.

I haven't been for a single walk yet as it is exercise enough to go from

1. Rajpati Kaul, Kamala Nehru's mother.

2. Kamala Nehru's health deteriorated in the summer of 1934. She was admitted to a sanatorium in Bhowali. As Jawaharlal was, at the time, in prison, Indira accompanied her mother to Bhowali.

3. A tourist spot in the hills in Uttar Pradesh. Tal means a lake.

4. A long coat reaching below the knees with a buttoned-up collar. The coat has a little flare.

5. Feroze Gandhi: a young political worker of Allahabad, who devoted himself to helping Kamala Nehru in her political activities. He married Indira Nehru in 1942.

one house to the other several times a day. But I propose beginning this evening, so expect to see me quite pink & fat.

The nurses are working satisfactorily and do not make as much fuss as we expected them to. We have of course done our best for their comfort, as they are next to Mums the most important people here & we cannot afford to have them in a bad humour.

My writing has always been bad, but you will have noticed that this time it is worse. This is due to my having hurt my thumb . . .

Always your loving,
Indu

90.   Almora District Jail,
                                                     30th October, 1934

Darling Indu,

We had a good run from Bhowali though it became a bit tiring towards the end. It took us just under three and a half hours from Bhowali to Almora. The road is very good up to Ranikhet and the mountains are wooded; after Ranikhet there is plenty of dust and bare and naked-looking hills succeed one another. But sometimes a huge pyramid of ice and snow rises up above the distant clouds and gives one a thrill. As we approached Almora memories of my early boyhood came up before me when I spent nearly a year at Almora.

I am installed here in a lordly chamber which is big enough probably to contain both your little cottages. It has fifteen windows of various sizes, and a door, so that there is no danger of my feeling cramped or stuffy. Here I sit in solitary grandeur and when I feel weary of this expanse of emptiness I can go out into a yard close by where I can trot up and down. It is a decent-sized yard and there are a few faded flowers there – chiefly marigolds and candytufts planted by some predecessor of mine. The jail is situated on the ridge of a mountain and I can only see the sky from here and just a bit of a distant mountain or the top of pine trees. This gives one a curious feeling of being high up on the top or roof of something, cut off from the world. The sky seems to be so near and to envelop us. It is a pity I can't see the snows from here – the walls intervene.

I have started my sunbaths, though it is warmer here than at Bhowali.

When you go to Allahabad please send me a pair of my pyjamas (sleeping suit). I think you will find at least one decent one. This will do. I can easily get another made from a sample.

You can come here to see me before you go down just when it suits you. Only send me intimation a day or two ahead. And before coming tell Dr Kakkar in case there is a chance of my being sent to Bhowali for a short visit. You had better make arrangements on the basis of my not going to Bhowali. Bul & Feroze will come with you of course and all of you will have to spend the night here as it is too much of a good thing to go back the same day. You might stay at the Dak Bungalow. Come & visit me the day you arrive – and that means that you should arrive early. If possible I should like you to visit Binsar from Almora before you return but I do not know if you can do so. Consult your landlord Hiralal.

You can write to me in answer to this when you like – say two or three days after you get this. If you have made your plans for the Almora visit by that time you can tell me of them in your letter.

I don't suppose it will matter much if you reach Santiniketan a day or two late. Do what you feel like in the matter.

Perhaps when you reach Allahabad Dol Amma & Puphi may have left for Bombay. Pupha however will be there & you had better wire to him your arrival.

Mummie has received a letter from Nanu (A. C. N. Nambiar)[1] which she showed me. As she cannot reply I think you might write a few lines to him telling him how Mummie is.

I hope you have paid a visit to Ranikhet.

I shall look forward to seeing you here soon.

Love,

Your loving,
Papu

---

91.   Bhowali,
                                          2nd November, 1934

Papu darling,

I have your letter.[2] As soon as it arrived I sent word to Dr Kakkar, and I enclose his note for you.

I know you will feel rather irritated when I tell you that we have not been to Ranikhet yet. But it could not be helped – the last few days have not been good ones for Mummie, her temperature began rising (it went up to 101.2 on the 30th & 31st) and she felt rather weak & low. Day before yesterday A.P.[3] was performed for the fifth time. As more air (380 c.c.) was pumped than ever before, she felt a little uncomfortable in the

---

1. A. C. N. Nambiar (Nanu): A journalist active in the struggle for freedom who was a close friend of the Nehrus.

2. Refers to letter No. 90.

3. Artificial Pneumothorax: a form of surgical treatment for pulmonary ailments in which the lung is collapsed by introducing sterile air or oil into the pleural cavity.

evening but the next morning showed improvement and since then she has been quite cheerful. We weighed her this morning and found that she had gained three lbs since last week. Her weight now is eighty lbs. Dr Kakkar wants to X-ray her on the 5th.

We, that is Bul, Feroze & myself, intend doing Ranikhet & Almora in one trip, if possible. We could go to Ranikhet in the morning, have a good look at the snows and buy the jams if we can get them – I hear the Government Gardens have stopped making them. Then we could proceed to Almora, spend the night in the Dak Bungalow & interview you the next morning.

We shall probably start on the 5th after the X-ray or perhaps on the 4th, if the doctor consents to X-ray Mummie a day earlier.

As we are having a sort of a test immediately after the college reopens I think I had better be in Santiniketan in time. As it is I have missed quite a lot.

Just before the holidays I had stopped attending the Chemistry classes, as they clashed with some other arts subject. And now I am at a loss as to what I should do. For the regular exam I must have a third subject – what do you suggest? Should I go back to Logic? I had thought of doing this but many of the Logic students discouraged me, saying that the Professor was a most uninteresting & boring person. Besides I have not much inclination for the subject. I meant to ask you when you were here for a few hours, but the time seemed to fly & soon you were on your way to Almora.

About your sleeping-suits, I think the best plan is that I will send some cloth & the pyjamas here from Allahabad. Bul or somebody will get them sewn and send them to you.

Bul & I go out for long walks but I'm afraid it is impossible to take sunbaths. Anyway there are only five days left, as I intend leaving Bhowali on the 7th or 8th.

I have sent your letter to the Puphis. As far as I know Bari Puphi is still in Allahabad. It was Rita's birthday some days ago and she sent us all that was left of the birthday cake.

The night nurse had been giving some trouble lately and said that she wanted to return to Allahabad as soon as her month was over on the 9th. We consulted Dr Kakkar and he says that there is no longer any need for a fully trained nurse to be on duty all night. So he is sending Dr Sah, his assistant to Nainital to get an Indian Christian child welfare or maternity worker, who would stay near Mummie in case she wants anything at night. The day nurse, of course, will stay on for the present.

We have some quite amusing jokes at the expense of Mrs Gutteridge – that's the night nurse. The latest is that *supari*[1] makes one passionate. Last

---

1. Areca nut.

night, at about nine, I was surprised to hear some shouting in the kitchen, as generally we are all in bed by that time. So I called Hari[1] to ask what the matter was & found that the nurse was lecturing the cook as to the effects *supari* had on one's temper!

Mummie sends you love – she is quite bucked up since she knows that she is gaining weight.

Ammaji, Bul & Feroze also send love, while Hari and the other old servants send salaams.

With lots of love.

Ever your loving,
Indu

We had a good shower of rain and it has become colder. We read in the *Hindustan Times* that you would be allowed to come thrice a week to Bhowali.

---

92.   Almora District Jail,
                                     12th November, 1934

Darling Indu,
Whether you are in Bhowali, Allahabad or Santiniketan I do not know. I presume you have adhered to your programme and so must have reached your destination. When you were leaving me, at the last interview, you threatened not to come back for six months. That is a terrible long time not to see you and I can't quite imagine that the threat will come off. You know the story of Mahomet & the mountain. If the mountain will not come to Mahomet, Mahomet will have to make the journey. However, this question does not arise just yet and so we need not bother about it. Your thoughts must be concerned with your new term, your work & play, and your companions.

About your subject in place of Chemistry, consult your Professors there and choose something that appeals to you. Logic is a dry subject, and though good in itself as it helps us to think straight, is not to be commended. As you know I fancy the sciences and I should like you to continue with at least one of them. It is not so much the facts one learns there as the method that is important. I should like you to develop that scientific method in all your work. But in choosing your additional subject, do not trouble about my preferences. It is foolish for me to try to advise you from a distance without knowing all the facts.

---

1. Hari Lal: Jawaharlal Nehru's personal attendant, elected to the U.P. Legislative Assembly in 1937.

Ever since I came to Almora – and it is over a fortnight now – I have been expecting a copy of *Glimpses* Vol. 1 to be sent to me from Allahabad. I asked Puphi to have it sent when I saw her just before coming here. I wrote to her about it too. But something has happened and it has not come yet. Will you please write a line to her and remind her of it. Of course if the book has already been sent she need not have another copy sent.

About the Hindi translation of the *Glimpses*, tell your friend that it is too late for me to make new arrangements now. Tewary[1] must have finished the work by this time. Ask the critic to write to Tewary direct and make suggestions.

I have no news of Mummie since you came here. I can't quite make out what was the good of my coming all the way from Allahabad to Almora when I am, in effect, as far away from her as ever.

If Raj Chachi[2] has come back from Europe, please ask Puphi to send her a copy of the *Glimpses*, Vol. 1.

Love,

Your loving,
Papu

---

93.   Santiniketan,
                                                        14th November, 1934

Darling Papu,

Well, here I am, back at Santiniketan, feeling bored stiff, as the classes won't begin till tomorrow and missing Mummie terribly. Of course I miss you too, but though I was much nearer the jail in Bhowali I could only see you once a fortnight and that for a short while, and with Mummie I used to spend most of my time. Since I left Bhowali on the 8th there is no news of her and even though I know that she is well on the way to recovery, one can't help feeling anxious.

After the lovely cold of Bhowali & pleasant weather of Allahabad, I feel quite warm here and have managed to lose most of the weight I had gained up there.

I am thinking of giving up the morning *chhota hazri*[3] given here. It

---

1. Venkatesh Narayan Tewary: a Hindi journalist and writer, who later edited *Nav-jivan*, a Hindi newspaper founded by Jawaharlal Nehru.
2. Raj Dulari Nehru: wife of Shri Shridhara Nehru, a cousin of Jawaharlal Nehru. ('Chachi' means 'aunt'.)
3. Breakfast.

consists of *puris*[1] and *dal*[2] generally. And this sort of meal at six in the morning does not agree with me. I don't know how I had gone on with it for so long. However, I have decided to have my own breakfast, consisting of brown bread & butter, milk and fresh fruits.

I would also like to have some sort of tuition in Hindi. We do have classes here but we are supposed to have studied it up to the Matric standard and so Panditji[3] only reads out great poems and things of that sort. As you know I have not had any grounding in Hindi and know nothing whatsoever about grammar and the like. I have never written a Hindi essay in my life and so I do not know what I'll do when the exam days are approaching.

About the other subjects I shall talk to Anilda[4] (Mr Chanda), and see what can be done.

I gave the list to Puphi. The two days I was in Allahabad, Kitabistan[5] was closed. So Puphi will send a copy of the *Glimpses* direct to Ghani.[6] I had one with me which I have given to our Visva–Bharati library. My special copy is not ready yet. It will be sent to me as soon as it is.

In Allahabad everybody was all right except Tara, who had a bad cold and Puphi, who was feeling rather low. Dol Amma is not going to Bombay till the 18th, as she wants to meet Bijji Bhai who is coming on the 16th or 17th.

15th November

Our classes began today and I feel settled. It seems that this is the best season here and the most enjoyable term. We shall have a week's holiday or so, during which there will be a big *mela*,[7] in December. If we are lucky we might also be taken on an excursion for eight or ten days.

Gurudev is going to Benares in the last week of November. I am not yet sure if he is taking his 'dancing party'[8] with him or not. I did not post this letter yesterday as I thought perhaps you might have written to me and I was waiting for the note to arrive from Bhowali. As yet nothing has come but I shall wait for one more day.

   1. Fried bread.
   2. Boiled lentils.
   3. The distinguished Hindi scholar, Hazari Prasad Dwivedy, who was on the faculty of Visva-Bharati in 1934 and taught Indira Nehru.
   4. Anil Kumar Chanda; in Bengal, the suffix 'da' (brother) is often added to the first name of a person by those younger to him.
   5. A leading publishing house of Allahabad, which published nationalist books, including those of Jawaharlal Nehru.
   6. Ghani Khan: the son of Abdul Ghaffar Khan and a freedom fighter.
   7. Fair.
   8. A troupe of dancers often accompanied Tagore.

16th November

No letters – so I am posting this. No news even from Bhowali since I arrived here.

Lots of love,

Ever your loving,
Indu

———◆———

94.   Almora District Jail,
                                          26th November, 1934

Indu *bien aimée*,

I have had a little outing from jail and have visited Bhowali and seen Mummie. I went on Friday last, spent the night there, and returned on Saturday morning. I was very glad to see Mummie again after nearly a month but I wish I had found her better than she was. She has not been keeping well lately.

Your letter[1] from Santiniketan, written soon after your arrival there, has reached me. I am glad you have decided to have a more sensible breakfast than *puris* and *dal*. *Puris* may be excellent but at six in the morning they are not very inviting.

I sent you a book – *Humanity Uprooted* by Hindus[2] – for your birthday. It must have reached you many days after the birthday. This was partly my fault and partly the jail's. It was not a book that I would have particularly selected for you but I had no choice in the matter. It came to me just then and I had no other more suitable book. I had read it two or three years ago and found it good, and so I hastened to send it on to you. It is supposed to be one of the best books on changing Russia. One must remember, however, that Russia is changing so rapidly that books get out of date very soon.

Padmaja sent me a number of books for my birthday and so did Dr Mahmud. I am always sure of birthday presents from these two! One of the books that Padmaja sent was a beautiful one about Pavlova[3] with scores of fine pictures. In my student days in England I had often seen her and I was very fond of her dancing. She was probably the best dancer of the Russian classical school. The book brought back the old days very vividly to me. I wish you would write to Bebee – as I cannot do so from here – and tell her how happy I was to get her books and especially how much I enjoyed the Pavlova book. I looked through its pictures again and again and, when I had read it, I took it to Mummie and left it with her.

1. Refers to letter No. 93.
2. Maurice Gerschon Hindus: journalist from the United States.
3. Anna Matveyevna Pavlova: Russian ballerina.

About Hindi, I think it will be a good thing for you to take some private tuition, as you suggest. You can consult your Panditji about this and Mr Chanda.

I hope you will enjoy your little excursion. I have no idea where you are going to.

All my love.

Your loving,
Papu

95.

[Almora District Jail]
New Year's Day,
1935

A Happy New Year to Indu darling from Papu & Mummie and may she grow up wise and strong and full of joy and with all the good gifts that the fairies can bestow.

[Papu]

96.

[Almora District Jail]
5th January, 1935

Send this message to Indu.

Darling – I have been thinking of Montana and Villars and Chesières and little Indu pottering about there in the snow. For we have had snow here also, not very much, but still enough to give the magic touch for a while even to the drab surroundings of jail. I hope you will continue sending your letters for me to Mummie. If I cannot see you, at least I want to have direct news of you and from you. Tell me how you liked Nalanda – was it not this place that you visited with Nandalal Bose? And how you are getting on with your work and play and friends at Santiniketan.

Love from,
Papu

97.

Santiniketan,
12th January, 1935

Darling Papu,
You have made a mistake regarding the place where we went with *master moshai*[1] – Nandalal Bose. We went to a village called Tribeni. First we

---

1. Respected teacher.

went by train to a place – Magra and then walked four miles to Tribeni. Here we camped on an island in the middle of the Ganges. It was a beautiful spot. After two days we shifted again to Hansheshwari temple. Just near this temple there was another very old one, beautifully carved but in ruins. We, all enjoyed ourselves immensely. I used to swim in the Ganges everyday.

It is quite cold here – of course nothing compared to the cold in Bhowali or Almora. When I read in Mummie's letter about the snow, my thoughts flew to Bex and Mlle Hemmerlin. I thought of the two of us climbing that hill near Chesières for the fair that is held there every year. I remember every detail of that day. Do you remember losing your walking stick and how we searched high and low for it – but in vain? Whenever I hear or see the word 'snow', the picture of myself – all wrapped up in a blanket with my nose flattened against a hotel window pane in Lausanne, and feeling excited at seeing snow falling for the first time in my life – comes to my mind. That was when I had bronchitis at the Hotel Mirabeau, where a French lady took a fancy to me and sent me flowers & chocolates and a card that I still have, on Easter day. If I were to write all that comes to my mind it would take pages and pages, for memories of little happenings and petty details not thought of these last six years are coming one after the other.

But now let us come back to the present. I am quite fit and have been reading quite an interesting book – *The Art of Thinking.*

Raj Chachi and Mami[1] came to see me a few days ago. Chachi said that I had changed very much. They stayed only one evening as Shridhara Chacha[2] and Raj Chachi had to catch the train to Allahabad the next morning.

We have as one of the matrons – Dr Margaret Spiegel.[3] You must have heard quite a lot about her, she was with Bapu for some time. I think it was Bapu who gave her the name Amalaben – as she now calls herself. She is a linguist – knows sixteen languages fluently – also Hindi and Gujerati. Amalaben takes the French and German classes here. She teaches quite well.

Our Hindi Panditji is going to give up teaching and we will have a new man from next week. I have not begun the extra classes yet.

My Bengali is improving considerably – so much so that when I went to see Gurudev the other day, he suggested attending Bengali Literature classes.

---

1. Sheila Kaul: wife of Kailas Nath Kaul, Kamala Nehru's brother and a political worker. ('Mami' means 'aunt'.)

2. Shri Shridhara Nehru: cousin of Jawaharlal, married to Raj Dulari.

3. Dr Margarete Spiegel (Amalaben): a German lady who was on the faculty of Santiniketan and a disciple of Mahatma Gandhi.

Leena Sarabhai is here since a week. She is as fat as ever but dances beautifully. There is to be a performance tomorrow evening for a party of Japanese arriving in the morning. Leena will also dance. Bharati & Suhrid were holiday-making on the Continent but have returned to Oxford for their studies.[1]

If the Japanese like the performance and think it will be appreciated in Japan, Gurudev will take his 'dancing and singing' troupe there in the near future. The old man is very weak and yet for the want of funds for the Visva-Bharati he has to rush about from place to place.

14th January, 1935

We had the performance last evening. It was quite good, though I do not know what the Japanese thought about it.

I have just received a card from Bhowali, which informed me that Dol Amma is not very well. I have written to Upadhyaya. It is so irritating not to get any news of any body when one is far away.

With ever such a lot of love,

                 Indu

———————◄■———————

98.   Almora District Jail,
                               4th February, 1935

Indu darling,

I have your letter.[2] I am glad you had a pleasant little holiday on the island in the Ganges and enjoyed yourself swimming about in the river and wandering among the ruins of ancient temples. I had imagined, from something you had written, that you were going to Nalanda, the old university town in Bihar, where Hiuen Tsang[3] went in the days of Harshavardhana.[4] Hence my mistake.

The snow was very pleasant to see and feel but it was a very temporary visitor and, like most good things, it left us too soon. The deodars and other trees laden with snowflakes were very beautiful and fairy-like. Snow whitens and beautifies even the ugly things of life; what then of those that have their own grace and beauty? But it vanished into nothing and it has not come again, and perhaps will not come again this winter, and we can only dream with the poet: Where are the snows of yester-year?

1. Leena, Bharati and Suridh (or Suhrid): members of the notable Sarabhai family of Gujarat, prominent in industry and culture.

2. Refers to letter No. 97.

3. Hiuen Tsang: a Buddhist traveller from China, who visited India in the seventh century. His chronicle is a major source for the history of that century.

4. Harshavardhana: Emperor of Kanauj, distinguished both for his military prowess and his patronage of literature and the arts.

I thought so much of you and of Switzerland with the snow all covering my prison surroundings. The Hotel Mirabeau and you lying ill, and the Danish lady who sent you flowers (she was Danish not French). I sent her some flowers also and quite by accident I chose the Danish national colours – I did not even know at the time what they were. The old lady was so pleased at what she considered my delicate and graceful compliment to her nationality! And then Geneva with our flat there (I have forgotten the name of the street but I think the number was 46) and the Ecole Internationale; and Chesières and Villars; and Montreux with its picture-like beauty with the Dents du Midi towering high up beyond the Castle of Chillon; and Chamonix and Mont Blanc; and your American camp by the lake-side (what was the name of the lake? How my memory fails me!) where you tried to learn swimming; and Bex; and the Etablissement Stephani at Montana.

How small you were then and how you have grown since, and what a lot has happened since then to all of us! Memories crowd back and fill the mind, memories of the past, especially in jail, where the present is too flat to offer any grip to the imagination and so the mind wanders back to the past or sometimes dreams of the future and builds magic castles in the air. Alas that these castles should be so ephemeral and, like the snow, should vanish so soon, leaving no trace behind.

I had quite forgotten that incident of the walking stick which you mention. But now I remember it and that village fair comes back to my mind, our climb up the mountain, and the people carrying their skis, and the crowds of holiday-makers in that expanse of snow.

There was much more snow round about Bhowali than here at Almora and Feroze had some exciting adventures. Ranjit Pupha was there also then and Madan Bhai and they used to go out for long walks. At one place a pond was frozen over and Feroze tried to skate or rather slide on it. The ice broke up under his weight and he disappeared suddenly up to his waist in freezing water. It was a job to come out.

The winter seems to be passing and there is already a faint smell of the spring in the air. In another four days it will be Vasanta Panchami.[1] Last year on this day Mummie and I were in Santiniketan and the Chandas gave us a pretty little present for, you must know, that this is an important anniversary for both of us – we were married on that day! A year ago that was and within a few days I was in prison and here I have been since then. Another year gone, another year still to pass. Heigh ho!

The clouds are my favourite companions here and I watch them daily. Sometimes they pay me a visit in the shape of mist and they fill my barrack with a damp and sticky feeling, but it isn't so bad. Usually they are high up,

---

1. A festival marking the coming of spring.

assuming the most fantastic shapes. I fancy I see shapes of animals in them, elephants and camels and lions, and even little pigs. Or they resemble the porpoises that hop about in the sea, or fish lying side by side, almost like sardines in a tin. And then they would change suddenly and coalesce and look like a mighty ocean, and at other times like a beach. The wind rustling through the deodars helps the illusion, for it sounds like the tide coming in and the waves breaking on a distant sea-front. It is a great game, this watching of the clouds. Once I saw some whiffs of them floating about and I was immediately reminded of Sir Prabhashanker Pattani's[1] peroxide beard. It was really a remarkable likeness and I was highly amused and laughed to myself for a long time. Have you seen this famous beard? It is worth seeing. Puphi – the elder one – knows it well and so you had better tell her of my experience here.

We shall have flowers soon, the dainty gifts of the spring season, and the hillsides will be covered with them, especially at Bhowali. Even here in my barrack yard I hope to raise a few. Just at present last year's plants and shrubs look shrivelled up on account of the cold.

Some time back, when I was at Bhowali, Mummie told me that you wanted to change your subjects and give up your present course. You were keen on giving more time to the Kala Bhavana and to languages. I asked Feroze to send you a message and also to write to Anil Kumar Chanda. I suggested that you might discuss the matter with Chanda and then make such alterations in your subjects as you think fit. I do not know if you got this message.

I am quite clear that if you have a clear bent in any direction, you should follow it. It is all wrong to spend too much time on subjects which do not interest. That is almost time wasted. Of course every cultured person must have some general knowledge about the world we live in and its problems. I have always attached importance to the study of science because without it, it is hardly possible to understand the modern world. But, as far as I can make out, you cannot do much in the way of science at Santiniketan. If you can carry on with Chemistry do so, but it is for you to decide. Biology is really more important than Chemistry but they are all related together. I sent you a fat tome on Biology by Wells a month ago.

If you are attracted to the Kala Bhavana I think it advisable for you to give more time to it. It is better to do some things well than many things indifferently. There is also this to be said for it, that art is the speciality of Santiniketan and Nandalal Bose is a fine artist and teacher. If the *master moshai* thinks you are a promising pupil you should profit by his teaching as much as possible. This is a thing which you cannot easily have elsewhere.

1. Sir Prabhashanker Dalpatram Pattani: civil servant and politician.

Languages are also desirable and languages are tricky things after a certain age. You will find it far easier to learn a new language now than say five years later. As one grows the capacity for learning languages weakens tremendously. The best time of course is babyhood. As Miss Spiegel (I refuse to call her by any other name. Why should people's names be changed?) is a good linguist take advantage of this. I do not know what languages you are doing at present. Of the Indian languages I understand you are taking up Bengali and Hindi. French of course you are taking and presumably English literature. Are you doing German also? I had no idea you were doing so but a mention of it in one of your letters made me think that you had taken it up. If you want to take it, do so by all means. It is for you to decide.

So that you can build up your studies round the Kala Bhaana and languages and any other subjects you choose. It will be a good thing if you could discuss the matter with A. K. Chanda. He might be of help in making up a programme.

I am not at all keen on your taking any particular examinations at Santiniketan. If they come in your way take them. You need not go out of your way for them. I look upon all these studies of yours as preparatory to specialisation, probably in Europe, for some particular line of work. I do not yet know what your own desires are in regard to this or whether they are clearly formed yet. In the ordinary course you will remain at Santiniketan till the summer of 1936. If possible I should like to go with you & Mummie then to Europe, but it is quite impossible to make any plans so far ahead. There are so many indeterminate factors – Mother's health, Dol Amma's condition, my own entanglements, etc. So for the present you had better not bother too much about the distant future and carry on at Santiniketan and learn as much as possible there.

You must have had news of Dol Amma. She has been through a big crisis and although she is much better now, she has to be carefully watched and taken care of. At one time there was some talk of my being transferred to a Bombay Jail so that I might see her. But now that she is a little better there is no immediate chance of my being sent. It is proposed to keep her in Bombay till the end of March and then to bring her to Allahabad. After ten days or so there the idea is to take her to Bhowali. If all goes well she ought to come up about the middle of April.

It is quite possible that Ranjit Pupha & Puphi & the children might also come up for the summer to these hills, probably somewhere near Almora. Ranjit has taken a fancy to a house in a beautiful spot about fourteen miles from Almora. It is much higher up and commands a magnificent view of the snows but it is far from civilisation and rather desolate.

Perhaps Raja & Chhoti Puphi might also come up. They will certainly come to see me, for I have not had a glimpse of them for a long time. And then there is the bawling infant who has to be displayed. You know of course of the new arrival [Harsha] who appeared in the world on the morning of February 1st. Bari Puphi must have been greatly relieved that the newcomer was a son. Our family had had too many daughters already for her taste!

Your next holidays, I suppose, begin in May. It is so long since I saw you and May seems to be a terrible distance off. However the months will pass and then I hope you will come up to Bhowali and pay a visit to your Papu in Almora Jail.

Upadhyaya will probably be coming up to Bhowali soon.

I hope you are keeping well. I want you not merely to keep well but to be aggressively fit and, as far as possible, to make yourself impervious to disease. What a terrible waste of energy is illness and how it disables us from doing useful work! One does not think about it much in one's youth but it is worthwhile doing so. A little care now might make such a lot of difference later on. Many people take various tonics but really the best thing, especially in youth, to build up a strong body is cod liver oil. Horrible stuff you will say and I entirely agree with you. But there is a very good substitute – halibut liver oil. This is as bad but the great advantage is that one has only to take two or three drops of this instead of the huge quantities of cod liver oil. It is quite easy to put these drops in any liquid or solid and not feel the taste. Even I have started taking them regularly! I would be glad if you followed your father's example in this respect at least. Ask your doctor there and tell him to get it for you from Calcutta. You can also get it in capsules or in a malt mixture. It is called Crooke's Colossal Halibut Liver Oil. I am sure it will do you a deal of good and make you strong and capable of resisting any disease.

I am glad you read *The Art of Thinking*. It is by an Abbé (Dimnet[1] I think) is it not? I read it some time ago and liked it. Do let me know from time to time what books you read. I am interested in books. And should you at any time want me to send you interesting books I shall gladly do so. Even from Almora Jail I can reach out for them.

Is Leena Sarabhai studying at Santiniketan? Or did she merely come to dance? I saw her dance four years ago in Ahmedabad and liked it very much. She must have grown a lot since then. She was plump enough then.

Gurudev must be going to Allahabad soon. When he returns give him my regards and love.

Who pays your college account? Is this done from Bombay or Allahabad? Mummie doesn't know. And do you get any pocket money? You must not run short of pocket cash.

---

1. Ernest Dimnet: French author and writer.

This is a fairly long letter but then I don't write to you very often do I?
With all my love,

Your loving,
Papu

---

99.   Santiniketan
                                                     [February 1935]

Darling Papu,
Your letter[1] is always so welcome and when it comes after such a long
absence, my delight is almost immeasurable.

All the little scenes you mention of our stay in Europe come so vividly to
my mind – the Geneva flat was at 46, Boulevard des Tranchées and the
name of the beautiful French lake was 'Lac d'Annecy'.

Some days ago Ragini Devi, the dancer, came here with her party. She
gave two performances. Her dancing was hardly worth looking at but
Gopinath, her partner was superb. His expression, his movements, and
the strength and vigour with which he danced were simply marvellous.
Some people go so far as to say that he is even better than the great Uday
Shankar.

On the 6th of the month, the Governor of Bengal paid a visit to
Gurudev and you should have seen the preparations. From the 4th
evening Santiniketan was crowded with red turbans and all our letters
were opened at the post office. On the 6th morning we were all (including
professors) packed off to Sriniketan where fortunately for us there was a
mela [fair] (it being the anniversary of that place). We were not allowed to
return before evening.

Amalaben (I'm so used to this name by now that the other one seems
strange) teaches quite well, though I'm afraid she's a bit queer in the head.
She has to look after the smaller girls and has already managed to make
herself thoroughly unpopular. She gets very little time. Several people
suggested my taking up German with her but I had not actually begun
attending the classes and then she cannot afford any time so I left it and
now I attend only my special French class.

Leena was here for about a week. She spent most of her time in the Kala
Bhavana talking to the students and looking at paintings – we have quite a
big and a very good collection. Also she exhibited her own paintings and
gave a performance of her dancing – it is the same style as is taught here,
but she has mixed it up with some poses from the Garba dance. I agree it
was very nice, but then she has devoted all her attention to that one dance

---

1. Refers to letter No. 98.

for eight whole years, so what other result would you expect? Leena has not changed one bit since I saw her last on the S.S. *Kalaghora* on our way back from the Karachi Congress.[1] She's just the same sweetly smiling plump little girl with the 'all dressed up and nowhere to go' look.

On receiving your message, I took the letter to Anilda who directed me to Mr Kripalani (perhaps you remember the gentleman who came to Allahabad with me, the first time I returned from Santiniketan). After a consultation I decided to leave the college classes except those of Politics & Economics. History I shall [read] by myself. Also I go to the Visva-Bharati English classes, in which we do Browning with one Professor and the essays of Emerson with another. And then of course there is French.

The rest of the time I devote to Kala Bhavana. In the evening we have our dancing class, which I should hate to miss. The arrangements made for science here are not at all satisfactory. The laboratory is small and the Professors not up to much.

It is fascinating to watch clouds. There are seldom any here, but down at Juhu and also sometimes on hot summer nights at home it used to be a favourite pastime of mine.

Here the summer is settling fast and there is only a faint hint in the atmosphere in the very early mornings to remind us that only a week or two ago it was winter. I'm afraid any form of cod liver oil will be too hot to take at this time of the year, so it will be better to begin the pills in Bhowali or anywhere where it is a bit cooler.

Interesting letters from the Puphis in Bombay keep me regularly informed of Dol Amma's condition as also of Chhoti Puphi's and that of the 'brawling infant' as you call him, though I hear he seldom cries and is very lovable.

I found the *Art of Thinking* rather interesting. Yes, it is by Ernest Dimnet. One does not often get good books here. So if you could, do send me some good ones whenever you get hold of them.

I do not know anything about my fees. I enquired at the office once, but did not get any clear reply – these Bengali Babus do get on my nerves sometimes. However I will ask again. As for pocket money I have more than enough of it. One doesn't need much here except for subscriptions and food-stuffs.

With ever such a lot of love and kisses.

From ever your loving,

Indu

---

1. The annual session of the Congress was held in Karachi in March 1931, presided over by Vallabhbhai Patel.

100.   Almora District Jail,
                                  22nd February, 1935

Darling Indu,
I have your letter.[1] I am glad you have fixed up your subjects in consultation with Kripalani. Your choice seems to be as good as was possible in Santiniketan. I do not quite understand what you mean by reading history by yourself. It is such an enormous ocean that one is rather apt to get lost in it without some expert help. Perhaps you will get this help from some of the Professors there. Classes are really far less important than this personal guidance from good professors. Indeed at Cambridge we attached little importance to the university lectures; far more helpful is the help given by college tutors, as they are called. This really applies to every subject – Literature, Politics, Economics. I do not know if there is any such system obtaining at Santiniketan or whether the Professors do this job apart from professing in classes. Even if the system does not prevail, there is no reason why you should not seek help from time to time from your Professors. Kripalani, for instance, will always be helpful.

You have accepted my suggestion that I should send you books from time to time. I shall do so. And yet when I came to think what I should send you, I was a little puzzled. Most of the books I get here are new books, just published. Some of them are good, and yet I wonder how many will survive after a few years. There was an old rule that was dinned into me when I was about your age: don't read books less than fifty years old. The idea obviously was that a lapse of that period will sift the good from the bad and the indifferent, and if a book survived, it was likely to be worth reading. It was a good rule. It cannot of course apply to scientific, historical, political, economic and similar subjects, in which continuous research work is resulting in an addition of knowledge. In these subjects such rapid changes are being made nowadays that a book written a generation back is completely out of date, though it may be interesting and important from other points of view. But in pure literature it is perfectly true that the avalanche of books that is descending on us in these days is very largely trash and it is not easy to separate the chaff from the grain. It is far safer to read the famous classics of old which have influenced thought and writing for so long. With that background it is easier to exercise a wise choice in modern literature. We must not of course ignore modern books, for without them we cannot understand our own age and its inner conflicts.

Then again the reading of books depends so much on the individual – his or her general tastes as well as special moods. To enjoy a book we must

1. Refers to letter No. 99.

not be forced to read it as a duty. That is the surest way of disliking it, as well as developing a prejudice against all reading. Our examinations and textbooks often have this result. Shakespeare, Milton, Goethe, Molière, Victor Hugo, etc., become terrible bores because of this association with examinations. And yet what wonderful stuff they have written!

I have yet another difficulty. Youth likes one kind of book, middle age another kind, and old age yet a third kind. As a boy I loved Scott's novels and Tennyson's poems. I could hardly stand them now. Then I became passionately fond of Swinburne and Shelley; my enthusiasm for them has considerably abated. Must I therefore, in recommending books to you, think of my youthful tastes or my present tastes? Probably neither would be a safe guide. What I would like to know is what books you read and how you like them. Do you like poetry and if so who are your favourite poets? Do you like history – sociology – current affairs – economics? Fiction – historical novels – utopias – essays? And so on. If you would write to me about these matters I could keep in touch with your mental moods and development and I would then find it easier to suggest further reading. I do not want to thrust books on you which you do not like.

Any outstanding new book that I come across and that I think will interest you I shall send you. Meanwhile I shall mention a number of good books and leave you to choose from them. As they are all well-known classics you ought to have them in your college library. If they are not there I can have any you want sent from Allahabad.

Most of Plato's books are very interesting and thought-provoking. Try one of them – say the *Republic* – and see how you like it. The old Greek plays are also fascinating. Some of them are so powerful that they make one shiver almost. Sophocles, Euripides, Aeschylus for tragedies – Aristophanes for delightful comedies. The plays are short and easy to read. There are many good English translations. And talking of plays – have you read *Shakuntala*? Not of course in Kalidas's original but in translation. It is worth reading.

Shakespeare again makes fascinating reading if one takes to him for pure pleasure and not for examination stunts. And his sonnets are extraordinarily beautiful.

I do not know if you are keen on poetry. I see that you have been studying Walt Whitman and Browning – excellent persons but not poets after my heart. Modern poetry is very different – some good, some totally incomprehensible to me. The most lyrical and musical of modern English poets is Walter de la Mare. I have just been reading him.

When we were together in Anand Bhawan last August you told me that you would read Tolstoy's *War and Peace*. Did you read it? It is supposed to be one of the greatest of novels. Another great novel by Tolstoy is *Anna Karenina*. Have you read much of Thackeray or Dickens? They are rather old-fashioned now but I remember how I used to enjoy them in the old days. You should certainly read Thackeray's *Vanity Fair*, a story of Waterloo days.

I have always been interested in utopias and books peeping into the future. William Morris's *News from Nowhere* was an early favourite of mine. Then there is Samuel Butler's *Erewhon* and a fairly recent book by H. G. Wells: *Men Like Gods*.

Bernard Shaw you have read a little. Read more of him. Almost all his plays are worth it and his prefaces to these plays are equally important.

A favourite author of mine is Bertrand Russell. He writes beautiful English and he is eminently sensible. I think you will like him. Except for his philosophical and mathematical books, you can take up any of his works.

This is just a brief list which strikes me at the moment. I can go on adding to it but for the time being I shall stop and leave you to make your choice. Probably within a few days you will get the second volume of *Glimpses* and you might honour it with a perusal, though I am told it is unconscionably long. Perhaps, if I am provoked, I might write another book for you!

Why does one read books? To instruct oneself, amuse oneself, train one's mind, etc., etc. Certainly all this and much more. Ultimately it is to understand life with its thousand facets and to learn how to live life. Our individual experiences are so narrow and limited, if we were to rely on them alone we would also remain narrow and limited. But books give us the experiences and thoughts of innumerable others, often the wisest of their generation, and lift us out of our narrow ruts. Gradually as we go up the mountainsides fresh vistas come into view, our vision extends further and further, and a sense of proportion comes to us. We are not overwhelmed by our petty and often transient loves and hates and we see them for what they are – petty and hardly noticeable ripples on the immense ocean of life. For all of us it is worthwhile to develop this larger vision, for it enables us to see life whole and to live it well. But for those who cherish the thought of rising above the common herd of unthinking humanity and playing a brave part in life's journey, this vision and sense of proportion are essential to keep us on the right path and steady us when storms and heavy winds bear down on us.

'Hear, hear,' I seem to hear you say, 'to these pious and noble sentiments, but why inflict them in a letter?' I agree with you – my pen strayed and it is admonished.

We shall return to a more profitable subject. I have been watching the kites here a good deal. There is a wide expanse of sky and quite fifty kites round about here. Every day they crowd right over this little jail, when the prisoners are fed, in the hope of getting scraps of bread. What is more interesting is to watch them glide gracefully high above almost without effort. Sometimes they rush past at amazing speed, borne by a current of air, or they go up and up, or swoop down at quite a tremendous pace. They seldom exert themselves, except to steer by their tails, and to balance themselves. The rest they leave to the wind. I can almost chart the air currents above me by watching these kites. Do you know much about 'gliding' – the new form of flying on light little aeroplanes without engines? This is based entirely on the knowledge and use of these air currents. There being no engine, there is no motive power behind the plane. It has to rely entirely on the wind and air currents. It is very light and usually has a single pilot, or at most two, whose function is to balance and to nose out the currents which lift him up. Then he gradually glides down till he is fortunate enough to pick up another upward current. People have flown twenty and thirty miles or more in this way. It is perfectly soundless flying – there being no engine – very like a bird. There is not very much danger in it as usually the plane glides down slowly to the ground. There is just a chance, of course, of a collision against a tree or telegraph wires or a house. This gliding is now taught in a large number of schools in Europe and America, especially in Germany. It is fairly cheap as the simple planes cost little. It is excellent training for boys and girls, both for their nerves and to make them efficient pilots of real aeroplanes later on. Why should not Santiniketan start a gliding class? Suggest it to the authorities. But I am afraid this innovation will not be welcomed by them.

Perhaps you are right about the cod liver oil. The summer in the plains is not a suitable time for it. Why not swallow Pangaduine[1] instead?

I went to Bhowali a few days ago. We have almost fixed on certain changes. The final touches will be given when I go there next. It is proposed to transfer Mummie from Chandra Bhawan to a cottage in the sanatorium itself. I visited the sanatorium and liked their little cottages. I think the sanatorium regime will be good for Mummie and I hope she will improve rapidly there. She will not have quite so much company there and might feel a little dull but her treatment will benefit. The nurse will live with her there and if necessary one other person can share the nurse's room. It is probable that quite a number of our family members will be coming up in summer and it will be better for them, as well as for Mummie, if she lived quietly in the sanatorium and saw visitors at fixed hours every day.

We are thinking of leaving our present cottages – Chandra Bhawan, etc. – and taking two other cottages. These latter are just above the Royal Oak Hotel. They are not so well situated but there are certain advantages. They are situated on a good bit of level ground and there is a plentiful

---

1. A patent medicine.

water supply. And then they are much cheaper. They are just the same size as the old cottages. Dol Amma when she comes up in April can occupy one of these cottages and Chhoti Puphi (with the brat) the other. You and others who come can fit in either of these. I should like Chhoti Puphi to stay in Bhowali for some time. This will be good for her and the kid. I do not know if she will like making a long stay in such a quiet place. Ranjit Pupha [Pandit] intends, I believe, taking a house in Binsar, high up above Almora. It must be delightful there but it is a wilderness. I have suggested to him to make a trip to the Pindari glacier. If he fixes this up I hope you will also go, and I shall renew my acquaintance with it vicariously through you. It is thirty-five or thirty-six years since I went there! I was about nine years old then.

I understand there is a great argument going on in Bombay as to what name should be given to the son and heir. Two names have been especially selected: Rahula and Harsha. I like both. I think Harsha is better in some ways; I like its meaning[1] and its sound. But it is fairly common. Rahula has the advantage of being rather uncommon and its association (being the name of Buddha's son) is in its favour also. I know only one Rahula and he is a very delightful and learned scholar who is a Buddhist monk and knows any number of out-of-the-way languages. So I find it a little difficult to choose. Harsha reminds me of some famous lines by Blake – Do you know them?

> 'I have no name:
> I am but two days old.'
> What shall I call thee?
> 'I happy am,
> Joy is my name.'
> Sweet joy befall thee!
>
> Pretty joy!
> Sweet joy but two days old,
> Sweet joy I call thee:
> Though dost smile,
> I sing the while
> Sweet joy befall thee!

Send these lines to Chhoti Puphi and tell her that I have so far been unable to choose between the two names. If she and Raja have no marked preference, why not toss for it?

---

1. Harsha means joy.

When does your term end? Early in May, I suppose. Do you have any terminal examinations?

All my love,

Your loving,
Papu

———————————◆—◼◼———————————

101.   [Almora District Jail]
22nd March, 1935

Darling Indu,
It is just over five weeks since I received your last letter,[1] and because yours is the only letter Mummie sends on to me here, I have received no letter at all, from her or through her, for this period. It is rather odd that I cannot take advantage even of the privilege of receiving letters every fortnight that I am allowed. Fortunately I have been able to see her twice during this period and so have had some news. But for this I would have been completely cut off from the family . . .

Love,

Your loving,
Papu

———————————◆—◼◼———————————

102.   Santiniketan,
27th March, 1935

Darling Papu,
I did not know that mine was the only letter you received, indeed I was under the impression that as enclosures are not allowed you did not always get my letter when I sent it, but much later. I am so sorry for this long delay in writing – I can well imagine how awful it must be to be expecting a letter every day and not receiving it.

About three weeks ago, Santiniketan looked perfectly lovely with all the spring flowers in bloom. Of course the beautiful English flowers you name are unknown in these parts but I think the ones we have here are not in any way less beautiful. I had never before seen or even heard of these Birbhum District flowers and I must say I was very attracted to them. I spent much time sketching & studying them. But now it is getting hotter and hotter and everything is dry and very few flowers are visible . . .

On the 20th we observed *Basant Utsav*.[2] Very early in the morning there

1. Refers to letter No. 99.
2. Festival of Spring.

was a sort of a *Prabhat Pheri*.[1] Then at eight thirty all the girls who learn dancing went in a procession, doing rather a pretty step, to our mango garden, where we had a meeting, in which Gurudev read out of a play of his on spring. In the evening there was a performance of dancing.

We had many guests & visitors from all parts of India. Pupha, Puphi and Chand arrived on the 19th and stayed for three days. I made arrangements for them at 'Uttarayan'.[2] They were charmed with the place. They left for Calcutta on the 22nd morning at four o'clock. I went with them as Uday Shanker was giving a performance in Calcutta and I was very eager to see him. At the 'Empire' the house was very crowded and not a single seat was available so Puphi had a talk with Harin Ghosh, the manager and Chand and I watched the show from a stage wing. I simply loved the dancing and the music and costumes were marvellous. But after having seen Gopinath's dance, (Gopinath is Ragini Devi's dancing partner) I was a bit disappointed – Gopinath is so much more graceful & his art is far superior to even the great Mr Shanker's. If Gopinath were to give a performance or two in Europe, his fame would be greater than that of Uday Shanker . . .

On the 10th March years ago just after Bapu had returned from Africa, he paid a visit to S [Santiniketan]. Since then every year that day is observed as 'Gandhi Day'. On this day no classes were held, all the servants in the whole Ashram were given a holiday and the students & professors did all their work. Batches were made. One batch undertook the cleaning of the grounds, another that of buildings and a third that of the latrines, etc. The other batches did the cooking, peeling vegetables, etc. It is quite fun.

I think I wrote to you or to Mummie that a party had come from Japan to see if the type of dancing we have here would appeal to the Japanese public or not. They saw one of our performances and liked it very much. After a few days they returned to Japan and now they have sent a gentleman to take the Tagore party over to their country. The party will give performances at some of the big towns in Japan & China. If all goes well they will leave sometime in August.

There is a Madrasi Professor here. It seems he is rather keen on translating the *Glimpses* into Tamil. Have you any objection? Or perhaps someone is already translating it into that language? Could you please let me know?

About the Hindi translation, there is some agitation here as well as in other places. Of course I'm not a Hindi Pandit or rather Panditani, but some phrases are ridiculous – for example Tewaryji has translated 'white

---

1. *Prabhat Pheri* traditionally means a morning procession or festival, etc. The tradition was utilised for political purposes in the national movement.
2. One of the main buildings of Visva-Bharati.

ant' as *safed chīntī*.[1] There are many such words & phrases in the book. Then in the introduction or preface or whatever it is that Tewaryji has written, he seems to have misunderstood you in certain places. In one place he quotes you *ham to bare bāp ke bete hain*.[2] I'm not sure whether you ever wrote this or not, anyway it sounds awful in Hindi.

At your suggestion I asked the people who were grumbling most to write to Tewaryji direct. They did so but received no reply whatsoever. I read the letter and did not find anything to get angry over. Then when Puphi came, the boys had a talk with her & showed her some of the most awful bits of translation and she promised to do what she could in the matter.

I received all the books you sent me. I have not yet read *Last & First Men*.[3] But I did not much care for the plays. Lately I have been reading Hardy. I like him. Nowadays I don't get much free time. And the little I get I spend in reading periodicals & newspapers – we get a good many of them here. Some of them are quite good.

Some of the U.P. [United Provinces] boys are very keen on my reading something of Hindi Literature – specially as my knowledge of it is rather weak – and occasionally lend me books which are supposed to be the best. I don't much like the Hindi novel but some poetical works are quite good. The idea just struck me to ask what you thought about this.

In my room in Anand Bhawan there are a great many useless stupid books – all the rubbish of two generations. What is to be done with them? They use up an awful lot of space and are of no earthly use to anyone.

About my going to Europe I can't say what will be best. Of course if I can be of any help to Mummie *en route* or at the sanatorium, I had better go. I'm not frightfully keen on going just yet, apart from the fact that I'd like to be with Mummie, specially during the operation.[4] However we can decide everything when I come to Bhowali in a month and a half.

The newest arrival in our family is still without a name, the chief objection to Harsha being that when the infant will go to an English school the children will call him Harris!

The Vile Parle School is fast becoming a miniature Santiniketan. They are copying most of our ceremonies and festivals and have the same kinds of performances and shows.

At Santiniketan we all seem to be having festivals. On the 13th or 14th April is the Bengali New Year. So we will naturally have a holiday and

1. The correct translation of white ant is *dīmak*.
2. Literally it means 'I am the son of an important father.' Indira Nehru was obviously unhappy about the translation.
3. *Last and First Men*: by Olaf Stapledon, one of the first books published by Pelican.
4. Kamala Nehru's condition had suddenly deteriorated and she was advised to undergo a chest operation.

some ceremonies will be performed. The Hindi Samaj[1] (did you know we had one here?) has invited all the big guns in Hindi literature to be present on that date, as at that time they will have a good opportunity to see the place & have a good talk with the Poet.

In the daytime it is terribly hot and it is almost impossible to eat the food that is given here – it has such a lot of *tel*[2] & spices in it. (We exist only on bread & butter and the parcels from home. Jamnalalji sent two huge packing cases of lovely big oranges from Wardha sometime ago. Two days after the arrival of the parcels he himself came with Jankiben[3] & another gentleman. He had come to Calcutta for ear treatment & just dropped in to see me.) But the nights are lovely, for generally we have a cool breeze blowing and it is very pleasant.

We also had an earthquake on the 21st morning, though a very slight one. Almost everybody felt it except my room-mates & myself, though I woke up only seven or eight minutes after it had happened.

There are two swimming tanks here, and a third huge one is in the process of being dug. But either there is no water or we are not allowed to go for a swim. So they are not much good to us & I am longing for a decent swim. I hope I shall get it in Allahabad. Did you know that Ghani has left this institution and has joined some sugar mill? At present he has gone to the Frontier with his cousin,[4] who is engaged to be married to Sofia Somji.

Isn't my writing getting awfully untidy? With ever such a lot of love & kisses.

Ever your loving,
Indu

---

103.   Almora District Jail,
                                                     4th April, 1935

Darling Indu,
I have got your letter[5] and I was happy to read it. Puphi also sent a description of the *Vasanta Utsava* and of the visit to Calcutta to see Uday Shankar. As you are by way of becoming an expert in matters relating to art and dancing I must bow down to your opinion about Uday Shanker. Besides I have not seen Gopinath dance. I liked Uday Shanker not so much because of his individual dancing as for the whole ensemble which was very pleasing.

1. Hindi Association.
2. Oil.
3. Janakidevi Bajaj: wife of Jamnalal Bajaj and a participant in the struggle for freedom.
4. Sadullah Khan: nephew of Abdul Ghaffar Khan. He later married Sofia Somji.
5. Refers to letter No. 102.

So in about a month or so you will be leaving Santiniketan for the vacation and a little later I shall see you. Or if the water famine persists you may depart earlier. I have something in common with you there for here also, in Almora, there is a great scarcity of water at present and I am troubled because of it as my seedlings and flower trees want plenty of water. I have to conserve the little water we get and pour it out gently on my thirsty little ones.

Gurudev's birthday is on the 7th May, you say. At one time I was under the mistaken impression, due to a misprint in a book, that it was on the 4th May. This struck me as a curious coincidence for that was the exact day and month and year (1861) when Dadu was born. But now it appears that Gurudev was born three days after Dadu.

I am inclined to agree with the U.P. [United Provinces] boys at Santiniketan about the Hindi translation of the *Glimpses*. There are some obvious howlers in it. I noticed *safed chīntī* myself and some others. I do not know what to do in the matter, especially from jail. I hesitate to interfere as I am no scholar of Hindi. The only thing that can be done is to draw Tewary's attention to some of the obvious mistakes. Most of these, I think, creep in because of a certain journalistic touch that Tewary has got. He does his work rapidly and sometimes carelessly. Very few writers in Hindi, as far as I can make out, pay real attention to the artistry of language, the beauty and significance of words and the images they convey. They get lost in high-sounding and vague language; there is little precision about it, and hence there is always a want of sincerity in the written word. They have not realised yet that true style comes from simplicity and sincerity. Nearly two years ago I pointed out to a small private gathering of Hindi writers in Benares that modern Hindi literature suffered from a *darbari*[1] style and as long as this continued it could not have real beauty or a mass appeal. My remarks were given publicity in the Hindi press and created quite an uproar. I was cursed and denounced for being an impertinent ignoramus. Nevertheless I hold to that opinion. All languages have passed through that stage and till they have shed it, they have not grown. Another great drawback in modern Hindi is the ignorance of most of its writers of world literature and new ideas. There must be something worthwhile at the back of what one writes. One must have knowledge and ideas. Just a mere spinning of words gracefully does not take one far.

You ask me about your reading Hindi literature. Why, of course you should do so. Hindi poetry is very beautiful but I find it a little monotonous and it seems to deal with a few limited topics. Old Hindi literature is good and it is not only desirable but necessary that we should know it. Only then can we build on it and develop it and make it absorb modern ideas. My

1. Literally means courtly but Jawaharlal Nehru's usage implies hagiographical.

own limited knowledge of that literature has been a great drawback to me and I hope you will not suffer thus. I could have improved that knowledge in prison – perhaps I shall still do so – if my mind was not full of the modern world with its problems. I want books dealing with these problems, with new ideas, with history, science, sociology and economics. And Hindi hardly has any decent books on these subjects. At most it has a few second-rate translations. But I am glad to find that new and interesting books are coming out.

As for novels and plays and the like modern Hindi is quite extraordinarily backward. I have made a great effort to read some of these novels & plays and almost invariably I have found them to be quite amazingly bad. Compare them to Tolstoy! The one Hindi writer who seemed to me hopeful as a novelist is Premchand[1] (he translated the *Letters from a Father to his Daughter*[2] and a good translation it was). But then I know so little of Hindi literature that I have no business to make generalisations. Latterly I have often read Hindi magazines. I find them a poor lot.

To revert to the *Glimpses*. So far as I know no one has undertaken the Tamil translation and I have no objection to your Madrasi Professor undertaking it. Being a Professor I suppose he is good enough for the job. I think the Professor had better write to Puphi about it to fix it up finally. Usually the arrangement for the publication of a translation is made with a publisher and not with a translator direct. I suppose your Professor has some publisher in view. There is no point in translating a book and then holding it up for want of a publisher.

I notice that you did not like the Soviet plays. None of them was great but I thought some fairly good in the modern style. But the main purpose of reading them was to understand the present atmosphere of Russia.

I am glad you like Hardy, though (may I whisper it to you?) I have hardly read him. My neglect of him is strange for I am tolerably well read in that class of books. I think you will also like Meredith, one of my favourites. He is a little heavy, but if one overcomes this initial difficulty, he is altogether delightful. You will find all his books in Anand Bhawan. *The Ordeal of Richard Feverel* is a good book to begin with. When one reads these books how strange their world seems when compared to today! They were not so strange in my boyhood but the last twenty years or more have made all the difference. And the changes continue at an amazing pace and the differences grow, and when you attain the advanced age in which your father does not rejoice in at present, no doubt you will look back on a changed world.

1. Dhanpatrai alias Munshi Premchand: Hindi writer and novelist.
2. *Letters from a Father to his Daughter*, Allahabad Law Journal Press, Allahabad, 1930. Collection of letters written by Jawaharlal to Indira in the summer of 1928. The letters deal with the early history of man and civilisation and are primarily meant for children.

You have been now nearly a full year at Santiniketan and I am very glad you went there. You have had, on the whole, a happy time there and have grown physically and mentally. Perhaps you are gradually finding your bent. It was my wish that you should spend two years there and then go to Europe. But I am beginning to doubt if that will be possible. I can quite understand that you are not keen on leaving Santiniketan in the near future. Nor am I. It would be a pity for you to interrupt or put a stop to some of your activities there. But there is that possibility of your having to go off soon with Mummie and that possibility grows. Nothing has so far been decided and I am in a hopelessly vague state of mind – a condition I dislike intensely. But the fault is hardly mine as the doctors have a major say in the matter. Perhaps we shall know more in a fortnight and certainly we ought to know definitely within a month.

It seems to me practically certain that Mummie will have to go – the only question is whether she is to go just before the monsoon or just after it is over. That is to say is she to go in May or September. May is very near, dreadfully near, and I am by no means sure that we can even get passages then. But if Mummie's treatment demands it, it is clear that go she must. And I feel clearly now that you should accompany her. You will be of the greatest help to her during the voyage and it is obviously desirable that you should be near her if operations have to be performed. As I wrote to you last time, I would not like you to stay long in a sanatorium. But that is a matter that can be attended to later. Meanwhile there is just the possibility of your being asked to pack up your toothbrush and march off!

I shall feel rather lonely here with both Mummie and you far away and inaccessible. But that cannot be helped and I shall at least look forward to Mummie at last recovering her health. And perhaps, if all goes well, I may fly over to you next year! Indeed I would have suggested that Mummie & you might go by air also but the doctors will not permit this.

But all this is about a problematical future. At present the question is: to go or not to go, and I await impatiently for the doctors' final advice in the matter. In the meantime I am making a few preliminary arrangements, like the taking of passports, etc. It is possible that you may have to sign some papers in this connection. It is as well to be prepared for contingencies.

You have asked me about your old books in Anand Bhawan. I do not know if you have thought of any special use for them. If not why not leave them where they are? They are doing no harm. Some of the utterly useless ones may be weeded out. I have a sentimental attachment to old books which I have liked some time or other and I suppose you have some such feeling also. They bring back old memories and visions of times gone by. But much as I love old books I prefer that they be used to their not being used, and if you want to give any of your books to some place or someone who will put them to use, why, go ahead and give them.

Dol Amma has not been well. If she recovers sufficiently she may come up to Bhowali with Puphi about the middle of April. Chhoti Puphi & Raja Bhai are also coming up soon after. And probably the whole Pandit *khandan*[1] will follow in May when the school closes. Perhaps you know that Ranjit Pupha has bought some property high up above Almora, right away from civilisation. By the time you come back from Santiniketan there may not be any of the family in Allahabad, and the sooner you come up to Bhowali the better.

I continue to amuse myself with my gardening operations. I am waiting impatiently for the seedlings to grow. It is very fascinating to watch the little shoot come out of the soil. One notices at first just a slight protuberance in the soil; something is obviously pushing it up from below. And then the tiny upstart breaks through and peeps out bravely at the strange wide world. It grows rapidly and is soon waving gracefully in the breeze. Some of the shoots resemble little swords or daggers cleaving through the earth. I don't think I had ever before quite realised this mystery of plant growth. And two other mysteries that prison has made me appreciate are: the sudden breaking out of leaves all over a banian tree in spring, and the equally sudden blossoming of trees.

I wrote to you a fortnight ago[2] of the peach and plum blossoms. Already they are disappearing. Even the red rhododendrons are not so aggressively noticeable now. The tender pink leaves have turned green and the look of childhood & early youth is giving place to one of maturity. In the Bhowali sanatorium there are some perfectly marvellous wistaria creepers. I had often read about these creepers but I had no clear idea what they were. Now I know and I am not likely to forget.

I have a number of iris plants in my yard here and I am greatly looking forward to their flowering for I like the iris flower. And then there is canna, that old native of India, a favourite even in the villages. Some of the so-called English flowers grow wild round about here. Do you remember the creeper – morning glory – which put up a brave show at 6, Cawnpore Road? It seems to be all over the place here, appearing even where it is not wanted.

There are very beautiful flowers all over the plains, probably not unlike the Birbhum varieties you mention, but unfortunately they have a short life because of the heat, unless special care is taken. Here in the hills flowers survive and are longer-lived.

Today is Nauroz and the new Samvat 1992 begins. And so a happy new year to you. I have celebrated it by putting on a new *kurta*[3] which has been

1. Family.
2. Refers to letter No. 101. Part of letter not published.
3. Shirt.

exceedingly uncomfortable as the stuff was almost unbleached & un-washed khadi and it irritated the skin. I hope you had better luck. The Bengali New Year will come ten days later and then you will have your great gathering of Hindi highbrows. I suppose you are an ornament of the Santiniketan Hindi Samaj.

Do you know if the Bengali translation of *Glimpses* is getting on? Chanda was supposed to be doing it. The second volume of *Glimpses* is not out yet. It has taken a mighty long time. But the first volume has resulted in the press conferring the wholly undeserved title of 'historian' on me. I claim no such distinction and I warned you of this in my letters. But such verbal honours come easily when one is supposed to have gained a measure of distinction in public affairs. It is so easy (and often so disastrous) for the politician to claim and receive distinction in a variety of fields!

Did I tell you that Manishy Dey,[1] who is I believe Rani Chanda's brother, presented a vast number of his sketches to Mummie in Bhowali? Some of these are good and I like them. I liked Manishy. Like all artists he is most unbusinesslike and emotional and he parted with two months' hard work although he is usually very hard up.

Love from your loving,
Papu

104.   Almora District Jail,
                                                         6th May, 1935

Darling Indu,
As I write this letter to you, on the evening of 6th May, you must be speeding to Allahabad. Probably you will not have returned to Bhowali by the time this reaches there. But that does not matter. You will get the letter a day or two later on your return. I feel like writing to you this evening and the thought strikes me that in all likelihood this will be my last letter to you before you sail with Mummie. When I write again probably you will be on the high seas and my letter will be addressed to some place in Switzerland. How far you will be from me then, moving away rapidly across the Arabian Sea, ever further away from this little corner of the world which I inhabit at present! And I wonder when and where I shall see you again. We create these distances in our minds, physically they are not really great. The world grows narrower daily and you in Switzerland will only be four or five days' flight from Allahabad. And as for meeting you, we have not seen too much of each other during these years, have we? We met at Bhowali last

---

1. Manishy Dey: student of Rabindranath Tagore at Santiniketan.

week after nearly six months. And yet old habit and our early ideas persist and Switzerland does seem a long way off and your going there makes you much more inaccessible. Perhaps all this is for the good, good for you and good for me. You will have to shift for yourself a little more and not rely on me or on others. Home is good but it has a tendency to narrow one and make one too much of a hothouse growth. It does not prepare one sufficiently for wider contacts and interests and when one goes out into the bigger world, it is apt to hurt. Other people do not take so much interest in us and we are apt to resent this. That of course is an unreasonable attitude and the fault lies not in others but in our own narrowness and selfishness, the product of a constricted home life. The sooner we get used to cooperation with others the better fitted we are for the ways of the world. It takes all sorts to make this world and it is folly to expect others to be after our fashion.

This letter is taking the shape of a farewell epistle but fortunately I shall see you once again to bid you farewell. But many thoughts come to my mind and it soothes me to put some of them down in black and white. I shall of course write to you more or less regularly to Switzerland within the limits of jail rules and regulations. These are not very liberal as you know and a curious difficulty arises. If I send Mummie and you my usual fortnightly letter, as I propose to do, and receive letters from you, I shall be cut off from people in India. Except for possible interviews, I shall not be in touch with them. Even interviews are not easy to arrange in Almora Jail. Thus in July when Dol Amma and the Puphis leave Bhowali for Allahabad these interviews will stop and I do not quite see how I am to have even news of them after that. As for Dol Amma she is too weak even to come from Bhowali to Almora for an interview. However, I suppose, we shall manage to fix up something when the time comes. We need not worry about it now. So far as you and Mummie are concerned I shall write to you by air mail every fortnight and I expect you to do likewise. Mummie is not strong enough to write much for some time at least. So I am afraid the burden of writing will fall on you.

I want you to leave India in a happy and expectant frame of mind. Do not worry at all about me. I am all right. I can manage to find a fair measure of peace of mind wherever I might be. The mind cannot be enchained and I have developed the habit of undertaking great journeys mentally. I am quite sure that I am happier and freer here than great numbers of people who are not physically restricted. My peace of mind would be almost complete if I was assured that Mummie and you were faring well in Europe.

Parents are a curious phenomenon. They seem to live their lives again in their children. I have many wider interests in life which sometimes envelop me and make me forget much else, but still I am not free from that preoccupation of parenthood and I am vastly interested in your growth and preparation for life. The fact that I cannot help you much personally does not lessen this preoccupation. Parents, again, have a tendency to mould their children after their own fashion and to impress them with their own ideas. To some extent I suppose this is inevitable, and yet the fact is that each individual stands out by himself or herself as a new experiment which life is working out. To force a growing person into a particular mould is to stultify him or her and to prevent growth. Bernard Shaw has called this the greatest of crimes. And so I have tried, with what success I cannot say, not to force my ideas and pattern of life on you. I want you to grow and develop after your own fashion and only so can you fulfil your life purpose. Inevitably you will carry through life certain hereditary habits and ideas which your home life has impressed upon you in your early days, and I am conceited enough to think that your hereditary background is rather good. But the foreground must be your own creation. I have often asked you what particular subjects of study interest you. The object of my questions was not so much to determine these subjects as to find out how your mind was working. It matters little what subjects you specialise in, provided they are such as interest you. What I am far more interested in is yourself. All round us we see people who have had brilliant academical careers and yet who are somehow unable to fit in anywhere. Partly the fault is not theirs, but certainly there is something seriously lacking in such a one-sided education.

Right education must be an all-round development of the human being, a harmonising of our internal conflicts and a capacity to cooperate with others. We are the mirror through which we see others and generally we shall find in others what we look for and expect. If we keep this mirror of our minds and hearts bright and clean the world and other men and women will have a pleasant aspect to us and we shall be agreeable companions and comrades to them. But if we cloud our mirror and make it murky and smoky how shall we see straight? We shall then become self-centred and selfish, oblivious of our own failings and always finding fault with others. And the others will come to the conclusion that we are highly disagreeable persons and pass us by.

I am afraid I am writing like a professor. Forgive me this while. I do not want to preach or profess but I do want to take you into my confidence. As I grow older and perhaps wiser I attach more and more importance to real education, and by that, you know, I do not mean examinations and the like. I think a proper intellectual training is essential to do any job efficiently. But far more important is the background of this training – the habits, ideals, ideas, objectives, the internal harmony, the capacity for cooper-ation, the strength to be true to what one considers to be right, the absence of fear. If one attains this internal freedom and fearlessness it is difficult for the world, harsh as it is, to suppress one. One may not be happy in the narrow sense of the word, for those who are sensitive can seldom be crudely happy, but the loss is not great, for something that is worthwhile takes its place, a sense of inner fulfilment.

For you these questions and problems are yet of the future. Do not trouble about them. It is a little foolish of me to write of them even and thus perhaps to burden your mind when it should be as free of burdens as possible. At your time of life you should grow in happiness, for otherwise your youth would be darkened with care and worry. I want you to be happy in your youth for so I renew my own youth and participate in your joy. I do not want you to be a quarrelsome and disgruntled specimen of humanity!

You cannot help carrying the burden of your family with you, not so much in Europe but very much so in India. As it happens, your family has attained a great deal of prominence in the Indian world and this has its advantages and disadvantages for you. I am proud of my father and the example of his life has often inspired me and strengthened me. Trying to judge him not as his son but independently of it, I believe he was a really great man. If your grandfather's example strengthens and inspires you in any way, that is your good fortune. If your feelings towards your father or mother also help you in that way, well and good. But your grandfather and father and mother, whatever their virtues may be, have many failings also, like all human beings. The public mind, however, especially in India, has a habit [of] idealising and dehumanising the persons it likes and this is apt to irritate, in particular those who are supposed to live up to these imaginary standards. The family and one's forebears thus become a nuisance and a burden. I do not want you to feel this way about us! Do not imagine that the family or family tradition wants you to do this or that or to refrain from doing something else.

You should go the way you think proper and right and if the thought of family tradition helps you in this, well, stick to it. Not otherwise. To some extent you cannot get rid of the family tradition, for it will pursue you and, whether you want to or not, it will give you a certain public position which you may have done nothing to deserve. That is unfortunate but you will have to put up with it. After all, it is not a bad thing to have a good family tradition. It helps us to keep looking up, it reminds us that we have to keep a torch burning and that we cannot cheapen ourselves or vulgarise ourselves.

There is a terrible lot of vulgarity in the world and we see it everywhere in India. And when I talk of vulgarity I do not refer to the poor; they are singularly free from it for they do not try to pose and appear to be something other than they are. It is our middle class that is often vulgar. It has no artistic standards and it has got rather lost between Eastern and Western culture. It is hardly to blame for it, for circumstances have forced this unhappy state of affairs on it. Political circumstances have largely made us what we are and then there is our narrow domestic life. And so when we go out into the world we are often making false gestures which jar on the sensitive. I confess that I find this very painful.

But enough of this professorial theorising! My pen runs away with me. I have little to say about your studies in Suisse. We have discussed them already and you will fix up with Mlle Hemmerlin. If unhappily Mlle Hemmerlin is not available, then you will be at a loose end. I think you had better consult Mlle Rolland[1] then. As you suggested, I think you had better take, besides languages, history & economics. If you join the university at Lausanne or Geneva you will have to choose some fixed course.

I don't think you will have any difficulty about opening a bank account in Switzerland. At any rate I had none in Cambridge although I was a minor – I was under eighteen then, about your age.

I do not know how you will fix up things at Allahabad. I hope you will finish with most of Mummie's packing so that she may have no trouble when she goes there. I suppose you know that Puphi and Pupha will occupy Anand Bhawan when you leave. I am very glad we have made this arrangement for it takes a burden off my mind and the house will be well looked after. The whole house will be at their disposal and no changes need be made. So far as Mummie's and my room upstairs is concerned it had better be kept for me whenever I might need it – that won't be for a long time yet. If you want to put any of your personal effects apart you can put them in our room. But I do not think it is necessary or desirable for you to shift many of your things across. They will be better off where they are and Puphi can look after them. I do not want my room to be converted into a luggage room! As for the other rooms in Anand Bhawan, they should remain as they are. Puphi & Pupha can make such changes in them as they like when they come.

You will remember that I told Puphi about the Hindi translation of the *Glimpses*. I have thought over this again and I am quite clear that the Tewary arrangement should continue.[2] I am not very satisfied with this and some of the errors are very irritating but we cannot make a change now. This would mean my breaking my word and I think this would be improper. Besides Tewary must have entered into arrangements and contracts with the publishers & printers and obviously we cannot upset the whole apple cart at this stage. One message, however, I should like to be conveyed to Tewary. This relates to the notes that are being given at the

---

1. Mlle Rolland was Romain Rolland's sister.
2. Tewary was translating *Glimpses* volume by volume, and the criticism was of his translation of Volume 1.

end of each monthly part. These notes are very copious and are entirely out of keeping with the spirit of the book. Some brief notes are necessary. For instance when I refer to *Alice in Wonderland* the Hindi reader ought to be told something about it. The notes should be briefly explanatory *not* additional. As it is, they are long extracts from some encyclopaedia giving all manner of dates and utterly unnecessary information. The whole purpose of my writing as I did was to ignore this useless information. Why then add it? It would seem that the gentleman who is thus reproducing pages of an encyclopaedia thinks that I had not done my job properly and is improving upon it. As a matter of fact he does nothing of the kind & his notes have little or no relation to the text. Please write to Puphi about this. You can quote this paragraph from my letter.

I understand that Raja is coming to Allahabad to see Mummie. He must of course stay in Anand Bhawan. I do not know what arrangement for food, etc., will be made there at the time. You will be busy with the packing and other arrangements and ought therefore to be free from the kitchen department. I think Puphi should be asked to take charge of this during your three days' stay in Anand Bhawan. This will relieve you. Puphi & Pupha had better feed in Anand Bhawan during those days. The children, I fancy, will be in Bhowali then. Amma & Bappi[1] will be in Anand Bhawan then but they will have a separate kind of food. I mention about Raja as he might think that owing to preparations for departure his staying at Anand Bhawan might be a burden. It would not be right for him to stay elsewhere.

Will you please ask Mr C. C. Das (who lives in the house adjoining our cottages at Bhowali) the address of Professor Neumann of Vienna?

Mummie or you need not write to me now from Bhowali as I am likely to see you on the 14th. I want you to write to me from Bombay prior to sailing and then from the ports of call. Please ask Madan Bhai to fix definitely your address in Switzerland – whether it is c/o Thomas Cook or the American Express Co – Lausanne or Geneva. Write this to me from Bombay or else I will not know where to write to.

I do hope you will be able to take with you Volume 2 of the *Glimpses*. It is really amazing how long this has been in the press. I was told in January that it was almost ready – and here we are in May. Please take three copies – one for yourself, one for Mummie & one for Madan Bhai. Even if the book is not quite ready, take it in an incomplete stage. But there is no reason why it should not be got ready within a few days. If this has not been fixed up already please write to Puphi to shake up Kitabistan and the *A.L.J. [Allahabad Law Journal]* Press. Also have a copy sent to me.

I have written more than enough & it is time I ended. My next letter will

---

1. Swarup Kathju (Bappi): Kamala Nehru's younger sister.

fly to you across the gardens and deserts and ruined cities of Western Asia –

Give my love to Dol Amma & Puphi & the infant. I am afraid I am not enamoured of the infant's name. I did think Rahula a lordly name.

Love,

Your loving,

Papu

I hope you will give a good deal of time during your last days at Bhowali to Dol Amma. She will not see you again for a long time. Did I give you Halide Edib's[1] address in Paris? It is as follows: Halide Edib Hanum, 2 rue Georges de Porto Riche, Paris (14).

---

105.   Almora District Jail,
26th May, 1935

Darling Indu,

Your letter[2] and Mummie's sent prior to sailing from Bombay, reached me today. I am replying to it immediately as my letter is already overdue. I shall send this by air mail, so also my future letters, which will of course go fortnightly. I have no idea when the air mail leaves but as there are frequent services now this does not matter much. I want you and Mummie also to write by air mail direct to Almora Jail. I don't suppose I shall be transferred from this jail for some time. In case of my transfer I shall try to inform you.

I shall send my letters c/o Thomas Cook, Geneva. Also any cable or wireless message that I might send. So please keep in constant touch with Cooks at Geneva. In the event of your settling down anywhere for some time, that address should immediately be communicated to me so that I can write direct. I have told Madan Bhai to send cables to Anand Bhawan and have arranged that they be sent on to me here. But tell him that in the event of an urgent message requiring a quick answer he might cable direct to me here. I don't suppose any special necessity for this will arise. After all, what can I advise or suggest from this distance? All decisions will have to be taken by you there and it is as well that this should be so. We should all be self-reliant and depend upon ourselves. You know my general views and I have gone even further than I might have done in giving all manner of unnecessary details. That is a bad habit I have got into, which even jail does not rid me of.

1. Halide Edib: Turkish writer and political activist.
2. Letter not traceable.

Our Bombay friends – and they are so many – were wonderfully good to you and did everything conceivable for your comfort in Bombay & during the voyage. That is very pleasing of course and yet I sometimes think there is danger in such abundant good will and help being showered on us! We get spoilt and begin to expect it everywhere as of right and when it is not forthcoming we feel grieved and cantankerous! We get into the habit of depending on others – a bad habit. Of course in Europe you cannot expect all this personal attendance and help. That indeed is one of the advantages of going there and getting out of one's shell.

I want you to write to Pilloo and give her a message on my behalf. Curious that I should send a message to Bombay via Europe but such is life at present for us. I cannot write to her direct. Indeed I cannot write to anyone but you & Mummie. Tell Pilloo that I think she is a perfect brick and that I am ever so grateful to her. And give her my love.

You must be in the Arabian Sea, as I write this, far from all land. On board also you will have [an] abundance of kindness. There are many friends and the Lloyd Triestino people are decent. Besides, with the Italian Consul's letter and Scarpa[1] at the other end you will have the shadow of Mussolini to help you and that is a mighty shade on an Italian boat. I have an idea that this is about the time when Mussolini's march on Rome took place and if so this will be celebrated on board. Do you remember the celebration on board the *Cracovia* in May 1931[2] with its songs and Blackshirts? One of the very few things I like about Italian Fascism is their song of youth – 'Giovinezza' – with its haunting refrain.

You have a number of big guns on board. They are pretty dull people as a rule and do not look quite so big from close quarters. I am glad you met Mrs S. K. Dutta. I gather she is taking a crowd of Indian girls for a European tour. She does so every year. So you must have plenty of agreeable company. I have never met Mrs Dutta but I know Dr S. K. Dutta[3] well and I think he is a very fine man. He was a friend and admirer of Dadu's. He felt Dadu's death so much that he gave up smoking, quietly without any fuss. This was a very touching and graceful tribute to a friend, and it was a sacrifice for a smoker to give up a lifelong habit.

I hope you are having a calm voyage and will escape the monsoon. And yet I almost wish that you – not Mummie – might have experience of the monsoon on the high seas. There is a magnificence about the sea then with its great waves tossing about the little ship and huge showers of spray enveloping the decks. The cloudbursts come with a peculiar fury and in

1. Gino Scarpa: Italian author. His works include *L'Asia e il Mondo Occidentale* (1959).
2. En route to Sri Lanka.
3. Dr S. K. Dutta: leader of the Christian community in India, who was a prominent educationist.

the distance you might see what look like huge columns connecting the sea with the clouds above. Apparently the water is sucked up through these columns. Twice in my student days I passed through the Arabian Sea monsoon. Almost everybody on board, that is the passengers, was laid low and groaned all the way from Aden to Bombay! But I survived with about half a dozen other passengers and regularly appeared for my feeds in the dining saloon. It was a job to walk about, clinging to various objects, and food sometimes would hop about.

So you are going to Trieste and Vienna or shall I say Wien as the Austrians call it? My mind goes back a quarter of a century or more – I think it was in 1909 – when I visited the place with Dadu & Shridhara Chacha. It was pre-war Vienna, charming and graceful, full of beauty and historic associations. It was the home of music of the gentler variety, of waltzes and comic operas and songs. Do you know the famous old Blue Danube waltz? Perhaps the younger generation have forgotten such dainty trifles in these days of the strident jazz. The Viennese were a peculiar and very happy mixture of the Germans and Italians! Somehow they had managed to get many of the good qualities of both, and life seemed to flow, at the top at least, with a charming grace. But this was long, long ago, not so much in point of time as of a succession of tragic events. Vienna, proud Vienna, thousand-year-old Vienna, was very badly hit by the Great War and ever since then it has gone down and gasped for breath. Today it leads a precarious life in the shadow of an ever-impending tragedy. No one can tell what its future will be. Only last year there was a dreadful civil war there.[1]

But of course you will have nothing to do with all this and during your brief stay there you will see the surface of the great city only and may not even realise what lies behind it. But the glory has departed from Vienna and I am sure that if I went there I would feel sad. It is or was one of the great cities which have a soul or a personality – like Rome and Paris and London – not Berlin. I remember being taken up a huge dome of a cathedral in Vienna from which we had a fine view of the city. And there on the dome were pointed out to us bullet-marks, caused hundreds of years before, by the invading Turks who besieged the city.

One thing modern Vienna produced after the war which was considered unique. This was a series of very fine workers' flats, beautiful palaces they were, where ordinary workers could live very cheaply. Many of these workers' buildings were knocked down in last year's civil war. Still, they are very well worth a visit to see what a go-ahead municipality can do for the poorest of its citizens. Compare them to our mud hovels. If you have a chance, go to see them. If Nanu is there he can easily take you.

---

1. The confrontation in 1935 between the socialists and the army.

I hope Nanu is there with you and that you sent him a telegram on arrival at Trieste. He will not only be of immense help to you but his presence will save you a deal of money for he knows the place & the people.

It is good to visit Vienna and other places but I do hope that you will all soon settle down in good old bourgeois Suisse. I do not at all fancy Mummie being carted about from place to place and I particularly hope that she will not have to go to Berlin. The sooner she gets settled down in Switzerland the sooner will you be able to settle down also with your work. Afterwards, when Mummie is better, of course I would like you both to tour about a little. But there is no fun in travelling when ill. Your present movements will naturally depend on Mummie's treatment and the possibility of an operation. Probably this matter will be decided within two or three weeks of your arrival. Will you please ask Madan Bhai to send me a fairly detailed cable about the advice of the Vienna physician on the desirability of an operation and future treatment?

Mummie and you will of course manage everything marvellously, as you say. You have no business to do otherwise for you have the family reputation to keep up! For the present the management will have to be done largely by you for Mummie will have enough to do to look after herself. But I do want you to take personal interest in the arrangements, whether it is engaging hotel rooms, reserving accommodation on the railway or the many other things that will be cropping up. Do not put too much of a burden on Madan Bhai. You must get used to shifting for yourself or else later on you will have difficulties. Interest yourself in the money side too, so that you may know what is happening and can take charge whenever Madan Bhai happens to be away. I suppose Madan Bhai will have an account at Cooks at Geneva. This might be in your joint names – yours & his.

Meanwhile keep in touch with Mlle Hemmerlin –

My dear, I do not worry. I am not the pining sort. If I had been inclined that way I would have pined away already. But instead I prosper and fatten in the face of difficulties and adversities and I find life worth living because of them. When any action or work faces me, I concentrate on it and try to do my best. When action is denied me I shut that drawer of my mind and open some other. And so now that I do little else I take a vast interest in my little jail garden and my flowers and seedlings and exercise such managing capacity as I possess on them and give them the benefit of my care and tenderness. The rain god has been playing us false and there has been practically no rain for two months. But I am fighting this perverse creature – for my pugnacity must find an outlet – and carefully utilising every little bit of water that I can lay hold of. Some of my little flower plants have dried up but on the whole I have kept my end up so far.

I live in my little tent, for my barrack is under repairs. It is very hot in the middle of the day but I prefer this tent to the barrack for I have the starlit night above me and the tent gives me an illusion of travel. And though you may plough through the great ocean, my imaginary journeys are vaster and take me to greater distances.

This morning I had an interview with Raja and Chhoti Puphi. They came to Almora yesterday and returned to Bhowali today. The call of the baby was insistent. In my next interview, a fortnight hence, I hope to see Chand & Tara & Rita. Dol Amma is not well. I hope you will send her a few lines regularly. These will cheer her up tremendously. Also write to the Puphis and keep them informed of your plans.

I have received a copy of Volume 2 of the *Glimpses* & I gather that you have taken a number of copies with you. The book is formidable to look at and handle. You must be terrified at the prospect of reading it! I wish it had been split up into two volumes. Unfortunately it is full of misprints and minor errors. As I could not correct the proofs this was inevitable but none the less it is irritating. Probably you will not miss the meaning anywhere.

And so *au revoir* again and all my love.

Your loving,
Papu

I had your telegram from Bombay. I am not writing separately to Madan Bhai. Tell him all that interests him and pertains to him in this letter.

106.　　　　　　　　　　　　　　　　　　　　　*Conte Rosso,*
28th [May 1935]

Darling Papu,

At last I am off and we have the huge Indian Ocean between us. And the distance goes on increasing every minute – every second. We are now in the Red Sea – our first stop is at Suez. We do not stop at Aden as the Triestino people are most probably trying to economise on port duty.

I have decided not go on the trip to Cairo as Mummie will be alone for a whole day and night and the night at Port Said is going to be extremely hot as the ship will be in port. Besides Madan Bhai wants to get down at Port Said to make various arrangements with the Thomas Cook people – and there will be nobody, with Mums. Old Chacha has offered to look after her but then what could he do.

At present I am in Chacha's favour. He is very pleased with me – thinks I am one of the few people with any sense on board! He informed Madan Bhai that he had written home a letter full of my praises, saying that

Madan Bhai tried to put wrong ideas into my head but that I refused to be spoiled. All this is because I have not cut my hair yet and do not go about in beach pyjamas!

Travelling in the second economy class is a Mrs S. K. Dutta. You must have heard of her husband. He is a professor at Lahore. She is an English woman – Pilloo knows her and introduced me to her in Bombay. I rather liked her. She came to see Mummie twice and has offered help if needed here or in Vienna. She is taking with her a group of twenty or twenty-six girls who are interested in educational work. She will take them to all the big cities and educational centres of Europe and return after two and a half months to India. She did the same thing last year and it was so successful that her friends asked her to do it again this year. She is not sure about next year – she might take a group of social workers.

I wonder if in my last letter I mentioned the story about Pilloo and the Italian Consul in Bombay. Pilloo went to the Italian Consul to tell him about Mummie's travelling and that the best arrangements should be made in Italy about the customs, etc. The Consul got quite mixed up with the names Nehru and Naidu and insisted that Mrs Nehru & Mrs Naidu were the same person. Pilloo got most annoyed, swore at the Consul and walked out of the office. She wrote a long letter to Scapa (is the spelling right?) telling him that such an ignoramus should not be kept as Consul!

Thanks to Pilloo the arrangements are excellent and the Pursers and other people most considerate and obliging. But we made a great mistake in having our cabin changed. The ones on D-deck have been made lately, so they are in the latest style – much bigger, smarter with special arrangements made for the air to come in, hence very much cooler, etc., etc. Our cabin, which is on the B-deck, is quite a good one but in the daytime it becomes terribly hot and the fans are fixed in such a way that no breeze comes on the beds. Otherwise everything is all right and so far the voyage has proved to be good.

The sea is beautifully calm and is a lovely shade of navy in colour. It is so beautiful and peaceful – I love to watch it. Occasionally we see other ships; these look awfully pretty at night. Yesterday morning a small steamer crowded with Italian troops whizzed past us quite close, while the sailors stood on the railings and cheered.

The company on board isn't very encouraging. A good number of the first-class passengers are Indians, almost all of whom are suffering from some disease or the other and are going to Vienna to consult the doctors there. Of the Europeans, very few are English. In the passenger list I saw a Mr & Mrs Vernade. I wonder if he is the same person as the magistrate at Allahabad. You know, the one who used to write about the orders from the U. P. Govt. [United Provinces Government] during your brief interlude out of prison.

This ship is very much like the *Cracovia* and the *Pilsina*, though not exactly. And every room reminds me of the fun we used to have on board those ships and I miss you so much. There is no one to talk to or walk about with and when I'm not with Mums I feel so lonely.

Birla[1] and his daughter-in-law are also on the ship. She is going for her health. As companion to her, Birla has brought an Anglo-Indian woman from Delhi. She is about four and a half feet in height and seventy years old, hunch-backed and horrible looking and paints her face quite brightly. Her talk is even worse. I pity the poor Birla girl and wonder that Birla couldn't find a better person in all India's thirty-five crores.

On board there is a Mrs Shivpori[2] – a Kashmiri lady from Gwalior. I think she is Col. Haksar's[3] sister. She is taking her husband who has got 'jaundice' badly, to Vienna. She is rather nice. She knows a little English, is going out of the country for the first time, doesn't like the food and the husband is too ill to leave the cabin, so she will have to manage everything by herself. I think it's plucky of her to come like this all alone. I asked her to sit on our table at meal times as she seemed rather lost by herself. So now Chacha, Mrs Shivpori, Madan Bhai & I sit at one table. Queer mixture, isn't it?

Everybody is very astonished that such a young person like Mummie should have a big daughter like me. People think we are sisters. She does really look so young and sweet – it is such a pity that she has had to spend so many dreary months in bed. But now let us hope those days are over and she will begin a fresh healthy life in Europe and that she will be happier than she has been.

The women here wear mostly pyjamas and low-necked or backless blouses. Of course this dress is more convenient than a sari – but as far as the appearance is concerned it needs a slim person to wear it. Some of the women with roly-poly figures look most comic. As it is too hot, the Captain has issued an order that it is not necessary to dress for dinner in the Red Sea, so in the dining hall you can see all sorts of clothes, varying from saris to shorts and it is very amusing to watch.

Every night we have either a cocktail dance or a cinema or something else. I don't go to these functions and I'm sure I don't miss much, though Mummie thinks that I am tied to the cabin because of her.

Just before leaving Bombay, Mums asked Bachhraj & Co.[4] to give us some mangoes for the voyage. When we arrived on the boat we found

1. Ghanshyam Das Birla: a leading industrialist.
2. Bilas Shivpori.
3. Col. Kailash Narain Haksar: civil servant who held high office in various Princely States.
4. Bachhraj & Co.: banking firm owned by Jamnalal Bajaj, a businessman and nationalist leader.

three packing-cases – full. One was a present from Mridula,[1] one from Mulraj. The third was from Mrs Hutheesing[2] and of course there was a fourth, the one we had ordered. We sent two back with Upadhyaya. (I wonder if you got any?) And have distributed most of the rest. There is a small boy here – probably German. He can't understand why Mummie does not walk about like the rest of the passengers. He always stares at her and once or twice tried to enter our cabin, but his mother pulled him away. Yesterday while Mummie was writing to you and I was reading with my back to the door we suddenly heard a shrill little voice, 'Why sleeping', and there was our friend in the doorway with a pair of very small red knickers and a puzzled expression in his eyes. He does not know English, so he did not understand when Mummie said, 'Because you don't play with me.'

Among the passengers there is a Mrs Woo; she is the wife of the Chinese delegate to the League of Nations – at least I think so. She is quite a nice person. She lives most of the time in Geneva.

Madan Bhai has made friends with almost everybody and feels very bucked up and gay. Up till now he has been wearing his *kurta* & pyjama, but intends to begin European clothes in the Mediterranean. Madan Bhai thought Raja Bhai looked very smart in his Russian shirt, so he has had some made for himself. I told him he had better reduce his tummy before wearing them. His night suits are rather smart but he has not got quite used to them yet and takes off the pyjamas after a while (so he whispered to Mummie, the other day).

I hope you have received a volume of the *Glimpses*. Rehman[3] came to see Mummie at Allahabad a few hours before we left and sent us a packet of six books on the station. Jal[4] looked through it and simply would not let us bring any with us – said it would cause trouble on the frontiers, specially if we had to go to Germany. So I have brought only one copy for myself.

The food here is not bad, though there is very little variety. After being a vegetarian for over two years, I eat meat and very little vegetables (they're not at all good) but it does not seem to be doing me any good.

By the time I next write to you – it will be either from Lausanne or Vienna – I will have met a number of people and I hope settled something about myself. Mummie's programme will probably be decided too.

With all my love,

Ever your loving,
Indu

1. Mridula Sarabhai: member of the Sarabhai family of Ahmedabad, who was active in the freedom struggle.
2. Mother-in-law of Krishna Hutheesing.
3. An employee of the *Allahabad Law Journal* Press.
4. Jal Naoroji: industrialist who was the grandson of Dadabhai Naoroji and a close friend of the Nehrus.

Madan is also writing. He will give the news about Mummie.

---

107.   Almora District Jail,
                                            7th June, 1935

Indu darling,
On 28th May I received your cable, probably sent from Aden or thereabouts, and forwarded to me from Bhowali. Day before yesterday came
the cable informing me of your safe arrival in Vienna. I was half expecting
news that day but I thought the cable would come from Venice. That you
had all already reached Vienna was a surprise. I am afraid I am getting a bit
out of date and am not keeping up with new developments in world travel.

So you have arrived at the end of your sea journey and are in Vienna
now. You will stick to the land now and may not have to cross the ocean
again for a long time. I have followed the course of the *Conte Rosso* since it
bore you away from Bombay, and have tried to find vicarious joy in the
voyage. Did not the dark water of the Indian Ocean sparkle with
phosphorescence in the night? And then Aden, drab and dull, with the
white glare of the hot sun, and little to see or do, except to visit the old
tanks, which are not worth a visit. Do you remember Djibouti near by?
That was bare enough and dreary, but it had some romance, for it is the
gateway to Abyssinia and the interior. The only thing worth seeing was
sometimes the magnificent body of a negro, like an ebony statue.

From Aden I accompanied you through the Red Sea and I could well
imagine the heat. It could not have been much hotter there than in Almora
at present. The *Conte Rosso* enters the Suez Canal with its sandy stretches
on either side and an occasional camel going by, slouching along with its
soundless feet. And Port Said with the statue of Ferdinand de Lesseps
pointing towards his great achievement.[1]

It was pleasant to enter the cool, blue Mediterranean with all its
memories of early civilisations. The isles of Greece – 'where burning
Sappho loved and sung' (Byron's lines[2] come back to me from the old days
in Harrow when I had to learn them by heart) – and Ithaca, home of
Ulysses. Your boat must have passed quite near to Ithaca, with its bare
rock standing out of the sea, but I doubt if anyone pointed it out to you. Up
the Adriatic, a troubled sea with rival nations on either side glaring at each
other. And Venice, queen of that sea, which once held 'the gorgeous East
in fee'.[3] But you could only have a fleeting glimpse of her for you were

1. The Suez Canal.
2. From *Don Juan*.
3. William Wordsworth: *On the Extinction of the Venetian Republic*.

bound for Trieste. I have never been to Trieste but I imagine that it has dwindled since the days before the war when it was Austria's chief port.

So we travelled together, you and Mummie and I, but now I do not know what your programme is and so I have to stay in Almora Jail. I am still in the tent – there is not a drop of rain and not a cloud in the sky, and the heat seems to grow worse. If it is so bad here what of the plains? *On dit* that this has been a record summer all over India and the heat has not been so intense and continuous for a long, long time. There is a permanent heatwave on and large numbers of people collapse daily, unable to bear this gift of the sun god. Soon after you sailed from Bombay temperatures went up everywhere and they have continued up ever since. Even in Almora it has been 100°F in the shade, and in Allahabad & Lucknow 115° and 116° have been touched.

It is June. 'What a tune, kind June, you are playing all the noon', says the Harrow song. But June is not kind here and the tune it plays is not pleasant or soothing. There is one consolation: the monsoon is slowly creeping up from Colombo and the south and perhaps in another two or three weeks we shall emerge from this Turkish bath and feel cool again.

But all this grousing about the heat seems trivial and out of place in view of the appalling catastrophe that has overwhelmed Quetta and North-West India. You must have heard of it. On the last day or night of May a terrific earthquake laid a fine city and numerous towns & villages low, and where Quetta stood is now a heap of ruins, a wilderness of brick and plaster and dust covering thousands of human bodies. These mighty disasters move us and yet, as a rule, they seem far removed from us. But last year's Bihar earthquake brought them very near to me and that insight has made me realise their horror far more than I had ever done before. The Quetta earthquake is evidently on a vaster scale even than the Bihar one and estimates of the dead alone exceed fifty thousand.

And this reminds me that you must feel rather cut off from India without Indian newspapers. It seems rather silly to get a daily from India and I am not aware of a decent weekly which gives a good summary of news. There is the semi-weekly *Leader* which is a perfect rag. I do not know if you or Mummie made any arrangements for papers before you left. Anyway I am arranging to have some periodicals sent to Mummie. They are not newspapers in the narrower sense and they cannot take the place of one. They are the *Hindu Illustrated Weekly* of Madras, the *Modern Review* and the *Vishal Bharat* (Hindi magazine). Besides these you might get an Indian paper, perhaps the *Bombay Chronicle*, but I leave that to you & Mummie.

Apart from Indian papers I would advise you to subscribe to the *Manchester Guardian Weekly*. This is cheap and good and will keep you in touch with important world happenings. You can order it through any newsagent on the Continent or send for it direct. You ought of course to read the local papers wherever you may be.

My flowers are fighting bravely for life but their thirst is seldom quenched. I ration out the little water I can get. I cannot complain when I know that people in Almora city have sometimes to fight for small quantities of water. Still we carry on, my flowers and I. Some of the sunflowers turned out to be enormous – nearly a foot across in diameter. The dahlias have also been a success and so also the zinnias and morning glory. Impatiently we all wait for the rains and scan the sky for signs of clouds. Meanwhile the flowers & plants wilt and dry up.

Perhaps *en route* you looked through the second volume of *Glimpses*. It is a fearsome object, enough to frighten the bravest. Yet I hope that the inside is not so bad or heavy, though it is long. I should like to know what parts of it interested you and what parts you found difficult to follow. Probably the letters dealing with economics and financial affairs you found dull. It is a new subject for you and it takes time to get one's bearings. My own private belief is that some of my last letters dealing with the world financial situation are rather good. I have tried to explain a rather complicated process in as simple language as I could. They are very elementary of course and yet, strange as it may sound, most of our big politicians and the like are hopelessly ignorant of the subject. If you read through those two volumes you will have a better knowledge of world history and affairs and the economic and financial basis of the modern world than many a well-known politician who holds forth eloquently on the platform. Nothing like blowing one's own trumpet! But remember that the world changes so rapidly nowadays that even these last two years, since I finished writing those letters, have made them a little out of date. So much has happened and is happening before our eyes.

Among my companions in this little tent – besides you and Mummie – is a picture of the Anuradhapura statue of the Buddha. For nearly three years I have had it with me and I gaze at it after finding comfort in its amazing strength and calm. You gave me a number of the *Visva–Bharati Quarterly* and in this I read a sonnet on a Buddha statue which I rather liked. I wonder if you read it. In case you did not, I shall quote it here. It is by E. H. d'Alvis, who is apparently a Sinhalese Buddhist.

> Nay, do not mock me with those carven eyes:
>   I too might grow, beneath that gaze of thine,
> Desireless, immortal, unerringly wise,
>   Disdaining human dreams. Lo, by thy shrine
> A multitude slow-worshipping still goes
>   Unsandalled, bearing perfumed offerings,
> While down the avenues of time still flows

The splendid pageant of all timeless things.
Nay, do not mock me with that ecstasy,
    Born of a peace abstracted from life's pain:
Love and its futile dream shall trouble me
    Too briefly – I shall find myself again,
And look on thee unpassioned, mute, alone,
    An agelessness invincible in stone.[1]

I am afraid I have no desire to be 'desireless, immortal, unerringly wise' and I certainly do not want to disdain human dreams. Indeed I do not believe that Gautama [Buddha] himself disdained them. But there is something extraordinarily attractive in that 'ecstasy, born of a peace abstracted from life's pain'. Of all the great men of the past, the Buddha attracts me more and more.

I have had no interview since I wrote to you last, nor have I had any news from anyone in India. My letters only go to and come from beyond the seas now! Day after tomorrow I am told Chhoti Puphi and Raja Bhai will come to see me. I had expected the big Puphi also and Ranjit Bhai but apparently they are not yet at Bhowali! What they are doing in Allahabad with the children in this heat I cannot imagine.

Soon I hope a letter will come from you from Aden, bringing me more news than the brief telegrams have done. Meanwhile I shall think of you in far-away Europe, busied with a hundred things, with new sights to engage your attention, while I go through my daily round and walk up and down my little yard and gaze at the young moon waxing bigger nightly.

Love,

Your loving,
Papu

---

108.   Hotel Bristol,
                                              Vienna,
                                        10th June, 1935

Darling Papu,
You must have received my letter[2] from the boat, and perhaps the Superintendent showed you the postcard[3] that I posted from Port Said.

We reached Suez at six in the morning. Madan Bhai brought Mummie out on deck so that she may have a look at the Canal and the shores of

1. Source not known.
2. Refers to letter No. 106.
3. Postcard not traceable.

Egypt. Everything has changed so much. Suez has grown and is full of big buildings. On the banks of the Canal – at least on one side – there were gardens and small cottages all along the way and it looked quite pretty.

At Port Said, the ship stopped about a mile away from the port. The ship reached there at eight p.m. It was nine before anybody was allowed to get off and we were told that the ladder would be kept down until two thirty, which meant that we could remain in town till that time – the boat was to leave at four the next morning. Madan Bhai & I got down. As soon as we got down from the launch, we were surrounded by about fifteen chattering guides. We managed to escape out of their circle, but having no idea whatsoever about Port Said, it did not take us long to get lost. However, I went into an Indian shop to enquire about Cook's office. The Sindhi gentleman who was serving recognised me, asked about Mummie & you and of course after that all was plain sailing. He accompanied us to Cooks, showed us all the best shops & bargained for us, so that we got the things cheap. When we were leaving, we were presented with three boxes of Turkish delight and a lovely bunch of roses for Mummie. Port Said town is much bigger now. There are cinemas and quite a number of big shops under English & French management – also several Indian ones. At every street corner there was a small restaurant with its cheap jazz band playing its loudest. On the roads were a large number of private cars & taxis. We returned to the *Conte Rosso* at about one thirty.

Except for the first day, the weather was not very hot on the Red Sea and when we entered the Mediterranean on the 31st morning it became quite cold & thus it remained till the 3rd, when we got down at Trieste.

In the Mediterranean, we passed several small Grecian islands quite closely. They looked beautiful. At Brindisi the President of the National Fascist Party, came with some members and a huge bouquet of lovely flowers to see Mums. None of the party knew English and so for sometime they went on talking in Italian & we replied in English, nobody knowing what the other was talking about. Suddenly I had a brainwave & I asked an old lady of the group, *'Est-ce que Madame parle le français?'*[1] Fortunately she did, in fact she was the only member of the party who would really speak it well. After this we managed a bit better. We also received a letter from Scarpa, saying that we were to write to him if we needed help of any sort.

At Venice we got Subhas Bose's[2] wire. We reached Trieste on the 3rd afternoon. Just as we were entering the harbour, another ship, much smaller than ours but containing 40,000 Italian soldiers, was leaving the

1. Do you speak French?
2. Subhas Chandra Bose: nationalist leader from Bengal who organised the Indian National Army in the Second World War.

docks, which were crowded with the relatives & friends of the soldiers. The ship was packed like a tin of sardines. It was bound for Abyssinia, where the troops were being sent to pacify the Abyssinian people.

An ambulance came for Mummie and we had no trouble with the Customs either. The wagon-lit we had reserved. We reached Vienna the next morning at nine. The journey was not very comfortable as the compartment shook a lot and Mummie could not sleep.

At the Vienna station we were met by Subhas Bose & some young Indian doctors who are studying here. They had made all the arrangements for Mummie. They took charge of our luggage, etc., and we had nothing to do except to come straight to the hotel. If they had not come we would have found it very difficult, not knowing German. Bose comes to see Mummie every day and another young Indian – he comes from the U.P. – a Dr Katyar is on constant attendance on Madan Bhai. He comes every morning at about nine and goes out with Madan Bhai, shopping, etc., the whole day. He finds enough time, as he has won an Italian scholarship and is leaving for Rome in a week or two – hence he has left off his work here.

Nanu [A. C. N. Nambiar] came here from Prague for two days on the 5th. I met him for the first time and rather liked him.

Soon after arrival in Wien, I wrote to Mlle Hemmerlin. Two days later I got a telegram from her, saying that her letter addressed to Venice must have missed me and that I could go to see her whenever it is convenient for me.

I have also a letter from her. She says she has replied to your letter. You must have received it . . .

We have received your note to Mummie but not yet the letter. We have written to Cooks and will probably get it tomorrow or the day after.

I have not seen much of Vienna yet. Most of the time I am with Mummie. And when I do go out it is for shopping or meals. The food at the hotel is terribly expensive so Madan Bhai & I generally go out to some restaurant. I have not done much shopping either. It is awful going out in a sari. Everybody turns round and stares and looks me up and down, till I want to just sink in the ground or run back to the hotel. A German lady on board had given Madan Bhai an introduction to a great friend of hers an Austrian lady in Wien. Madan Bhai wrote to her to come and see us & she said she would help me in shopping. She took me to dress shop & I have ordered two. I am so thin that it is very difficult to get ready-made clothes to fit me. I take any amount of foodstuffs & get plenty of fresh air and enough exercise – so I really ought to gain weight. If I don't it isn't my fault.

You will be surprised to hear that there is as much bargaining here in the big shops as well as the small ones as we have in our Indian bazaars.

Madan Bhai bought some leather photograph-frames the other day at quite a smart shop (the leather goods of Vienna are far superior to those of other towns on the Continent). The bill came to eighty-eight Austrian Schillings. M.B. said it was too much and at once the man was ready to give them for seventy Schillings.

At the dress-makers there was a dress for 600 Schs. I said I could not afford it & the saleswoman reduced the price to 550.

After the quiet & peacefulness of Bhowali, this is rather noisy, even though our room is on a small road, where there is not so much traffic, and Mummie finds it hard to sleep. However I suppose we will get used to it soon.

It is very hot here – even at night. All the arrangements are for heating the room during the cold weather but there is nothing whatsoever for the summer.

Yesterday afternoon I went and had my hair cut, partly because it was hot and partly because my *jūrā*[1] became untied about ten times a day and it was a nuisance making it. Besides it did not go at all well with European clothes.

Bose & the other Indians are terribly prejudiced against my leaving off the sari. They say that people only stare because they admire it so much. I have not told them yet that I am going to wear frocks because it isn't necessary. My clothes aren't ready yet & won't be till we leave for Berlin. In Berlin I will buy more . . .

12th June

The arrangements made for letters to be redirected from Cooks are something terrible. Your letter must have reached days ago, but we have not received it yet and probably won't get it in Vienna. This is due to the fact that the letter telling Cooks to send our mail here must have reached them on Sunday, saying that our mail was to be sent here till the 10th. I did not know this arrangement was being made or I would have written myself. Madan Bhai has no idea whatsoever about time. Yesterday he said he would take me out at ten a.m. I had another engagement but postponed it to two o'clock. Madan Bhai came to fetch me at twelve forty-five. But of course I couldn't go out then for by the time we had finished lunch it was one thirty. This sort of thing happens almost every day. And if there is anything I can't bear, it's unpunctuality. This letter ought to have been posted yesterday, but I expected your letter today, so I kept it. Now it will have to be sent.

Madan Bhai is leaving for Berlin tomorrow to make various arrangements with the doctor, etc. Mummie & I will go on Sunday, the 16th.

1. Bun-shaped hair-do.

Chacha was staying at this hotel up to now. This morning he has shifted to the Cottage Sanatorium.

A friend of Nanu's – a Fräulein Eva Geissler – lives in Berlin. He has asked her to help me in shopping, etc. So I will have no difficulty in Berlin in that direction.

By the time I write the next letter, Mums' operation will be over. I will probably write from Berlin.

How are you? Is the building finished or are [you] still living in a tent? What about the interviews?

With lots of love from Mummie & myself.

Ever your loving,
Indu

———————————◄►———————————

109.

Hotel Adlon,
Berlin,
27th June [1935]

Darling Papu,

I have your letter. About our permanent address – Madan Bhai's letters come c/o the American Express & Mummie's & mine c/o T. Cooks. But we have since discovered as you would say, *dhokhā ho gayā.*[1] American Express is by far the more efficient, obliging and less expensive firm, though Cooks is an older one. However now it will be more convenient for all of us if you send your letters direct to Badenweiler. I do not know the exact address yet, as we will have to go flat-hunting or look out for good pensions before that can be settled. I will send you a postcard by airmail from Badenweiler & let you know.

You will be, perhaps, surprised to see that I am at the Adlon. And perhaps you will not like the explanation. I had ordered a number of frocks and was to try on last evening, but the woman misunderstood me and when she did not arrive I phoned to her. She said nothing was ready and she could not possibly come before Thursday evening. Now, we had already decided to leave Berlin on Thursday morning. Everything was packed and the tickets bought. I decided to stay on for two days. By the end of this period I will be able to get my clothes, do some shopping & have a look round Berlin. Of course I have been on most of the big streets but have not seen anything such as zoo, etc. And Mummie used to be quite alone & used to feel very lonely so I did not like to leave her.

So I went to the station and saw Mummie & Madan Bhai off, and then came here and engaged a room for myself. Mummie was rather worried that I might be nervous & frightened and would shut myself in my room &

—————

1. We have been cheated.

do without food, etc. But as I told her, I am very lazy; when there is someone to do things & run about, why should I exert myself and so I do nothing. But when left to myself, with nobody to help me, I manage everything quite well!

Badenweiler is a small town in the Black Forest, very near the Swiss frontier and still nearer the French. It is said to be a beautiful place. For the first week Mummie will remain in the sanatorium and then shift to wherever Madan Bhai & I am staying.

Nanu has arranged for a companion for Mummie. She is a German girl – now a Swiss subject and knows German, French and English perfectly. She is a great friend of Nanu's and he says she will be the best person for Mummie, as she is very capable, as well as jolly. She is a Mrs Geissler.[1] She has met many Indians and knows all about India. Mrs Geissler will meet Mummie at the sanatorium in Badenweiler on Friday morning (28th). We met her sister, who lives here. She was a great help to us & a very nice person.

I shall spend two or three days at Badenweiler and then go to Mlle Hemmerlin. From Bex I shall go to Villeneuve to Mlle Rolland, who has sent a very nice reply to my letter and sends you her best regards. She might come to visit Mums. Nanu advises me not to stay too long at these places but to stay with Mums till September, during which time Mrs Geissler will be a teacher to me & teach me German & French.

In September the universities open. Nanu agreed with me that Economics and Sociology would be the best thing for me to study. The problem now is where to settle? The best professors are in Berlin, but I do not care for the idea of settling in Germany and I don't suppose you do either. Next comes Zurich in Switzerland. But everybody says that living in Suisse will be very expensive. The universities at Rome & Paris come next on the list. However I have three months to decide in.

To be a regular student at any continental university one has to pass an exam – it has a long name. But one can also study there without giving the exam. Nanu says that I could join any univ. in Sept. without giving the exam and at home I could prepare for the exam. Whenever I am ready for it I could give it. In this case I would become a regular student & even the lectures I attended before the exam would be counted. Thus no time would be wasted. I think it is a good plan – to you it must seem rather complicated in writing. But I don't know how to make it clearer.

I have seen more of Berlin than Vienna, but Vienna is by far the more beautiful city and I liked it. The people there are so terribly polite that sometimes I used to feel quite upset – but they are very poor. The biggest hotels and restaurants look dowdy and in the evening most of the people –

---

1. Louise Geissler: a German lady who helped Indians in Germany in the 1920s.

well-to-do people – take only biscuits and coffee or an egg. The waiter was telling us that it is only the foreigners who have a decent-sized dinner and very few Austrians! Of course now Austria is so weak it has no future – Hitler is keen or rather mad on it, it will probably become part of Germany soon.

In Berlin one really feels as if Europe were on the eve of war. Aeroplanes are buzzing overhead all day and night. They fly rather low and at first it was impossible to sleep, until one got used to the sound. All night they throw searchlights – I was rather fascinated by the queer symmetrical designs in the sky. A week or two before we arrived they had a mock air raid – the people were told to keep shut up in their houses, cars were set fire to, etc. . . . .

It is very hot – like India. Not a breath of air; it was almost impossible to sleep last night. And nothing is more exasperating than when some European says, 'You must be happy to have the climate as it is in India.' I miss the *tattīs*[1] and the fans so much . . .

> *Badenweiler,*
> *2nd July*

You must be anxious, for this letter ought to have been posted some time ago. In Berlin my cold, which I had caught a few days before Mummie left, became much worse & my head was in a terrible state, hence the delay.

Three days all alone in Berlin did me a world of good. I used to be out all day, the result being that I could find my way about there now easily and I have increased my German vocabulary. The journey here was a bore & very tiring. I had only a small suitcase (your old one which you saw in Bhowali) & a small hat box. It was a brainwave to bring this suitcase, as it is very light & a convenient size for a few days – what does it matter if it looks pretty ancient? I carried the things myself (engaged no porter). The things were quite light and made me feel more like everybody else.

This is a delightful little place. We are surrounded by trees except on the west side. From this side we get a beautiful view of two or three villages & towns on a slightly lower level than ours. The air is very refreshing and there is a lovely smell of fir.

Mummie is in the sanatorium and will probably stay there for some time. It is a nice place and the management is good. The nurses & the doctor are nice persons & do their utmost for the patient. The doctor comes to see Mummie twice a day and himself makes her menu for the day, with her. And she was telling me that the food is excellent.

Madan Bhai & I are in a pension which is half an hour's fast walk from the sanatorium. Badenweiler, because of its climate, is a well-known &

1. *Khas tattīs*: screens made of the scented root of a grass, used for cooling purposes.

quite popular place and June, July & August is the season here. At this time it is quite crowded. Except for two lines of shops, all the houses are pensions and two or three hotels. But it was with the greatest of difficulty, after knocking at every door, that we at last found this pension where they had room for us. Even then we have got two double rooms as no single room was free. The food is eatable and we have a wee garden, but this is not at all necessary, for the whole place seems so crowded with trees & grass (wild) that to plant other things makes it seem overcrowded.

There is a lovely swimming pool nearby and I will go tomorrow and then everyday. Madan Bhai has just bought a bathing costume also as he wants to reduce his tummy. Of course he doesn't know a stroke of swimming.

For our shopping we will have to go to Freiburg which is quite near.

Mrs Geissler tells me that the plan Nanu suggested about my studies was an excellent one except that the exam necessary is so difficult that it will be impossible to prepare for it as well as attend the lectures. She knows most of the professors at Zurich & is writing to one of them to send full particulars.

Apart from all this she says she will strongly advise me not to do anything for some time, till I am much stronger and have a good command of German. She says if I join now I will probably have to leave off in a few months. I think she may be right – I have become weak lately – more than I was in India. Perhaps it is the strain of so much travelling – I don't know but I do know that I look and feel awfully tired all the time & have aches & pains all over.

Mummie is very pleased with her companion, for she is full of life and funny stories about Nanu and other people we know and keeps Mummie in high spirits . . .

In future I think it would be best if you write to us direct. The following is the Sanatorium address. It will be the safest as Mummie will be there all the time, whereas we might change the pension.

This is the address:

> Nehru,
> Badenweiler,
> Baden,
> Hans Waldeck,
> Germany.

This is the German way of writing it – the town first. With lots & lots of love from Mums & me.

> Ever your loving,
> Indu

110.   [Almora District Jail]
                                             5th July, 1935

Darling Indu,

The last fortnight has been a blank one so far as any letter from you is concerned. I suppose you wanted to make up for your extravagance of the fortnight before. Mummie of course could not write because of her operation. I have had, however, two letters from Madan Bhai from Berlin. He has given me a full account of the operation. He also told me that you were not exactly flourishing like the green bay tree. You have been made to swallow bismuth meal and have been screened and radiographed, and your appendix has been held to blame, and a threat to cut it off has been held forth. Poor appendix! But the latest news is that a reprieve has been granted to it, and you are going to be (or more probably, are being at the present moment) stuffed with tonics and powerful foods and drinks.

I do not particularly fancy your hob-nobbing too closely with the tribe of doctors. They are excellent people and I admire them greatly but, on the whole, I prefer to keep at a distance from them professionally, and I have a feeling that medicine is usually better outside me than inside me. Of course under certain circumstance one must go to them and even swallow medicine, or get cut up. Surgery attracts me rather more than medicine. You can yourself form some idea of what wonderful progress it has made. For the matter of that even medicine has gone ahead pretty fast in a variety of ways – but not so far in our beloved country.

However, all this is an aside. You must of course follow doctors' advice and if they insist on cutting you up, submit to their will. An operation for appendicitis is not very terrible after all. When I was a student in England it used to be quite fashionable especially among society women, and even quite healthy women would, perfectly needlessly, have their appendices cut out, paying heavily for this gratification of their desire to be up to date and smart. Probably there is no such passion for this operation now but nevertheless it is common enough. Medical men have come to the conclusion that the appendix is a totally useless organ. There is a theory, I believe, that it is remotely connected with a tail which our simian ancestors had – a perpetual reminder of what we were. The tail has gone but the appendix still carries on uselessly. Perhaps in the course of a few thousand years this will also go.

Still, I am glad that no present operation is indicated for you. I am afraid I have no use for such 'fashion' and to cut up the body is not to be encouraged unless necessity compels one. More and more I feel that health comes from inside rather than outside, from the observance of simple rules of life and activity, and at the same time from almost forgetting the body rather than tending it carefully like a hothouse plant.

The body must be looked after, that is its due and is essential for our proper functioning. But to make of it an invalid and to think and speak continually of its pains and troubles is not only a most distressing habit (alas, so prevalent in our country!) but is calculated to make its condition worse. I sometimes feel that speaking about disease and illness, except in the case of necessity, should be forbidden by law. If such a law was passed in India, I am afraid quite fifty per cent of our subjects for conversation and small talk would disappear and many of our middle-class folk would be tongue-tied. Is it not terrible how they discuss repeatedly and at length their painful and unsavoury ailments?

I remember a book, a famous one – Samuel Butler's *Erewhon* – in which a society is described where illness itself was made a crime; the more serious the illness, the heavier the sentence. On the other hand, crime, so-called now, was treated as a social disease to be treated by experts and not to be punished. The idea was carried to an extreme in the book, with some inevitable absurdities, but the way it pointed was correct. Read the book, it is worth it.

Where are you to get the books I suggest to you, you might well ask. You must know the Tauchnitz edition of English and American works published, I think, in Leipzig and for sale all over the Continent. This is a wonderfully complete edition of almost all worthwhile books in the English language and it is far cheaper than the original edition in England or America. Any local bookseller will get Tauchnitz books for you and you can keep their fat catalogue.

So you are all in Badenweiler now and likely to remain there for two or three months more. I do not know that little town but I know well enough that all that neighbourhood is very beautiful, perhaps the best part of Germany, from nature's point of view. Very near you is the Black Forest, the Schwarzwald, full of beauty spots. Not far is the Rhineland and the banks of the Rhine must be covered with the vine in these summer days (or am I mistaken about the season?). You were with us, were you not, when we steamed up the Rhine, following its winding course through town and countryside, passing its great rocks with frowning castles seated atop of them, and legends of long ago clinging to them. There was the great rock where the Lorelei used to sit and sing and lure unhappy sailors to their destruction. And so we passed from Cologne to Mainz and thence to the old delightful city of Heidelberg. Do you not remember it, and the River Neckar and the professor of geology who took us reverently and proudly to his cabinet to show the ancient skull of the Homo Heidelbergiensis, that half-ape, half-man, one of the links in the missing chain of early human development? I am very fond of Heidelberg and several times I have been there, once with Dadu so long ago as 1909 to pay a visit to Shridhar Chacha who studied there and lived in a pension run by a professor over eighty years old. That professor's one consuming passion was hatred for England and I believe he died during the war years through very excess of anger and hatred.

Freiburg is of course your very near neighbour and I suppose Wiesbaden cannot be far off. Bad Ems and Hamburg, if I remember aright, must also be round about somewhere. To both these places Dadu and Dol Amma went when they first put me at Harrow. It was at Ems that Puphi's (the elder one's – there was only one then) fifth birthday was celebrated, and Dadu gave a party to all the municipal school children of the place and the mayor or burgomaster, or whatever he is called, attended in state. Old memories come back to me and I write them down, thinking that they might interest you.

So you are in a beautiful land and the early summer must have covered the hillsides with flowers. I hope you will take some advantage of your position and have an occasional excursion. I am sure you will give pleasure to Mummie if you do so, rather than if you remain with her all the time.

You have been now just over a month in Europe and you have seen something – not much, I am afraid – of two of its great capitals. How did you like them, Vienna and Berlin? Berlin, with all its pomp and circumstance, is not very impressive. Munich, I think, is a more fascinating German town, and the Germans themselves have a saying: see Munich and die. Apart from its old fascination it has got a new and a wonderful appeal – the great Deutsches Museum, built since the war. This is really something magnificent and worth going all the way from India to see.

When you were in Vienna it struck me how foolish I had been in omitting to have Czechoslovakia added in your passports. I hope you will get this defect remedied at some British Consulate. There will be no difficulty and it is as well to be prepared. You might also add Belgium and Holland. Suppose you want to pay a visit to Nanu at Prague or Praha as they call it? The city is said to be very beautiful. I have never seen it although I spent a month quite near it with Dadu at Carlsbad. Dadu wanted to go there because he said a resident of Prayag in India ought to visit this Prague of Europe! But he couldn't manage it. He was taking the 'cure' then at Carlsbad for his asthma, etc. Most people there come to get thin – so did old King Edward VII who used to visit Marienbad nearby regularly. It was rather comic to see crowds of people moving up and down every morning and evening before the springs with little mugs sipping the particular spring water that had been prescribed for them. I tasted this stuff once and turned away from it in disgust.

Then there were the baths at Carlsbad, a tremendous variety of them. One of the popular baths for getting thin was a mud bath. Another bath, and I tried this for the fun of it, was a carbonic acid bath, that is, soda water. This was a delightful affair and it filled one with energy.

I suppose Badenweiler has also got, on a smaller scale, its baths and springs. All these 'Bads' have them. I remember to have read in stories and accounts of Central and Western Europe in the old days how the feudal lords and the Jewish financiers and the petty chiefs of German principalities – there were so many of these then – used to crowd at Baden Baden.

I read the other day in the papers with immense surprise that there had been an earthquake shock in Wurtemberg and west Switzerland; I wonder if you in Badenweiler felt it.

It is seventeen days since Mummie's operation and I hope that she can walk about a little now. I am very keen on her leaving her bed and getting out of the perpetual invalid atmosphere which bed always carries with it. Of course she must take care for a long time and carry out carefully doctors' orders and in this matter Professor Unverricht, the surgeon who operated, must have the last word. He is now more or less in charge of Mummie and his advice should therefore be taken. I hope she will make good progress and by next month go about a little.

This stay in Badenweiler is somewhat different from what we had anticipated and I do not quite know how it will affect your programme. But in this matter I must not interfere, for any advice that I may give is sure to be belated and out of place. You must yourself decide, having regard to Mummie's condition, your own health and other factors. There is of course no hurry for you to leave Mummie. Remain with her as long as necessary. From your own health point of view I think regular mental occupation and companionship of fellow students is more important than tonics and the like. Such occupation and companionship draw us out of ourselves and we forget our narrow selves in cooperative habits and wider questions. We grow and health comes to us unasked. I am convinced that the mind plays a most important part in our physical make-up.

Badenweiler is near the Swiss and French frontiers, but still it is a longish journey to Lausanne. I imagine you will have to go to Basle and then to Berne, the Swiss federal capital, a delightful city with arcades and covered footpaths. I have an idea that a light railway goes from Berne to Lausanne over the mountains and the route is a very beautiful one. I have passed through it both in winter and summer. So although near on the map, you are really further away from Lausanne or Bex than you would be if you were in Paris or Milan. Still you are not very far. It might be worthwhile for you, when you can conveniently manage it, to pay a weekend visit to Mlle Hemmerlin.

Should you be staying on in Badenweiler for a considerable time why not utilise your time there to pick up some German and improve your French? If not at Badenweiler, you could go to Freiburg for it. The best way to learn a new language is to grow up with it, almost like a child does. If you could get to know some German family, make friends with a Fräulein, you could not only have some lessons from them but mix with them and listen to their talk. Indeed such friendship would be good in many ways. You could have companions of your age to go about with and the way to know a country is to know its people and try to understand them. It is an English habit to live in a stuck-up stand-offish way in foreign countries. It is not a good habit. We should indeed go out of our way to make friends. That is a courtesy we owe to the country we are in and it pays well, for it brings us intimate glimpses and friendship, and it helps us to grow out of our narrow national selves.

To come to a less interesting topic – myself. Here I am still in my little tent and the big *barsat*[1] seems to have come. We have had only one really heavy rain so far here but probably there will be plenty more soon to follow, and I shall get fed up with it and yearn for a clear sky. The air has definitely changed, it is the atmosphere of the *Chaumasa* as the monsoon season is called in our countryside. In Allahabad, reports say that the monsoon gave a grand kick-off with over four inches of rain, with the result that George Town was overwhelmed and half its streets are cracked and sunk in.

The delayed monsoon and the long hot weather was favourable for mangoes, *on dit*, and the mango crop has been most abundant. I tell you of this just to make you green with envy.

What do I do? Perhaps you have heard the story of the old villager who when asked how he spent his time after he had been pensioned off, made answer: 'Well, Miss, sometimes I sits and thinks, and sometimes I just sits.' That is the favourite occupation not only of our peasantry but of most of our so-called educated classes and mostly, I imagine, 'they just sit'. I have not quite got to the stage of just sitting, even though I am in prison, but a subtle change has come over me during the past few months. It has not come uninvited. I asked for it. The change consists of a diversion of interest from purely intellectual pursuits to manual ones. I had become too much of a bookworm, reading, reading and writing for most of my time. Outside, strenuous activity and moving about prevented me from becoming too lop-sided. In prison, that activity being denied, my interests became too intellectual. Of course I had relief in the past by spinning and weaving, etc. I liked them but they seemed to be extraneous activities, my main function being reading and writing, and as you know to your cost I produced 1500 printed pages during my last term! That is not so now. I have read relatively little and at the slightest pretext I put aside my book. Living in the tent has helped in the process and the cloudy weather has also lured me out. When I used to be locked up soon after five in the

1. Monsoon.

evening I had no alternative but to read. Now I can stroll up and down my yard, usually armed with a *khurpi*,[1] messing about my flowers.

I have always been a bit of a student, trying to learn to understand, but largely this effort was intellectual. There was also the emotional element in it, the learning from crowds, the appreciation of mass psychology. Latterly I have felt drawn more and more towards nature – to plants and animals. Maybe it is a relief and an escape from human folly, human cowardice and human knavery! I feel more in tune with nature. I notice little things that I had not noticed before. I sense the pulsating and throbbing life round about me. I notice the sensitive growing tip of a creeper plant, how full of life and energy it is! Animal-like it seems, and sometimes almost sinister looking; even the feel is hairy as that of a young animal. It stands up seeking for something to catch hold of. See, it looks just like a snake, with a snake's rounded nose and small eyes! Or it coils up, catching something in its grasp. Fascinated, I watch it.

I feel that this is a hopeful sign in me. I am growing still, getting more educated, more in harmony with life. If only human beings were not such spots of disharmony! Three years ago died a very great man, though he is not very well known. He was a Scot, Patrick Geddes, and he was a genius in many fields. He even came to Allahabad once and drew up a scheme for its town planning! He was a great educator and instead of the three Rs he used to lay stress on the three Hs – heart, hand, head. He wanted children to grow up with a first-hand knowledge of the worlds of nature and of man and to develop an unspoiled appreciation of life, the beauty of nature, of the human mind, etc. The first approach for the child thus came through the heart, through the emotions – the affection of parents, the enjoyment of fresh air, sunshine, etc. Then came the hand as the child grew older. Petty manual tasks in the garden or some craft. Then at last came the head and, curiously, the intellectual development of the child who had gone through the course of heart and hand was very rapid – far quicker than the child who began with intellectual teaching only. More important still, such children developed what is called a well-integrated personality, something in harmony with life and nature, the very reverse of the quarrelsome, dissatisfied, ever-complaining type that we see so often today.

Towards the end of his long life Geddes started a 'Cité Universitaire' at Montpellier in the South of France, where every type of student came to him – the Ph.D., graduate and undergraduate. However learned the student, his first job was digging in the garden, his second, observation of the sea and the country from a watch-tower and by wandering about and then came intellectual study.

1. Trowel.

I sometimes console myself that I am in my own topsy-turvy way following Geddes's course and so trying to develop that integrated personality. Having become somewhat of a highbrow, I have tried to lay more stress on the hands. Whether the result is going to be satisfactory it will be for others to judge. Let us hope it will not be too much of a mongrel type, neither here nor there! To a large extent Tolstoy and Ruskin advocated manual labour for this purpose. And the real psychological basis of Bapu's *charkha*[1] is also this.

Are you not tired of me, Indu-boy, writing all this stuff to you and wearying you even at this great distance with my wordy chatter? Once a fortnight I have the chance and I let my pen run on. You will have to bear with me. But I have written so much already today that I really must put a brake on, though my pen protests and wants to scratch on. Share this letter with Mummie and Madan Bhai.

I am sending separately to Mummie three snaps of Anand Bhawan and Swaraj Bhawan. Someone whom I don't know sent them to me (having signed them!). Perhaps they might interest you so I am sending them.

　　Love,

Your loving,
Papu

——————— ▬ ▪ ———————

111.

Hans Waldeck,
Badenweiler,
Schwarzwald,
Germany,
18th July [1935]

Darling Papu,

Your letter dated 5th July[2] arrived last night – we get two posts here one at nine in the morning and the other at eight in the evening. This was the second letter we had from you. The first was dated 26th May.[3] I had calculated that the next letter would be written on 11th June and then another on 26th June. Hence when we did not receive any letter till 15th July I was anxious and Madan Bhai wired to you. 26th May to 5th July is rather more than a fortnight, is it not?

As for my letters, I wonder how many you have received. Since leaving India, I wrote first from Port Said by ordinary mail. Then I posted a letter in Vienna by air mail and the third I sent from here, Badenweiler on the 3rd July . . .

1. Spinning wheel.
2. Refers to letter No. 110.
3. Refers to letter No. 105.

I give you Mummie's address above though I don't suppose you will be able to write there, as you will probably send your next letter before this reaches you.

Yes, we have a swimming bath here. The spring which supplies the water comes from 700 metres below the surface of the earth. The temperature of the water is 27°C. It is said to be very healthy to bathe in this water. The bath is not very big and only a part is deep. But all the people go there everyday, hence it is too crowded to swim, unless one goes at seven thirty (just when it opens) a.m. It is fun to watch the people – the great German race! All ages, shapes and sizes, mostly bulging out of their costumes – unfortunately people do not look their best in bathing costumes. I go every morning early with the Geissler sisters. After swimming, we laze around in the sun and return home in time for breakfast at nine fifteen.

A few yards away is a bathing place in ruins, where it is said the Romans used to bathe in 2000 years ago.

There are lovely walks here in the woods. And the smell of the pines is delicious. At first I used to go alone, but now Eva, the companion's sister, who has come here to spend her holidays, accompanies me. We go morning & evening and talk only in German.

I have made marvellous progress in German. Everybody is quite impressed.

I had made enquiries about the visas at Vienna and found it was not at all difficult to get them. Yes, I intend visiting Praha some day. Nanu is full of its praises and I hear the Czechoslovakian University there is quite good. I once expressed a desire to learn Russian to Nanu and since it has been agreed by all that I have a talent for languages and that this talent must not be wasted, it was decided that I should spend some time at Praha. Of course all this is still in the air.

Mrs Geissler lives in Zurich and knows many people and good families including several professors at the University. Besides this Zurich is one of the most beautiful cities of good old Suisse and its university is one of the best on the Continent. Hence we decided that it would be the best place for me at present.

Mrs G. knows the Prof who is lecturer on Economics very well, and she wrote to him all about me, how much & what I had studied, etc., and he has replied that in any case I shall have to give the Continental school-leaving exam – the Matura as it is called. This is a pretty stiff exam, specially as it will have to be given in German, but Mrs G. thinks I will be able to manage it in a year (the period that it is compulsory to attend the school before giving the exam).

I could not go to Mlle Hemmerlin yet, as I had a slight attack of influenza. But I intend going in a few days. On my way back I might go to

Zurich and meet some people, etc., to decide where I shall stay. There are some good families, Germans who have left Germany and also Suisse whom Nanu and the Geisslers know well.

Madan Bhai was very enthusiastic about German the first few days but has lost all interest now, although he does not know very much more now than he did before. He is now more keen on improving his figure. His tummy was large enough as it was, but he increased it by a good inch on board the *Conte Rosso*. Now he has seriously begun reducing. He takes long walks and is learning swimming, has Fango baths[1] and mud baths and does gymnastics with those electrical machines that pull you and push you and heavens knows what else. And, the most important, has dropped a good deal of the meat and eggs he used to consume daily.

I have changed my pension. I now share a double bedroom with Mrs Geissler in Pension Ehrhardt, which is half way between the sanatorium and the place where Madan Bhai stays (and where I stayed the first three days). Mrs G's sister is also with us. So I do not need a German family. There is a lot of propaganda against Indians in the papers because of the foreign policy to be friends with England. Hence it is not very agreeable sometimes.

There is a beautiful garden here called the Kurpark. The baths are all in this. And there is a band every day. I have made friends with some of the little birds and take some bread for them every day, though one of them was very angry with me today because I would not let it eat a grasshopper which was wounded & could not hop away.

We have been getting occasional showers and today it is cold & cloudy, though lately it has been very hot. It is always lovely in the shade.

I feel and look much better now. We get good food (this pension is well known in Badenweiler for that) and plenty of rest & fresh air. I am out all day almost, except the two hours' rest in the afternoon and half an hour in the morning with Mummie & half an hour in the evening.

I have but a faint recollection of the Rhine trip and Heidelberg but I seem to remember the cathedral at Cologne. But that's all.

Mummie came here three days before I did and while I was in Berlin I heard there had been an earthquake in the Schwarzwald. I wrote to Mums if she had felt it, but it seems it did not extend to Badenweiler.

We have almost no news about India. We get no Indian paper, only the *Daily Telegraph* of London. The German papers of course are hopeless. And very few foreign papers are allowed in.

I might go with Mrs Geissler to attend the 'Rendezvous of East & West' Conference at Ascona on the Lago Maggiore. It will be interesting as many big guns from all over Europe are going to speak. From there we will

---

1. Medicinal bath.

go perhaps to see Lago Lugano; it is only half an hour's run from Lago M. Lugano is also a health resort for people with lung troubles and besides it is the most beautiful place in Switzerland. Mrs G. thinks it will be a good place for Mummie, when she need not any longer stay in a sanatorium.

I hear it has been decided to transfer you to Allahabad. Please let us know when, so that I can write direct there.

The people here like to show off their English. They generally only know two or three words, but at the first opportunity they get, they say them. There is one old porter, who was in Texas and England, for over two years and speaks English perfectly & with very good pronunciation. He is a nice person & was very helpful the day Mums arrived. He is the head porter, guide, interpreter & two or three other things as well.

Mummie sends her love, she is not yet allowed to write, but she sits out for a while on the balcony every day. Dr Steffan is a nice person. (He has been in Badenweiler the last fourteen years.) He makes Mums' menus himself and takes special care of her. Oh, I forgot to tell you, Mums' name on the register here & also in Berlin was written as Princezzin[1] [sic] Nehru, in spite of our protests!

How are you keeping? Puphi wrote you did not look well at all.

With lots of love,
Always your loving,
Indu

Love from Nanu & Madan Bhai.

———————— ◆ ————————

112.   Almora District Jail,
                        19th July, 1935

Indu dear,
I sit down to write to you and cover sheet after sheet of thin airmail paper, trying somehow to bridge the many thousand miles that separate us. I hope that my letters will carry with them, somewhere hidden away between the lines, a bit of me to you, and that if you care to look for it, you will find it; just as I seek for you in your letters, behind and between the lines that you have written. What indeed are letters? Not surely just budgets of news, although they contain news. Not a record of illness and birth & marriage and death & humdrum domestic happenings, such as are most of the letters that people write. They are something far more; they are, or ought to be, bits of the personality of the writer, quivering shadows

1. Correct spelling is Prinzessin (means Princess).

of the real self. They are also, or they at least endeavour to represent and to mirror, something of the personality of the person written to, for the writer is full of the person he is writing to. Thus a real letter is a strange and revealing amalgam of the two – the one who writes and the one who receives. If it is such a real letter it has considerable value for both the persons concerned.

I have been led to this musing on letters because I have learnt that my letters have not been reaching you and I have been pained at this unexpected and unwelcome news. Cables from Madan Bhai have informed me of it and I am at a loss to know why this has happened. I have been pained at the thought of Mummie and you expecting my letters, waiting day after day for them, and waiting in vain. Few things are more distressing than to expect something which does not come. It upsets one, irritates and worries. So you must have been put out. I was pained also at the thought that my letters, which I had sent out with so many messages and loving thoughts, to fly over two continents to you, should have gone astray. I felt almost as if I had been physically hurt. And then it was disheartening. To have to write once a fortnight only is a poor enough bond, but if even that snaps?

I can't make out what can have happened to my letters. They have been sent regularly every fortnight. Ever since you people went away I have written to no one in India. Every two weeks my letter has gone addressed to Mummie with a long enclosure in it for you. They were addressed care of Thos. Cook, Geneva, but the last one went care of the American Express, Berlin, as desired by Madan. I am a methodical person as a rule anywhere; in prison I am even more so and my life is governed by a routine. As for letters, I write them with the regularity of a good clock. You may rest assured that I have sent my letter on the appointed day whether you receive it or not. And you may also rest assured that not receiving a letter cannot mean that I am unwell for in that event also I shall write to you or have a message sent. So far as I can make out, my letters have been despatched regularly from here. Enquiries were made at the post office also. The probability therefore is that something went wrong at the other end. You have been moving about. Perhaps Cooks forwarded the letters to Vienna or Berlin after you left, in spite of your instructions. Such mistakes are often made. You should always take care to leave your address at every hotel you stay at . . .

To get on to your last letter.[1] Yes I was a little surprised to see the superscription – Hotel Adlon. I had expected you to be in Badenweiler. Also I was a little surprised at the choice of hotel, for the Adlon is

1. Refers to letter No. 109.

supposed to be the most expensive hotel in Berlin and rather a flashy kind of place, frequented by the newly-rich, intent on display. It is not considered a select place. Probably the Kaiserhof is better in that respect. But these are very petty considerations and for a short stay for one or two persons there is not much difference in the charges so far as the ordinary rooms are concerned. The real difference comes in the suites and, above all, in food. Personally I think it is always safer in a new city to go to a good well-known hotel even though it may be expensive. If necessary feed outside more cheaply. If a longer stay has to be made then one can shift to less expensive quarters. So I am glad you went to the Adlon rather than to a cheaper hotel. I am also glad you stayed on in Berlin for a few days after Mummie left and had a look round. I want you to shift for yourself as much as possible.

I am not very happy about your health. Madan Bhai wrote to me that the doctors were of opinion that there was nothing fundamentally wrong with you. So far so good; but it is not good enough. You must not feel weak and headachey and have frequent pains. This has to be seen to or otherwise both your physical and intellectual development will be interfered with. My own attitude to ill health is I am afraid rather intolerant and aggressive – it is, as I wrote to you in a previous letter (which you have not got!) – the very opposite of the usual valetudinarian attitude prevalent in India. I dislike it, consider it almost indecent and do not feel much sympathy for the person who willingly indulges in it. Perhaps this is due to my own youthful record. After I had got rid of certain infantile ailments I developed a healthy body and during all the long years I was at Harrow, Cambridge & in London I never spent a day in bed owing to illness. My one visit to a doctor was at Harrow when my shins had been rather badly kicked at football. I paid no special attention to my health. I simply lived a normal life and looked down upon those who were often ill or who frequently complained of their bodily troubles. (One of the trials of my existence in India is that people will insist on discussing their physical ailments when I am not at all interested in them.) So I grew up rather conceited about my bodily fitness and with the belief that anybody who wanted to be fit could certainly keep so. Illness only came as a rule when invited to do so. In later years in India I taxed my body very hard and took a lot of physical and intellectual work out of it and I must say that it behaved very well.

During the last four or five years, however, that conceit and assurance of good health has partly left me. This has been so ever since I have had some pleuritic trouble. But I do believe that it has been my general, good health and habits of life that have kept down this trouble to very small proportions. In another person not so fit or not so aggressively disliking illness as I do, the trouble would have probably grown. Even now I am confident that I can keep it in check and carry on normally for a long time to come.

Now I do not want you to worry or grow morbid about your little physical troubles. These growing pains do not mean much. But at the same time they should be attended to so that they may not weaken your constitution. Doctors will advise you and you should follow their advice, but personally I attach far more importance to healthy surroundings & healthy life & habits. Live in a good place with decent food, exercise, etc., and devote yourself to intellectual and other pursuits without thinking too much of the body. But do not overdo anything – do not tire yourself.

Regarding your future studies, the question of your health has to be borne in mind, and this was one of the reasons why I wanted you to stick to Suisse. There were other reasons also. I did not fancy most of the other possible university towns. Germany seems to me out of the question even if it be true that Berlin has the best professors. But I doubt that statement now – the best German professors are out of Germany and the whole atmosphere of German education today is oppressive and stifling and altogether wrong. You mention Rome – why you thought of it I do not know for there is not special argument in its favour and there are many against it. Then there is Paris and much can be said for it but I am sure that for the present it must be ruled out. I do not fancy these great big cities as educational centres. There is too much else doing there. But the reason that weighs with me more is the one of health. Paris is not a particularly healthy place. For the moment I am not thinking of the English universities. You may of course go to them later. So we are left with Suisse. I am not a particular admirer of the very middle-class, bourgeois, stodgy Swiss character. It is rather commonplace, but then it is so easy to criticise everybody and everything!

I feel sure that Switzerland is indicated for you at present and at least for a year or so. Afterwards we shall see. I have got out of the habit of making long-distance decisions. Suisse is certainly more expensive than neighbouring countries but for a student this will not make much difference; and then in these days of currency fluctuations one can never tell which country will be more or less expensive. Another reason why I prefer Suisse is because of Mlle Hemmerlin . . . It will be better if you are within easy distance of her and can consult her from time to time.

In Suisse there are three possible universities – Geneva, Lausanne and Zurich, the two former more French, Zurich more German. You will find that people connected with Germany will naturally favour Zurich, while those connected with France will recommend Geneva & Lausanne. In the matter I think you had best follow Mlle Hemmerlin's advice. It is always possible on the Continent to change universities – it is a good practice.

As for the course you should take, I should not bother very much just at present. Nanu's advice was good that you should join a university & give the Entrance exam later. But Mrs Geissler's criticism is sound. The burden on you will be too much – to attend lectures and at the same time to prepare for the entrance exam – and all this in new languages. Therefore you must not bother about the entrance exam or even regular courses of lectures. Your first job is to feel at home with the languages and get healthy. When you can easily continue with these, the attendance of lectures or any other work, do so. But not till then. Remember that students on the Continent – both at school and university – have to work far harder than students in England. I do not want you to join this treadmill too soon. Take your time and fit yourself for it before you do so. I am not keen on examinations and I do not believe that true education consists in passing them. To some extent one has to face them in the modern world as it is, but let us not make a fetish of them.

Therefore do not worry about exams at present. Have an easy time and stick to languages. Where are you [going to] stay for this? Certainly you can stay at Badenweiler near Mummie and work with Mrs Geissler at the languages. From the health point of view this would be good. Or you can go to Mlle Hemmerlin. Or you can spend part of your time at one place and part at the other. Decide for yourself in consultation with Mlle Hemmerlin. You have other people to advise you too – Nanu & others – and you should consult them whenever you feel like it, but on the whole it would be desirable to follow Mlle Hemmerlin's advice.

I am very glad Mummie is pleased with her new companion, Mrs Geissler. The name seems to be familiar to me. I wonder where I came across it before.

Puphi told me that a letter had come for me from Mlle Hemmerlin. I am asking Puphi to write to her. When you meet Romain Rolland and his sister give my regards to them.

I am sending you through Mummie a little book – J. F. Horrabin's[1] *Atlas of European History*. This is an excellent collection of historical maps and it will help you with the *Glimpses*. Horrabin has also prepared a very good *Atlas of Current Affairs* which I would advise you to get. It is a cheap book but it helps greatly in understanding current problems. If Horrabin would bring out similar atlases for Asia & America the whole of *Glimpses* would be covered!

I have asked Upadhyaya to send you lists of corrections in Vols. 1 and 2 of *Glimpses* – there are crowds of errors and some of these are extraordinary and misleading. When you get them it would be worthwhile for you to

1. James Francis Horrabin: English journalist and illustrator who created an Atlas series.

make the corrections in the body of the book. The petty corrections can be ignored.

Betty[1] has sent me some snaps taken by Raja at the sanatorium. They are rather good, especially one of yours standing. Probably she has sent you copies also. Why not get yourself photographed at a decent photographer's? I should love to have a good photograph.

My future letters will be sent to Badenweiler, Hans Waldeck, addressed to Mummie, till I hear to the contrary.

I hope the pine-clad hillsides of the Black Forest have done you good – and the swimming. You are in Baden at the best time of the year.

It was the full moon two or three nights back and the magic of its radiance drew me out of my little tent (for I am still encamped). For a long time I watched it playing hide and seek in the clouds, seemingly hurrying away at times and then standing serenely still, peeping at me through a rift in the clouds or over their edge, sometimes so near and dazzling and then far away, distant and vague, behind a dark veil. It was a great game. In the moonlight even the ugly jail walls toned down and lost their hardness. Everything was soft and dreamy – I thought of some lines of a vagabond or hiker's song:

> Heigh! brother mine, art a-waking or a-sleeping:
> Minds't thou the merry moon a many summers fled?
> Minds't thou the green and the dancing and the leaping:
> Minds't thou the haycocks and the moon above them creeping?

I suddenly thought of you and wondered if you might not also be enjoying the moonlight and looking up at the same old moon. But, foolish thought! While it was night here, it must have been the late afternoon in Baden, with the sun shining brightly and the moon and the stars invisible, awaiting the coming of night.

With the full moon passed the month of *Asādha*[2] and *Sravana*[3] began, the typical month of the rainy season. With it also ended my seventeenth month in prison this time!

Love,

Your loving,
Papu

---

1. The anglicised form of Beti (daughter), another name for Krishna Hutheesing.
2. Fourth month of the Indian Calendar.
3. Fifth month of the Indian Calendar.

I think it is desirable that all of you should have a permanent address whilst in Europe, otherwise there will always be difficulties about correspondence. You may keep me informed of changes but what of many others? Therefore please ask Madan Bhai to fix upon some such address & let us know. Usually the best address is the bank with which you deal. Have you opened accounts?

Dhan Gopal Mukerji[1] wants to know Mummie's address. What is one to tell him?

113.   [La Pelouse]
Bex,
1st August [1935]

Darling Papu,

I arrived here last night. The journey was comfortable, not at all tiring and the scenery was beautiful. I left Badenweiler at eleven thirty-three. To go anywhere from B'weiler one has to change at least once at Mulheim. The train from B'weiler to Mulheim has only two carriages, one third & one second, and when I called it a tram the conductor was almost insulted. I had to stay two hours in Bâle (Basel). Here I collected my money (which Madan Bhai had sent from London) at the American Express & had lunch. Then I had to change again at Lausanne.

At Bâle the American Express office is rather far from the station and on my way there I had a look at the buildings, statues, etc. It is a beautiful, clean & very rich town. After Bâle, the train passed alongside two beautiful lakes, those of Biel and Neuchâtel. All along the bank were vineyards. At Lausanne we came to the Lac Leman and were alongside it till its end, a little further than Vevey. We passed Montreux and from my window I saw the G. Hotel Suisse. That is where we used to stay in Montreux. Do you remember? And then we passed quite close to the Château de Chillon and, looking at the lovely lake, with the swans & seagulls and the mountain ranges, and behind them the snow-covered peak of the Dent du Midi (at least that is what I thought it to be) I thought of you & Mummie and missed you.

After Bâle everybody spoke French and although I can speak very little of that language, I understood everything that was being said and somehow felt I had arrived home and then the lake & Chillon & everything seemed so familiar.

At Bex, Mlle Hemmerlin came to the station, she introduced me to a French lady who had also been at the École Nouvelle, though a few [years]

1. Dhan Gopal Mukherjee: Indian littérateur settled in the United States.

before my time. All the old memories came crowding to my mind and I was quite excited as I remembered the café where I had so often sat with you & Mummie, as well as with the schoolchildren, and the roads, the garden. I remembered the old house perfectly – every room and what we did there. Mlle Hemmerlin is still the same sweet and gentle lady whom we used to love so much. She has not aged as much as I had expected. She is very pleased to have me here and is taking a lot of bother, in spite of my protests, to make me feel absolutely at home and comfortable. We talked about the old days (one would think I was at least sixty) and you & Bapu. She sends you her best regards.

The hot days are over and autumn is beginning. The last two days in Badenweiler were quite chilly and here the weather is very pleasant.

We have quite a nice view from my balcony, at night it is more beautiful, for we can see the lights of Vevey & Montreux reflected on the lakes. And La Dent du Midi is just behind. We can also see a corner of Mont Blanc.

4th August

Le premier août.[1] Do you remember this great Suisse National day? Fires are lighted at night and Suisse songs sung and everybody goes about with little paper lamps with candles inside. It looked so beautiful. All along the mountainside there were huge fires and Leysin, which is just opposite, was lighted up with coloured bulbs of blue, green and red. We also had a big fire and the maids sang songs – these are the summer holidays and there are very few children.

In my last letter I forgot to tell you one story. When I first arrived in Badenweiler I asked the landlady where the bathroom was as I wanted to bathe. She looked surprised and then said that people did not bathe at her place and that there was a bathroom attached to her room, but it would be very difficult if I had a bath and would cost much extra. So I used to bathe at the sanatorium, as we had taken a room with bathroom attached, for Mummie. Fortunately in Suisse baths are not such rare luxuries.

About a week or so ago Mummie received a letter from a German countess, saying that she was thinking of opening a home for Indian convalescents in Berlin or somewhere else in Germany under the patronage of Mrs Goering[2] and would Mummie give her name from the Indian side? Of course we wrote a very polite letter refusing.

9th August

Day before yesterday we all went to see the saltmines of Vaud. By we all I mean the children (there are very few as these are holidays), the mistress

1. The 1st of August.
2. Emmy Goering, née Sonnemann: wife of the Nazi leader, Hermann Goering.

who is in charge of excursions, walks, etc., a German lady who has come here to learn French and a Signorina from Milan who is here for the same purpose and I. We left La Pelouse at ten fifteen a.m. and although we walked fairly fast in the beginning and even later, not slow, and took all the short cuts we could find we reached the place at one o'clock. Then we had dinner and entered the mines at one thirty. We walked under the ground in a tunnel with little miners' lamps for a little [over] two hours. We reached home at six thirty and although it was a pleasant trip we were all tired & glad to sleep.

Yesterday everybody, including Mlle Hemmerlin and several other old ladies, went on a bus excursion to a place called Champeri. The route was very beautiful. Champeri itself is not very nice as big hotels and restaurants have sprung up due to the popularity of the place, but the surroundings are lovely. We first went to a charming spot called 'Petit Paradis'. There was a brook and some of the children played about among the rocks & in the water and then we lunched. Then, after resting for a while, we packed the rucksacks and went to 'Grand Paradis', which was lovely, but I did not like it as much as 'Petit Paradis'. From there some of us climbed a mountain . . . ; it took us two and a half hours. On our return we had coffee and sandwiches and then at five thirty we started back. It was six by the time we reached the bus and seven thirty by the time we were home. We all enjoyed ourselves immensely.

Mlle Hemmerlin has recd. Puphi's letter. But we have not yet come to any definite decision. In two days I am leaving for Ascona. There I will meet several university professors and shall talk with them about my course. Then I shall go to Zurich and spend some time there & then I propose to pay a visit to Mummie at B'weiler. At Zurich I shall decide whether to remain there or to settle in Lausanne or if possible to come back here to the Pelouse. Geneva is not at all healthy, Mlle says. She knows good families in Lausanne & Zurich and has also given me some introductions to people in Ascona.

Mummie wanted me to write to Dhan Gopal Mukerji, but we did not know his address. Is he still in America? Mlle Hemmerlin says he was thinking of coming to Europe.

Our permanent address is c/o Thomas Cook, Geneva. All the Indian mail still comes by that address, except your letters.

I have just got a short note from Mummie. She says your two letters dated 7th & 21st June, which were missing, have arrived, but she has not sent them yet. I had advised Mummie to get a new companion (Mrs Geissler had to go away as she had work) as Madan Bhai was busy with his reducing stunts and she used to be quite alone almost all day long. Mrs Geissler wrote to a young girl who was working but would be free by 4th August, to stop at Badenweiler for a few days, as it was on her way home.

Mummie writes that she did not like her and that she was not a patch on Mrs G., so she sent her away. But fortunately Dr Steffan has given the sanatorium sister who is very good and is fond of Mummie, to work for her. And a new sister will do the sanatorium work. So everything is all right now . . .

I am so glad your missing letters have come. It was so irritating to think that your short messages of love, (for though they be eight or nine pages, to me they are always short, for they are read so soon and then again to wait for the next) the only bonds between us, should be lying in some dead letter office.

Ascona,
13th August

I am so sorry for this delay in sending your letter – you must be waiting for it.

I arrived here on the 11th. The journey was not as beautiful as I had expected, but the view from my pension window is perfectly glorious. The lake looks charming in every weather. The first day I saw it I remarked how lovely it looked with the sunlight dancing on its waves. The next day I thought it looked much more beautiful with the reflections of clouds & at night it looks its best with its waves playing with the moonbeams & the reflected lights of several towns.

I have just had a letter from Puphi. She says that when she was in Lucknow, she heard that Bhabhi Saheb Takru[1] had passed away of heart failure on the 24th of last month! Maharaj Bhai has practically lost his sight – poor old man – and is quite thin. Radha,[2] it appears has lost her radiant beauty and looks quite old. Her two kids are sweet.

Chhoti Puphi seems to be having a very gay time but is fed up of the rain. She gave a huge stand-up party in honour of Bharati & Suhrid, who went to Bombay specially for it!

Since I left B'weiler I have not read a newspaper and feel terribly far from the rest of the world. At Bex we used to get a Lausanne paper but everybody used to read it by turns and by the time my turn came, it had disappeared or got lost or something. And of course there was no chance of hearing anything about India.

Mlle Hemmerlin & Mlle Rolland both asked me to send you their best regards. I could not go to visit Mlle Rolland, as somebody in her house had mumps which is very infectious. But I shall go sometime later, Romain Rolland is at present in Moscow, he is expected back in September. I hear he has married his secretary, who was a Russian

1. Bhabhi Saheb Takru: wife of Maharaj Bahadur Takru, a cousin of Jawaharlal Nehru.
2. Daughter of Maharaj Bahadur Takru.

countess & ran away to Suisse during the Revolution, but is now a confirmed Communist and under her influence so is he.

I am afraid this letter, as a letter, is not a good one at all – everything is so disconnected and untidy. But at present I can't manage anything better. So *au revoir* – when will it be?

With lots of love from Mummie &
ever your loving,
Indu

<table>
<tr><td>114.</td><td>Letter No. 6</td><td>[Almora District Jail]
2nd August, 1935</td></tr>
</table>

Darling Indu,

Fridays are special days for me. On Fridays, alternate ones, I write to you and Mummie, and on the intervening Fridays I expect your letters. And so, last Friday I waited for your letter and my desire for it was greater even than usual for I was worried about the disappearance of my letters to you people and hoped to have some information on this point. Also an item of news in the papers about Mummie's health had been disturbing. Your letter[1] however did not come on that day and I was a little disappointed. It came, however, three days later. It was dated 18th July but had evidently been posted much later for it bore the postmark 22nd July. Fortunately now even missing an airmail does not mean much delay. I believe there are at least five airmail services every week from Europe to India and beyond – two British, two Dutch, and one French. They all pass through Allahabad. But I suppose our letters are carried only by the British line.

You will note, perhaps with some surprise, the superscription: Letter No. 6. This is to indicate that this is the sixth letter I have written to you since your departure, and I propose to number my subsequent letters also accordingly, so that if any letter is missed by you, you can immediately tell. Indeed you could have presumed as much, but after the unfortunate experience we have had I propose to take no risks. Of the letters I have already sent you it appears that you have not received Nos. 2 and 3, dated June 7th[2] and 21st.[3] The first of these must have reached Cook's in Geneva while you were still in Vienna and it is quite possible that it was forwarded to your Vienna address – Hotel Bristol. The second might have also gone there by mistake or to Berlin. You should enquire at both places. Cook's are no doubt to blame but you should also be more wide awake in

1. Refers to letter No. 111.
2. Refers to letter No. 107.
3. Not published.

such matters. Wherever you may go to, even for a day, you should leave your address for letters and special instructions.

I am very happy to learn of your progress in the German language. Evidently you have a linguistic bent which certainly you have not inherited from your father. German is a fine language and the Germans are in many ways a fine people – brave, hard-working, disciplined, learned. But – there are always buts of course – learning does not sit lightly on them, nor is humour a failing of theirs. They are apt to be a little heavy, slow on the uptake, as the Americans say. I hope you will imbibe the many virtues of the Germans but there is no reason why you should also follow them in their failings and become mentally a little obese. In this respect the mental quickness and lightness of touch of the French is preferable.

You will wonder why I am indulging in this digression. Your last letter[1] is the immediate cause of it. It made me feel that you did not display what might be called the qualities of a Sherlock Holmes in regard to the non-receipt of my letters, and even after my telegram you seem to take it for granted that I had written after five or six weeks. You chide me gently: '26th May to 5th July is rather more than a fortnight, is it not?' Yes it is, my dear, even my arithmetic is capable of that intricate calculation. But, I wondered, did you know me so little as to think that I would refrain from writing to you and Mummie for five weeks? And, even so, did the idea not strike you when you received my letter after all this interval, that I would at least explain the delay? And then in my cable I had said that 'letters' sent care Cook's – that meant more than one letter, and you have so far received only one letter from Geneva. Finally if you read my letter dated 5th July carefully you will find internal evidence in it that previous letters were sent. I must confess to having sent much too brief and vague a cable in reply to Madan Bhai's. I wish I had sent a clearer message; but the desire to be economical influenced me at the wrong time.

As you are evidently linguistically inclined it is as well for you to encourage this bent and acquire languages. We lack linguists in India and we need them. It is one of my secret sorrows that I am not good at languages. The amount of trouble I have taken over French and German ought to have made me know them far more than I do. I have nourished a grievance against my old childhood tutor, F. T. Brooks, who might have easily taught me French well at the right age. His mother was French and he knew the language perfectly. At that age I could have picked it up rapidly and naturally. But he thought otherwise. In prison I have laboured fairly hard at German and I have gone through carefully and laboriously Otto's fat grammar. After that, in theory at least, I ought to be able to read and write German with some ease. As a matter of fact I seem to have

1. Refers to letter No. 111.

forgotten most of it and I can't read the simplest book in it. Perhaps the labour has not been wasted altogether and somewhere at the back of my mind there is buried a vague knowledge of German which can be unearthed with a pick and shovel if real need arises. However that may be, it is clear that I am no linguist and I rather admire those who are – at the same time I have a suspicion that people who dabble in many languages are often rather superficial and lack depth. They become Jacks at many tongues and master none.

So, by all means, concentrate on languages – German and French – for the moment. I should not trouble myself, if I were you, about the university entrance exam at this stage. Certainly you can attend lectures in subjects of your interest as soon as you can follow them. But if you prepare for the exam you may have to do all manner of subjects – perhaps Latin for aught I know. I really don't see why you should learn Latin. You will do a good year's work if by next summer you have got a fairly good knowledge of the languages plus such odd knowledge of special subjects as you may acquire. I suppose I shall meet you before then. Somehow I cannot imagine your spending the next three or four years at a Swiss university. Therefore, the exam is less important than the languages, etc.

I like Nanu's suggestion (or was it your idea?) that you might learn Russian at Praha or elsewhere. Among present-day languages it is one of the most important and it grows in importance. Remember that it is the language of a territory bordering our country – our neighbours speak it. Its past literature is fascinating, its new literature is unique of its kind. Sometime or other I would like you to go to the country from the educational point of view and a knowledge of the language would of course make a tremendous difference. The education there is the most scientifically up to date that can be found anywhere. This really applies not to the university stage but to the very early stages, beginning from babyhood and the creche period. The best time to learn anything is, it is said, when the babe begins to crawl! I am afraid you are too old for that now! What I like about Russian education is the attempt at producing harmony between hand and mind and heart. They want to produce harmonised, integrated, poised human beings, not the lop-sided people, unhappy and irritable persons that are so often met with. The ultimate success of this education remains still to be seen but already rather remarkable results have been obtained. Neurosis, the common disease of our civilisation, is very rare in Russia now. Partly no doubt the change is due to a new and fairer social structure.

It surprises me more and more how people go through life with their eyes shut to its varied beauty as well as its terrible misery. It is extraordinary how blind and insensitive they can be, and I imagine that our middle classes in India take the cake in this respect. Which reminds me of a bright little poem which might interest you. It is a modern poem – I forget the name of the author. It is said to have been written to a woman seen from a train:

> O why do you walk through the fields in gloves,
>   Missing so much and so much?
> O fat white woman whom nobody loves,
> Why do you walk through the fields in gloves
> When the grass is soft as the breast of doves
> And shivering-sweet to the touch?
> O why do you walk through the fields in gloves,
>   Missing so much and so much?[1]

No doubt you see plenty of such men and women in Badenweiler. But, though gloves are not sported in India, such people swarm here.

In one of my letters[2] I asked you to subscribe to the *Manchester Guardian Weekly*. Perhaps that was one of the letters you missed. It is really awful for you to be cut off regarding news from India as well as the rest of the world and have to rely on the stodgy and heavy *Daily Telegraph*. Most other English papers would be more interesting than this, but as you point out, many of them are *verboten* [forbidden]. I have now sent instructions to Upadhyaya to arrange the supply of a number of papers to you from India and England. The Indian periodicals are the: *Hindu Illustrated Weekly* (from Madras), the *Times of India Weekly* (this is *not* the *Illustrated Weekly*), the *Pratap* (Hindi weekly of Cawnpore), the *Modern Review* and the *Vishal Bharat*.

This bunch will give you some Indian news. I am not entirely satisfied with it but I can think of no better. It is rather silly getting a daily from India. All these papers will be addressed to Mummie.

The Times Book Club, London, is being asked to send Mummie: *The Times* (weekly edition), the *Manchester Guardian Weekly* and *The Listener* (weekly) – but I am not sure if the *Manchester Guardian* is permitted in Germany. Anyhow you will get a fair bunch every week. *The Listener* is the organ of the British Broadcasting Corporation. It contains broadcasts and articles and many of these are good. I wonder if you can get the British broadcasts in Badenweiler. Probably you have no private radio at your disposal and the public radios are full of German broadcasts.

All these papers from India and England will be addressed to Mummie to the Badenweiler address. Whenever an address is going to be changed you must write to Upadhyaya to inform the Indian periodicals concerned, and you should yourself write directly to the English papers or the Times

---

1. 'To a Fat Lady seen from the Train' by Frances Cornford.
2. Refers to letter No. 107.

Book Club (address: 42 Wigmore Street, London W1). The Times Book Club can also supply you with books or other papers. If you feel like it, you can open an account with them. Or I could authorise you to operate my account with them. I have dealt with them since they began twenty-five years ago or more. Probably it would be best if you dealt with them independently.

I do not know anything about the 'Rendezvous of East and West' at Ascona. It sounds inviting enough and it would be worthwhile your going. Even if the people are uninteresting, the neighbourhood – the Lago Maggiore and Lugano, etc., are enchanting in their beauty. Where Mummie will go when she leaves the sanatorium I cannot say. It will be for the doctors to decide. My own feeling is that during winter she ought to be on the hills and in the snows. The crisp and dry Alpine winter is far more beneficial than the gentle summer of the health resorts.

I am alarmed to learn that Mummie is described as *Princezzin*[1] (is this spelling you give correct?) in the sanatorium register. This is bad enough anyhow and I dislike it. Apart from my likes and dislikes, it is likely to mean higher charges everywhere. So you had better beware!

I am still in Almora Jail in the little tent and outside – the rain, it raineth every day. I know nothing yet about my transfer. Of course you will be informed as soon as this takes place.

Your account of the grasshopper and the angry little bird reminds me of a somewhat similar incident here. Some time back I caught a huge black centipede. I did not know what to do with it when a myna came and put an end to my mental debate by swallowing it with great relish.

I hope that now that you have got rid of your flu you will soon get quite fit. Has Nanu been in Badenweiler?

What about your sending me a photograph?

Love,

Your loving,
Papu

---

115.   Letter No. 7   Almora District Jail,
16th August, 1935

Darling Indu,

There has been no letter from you for nearly three weeks now. Yesterday I had a brief note from Madan Bhai, giving me some information about Mummie. He said nothing about you as apparently he expected you to write to me separately and give me all the other news.

It is sad that Mummie has not been making good progress lately. I hope

---

1. See footnote on p. 191.

the setback was not of long duration and she is pulling up again. These ups and downs are inevitable but nevertheless they annoy and I can quite understand Mummie feeling rather fed up occasionally. But she must not lose heart or allow herself to feel depressed. What a long time it is since she was confined to bed! Just a year ago I was with her in Anand Bhawan for eleven short days. That brief period together was ended all too suddenly and ever since we have continued in our respective prisons, and hers is far the narrower and worse one.

I wonder if you have remained at Badenweiler all the while or paid a visit to Bex and Villeneuve & Zurich as you intended to. I have been so much cut off from modern educational developments in Europe that I find it difficult to advise you. Indeed I never knew much about Continental universities. Being myself a product of one of the older British universities, I am unconsciously partial to them for the simple reason that I know something about them. In my last letter – or was it in the one before? – I said that I could not readily imagine your spending several years at Zurich or any other Swiss university. What I meant was that I did not look forward to your education being confined to some such place. My own idea was, and vaguely is, that a period in an English university is desirable from many points of view. To confine oneself to an English university has its drawbacks, for it means ignoring almost the non-British viewpoint in life & affairs. That difficulty crops up in another way if you confine yourself to a Swiss or other Continental university. How can we have the best of both? A difficult job.

When you were at Bhowali you will remember that I mentioned the possibility of your going to Oxford sometime or other. At that time I was thinking that after a year or so spent at a Continental university you might shift to Oxford. I do not believe in people joining universities like Oxford or Cambridge – I do not know much about the Continent – at too early an age. I myself went too early as I was under eighteen at the time. I think nineteen or twenty is a better age to join and one can profit more by the opportunities one gets then. As between Oxford & Cambridge I would slightly prefer the former for you. I think it has a better Economics school. There is also a well-known place for Economics in London – the London School of Economics. There again, I would prefer the life of Oxford to London and I am sure so would you.

I had all this background to my thought when I told you not to bother about appearing or even preparing specially for the entrance examination of a Swiss university. This would mean an unnecessary burden for you. You can attend any lectures you choose to without this exam and in particular you should try to improve your knowledge of languages, French, German &, if possible, Russian. There's a stiff year's work for you.

What is to follow? There are so many uncertainties in our life that I am unable to say definitely. But we can & should be prepared for various contingencies. One of these is the possibility of your joining an Oxford college. Probably this will involve also your having to pass some kind of an entrance examination, though this is likely to be easier than the Zurich one, even apart from the question of language. Another fact to be remembered is that Oxford colleges do not take an unlimited number of persons. One has therefore to make sure some time ahead. There may be other difficulties, especially for Indians. I think you might write to Bharati Sarabhai and find out from her what is supposed to be done. She can enquire from her own college people – Somerville College. There are I believe only two women's colleges at Oxford[1] and so there is not much choice. Tell Bharati that there is a possibility of your going to Oxford next year – that is *October 1936*. Till then you are likely to remain on the Continent learning languages and odd subjects. Will it be possible for you to join Somerville College then? And if so on what conditions of passing examinations, etc. Tell her that you have passed the Bombay Matriculation & then spent a year at Santiniketan & now intend spending a year at Zurich. All this will not let you off the Oxford Entrance – Responsions I think it is called. If you had gone in for the Cambridge Senior you might have got off Responsions.

Find all this out from Bharati and if it is possible ask her to get your name provisionally entered at Somerville for next year. This will not bind you in any way. Also find out details about the entrance exam, etc., so that you may know what it is like. You might inform Bharati also that you propose to take up Economics & allied subjects.

I do not know where Bharati is likely to be now, for it is vacation time at Oxford. For aught I know she might be in India with her parents. Anyway she is likely to return to Oxford next month for the new term which begins early in October. If you address your letter to Somerville College, Oxford, it will find her.

Having dealt with the important subject of your education, I must now come back to my usual topic – jail gossip. What am I to do? The range of my subjects is limited here and so I seek to interest you in my birds & flowers. Or at any rate I try to find an excuse in them for writing to you. Morning and evening a crowd of birds – they are mostly mynas & sparrows – sit in front of my little tent waiting for their food. If there is delay in supplying it, they make their presence and their impatience obvious enough by their noises. I share my morning *dallia*[2] with them and breadcrumbs of course. The sparrows and I are old friends, for we shared

---

1. In fact there were four women's colleges at Oxford at this time.
2. Porridge.

the barrack building for many months. Thirty or forty of them lived in the old roof and when this roof was taken down there were some tragedies. But fortunately most of them escaped and now I find that they have made themselves at home under the eaves of the new roof. Some of them have become greatly daring. They come quite near to me and even enter my tent. Then there are swallows and bulbuls and other birds that I do not know. The other day a new visitor – a charming little creature – came and sat down within three or four feet of me as I sat reading in the tent, and had a good look at me. I do not know if I was approved or not. I gazed at it fascinated and delighted and when it flew away to another part of my yard I followed at a respectful distance. I did not know its name and no one could tell it to me. And then it flew right away and has not returned again.

I am afraid my companions here are not exactly noted for bird-lore. Some time back I wanted to find out the name of a strange bird. I asked a warder – for warders are my constant companions – if he could recognise birds and knew their names. 'Well,' he replied after some hesitation, '*kauon ko ham pahchānte hain*'![1]

There was a swift tragedy two days ago. I was standing some distance away from my tent, looking away. Suddenly there was a noise in front of the tent. There was a whirr and a squeak – and that was the end of the story. A hawk had swooped down and seized & carried away a bird. It was done so swiftly that I could not even see what kind of bird it had got or do anything else in the matter. The story had ended, but the aftermath continued for long, for the other birds sat in rows on the barrack roofs & walls, terrified at this strange fate and croaking out their warning cry.

I saw another sight – this was last year in Dehra Jail – which surprised me. A crow came down into my yard and carried off with ease quite a decent sized frog. It was all done very smartly as if the old villain had practised at the job. He came down, tipped the frog over on his back so as to prevent him hopping away, and then seized him by a leg and flew away.

You write to me of the pines that surround you in Badenweiler and of the delicious piny smell. There are pines enough round about here too, as you know, but the smell is not so marked. Or it may be that I have got used to it. For the last month or so I have been living on top of pine-needles. A thick layer of them has been spread in my tent to prevent the damp from creeping up. These needles give a faint but pleasant smell. You must have a variety of pines and firs in the Black Forest. Have you got the monkey-puzzle tree anywhere about there? I like this tree and its name always amuses me. It is hardly native to those parts but I remember seeing it on the promenade at Montreux.

A few days ago I had a curious experience. I was looking at my zinnias

1. We recognise the crows.

early in the morning when I was taken aback and I almost gasped at a sight of extraordinary beauty. It was just a spider's web with the dew drops hanging on to it but in that half-light of the dawn it seemed like a wonderful pearl necklace, shimmering and full of lustre. Why do I compare it with a pearl necklace? It was far more beautiful. I gazed at it much moved, and then after a while I felt like sharing my emotion with a prisoner who was passing by. I drew his attention to the glistening wonder. He said something excessively stupid and banal which jarred upon me and almost upset me. The magic moment passed and I came down from the heavens and bumped on the too solid earth.

I felt irritated at my companion's blindness and indifference. Yet it was no fault of his. What chance had he had, poor fellow, to develop his artistic and aesthetic self? For generations he and his kind had been crushed, sat upon, till the light had gone out of their eyes and on their faces had come the 'emptiness of ages'. And I thought that for any real understanding or contact with another how essential it was that there should be not only a similar intellectual but an emotional background. Individuals & nations grow up with different backgrounds and then fail to understand each other.

To come back to earthy topics. I hope you are keeping physically fit now. You swim & walk and both of these exercises are excellent. I imagine that swimming is probably the best all-round exercise; it tones up every part of the body. But only if you swim enough. In small swimming pools little real swimming is possible and one is apt to laze more than swim. Apart from these open-air exercises, I wish you would keep up some of the *āsans*, especially the *shirshāsana* and the *sarvangāsana*.[1] I am a great believer in both of these. They are good for the back, the shoulders, the head & the eyes. The back is really very important, and a really strong and at the same time supple back is not only good for health but helps in a graceful carriage. Swimming is good for this. But it is not always possible to get a swim. If you practise these two *āsans* and a few bending & stretching exercises daily for say ten minutes, you will feel delightfully supple and fit. Your back is not strong enough physically, though metaphorically you may have a stiff backbone. At your age it should be very easy to get absolutely supple but if you are not careful a gradual stiffness creeps on as one grows older.

I do not want you to overdo these indoor exercises. Spend as little time over them as you like but try to give a few minutes daily. Remember not to strain or tire yourself in the least, and this applies very specially to the *āsans*. The point is to do them, not to overdo them. The test of any exercise is that you should feel fresh and energetic afterwards. If you feel tired

1. Refers to Yogic exercises.

there is something wrong with you or the exercise, or you are overdoing it. Begin with only half a minute of the *shirshāsana* and see how you feel. Apart from all this, try to keep up your swimming. If you have the chance go in for lawn tennis.

A line at the end of Madan's letter informs me that my two old letters which had gone astray have reached you. He does not mention if my fifth letter, dated 20th July,[1] reached. I presume it did.

Love from your loving,
Papu

When you write to me ask Mummie to dictate to you a line or two to me – write them down in Hindi – this will cheer me & it might also cheer her. Let me know what periodicals you are getting from India & London.

---

116.   Ascona,
                                                 19th August, 1935

Darling Papu,
Your letter[2] No. 6 was sent by Mummie a few days ago. As a matter of fact I wrote to all the places we had stayed at, giving the Badenweiler address – immediately on receipt of your telegram. Besides anybody would know after reading your letter of 5th July that several letters had preceded it. However now the letters have reached Mummie.

Two or three days before your letter came, I remarked to someone the difference between the French and Germans. But in respect to their knowledge of India almost all the Europeans I have so far met are terribly ignorant. They have all sorts of funny and wild ideas. And it is so exasperating to explain the same thing over and over again to different people. And worst of all are those so-called 'interested in India'.

Most of the lectures at the Conference are in German. But by putting all my attention on the speaker & his words I manage to understand the drift of the thing, though of course this is very tiring and at the end of the lecture I can't read or do any mental work.

The two most popular lecturers struck me as being rather coarse and I'm afraid I thought their jokes rather stupid, though most of the audience roared with laughter. Their theory was that one must act on impulse and damn the consequences – sort of thing. The one I liked best (who I afterwards learnt had delivered a really fine lecture – because as I do not know the language well enough I can't really judge) preached about

---

1. Letter not traceable.
2. Refers to letter No. 114.

looking into oneself and bettering oneself and thinking & not to act like primitive men – he also quoted some beautiful poems of Laotse[1] (This is how the Germans spell his name) the Chinese poet. However he was not appreciated & after the lecture I heard a neighbour saying *sehr schwach*,[2] while during the other two lectures *wunderbar*[3] could be distinctly heard.

The correct spelling of Princess in German is 'Prinzessin', I find, after consulting my dictionary.

I was under the impression that as I had done very little French all these years (the lessons with Amalaben, or rather Dr Spiegel, were not up to much, conversationally) I would have to begin all over again, but to my surprise after two days in Bex I could not only understand every word but could also speak, quite fluently – without having to think or to translate from the English. Though of course I made quite a number of mistakes in describing things, etc., and it would do me good to have it well brushed.

Mlle Hemmerlin – by the way I heard in Bex that it was considered impolite to write Mlle on the address or even in a letter, one must always write Mademoiselle. However to come back to what I was saying – Mlle Hemmerlin has given me a letter of introduction to a Madame Bara who lives here. She is a famous dancer or rather was, for I don't think she gives performances now. Mlle H. has written to her to show me a dance if possible, especially her Indian dance, so that I may be able to tell her at least, if it is at all like Indian dancing for she has invented it without studying Indian dancing. I hear she is a very nice person, though some people say she is a bit queer in the head. I have not had much time lately and so was unable to go to her place but shall try and visit her before leaving Ascona.

Yesterday, while out on a walk, we passed a nice little cottage, which I was told was the residence of Erich Maria Remarque, the author of that famous book, *All Quiet on the Western Front*.

I wonder if you have read a book, *Not so Quiet?* It is written by an English lady and deals with the part the women played during the war. I thought it very well written & liked it.

Just near the lecture hall, in the garden of Mrs Frolie, the Dutch lady who organised the lectures, there is a simple lotus bloom. It has been very carefully grown and is tended very delicately. Two days ago, when the bud opened, there was a terrible excitement among the people – there was a crowd around the flower photographing it from every angle and murmuring praises of its beauty. And I thought of the hundreds of lovelier lotuses growing wild in the dirty pools of Bengal and elsewhere in India, of which nobody took any notice.

1. Lao-tze or Lao-tzu: Chinese poet and philosopher.
2. Very poor.
3. Wonderful.

Almost in the middle of the lake there is an island, with a huge ugly house on it. By watching this island we can tell what sort of weather we will have – it's great fun. When the island seems to be very near we can be sure that we will have a cloudy day and perhaps rain. When it appears to be further away, it means a bright and sunny day. So far – and that is over a week – my prophecies have always come true.

So far I have not had the chance to be photographed. In Berlin and Wien I used to be with Mummie all the time and since then I have only been in small places. On my way to Badenweiler I am stopping at Zurich, so perhaps then I could go to a good photographer.

On Sunday last, I went to Lugano with friends. We went by car – the route was lovely and Lago Lugano more beautiful than the lake here and on the whole I had quite a topping time.

I am leaving Ascona on the 22nd. The train only comes till Locarno. So while coming here, I took my ticket for the steam launch that goes to all the little towns bordering the Lago. But on my return I shall go by bus.

These parts are full of Germans who have had to run away from Germany. Very few have gone to the French part of Switzerland. Most of them go to Zurich & the rest to the Lago Lugano & Maggiore. I was surprised to find quite a number of Indians in the streets of Lugano & Locarno. Yesterday we saw two fat Indians in a lovely Berlin car.

Nanu was in Badenweiler for about a week before my leaving for Bex. He left two or three days after my departure. He would have liked to have stayed on, but had a lot of work waiting for him in Praha & so had to return. I hear he is going there again in a short time.

On my way to Bex I was for two and a half hours in Bâle (or Basel as it is called in German). Most of this time was taken up in having lunch and going to the American Express for my money. But I liked the town – the little that I saw. And this time I would like to stop there for a few hours and visit the zoo, which is said to be the best in Switzerland. There is a special enclosure for the little ones of almost all the animals and here the children are allowed to enter & play with them. It must be nice.

Travelling in Suisse is so nice – the trains are quick &, as they are electric, there is no danger getting pieces of coal in your eyes and all over you. And the scenery is always gorgeous, the mountains with dinky little chalets. Besides the distance is never very long.

I am sending this letter to Mummie. She will send it on to you.

I myself, intend going to Badenweiler in a few days.

With lots of love,

Always yours,
Indu

117.   Badenweiler,
                                                      29th August [1935]

Papu darling,
Letter No. 7[1] arrived day before yesterday. I am so sorry for my letter
being so late and I am writing this to make up, for by my stupid
carelessness, you missed a letter, though I am not sure that you'll get this.

There seems hardly anything to write about, in spite of my travelling &
seeing new places. Had I been a good writer I would certainly have found
enough material to write pages, even if I had stayed on in Badenweiler,
doing nothing special. But as I am not one (in spite of Mr Vakil's hopes &
mine a few years ago) it is very difficult.

From Ascona, I have brought back a tan, two or three shades darker
than it was formerly and what Madan Bhai describes as a healthy look. But
my knowledge of German has not increased much, [for] though there
were many Germans there & I was surrounded by them most of the time,
the Italians – I mean the Swiss, knew more French than German. I must
say I felt more at home on the Lago Maggiore than anywhere else in
Europe so far – my black hair (people here insist on calling it black, though
I'm sure it's dark brown) & dark skin were hardly noticed there, and
people did not look so much. Only they were very astonished when they
found that I could not speak Italian or Spanish. 'Then what are you?' was
the inevitable question. And when I replied Indian – *'Mais c'est si loin.'*[2]

Besides Ascona, I saw a few other villages bordering the Lago. They
were built on more or less the same style & had the same view.

We left Ascona over a week ago & came to Zurich. I was three days in
Zurich. I was staying quite near the lake. It was not possible to see much of
the town as it was raining most of the time.

I came here on Sunday. My visit was quite a surprise to everybody, for
although I had dropped a card to Mummie & my pension landlady, they
had only received it a little while before my arrival.

I found Mummie looking thin & tired and very weak. It was quite a
shock to see her thus, for when I had left nearly a month ago she was
looking well, in spite of her temperature . . .

Since my arrival here I saw the sun for the first time this morning and
even then only for two minutes. It has been raining like the Deluge since
two days & nights and still it shows no signs of stopping. The houses and
lawns & trees look so fresh and clean and beautiful but a chilly wind has
been howling all night and is still blowing quite hard and it is quite cold. It

1. Refers to letter No. 115.
2. But it (India) is so far away.

is not pleasant walking to and from Hans Waldeck twice a day, every day, in this sort of weather.

During my absence, a Greek princess[1] who is living in Freiburg, visited Mummie. She is a great disciple of Bapu and corresponds regularly with him. Her dream is to go to India, but she cannot do so, as she is looking after her old mother. Mummie says she seemed to be a nice person. She might come again soon, as Freiburg is very near here.

Your paper is really too thick for the airmail and writing on one side only. I am asking Upadhyaya to send you airmail pad & envelopes.

Mrs Geissler was here for a little over a month. She had to go away at the beginning of August as she had some work somewhere waiting for her. Madan Bhai has however asked her to come back at least for a month, as Mummie is feeling rather depressed – and I don't blame her. Fourteen months in bed, and Unverricht[2] had promised her that she would be up and about within a month of her [reaching] Berlin after the operation. Lu is marvellous for chasing away the frown. (Lu is how Mrs Geissler is known to her friends.) So is her sister, Eva. Let me relate you an incident had happened when Nanu, Eva, Lu & all of us were in Badenweiler. One morning there was a discussion about Abyssinia – Madan Bhai said he wanted Italy to win, for that would be a defeat for England. All our efforts at explaining that it would also be a defeat for all the coloured races as well were in vain, he stuck to his opinion and Mummie got rather excited. This was very bad for her but if anyone had said so she would not have liked [it] for it was a reminder to her that she was ill. How else could we stop the discussion? Suddenly Eva said to Madan Bhai, 'All right, I am the white man, the Italian & you are the black man, the Abyssinian. Now see how you feel.' And like a tigress she jumped on him & sat on him and ordered him [about]. M.B. was quite taken aback. Everybody rocked with laughter and no more was heard about Abyssinia that day. And then her stories about various Indian students in Berlin, in the days when she says 'Berlin was one of the most wonderful cities of Europe, where it was well worth living,' are really wonderful. Also those about Baba[3] & Chatto.[4] By the way, you must have heard that Baba is in Hyderabad and has married a German girl called Eva.

On my arrival here I found your two missing letters. All I remember about Djibouti are the little boys diving from the ship and stuffing the coins they received into their mouths – and their quaint cries such as 'Singapore Ho-Ho'. Do you remember that? And the huge Negro who

1. F. E. Aristarchi.
2. Professor Unverricht: surgeon who attended Kamala Nehru during her illness.
3. Dr N. M. Jaisoorya (Baba): doctor, the son of Sarojini Naidu.
4. Virendranath Chattopadhyaya (Chatto): radical nationalist who was active as an emigré in Europe. He was the brother of Sarojini Naidu.

was standing so still & his body was shining so that I thought he was statue and was quite frightened when he moved or yawned or something.

I think we are getting all the newspapers you ordered. We get the *Hindu Weekly* of Madras, the *Modern Review*, the *Vishal Bharat*. Also the *Hindustan Times* and the *Sunday Chronicle* of Bombay. This from India. From London we get *The Listener* – sent by the Times Book Club – the *Manchester Guardian* and every day, the *Daily Telegraph*. Till I arrived they were all lying practically untouched. Madan Bhai is quite content with his *Daily Telegraph* and the *Hindustan Times* and does not care much for the others.

By the way, Devadas[1] wrote to me asking me to write articles (for the *Hindustan Times*) on the Indians here or some such thing. First of all, the subject did not attract me in the least and then, as I have mentioned before in this letter, I am no good at writing. So I politely declined.

The *Glimpses* are very inconvenient for travelling. The second volume takes almost half the place in a small suitcase. But I liked the parts I have read – I have not been reading from the beginning – though I suppose in a book of history that is what one ought to do. Mlle Hemmerlin was excited and pleased on seeing my copy – she has not been sent even the first volume and had no idea that you had written any book. I have written to Upadhyaya to have them sent to her.

At last the rain has stopped and the sun is peeping from behind a cloud. I'm glad for it is not very nice to get cold wet feet when it's cold & windy.

Mummie is always very tired & exhausted because of the continuous high temperature and so she doesn't talk and hardly listens when anyone else talks. She says she will write to you herself when she is well enough to do so.

My love to your flowers and the birdies.

With lots of love & kisses,

Deine,[2]
Indu

---

118.   Letter No. 8   Almora District Jail,
30th August, 1935

Darling Indu,

So at last your letter[3] came to me, a month after the one that preceded it, a fortnight after it was due. You began it in style on 1st August but it took you two weeks to finish it and it was not posted till the 15th August at Locarno. I did not even know, till your letter came, that you were travelling

---

1. Devadas Gandhi: nationalist and journalist, the youngest son of Mahatma Gandhi.
2. Yours.   3. Refers to letter No. 113.

or else I would have made allowances for the delay. Madan Bhai had written to me but he had not mentioned that you were away.

I am glad you have visited Bex and met Mlle Hemmerlin. I have only met her on three or four brief occasions but she has always struck me as a very fine woman. You will have many friends in Europe and you will never lack for advice and help. But somehow what comforts me most is the presence of Mlle H.

I do not know yet if you have come to any decision about your future studies. Probably you are back now in Badenweiler after your jaunt: Bex – Ascona – Zurich, and have met the people you wished to consult. I am still inclined to think that you should concentrate on languages during the next year and not bother yourself about the entrance exam of Zurich or elsewhere. European & for the matter of that, world conditions are peculiarly unstable at present and it is impossible to tell what the near future holds. It is quite possible that you may find it undesirable or impracticable later on to stick to a Continental university. The labour involved in an entrance exam would then be largely, or at least partly, wasted. But a knowledge of languages acquired will always be a gain. Of course the two cannot be separated. In any event you have to spend the next year on the Continent and the choice seems to be confined to Zurich or Lausanne. Zurich is probably the more advanced university centre but for the present and for my purpose, as suggested above, it does not matter much which you prefer. It is the choice between a German language background & a French language one. Fix up whichever you fancy.

In my last letter,[1] I think, I suggested your writing to Bharati about the Oxford college. Later on I found from your letter that she was in India for her holidays. I suppose she will be going back soon, for term begins at Oxford early in October. Zurich & Lausanne are all very well in their own way but they are, after all, rather narrow places with a limited outlook. For a wider world outlook, Paris, Oxford or some of the American universities are better. I rule out Berlin for the present. You might therefore write to Bharati anyhow and get all the facts. Later on, if we consider necessary, we can take a more formal step.

The papers are full of war rumours. For the time being there is talk of an Italo-Abyssinian war and it is possible that the next two or three weeks might see the beginning of this. I don't think there is any immediate danger of war in Europe. But one can never be certain and, in any event, war in East Africa will produce a continuing crisis in Europe. This will inevitably affect almost all activities there and foreigners, whether they are students or not, cannot escape this. Mummie's treatment may be affected, so also your educational course. The plan you may carefully lay down now

---

1. Refers to letter No. 115.

may have to be altered materially then. So you must all keep wide-awake and not be caught in any of the little difficulties that crop up during times of crisis. If such a crisis arises you & Madan Bhai had better consult the American Express people & Thomas Cook about money transfers, etc. It is possible that our correspondence may also be affected, though I imagine that air services will continue.

I have made arrangements from time to time for various newspapers and magazines to be sent to Mummie from India & England. But not a mention of them is made in your letters. I am intrigued. Are you not receiving them? In the event of your leaving Mummie to go to Zurich or Lausanne, you might arrange that a weekly packet of these papers is sent to you from Badenweiler after Mummie & Madan Bhai have seen them. You can choose the papers you want. Perhaps others – Indian students there – might also be interested in the Indian papers. They are rare enough on the Continent and you could arrange to send them on to some students' centre. It would be a pity to throw these papers away when others would welcome them.

I am rather vague about the purpose of your visit to Ascona, although the desire to visit a beautiful place is purpose enough. Still I have an idea that you mentioned some kind of a reunion of East & West. What this is I do not know and I await your next letter to find out all about it, and who you found there.

It is sad that Mummie is not making as good progress as she ought and odd complications are turning up. I was hoping that by this time she would be up and about and looking forward to an autumn and winter in Suisse to set her up. But it appears that she must stay on in Badenweiler for the present and till she gets better. It is a pity that Mrs Geissler has left her. If the new arrangement at Badenweiler is satisfactory, well and good, but later on some other arrangement will be necessary. I do feel so helpless sitting here, all enclosed in the mountains, unable to be of much use to you or to Mummie or to anyone else. Dol Amma, it appears, is again unwell and her blood pressure has gone up.

You were quite right in not getting Mummie involved in the proposed home for Indian convalescents in Berlin. It is best to keep at a safe distance from all public activities in Germany. Mummie is there for her treatment and for nothing else. Mrs Goering, as of course you know, is one of the big women of the Third Reich. I read about her marriage some months back. Was she not an opera singer?

Dhan Gopal Mukerji's New York address is 325 East 72nd Street, New York City. In summer he lives in a cottage elsewhere but I suppose he will be back in N.Y. soon, if he has not gone over to Europe as you suggest, on the strength of Mlle Hemmerlin.

This address reminds me of your address. This is going to continue, so far as I am concerned, to be Badenweiler until I am definitely told to write elsewhere.

Some days back I had a card from Ratan & Rajan[1] from somewhere in the Arctic Circle – latitude 80.10° it said, and you can look it up in an atlas to find out how far from the North Pole this is. They had been to Iceland & Spitzbergen on a pleasure cruise and they wrote, facing the great ice barrier and with the midnight sun shining down upon them, or rather sideways, for the midnight sun is just over the horizon. The picture card of a semi-frozen sea brought a sense of nostalgia to me. It reminded me of my own visit to Norway just twenty-five years ago. I had just taken my degree at Cambridge and I went with a friend on a modest trip to the Norwegian fjords. I did not go nearly as far as Ratan & Rajan but I loved those fjords and the blue ice coming right down to the sea. And though I did not see the midnight sun, I saw it set at eleven thirty p.m. and pop out again an hour or so later. I made up my mind to return soon and do the grand trip to Spitzbergen, that is as far as ordinary travellers can go. Beyond that is the preserve of Arctic explorers. But this ambition and desire of my heart, like so many others, remains unfulfilled. I am far enough from the Arctic seas in point of space, I am even further away if opportunity to visit them is a criterion. Ratan writes: 'You must do this wonderful trip before you resume work.' 'Must' indeed! How I would love to go there with Mummie & you and sail those silent and unruffled waters of the fjords, winding in and out between the high mountains, every turn bringing a new surprise. Indeed I would like to go further north still; it will be cold there of course with chunks of ice floating about in the sea, and icebergs, but the sun puts in a double shift of work and shines away night and day.

The Arctic regions have attracted me ever since I was a kid and read Fridtjof Nansen's[2] *Farthest North* – the Pole had still to be reached then. The polar regions and the Himalayan glaciers, these have beckoned to me for long years past. How many plans I have made to wander about in Ladakh and Skardo and Baltistan and Central Asia, and pass on to Tibet, to visit Mansarovar and Kailas! But so far my nearest approach to Kailas & Mansarovar is Almora Jail – for the pilgrim route passes through Almora and it is a bare three weeks' journey from here to that wonderful lake.

The rains continue here but they are less frequent and when the sun comes out it is very hot. But the nights are cool and there is often a bite in the air in the early mornings. The weather is slowly changing with autumn, but of course the rainy season does not allow the real autumn to

1. Ratan Kumar Nehru: a nephew of Jawaharlal Nehru. A member of the Indian Civil Service, he rose to a senior position in independent India's foreign service. Rajan is his wife.

2. Fridtjof Nansen: scientist and Norwegian explorer of the Arctic.

develop till October. Meanwhile I live in my tent and watch my flowers and feed my birds. The other day, as I was digging with the intention of making a new flower plot, I came up against a stone. It was no ordinary stone and I dug, and others dug, and we all dug, and the more we dug the bigger appeared the stone. At last we uncovered it; it was a hefty affair about six feet in length and broad and strong. With the help of numerous men, it was made to stand up on one end and then nearly half of it was covered up with the loose earth. The rest stands out of the ground now, a worthy sight with graceful curves and jagged corners, an embodiment of quiet strength. I hope it will remain there for many a long day, a reminder of my long stay in this jail! It is over ten months now since I came here! What a long time it has been, especially since you people sailed away from Bombay to the far West and my fortnightly visits to Bhowali ended.

Some of my friends, the birds, are sitting or standing near me as I write, trying to draw my attention to the fact that it is time I fed them. It is the new generation and it has not been properly trained. I am afraid I am partly responsible for their bad habits, for they want to be fed at odd hours and I humour them.

Some of the phrases in your last letter amused me. They bear evidence of your German or French background, and the 'wills' and 'shalls' get rather mixed up. It is a small matter and it is bound to happen when one changes over from one language to another. Chhoti Puphi, you tell me, was 'fed up *of* the rain'.

I learned about Romain Rolland's marriage to his secretary some time ago. Rather late in the day for a marriage, I should have thought, but the parties concerned are the best judges. I have just been reading one of his later books in translation. He writes beautifully. I have now sent for some more of his books in the original French from the Times Book Club, London.

I hope you gave my love to Mont Blanc and the Dents du Midi, & Lac Leman & our many friends in that part of the world.

Love,

Your loving,
Papu

Puphi has sent me, at my request, an enlargement of the snap of you that Raja took at Bhowali. It is quite good. I have also got a copy of the photograph someone took of Bapu & you in Bombay. You are grinning in it and the picture is good. Bapu has his back to the camera.

I wish you would let me know if the books I have sent to Mummie have reached her. Also the cable I sent on 31st July. I like to be definite about these matters. Uncertainty is not a pleasant sensation.

119.

La Pelouse,
Bex,
24th November, 1935

Darling Papu[1] and Mummie,

In case you ever travel by the '*Vor Sonntag*' train, it might interest you to know that it does not go any further than the German Basel station. The Badenweiler train and the Basel one arrived together. There were no signs of the porter so the conductor took my luggage. We had to race to catch the train and got in panting, half a second before it left. Imagine my face, when feeling so hot and bothered I was clutching my three suitcases and the hat box, and the bag and my ticket and trying to get into the compartment, the conductor (a huge fat fellow) bumps into me – nearly knocking me over – and gives me the above news! However he was very considerate and looked up the timings of the next train, which I could take at the Reich Bf [Bahnhof]. At the German station he related the story of my plight to the porter, who was of opinion that it would be better for me to take a taxi to the Swiss station. Then the two began arguing (needless to say my opinion was not asked). However, my patience being exhausted, I interrupted their discussion and said I would go by tram. At the Swiss station I had to wait for over an hour. So I sat in the waiting room and read. The journey from Basel was uneventful and uncomfortable.

Papu, I have given your letter to Mlle H. and have unpacked and arranged my things – (people here had never seen anybody with so many boxes). But nothing has been decided yet about my studies.

I share a room with a girl from Oxford – we had to solemnly promise not to speak in English.

It is quite cold. But there is no snow yet. On several stations yesterday I saw groups of skiers with their ski costumes & skis complete, and of course rucksacks. As I write I see the snow-covered mountains – and it is still snowing there, as far as I can make out.

I expect I shall be a bit of a misfit here – for the girls are younger than I am (except one, who is nineteen & with whom I have not yet talked – she is a Swede) and the teachers are older. But this is my first day and a Sunday so one can't really say what it will be like later & when I have glued myself to Latin & German.

An occasional letter or postcard to me will not require much brain work so Papu will you please write sometimes? Besides I shall want news about

---

1. Since Kamala Nehru's health deteriorated in the autumn of 1935, Jawaharlal was released from prison and joined his wife at Badenweiler. Indira was then sent to her former school in Bex.

Mummie – I hope she is smiling and chasing away the pains and behaving generally like a little lioness.

With lots of love to both of you.

Ever your loving,
Indu

---

120.   [La Pelouse]
Bex,
24th November, 1935

Darling Mummie and Papu,

I wrote to you this morning but I do not think the letter[1] will be posted at the Bex pillar box till tomorrow. Things like that will happen from here so don't get agitated.

My timetable has been made up. I think the routine is going to be terrible. I don't mind the getting up and going to sleep parts – but there is only half an hour for letters on Thursday and some time on Sundays. Hours will be spent in the singing and drawing classes. At present I'm not interested in them and shall probably feel miserable. '*Couture*',[2] whatever it is, also takes up time. When one leaves school one expects to have done with this sort of thing and compulsory walks, etc. Even if you like going it feels so awful to be told you have to go. I don't know what I'm going to do.

The whole day today was spent in arranging my things, talking to Mlle H. and others, writing a number of letters to India (I have written to Psyche about Mums' letter) and finishing the book on China. Just now I have come from the tea-table. I did not go for the walk as I am not feeling well.

I shall continue this letter tomorrow. Papu, did you write to Oxford for my books? And have you given them the Bex address? From tomorrow I will do all subjects, except the English text, which I begin in January.

25th November

I have had my first lesson in French and have written an essay in English.

Today it is very cold. I hope I don't freeze. Shall post this tomorrow morning.

26th November

There is no letter from you – I wonder why.

I am thinking of leaving the drawing, singing & rhythmic classes because there is such a lot to do and no free time. At this rate I shan't be

1. Refers to letter No. 119.
2. Sewing or needlework.

able to open any of the books I have brought with me – to say nothing of the homework I get. At the same time I do not want to have less classes or homework in my subjects because then it will take longer and that is a very tedious business. I have not talked about all this to Mlle H. but I hope to do so soon & I do hope she will agree. Of course I had told her the last time I came here that I loved drawing & music – and I do – but I don't think there is any time for them now. Will you please write to her something about this? Please do.

How has Mummie been keeping? Give her all my love.

Your loving,
Indu

I have received some books from Oxford.

---

121.   Badenweiler,
                                               27th November, 1935

Darling Indu,
Your letter[1] of various dates came this evening.

I can quite understand your feeling about the timetable. School timetables are apt to irritate as one grows up and especially when one has special work to do. Still, they have their uses and when one lives in any establishment a disciplined life in harmony with the other residents is helpful and desirable. Otherwise one becomes an odd number, not fitting in with the others. This does not produce much peace of mind. The real difficulty is that you are educationally and physically in a transition stage – between school and university. You are just beyond school and not quite of the university standard. You could of course have gone to a university straight off but you would have felt somewhat out of it for a while. It is far better to go there when you can take a leading part in the intellectual and social life there. That time will come soon enough – nine or ten months will go rapidly enough. Meanwhile I think it would be a good thing if you tried to fit in with the routine of La Pelouse in so far as you can do so conveniently.

This of course does not mean that you must do everything that the other girls or boys do. Anything that does not fit in, you can avoid. Usually I imagine it will be pleasant for you to go for the communal walks. Is it not better to go in a group than alone? When you do not feel like it, you need not go. As I have often said, a very desirable habit to cultivate is the habit of cooperation, and culture is partly the capacity to fit in with any new environment. If we are too individualistic we do not develop the social and communal virtues.

1. Refers to letter No. 120.

But the point is that you should decide for yourself what you can do and what you cannot without interfering with more important work. This applies to the subjects you have taken up. I am sure that Mlle Hemmerlin will help you in rearranging your timetable in order to make it most profitable to you. After a few days you will know better how to read just this timetable and you can then speak to Mlle H.

Of course if you want me to I shall write to Mlle H. But it would be so much better if you had a talk with her and pointed out your difficulties. Obviously your main preoccupation should be preparation for Responsions and languages. Music and painting are very desirable in themselves and add to our joy of life. Whether you can carry on with them or not it is for you to decide. Perhaps you can stick to one.

Anyway it will be a good thing if you had a little free time for reading, etc. For the rest a strict timetable is really very necessary to get work done regularly and efficiently. Otherwise one drifts. One of my virtues (so I think!) is that I work to a timetable.

Mummie is much the same, though her temperature was slightly higher today – not much but still I don't fancy it.

Madan Bhai has gone to Paris today and I suppose he is there by this time.

I enclose a letter for Lu Geissler – or rather two letters, one from me and one from another person. Will you please send them to her? Tell her that she can either reply to me direct or through you, as she prefers.

I have heard from Eva about the typewriter. I expect to get the machine soon.

Do not forget to let me know what bank you have finally selected. You will then have to write to India.

Today I had a visit from Raja Rao,[1] a young South Indian who lives near Paris and has married a French girl. He came alone from Mulhouse across the Rhine where he is spending some days. I liked him. I am thinking of going over to Mulhouse one afternoon for a few hours as I am told that it is a very enterprising municipality and has got all manner of socialistic and communal schemes working. Probably I shall go on Saturday next.

If you want any more books for your course you will let me know.

We have been having delightful weather here – cold and dry & sunny. This evening there was a little snow but it turned to sleet.

Love,

Your loving,
Papu

1. Raja Rao: writer and novelist.

122.   Badenweiler,
                                              3rd/4th December, 1935

Darling,
I have not written to you for some days. Indeed I have not written to
anybody. I have created quite a record by not going to the post office for
five days. I have been working very hard. A great deal of my time has been
spent with Mummie who has not been well at all and as Madan Bhai also is
not here I have to spend practically the whole day with her. Yesterday I did
not even come back for lunch. Today I went back after a hurried dinner
and returned at nine thirty. The aspiration[1] took place this evening. I hope
she will be better tomorrow. Her temperature has been keeping up and
she has had several sleepless nights.

The rest of my time has been given, almost every minute of it till late at
night, to revising my manuscript of *In & Out*.[2] This has become a terrible
job. I have got through over half of it and I hope to finish it in another
week. Meanwhile letters and other work are accumulating. I feel rather
tired and am already looking forward to a brief holiday at Christmas time
when you will be here. In between, I propose to go to Paris for a week if
Mummie's health permits.

Frau Ehrhardt[3] gave me quite a lecture two days ago. She told me that I
was not eating enough or sleeping enough and was developing nerves as a
result of over-work. She said she had observed that I shook my head
unconsciously during meals!

On Sunday I went to Mulhouse or Mulhausen. It was the very worst day
I could have chosen. It rained hard continuously and the wind blew as if it
wanted to blow us off. When I reached there I found that my host Dr
Dumesnil had developed influenza. Still I was glad I went and I saw a very
interesting municipal school for poor and weak children. Madame
Dumesnil asked me about you and when I mentioned Bex, immediately
she asked if you were with Mlle H. She praised H. greatly and said that I
had chosen excellently and could not have done better. She has never met
Mlle H. but they correspond with each other.

Mummie wants me to remind you to send some present to the girl in
Paris who frequently sends you gifts.

You can throw away *The Statesman* and *Manchester Guardian* and *Times*
after you have finished with them.

1. The withdrawal of fluids from the pleural cavity by means of suction. This treatment
is given in pulmonary ailments.
2. *In and Out of Prison*: this was the title which Jawaharlal initially gave to his memoirs
when he wrote them in prison from June 1934 to February 1935. These memoirs were
later published as *An Autobiography* (John Lane, The Bodley Head Ltd, London, 1936).
3. The landlady.

Hari is standing for election to the Allahabad Municipality on behalf of the Congress! The local lawyers, etc., are furious.

Love from,

Your loving,
Papu

———————

123.   La Pelouse,
Bex,
5th December, 1935

Darling Mums & Papu,

I have your letter[1] and p.c. You must be having rather a terrible time with *In & Out*. I hope it's nearly finished – you simply must have more rest. The typewriter is sure to be a great relief. I expect it has reached you by now. Is it a Remington?

On the 3rd morning at six forty-five, when Mlle switched on the light, everybody was frightfully sleepy and angry – but two little words had the effect of magic that no amount of scolding could ever have – *il neige*[2] – Hoop la! Out we jumped and there was a rush for the balcony. Since then it has hardly ceased. We have had two days of lugeing and skiing – isn't it lovely? (Everything is white and beautiful and it is very cold today.) I'm still rather clumsy on my skis and tumble almost every time – but I suppose it will be all right in a few days.

The Christmas vacation begins on the 20th – that is we shall be allowed to leave Bex on the 21st. The school reopens on the 10th or 11th Jan.

I received Lu's reply to my letter this morning – I enclose her letter to you. I do not think she is very happy about the news of her sister & other friends. She sends her love to Mums.

I have left the Rhythmics class – Mlle H. was not terribly pleased about it, but that cannot be helped. This gives me three hours free every week and I assure you they are welcome.

Mlle H. recommends the Bank Cantonale at Lausanne. She says it is a good one and has a branch at Bex, which would be exceedingly convenient. The Zurich bank is: – Julius Baer & Co., Bahnhof str. 36, Zurich. I shall write to Lu about the money.

The other day Mlle H. took me into a room and told me to write to you – about Chand & Tara's coming here. She said that she had no idea how much Puphi could afford and if Puphi thought her fees too high, she would willingly charge less.

I can hardly buy any present at Bex, so I'm afraid your suggestion is no use. I shall however send a Christmas & New Year card to my girlfriend in France.

1. Refers to letter No. 122.   2. It's snowing.

I do hope Mums is better. And please take care of yourself & don't overwork.

With all my love to you both. Can you tell me for how much was the cheque for Mlle H. you gave me on starting?

Your loving,
Indu

124.

[La Pelouse]
Bex,
8th December, 1935

Darling Mummie and Papu,

The snow is more wonderful every day and yesterday it was the best possible for skiing. We have the sun from about ten thirty to three every day and go skiing every afternoon. Our gymnastics master is an expert skier and now, since we have snow, we do skiing during the gymnastics period – this is lucky for us beginners as he supervises us and gives useful hints and tips from time to time. This afternoon he is taking the older girls who can ski well on a 'ski-promenade'. I don't think I shall go as it will [be] too difficult for me to climb and do steep slopes yet. I shall attend the ski lesson of the smaller children.

Last night Mlle H., three teachers and three girls, including me, went to the theatre in Lausanne. We went by car at seven and returned home by twelve thirty. It was a play of Ibsen's – *Jean-Gabrielle Borkman*. It was quite good – though exaggerated. I had no difficulty whatsoever in understanding the French. The theatre was a tiny and very charming little place. And the drive on snow-covered roads – with the surrounding mountains covered with snow, glistening with the night lights – was perfectly lovely.

During the vacation, Mlle H., with the girls who are not going home, is going to [a place] . . . which is very near Montana, though perhaps a wee bit higher. She is going there tomorrow to see the place & to have a look at the rooms they are going to stay at.

It is very cold here – but people say the weather will change soon. What is it like in Badenweiler? Have you still that awful howling wind? It has been rather windy here lately. The wind enters through the cracks in the door & windows and that is what makes it so cold. The balcony door and window in our room has to be open all night and the whole day until four p.m. When the windows are open, the heater does not work – so you can imagine how wonderfully cold it is in our room. I daren't enter. The study rooms are closed & heated.

I have written to Lu about the money and also to the bank at Lausanne. When do you leave for Paris? And what about Praha? Shall we go there this Xmas? I hear Nanu is spending Christmas in Zurich. Lu also invited me but I do not want to go there.

    With lots of love,

Your loving,
Indu

Could you send me the snaps of the children Puphi has sent, please?
    What about Vidya?[1] When is she coming? Have you written to her?

---

125.   Badenweiler,
9th December, 1935

Darling Indu,
This packet arrived in a torn condition.

    Mummie's temperature is not behaving well. Otherwise she is much the same.

    I am going to Paris tomorrow.

Your loving,
Papu

---

126.   [Badenweiler]
21st December [1935]

Darling,
I do not know when you are arriving.

    Mummie's condition took a turn for the worse this morning. It is rather serious. So you must be brave. Come up to Waldeck.

Your loving,
Papu

There is no immediate danger. A specialist is coming from Heidelberg.

---

127.   [Postcard]   Badenweiler,
12th January, 1936

Darling,
Mummie is much the same. She has been having rather bad & restless nights and so she sleeps till late in the day. This upsets the day's programme. I think it is time she had another aspiration.

---

    1. Vidya Dutt (née Nehru): a niece of Jawaharlal Nehru.

Hope you had a good journey. It is raining here.
Love,

Your loving,
Papu

---

128.   Badenweiler,
                                        13th January, 1936

Indu darling,
Mummie had an aspiration this afternoon and for the first time oil was put
in. The aspiration itself was a success, though for some time afterwards
Mummie had great pain. The next two days will show what the immediate
reactions are.

Madan Bhai saw a sanatorium near Lausanne and one in Leysin. He
preferred the Lausanne one. I am in a fix what to do. I do not think that
from the point of view of treatment a change makes much difference. In
fact there are certain advantages in carrying on here. But the fact that
Mummie herself wants to go elsewhere is very important and therefore I
think that she ought to be removed. I should like to take her away before I
go to India. Probably I shall now sail about the 23rd February or
thereabouts. I shall go to London in the last week of January (the date
is still uncertain) and return early in February. Till then Mummie
will anyhow remain here. The change over might take place after my
return from London. Meanwhile we shall watch the results of the oil
injection.

I have not heard from Vidya.
Love,

Your loving,
Papu

14th January
Mummie passed a good night and is feeling & looking brighter.

---

129.   La Pelouse,
                                                       Bex,
                                        14th January, 1936

Darling Papu,
I have your p.c.[1]

I do hope Mummie is having better nights now. If you have time please
do write and tell me about Madan Bhai's trip to Lausanne.

1. Refers to letter No. 127.

Since this morning I am most awfully upset. I had simply made up my mind to give Responsions in March and I was sure I could do it – I am still. But Mlle H. insists that it should be left till July. Of course I had thought that I would try my hardest for March and if even then I was not ready, I'd wait till July – but she says the idea of March must be given up altogether. I am so sure I can do it – why can't I be left alone to try it? In Poona I knew much less about my subjects but I was allowed to study as much as I wanted to – I left all other classes and put myself to it and I won. And it did not ruin my health either – I gained weight because I felt happy. Mlle H. just doesn't understand anything . . .

With tons of love to Mummie & you,
Your loving,
Indu

130.   Badenweiler,
15th January, 1936

Indu dear,

Yesterday morning I wrote[1] to you that Mummie was looking better. The aspiration with oil had been a success. In the afternoon she had a bad time with a cough, trying to bring out a lot of slimy stuff which was troubling her. This seems to have been due to weakness of the heart which was not functioning properly. It was an attack of the kind she had on 22nd December, only milder. It may have been partly due to the reaction from the oil, but chiefly, I suppose, from the exhaustion of high temperatures for a long time. The attack did not seem to involve immediate danger but it was very exhausting indeed as it lasted for three or four hours. The night was a restless one with little sleep. It was not considered desirable to give her a strong sleeping draught as this has a numbing effect on the heart. The temperature also went up high during the night. Early in the morning – about four – she fell sound asleep and she still sleeps as I write at ten thirty.

I wrote to you about your German that you should do what you think proper after consultation with Mlle H. It is difficult for me to advise without knowing much more of the kind of teaching that is given here. Generally speaking, it is desirable to keep up the thread of learning a language, as once broken, one has to begin afresh. It is preferable to give less time to it, to giving it up altogether. But these vague considerations must be applied to concrete facts. These facts can be considered best by you & Mlle H.

I have received a provisional programme from London about my

1. Refers to letter No. 128.

forthcoming visit. It is already pretty full and is likely to be a heavier one than [the] last one. But it is more scientifically arranged and so easier to manage. I shall probably meet a number of authors & writers. You see I am myself supposed to be one of that fraternity since I wrote the *Glimpses*. It would have been a good thing if you had also met some of these people, for they are interesting. But you will have plenty of chances in future of meeting them. One must make oneself interesting – intellectually and otherwise – before one can meet other attractive folk on an equal footing. There is no reason why the interest should be on one side only.

We have been having misty & rainy days. I suppose that is so in the greater part of Europe. But the weather seems to be changing. Last night there was a slight frost here. I imagine that the snow will be back within a few days.

Love from Mummie and

Your loving,
Papu

———————

131.   La Pelouse,
                                                    Bex,
                                       16th January, 1936

Darling ones,
I have Papu's letters.

I am rather anxious about Mums, I do hope she is better now. It will be difficult to move her in this very weak condition.

This evening a Russian lady – an *emigré* – gave a *soirée de chansons*.[1] Ever since the Revolution she has been living in France & Switzerland. Every now and then she goes on tours, giving a programme of Russian songs and piano music. She knows Mlle H. rather well and so comes here every time she is anywhere near. I loved the Russian songs – she sings with great expression. And the piano pieces were not bad. She is of course very much against the new regime and at the dinner table there was quite a discussion between her and Miss Lynham – my English teacher who has just returned from Russia & is very enthusiastic about it – she has a journalist sister there.

Since this afternoon the awful wind from the south is bellowing and howling away. It is colder than it was. Personally I would rather it remained as it is – except for the wind of course – than to have rain or even snow.

You write you will sail on the 23rd. Does it mean you are going by sea?

_____

1. An evening of songs.

The girl who teaches German is perfectly hopeless. I don't know [how] to tell Mlle H. so. I am sure she would be very wild if I ventured to do anything of the sort. At the lesson I always feel I am going back to what I know already – besides I never can learn languages with grammar books, until I can speak it.

In French I have made a good deal of progress and am now in quite a high class!

I had a letter from Puphi. Chand is going to Woodstock. But they hope to come here next year. I believe she has also written to Mlle H.

I wrote to Vidya but have no reply. Lots of love to you both & to Madan Bhai.

Your loving,
Indu

132.   Badenweiler,
16th January, 1936

Darling Indu,
Your letter of the 14th[1] came this evening.

Mummie had a fairly good day and at last she is asleep now. I do hope she sleeps well tonight. She wants it badly.

My dear, why do you get upset over little matters? It is not worth it. To be upset is a waste of energy and we have to conserve our energy for bigger things. It does not matter a rap whether you appear for Responsions in March or July. If you were keen on appearing in March certainly I would tell you to go ahead. I myself was under the impression that you had fixed on July and I always spoke to you accordingly. You did not tell me of your desire to appear in March. I am glad however you have written to me now. Of course you should write to me whenever you are troubled about anything. What am I for?

It is a small matter. But one thing about it worries me slightly, and that is a hint that you are not quite happy at Bex. Health & happiness depend of course on the state of mind far more than on anything else, and if you feel that your state of mind is not as it should be your health will not prosper. But if the mind gets easily upset, it is difficult to cultivate the proper state of mind anywhere.

About your taking the exam in March or July there is something to be said on both sides. For the earlier date, it is certainly desirable to get over the exam as soon as possible. On the other hand that is no special gain in time as according to the timetable we made you would in any event take

---

1. Refers to letter No. 129.

the last part of Responsions in October. We had decided, had we not, that you should remain at Bex till September? There is also this to be said for the July exam that this will enable you to prepare well for it and do better than otherwise, meanwhile of course doing languages & other subjects. You know that the next month or two may not be easy months for you owing to Mummie's illness & there is the possibility of interruptions. You will also come here to say goodbye to me. It would thus be certainly safer to stick to July rather than to fix March and thus have to shift it. Anyway do not attach too much importance to this matter.

I know that you have no suitable companions of your age at Bex. But for a few months does it matter much? You will soon be going out into the wider world and for the present you prepare for it.

Thanks for the snapshots.

Love,

> Your loving,
> Papu

17th January
Morning

Mummie spent a good night & had sleep. She is feeling refreshed this morning.

Have you heard from Vidya? She has not written a word to us.

---

133.   Badenweiler,
                                                17th January, 1936

Darling,

Mummie had a fairly good day today. She looked brighter. I am continuing my reading out to her. We have just finished an Oppenheim[1] thriller!

I had a talk with [Dr] Steffan today about our shifting to Switzerland. To my surprise he agreed. So now we intend moving as soon as I return from London. That will be at the end of the first week of February. We do not yet know where we shall go but I imagine it will be near Lausanne.

One thing I did not mention in my letter to you yesterday. Although you are preparing for Responsions, one of the chief objects of your studying in Suisse is languages. I hope you will keep this in mind. You may not have many opportunities of studying languages later.

Love,

> Your loving,
> Papu

---

1. Edward Phillips Oppenheim: English novelist.

18th January

Mummie spent a good night. Her temperature did not go so high . . .

———————◆◆———————

134.　　　　　　　　　　　　　　　　　　　　Badenweiler,
　　　　　　　　　　　　　　　　　　　　20th January, 1936

Darling Indu,

Mummie had a bad night last night, but tonight as I write at twelve forty-five she is fast asleep and I hope she will be much better in the morning. As I wrote to you we have decided to take her to Lausanne. I had intended doing so after my return from London but now I am inclined to hurry this, if it is possible. We shall have another talk with Steffan tomorrow. Perhaps Madan Bhai may take her there during my absence in London, about the end of this month, and I can go straight to Lausanne from London. At Lausanne she will go to the Sanatorium Sylvana. This is, I believe, a little high up the town. It will be convenient for you to see her there sometimes.

I enclose some snaps & flags which Puphi has sent me.

Love,

　　　　　Your loving,
　　　　　Papu

———————◆◆———————

135.　　　　　　　　　　　　　　　　　　　　Badenweiler,
　　　　　　　　　　　　　　　　　　　　22nd January, 1936

Sweetheart,

Mummie kept going well today. Last night also was a restful one. She is eating well. We are now busy making arrangements for the removal to Lausanne. It is a complicated affair and requires a lot of staff work. Madan Bhai went to Freiburg today to enquire about an ambulance car and to his great satisfaction found that he could get one there at about half the price which had been demanded at Lausanne. Tomorrow he is going to Lausanne to fix up things at the sanatorium there as well as to take our heavy luggage in advance. Indeed he is taking nearly all the luggage – sixteen pieces – leaving only bare necessaries here for another week's stay. He need not have gone quite so soon but he wanted to finish this job and come back before I went to London, so that one of us might be with Mummie. He has been ever so helpful. It is difficult to know what I would have done without him.

I have been busy all day with the packing. It was not an easy matter as part of our things were at Ehrhardt's. However I have managed somehow.

Most of my books have gone into one of the famous crocodile cases of Madan Bhai. I thought this would be strong enough for this weight. I have not generally interfered with your previous packing – the big trunk is as it was except for the tray which contains my clothes. One change I have made which might inconvenience you a little – though not much I hope. I have transferred Mummie's valuables to the dressing case which you took to Zurich. Such of your articles as I found in this have been placed in the other suitcase. I hope you do not mind. The Zurich case is going to remain here and will accompany Mummie. The other goes to Lausanne tomorrow.

All this luggage will be stored for a week or so in Lausanne till Mummie arrives there. Afterwards it will be distributed to the various places where we stay. It may be that the big trunk and one or two other boxes might remain in storage for a while longer.

I am not happy at the thought of my being in London when Mummie is being removed. Not that I would do much for I would have to travel separately by train. Still it will be a big burden for Madan Bhai. However I have to put up with this. One gets entangled in life's coils and cannot easily get out of them.

Provisionally we have fixed the 30th January for the removal. It may be a day or two later. I am going to London on the 25th and in the ordinary course I shall be in Lausanne on the 7th February morning – just a week after Mummie's arrival there. I think it would be a good thing if you could pay Mummie a brief visit soon after her arrival at Lausanne. February 2nd is a Sunday and you might come in the morning and return in the evening to Bex. You will be informed of course of Mummie's arrival at Lausanne by wire and then you can fix up a suitable day. I shall try to send you the exact address of the sanatorium. I am told it is some distance from the town – about twenty minutes' car drive. Trams run to it but they are very infrequent and for the first time at least it would be advisable for you to take a taxi to the Sanatorium Sylvana. I do not know yet where Madan Bhai, or later on I, are going to stay.

If necessary you could get into touch with Mummie on the phone.

I have had a letter from Bachhraj & Co. to say that they have sent £50 to the Bank Cantonale at Lausanne to your account. I suppose you have also heard from them. You can now pay Mlle H. Perhaps it will be necessary for you to get the money transferred to the Bex branch.

Now that we are going to be in Lausanne I hope I shall have the chance of seeing a little more of you before I return to India. Perhaps I might even pay you a little visit at Bex later on – if you will invite me!

Owing to heavy expenses we have rather unexpectedly run short of money just when we wanted it for the removal, etc. I am expecting some, however, during the next four or five days. Meanwhile I am going to

London with practically nothing except my ticket. That is not much of a risk as I can easily raise some funds there if necessary. Here the calculation as to how many registered marks are necessary and how much other money is a delicate and intricate affair.

Should you want any book or anything else from London write to me there.

Love,

Your loving,
Papu

Madan Bhai & I are going to Mulheim tomorrow morning early in a luggage lorry, probably perched up on the top of the sixteen boxes, etc. I shall see him off from there and then return.

Tomorrow also at last I shall vacate my room at Ehrhardt's after four and a half months. Frau Ehrhardt junior is still away.

———————————————

136.   La Pelouse,
Bex,
23rd January, 1936

Darling,
Since I last wrote to you, I have received three letters[1] of yours. Thank you.

I am so glad Mummie can come to Switzerland – for so many months she has been so keen on leaving Badenweiler that it is sure to do her good. But the journey is going to be an awful strain and I should feel happier if you were accompanying her, though I suppose with an ambulance car Madan Bhai and Annette[2] will manage quite well.

Now that Mummie is leaving Badenweiler so soon, it seems hardly worthwhile changing rooms. Mummie's leaving B'weiler will be bad for my German (and of course the end of Madan Bhai's) for the daily conversations with Frau Ehrhardt & family, and the various shop-girls and assistants that we visited daily, did me no end of good . . .

I woke up on Sunday morning with a queer singing feeling in my heart. At first I was not quite sure whether it indicated sorrow or joy – later I decided it is always best to assume the feeling is one of joy. I lay in bed till nine thinking all sorts of things of the past and what the years to come would bring. I thought of you and Mummie. I felt curiously peaceful. Where and when had I felt like this before? Then I remembered it was at

1. Refers to letters Nos. 132, 133, 134.
2. Sister Annette: the nurse attending Kamala Nehru.

Badenweiler . . . Like that night I felt at perfect peace with the world as well as with myself. Since then, the feeling has remained. I love everything – the horrible south wind included – and I am feeling happy and frightfully optimistic about everything.

The teacher who puts us to bed is like the crocodile in Peter Pan. One hears her singing when she is a mile off. I hear her approaching now. In two minutes she will be here, saying, '*Il est temps*'.[1] So I must stop.

With lots of love to Mummie & you.

Ever yours,
Indu

137.   Badenweiler,
                                        23rd January, 1936

Bien aimée,
Our belongings – or most of them – are off to Lausanne. They went in state this morning, piled up in the vegetable lorry which you must have often seen here – with Madan Bhai & me squeezing ourselves in beside the driver. We went down to Mulheim in this fashion and I sent him off, returning by the *Lokalbahn*[2]. I feel much lighter now.

Ehrhardts' are apparently preparing for the next season. My room, I was told, is being taken by somebody today. One of the old maids is back there, also busy with cleaning up.

Mummie has spent a good day. Her chief trouble is a cough which tires her out. Her temperature is a little better, though still high.

The full name and address of the Lausanne sanatorium is:

Clinique Sylvana
Epalinges sur Lausanne

For telegrams Clinique Sylvana, Lausanne, is probably enough. You can find out the telephone number from the book.

The place is situated a little above Lausanne on the road to Berne. By car it is ten minutes, by tram twenty minutes. The trams which go to it are those of Châlet-à-Gobet and Savigny (station Epalinges-Colleges). I give you this detailed information to save you trouble. But for the first time you had better go by taxi.

We had a little snow last night and today it is colder.

Love,

Your loving,
Papu

1. It is time.
2. Suburban train.

My London address will be:

> Artillery Mansions
> Westminster, London

I believe it is a flat.

———————————◄►———————————

138.   [La Pelouse]
Bex,
26th January, 1936

Darling Papu,
I have your letters.[1]

Thank you so much for all the details about the tram, etc. It will save me endless bother.

You must be awfully busy, though perhaps you might have to cancel some of your engagements on account of the death of our King-Emperor.[2] It is unfortunate that there is something on in England each time you visit it, so that you cannot meet all the people you would like to.

Meanwhile Nature, irrespective of the death of a great king and the quarrels of statesmen and ministers, not caring for wars and meetings and elections that loom large on man's horizon, carries on as before. The wind that blows and howls every winter and has been blowing hard for months continues. I believe it is called the 'Fern' (I am not sure of the spelling). The Mistral comes from the north. It is cold, but there is no snow.

In search of snow we went on an excursion to Bretaye – 1,800 metres above sea-level. We found enough of it – over two feet deep. Those of the party who could ski well climbed to the top of the mountain – Chamossaire – and came down to Villars on skis. I, along with some others, did some skiing at Bretaye and returned home by train. We all enjoyed ourselves and when we reached home at seven p.m. were almost dead with fatigue.

I received Vidya's reply to my letter a few days ago. She says she had no difficulty about anything and had an extremely comfortable journey. Perhaps you will meet her in London. Give her my love.

With lots of love.

> Ever your loving,
> Indu

———————————◄►———————————

1. Refers to letters No. 135, 137.
2. George V died on 20th January, 1936.

139.   Clinique Sylvana,
                                         [Lausanne]
                             2nd February, 1936

Darling Papu,

I waited anxiously till eight p.m. on the 31st. But no telegram came. Then I decided to phone to this clinique. I was told that Mummie had just arrived. I spoke a few minutes with Madan Bhai.

I came here this morning. Mummie did not have a very good night and this morning she was given a bath. And of course the effects of the journey are still there – so she does not look very cheerful. She has been coughing rather a lot. She has no temperature just now, but yesterday & at night it was high.

Her room here is large & spacious and has a balcony with a lovely view of the lake & mountains. There is a bathroom on one side & Sister Annette's room on the other. Next to the nurse's room is Madan Bhai's.

I hear Sister Annette has got a job in Paris & will be leaving soon – it is a pity. If you had known this before you might have stuck to Anna. I'm afraid I don't fancy the idea of having a new nurse every now and then.

Immediately after arrival I had to read out all your letters to Mums. Madan Bhai has some difficulty with your handwriting. So you had better write in English. Anyway reading those letters gave me news of you & I had a peep into your programme. I am glad you saw the Chinese Exhibition. I am looking forward to seeing the pictures.

As a gift from spring, I brought for Mummie, a tiny bunch of the first spring flowers that are now blooming in all the fields – *des petits épatiques violets et des primevères jaunes et naturellement des pagrets.*[1] The name of the wind I told you is spelt '*Foehn*'[2]. Princess Aristarchi has sent a bunch of roses to Mums.

                         With tons of love,
                               Indu

Mummie sends her love.
I enclose a letter that has come for you.

---

140.   London,
                                       6th February, 1936

Darling,

I have almost finished with my work here, although I have to face another day of it. But all the difficult and tiring jobs are done and I am so glad. I often wished you were here with me for you could have helped me a little

1. Tiny pretty violets and yellow primroses and naturally some daisies.
2. See letter No. 138.

about answering letters, etc. I had a great deal of competent assistance –
there were several girls who functioned as secretaries in turn – but I had
no time to sit down and tell them what to do.

The two most tiring jobs were a public reception at Caxton Hall and
addressing the House of Commons members. The former meeting was
too much of a success. There was not enough room for all that came and
even I had difficulty in getting in.

I am going tomorrow to Lausanne, reaching there on Saturday.

I wonder if you could come over to Lausanne for a day on the Sunday a
week later – the 16th. It would be better still if you came on Saturday
evening and spent the night there.

The enclosed picture in a London daily surprised me. There seemed to
be no particular occasion for it.

Love,
Your loving,
Papu

141.
La Pelouse,
Bex,
11th February, 1936

Darling Papu and Mums,
It was lovely to see both of you again and a week seems an awfully long
time to wait. I'm afraid I have really got all the bad qualities of the only
child and feel so dependent on you. I don't know what I'm going to do
when I shall be left all alone.

Mlle H. sends you both her best regards and thanks for the peaches. I
told her about your intended visit to Bex. She might go to Lausanne and
would have liked to pay Mums a visit. I am not quite sure when she intends
going. I shall find out and let you know – if she goes in the near future, you
need not come here.

I am continuing as usual with my work. And am feeling very fit and
kicking. As there is not enough snow for skiing we did lugeing – it was fun.
But it was a cloudy day today so perhaps it might snow at night – it is
certainly cold enough.

Tell Madan Bhai that his present from Berlin – the little red & blue
pencil – is at last coming in useful. My Latin teacher does not possess one
and so borrows it at every class to mark my work.

I hope Mummie is feeling much better.

With tons of love & kisses,
Ever your loving,
Indu

I have paid my bill up to the 23rd February.

NOTE: Soon after her move to the Clinique Sylvana, near Lausanne, towards the end of February, 1936, Kamala Nehru's condition took a sudden turn for the worse. She died peacefully on the morning of 28th February. With her, when she died, were Jawaharlal Nehru and Dr Atal. Indira Nehru, too, was close by. Kamala was cremated in Lausanne. Afterwards, Jawaharlal carried her ashes for immersion, according to Hindu custom, to the *Sangam* at Allahabad.

Two days before her death Jawaharlal Nehru wrote a poignant letter about Kamala to Swami Abhayanandaji. Kamala had often turned to Swamiji for spiritual solace during the last years of her life.

> Sylvana,
> Lausanne,
> 26th February, 1936

Dear Swami Abhayanandaji,
Your letter of the 17th came today and it came opportunely. I read it out to Kamalaji and it gave peace and joy and a forgetfulness of pain for a while.

She had been keeping fairly well for over two weeks. There had been no rise in temperature and it seemed that she was getting over her pleural trouble. But gradually, unnoticed almost, other troubles grew and yesterday her temperature shot up again. Her body, after the terrible long fight it has put up with, seems to have exhausted all its strength and is deteriorating. It cannot cope with little ills even and they grow. One never knows what she may not be capable of even now but, ordinarily speaking, there is no hope.

I was to have left her day after tomorrow for India but now I have postponed my departure for ten or eleven days.

With regards,
> Yours sincerely,
> Jawaharlal Nehru

142.   Heliopolis Hotel,
                                              Cairo,
                                              8th March, 1936

Darling,
Here am I again stopping at a very fashionable hotel, reeking of luxury and jazz and dancing, and enormous public rooms, and wide corridors, and crowds of waiters and dragomans & page-boys dashing about. I take advantage of the lovely bathrooms by having two baths during my short stay.

When I left Marseilles I could see in the distance the snow-covered Alps, probably Mont Blanc was one of the peaks. Today on rising from Rome we had a fine view of the city and of St Peter's. Later in South Italy we crossed the Apennines with their peaks covered with snow & ice. We were flying high – about 4500 metres which is, I think, over 14,000 ft. This means that we were not very much below the height of Mont Blanc. Our window-panes got covered with frost and it was difficult to see out. Again in Greece there were snow-covered mountains below us. The Athens landing-ground was far from the city but we passed over the city and had a good and rather unusual view of the Acropolis.

The Mediterranean was of a wonderful colour – deep blue, sometimes turning to emerald green near the coastline. A spot moved rapidly across the face of the waters – it was our shadow. Little islands were continually appearing and disappearing, cunningly shaped they were, fantastic little things dotted about over the blue sea, which crept inside them and sent its arms to embrace them. Over above them floated tiny wisps of clouds.

The great height at which we were flying made it just a little difficult to breathe with ease. The pressure of the atmosphere was less. At any rate I experienced some slight discomfort. It was not much. Our plane is a beauty. It is a great big aluminium bug with two eyes sticking out over its nose and graceful wings stretching out on either side. It bears the name *Perkoetet*, which in Dutch means, I think, wood pigeon or some such thing.

The height played strange tricks. A fellow passenger took out his fountain-pen. As he unscrewed the cap a fountain of ink splashed out. The lessening of atmospheric pressure had induced the ink to jump out in this way. The poor man's clothes were spoilt.

We had five passengers in all, including myself. Two dropped out at Athens. So now we are three. One, a woman, is bound for Batavia. She is Dutch. The other, an Englishman, is going to Calcutta.

On arrival at the Cairo airport I found Fouad Bey waiting for me. He was the same as ever and embraced and kissed me. One of his first questions was about you. He told me that he might be going to Suisse next summer and if so he would visit you. I gave him your address. Also he impressed upon me that whenever you passed this way to India you must visit him or at least let him know so that he can come to see you. You might keep this in mind and note down his address. Here is the address: M. Fouad Selim Bey Al-Higazi, 33 Sharia Dawawine, Cairo.

His wife is away and so I did not see her. But Bobby, his son, came round later and we had a long talk. He has grown of course and is a nice-looking boy. Fouad Bey told me that he was too full of politics to attend to his studies. He belongs to the *Bazis* (after the Nazis) – from *Baz*, a hawk. I was surprised to find how extremely naive he & others were about political matters. They seemed to know precious little and chiefly lived on enthusiasm. Even a little conversation with me was a revelation to him and he said that many of his old notions were upset and he was beginning to think on new lines.

It would be a graceful thing if you would send a few lines to Fouad Bey and tell him that you would be happy to see him when he comes to Suisse. This would cheer him up no end.

From tomorrow the deserts and the day after, India.

Love from,
Papu

143.

[La Pelouse]
[Bex]
8th March, 1936

Darling,

I sent you two days ago a letter by ordinary post. One was from Cedric Dover. It was expressing his sympathy. The other was a wire from Ellen Gotschalk.[1] This morning I received another bundle of letters addressed to you, of the same kind. They are from C. K. Narayanswami[2] & B. Das of Delhi. There is one from Eric Einan, somebody from the League of Nations. He says he would be glad to see you any time when you are passing through Geneva. It is dated the 5th March. The last letter is from S. D. Deo,[3] President of the Maharashtra Provincial Congress Committee. He requests you to consider the resolution passed by the Maharashtra P.C.C. at its annual general meeting held at Thana, 25th January, 1936, inviting the next (1937) session of the Congress to be held in Maharashtra. He says the claim is long overdue as the first & last session of the Congress held in Maharashtra was in Poona forty years ago. Rajendra Babu[4] & several Provincial C.Cs are supporting this claim.

Amiya Chakravarty has sent an article of his 'Events in India'.

I am sending all this by ordinary post. I give you a sort of summary of the contents in case you might receive other letters from these people.

This morning during the 'news hour' on the radio we heard Hitler's new peace terms – that he is demanding of France. He sounded very threatening. It seems the French have already sent troops to the frontier –

1. Ellen Gotschalk: American political activist who married M. N. Roy, the Indian revolutionary, in 1937.

2. C. K. Narayanswami: Bombay journalist.

3. Shankarrao Dattatraya Deo: close associate of Mahatma Gandhi, who was actively involved in the struggle for freedom.

4. Dr Rajendra Prasad: one of the leaders of the freedom movement, and later first President of the Indian Republic.

just to have a look round! Hatred of the Germans is much in evidence since this news – in Bex as well as elsewhere – & there is great talk of defending one's country.

The clouds apparently were waiting for you to leave Europe before they disappeared. Since yesterday the sun is out and the sky is of a spotless blue. But the wind is blowing and it is not very warm.

With tons of love,
Indu

For Mlle H. I have to write an essay in French *Faut-il cultiver ou combattre l'instinct de la propriété?*[1] in children of course. What do you think? Have you ever noticed how happy a young child is when he has something which he can call his very own? How delighted he is to take care of it. A friend of Mlle H. who was here sometime ago and who has a children's home – on a very small scale of course – tried to destroy this instinct and everything in her home was common property of all the children, even clothes. She says the children were miserable & the experiment was not a success. In Russia in the nursery schools there is also only common property and yet the children do not seem to be any the worse for it.

144.
River Front Hotel,
Baghdad,
9th March, 1936

Darling,

We are in Asia now, in famous Baghdad, but famous in history only for today it is a miserable enough place. We left Cairo at eight in the morning and Bobby (Fouad Bey's son) came to see me off at the aerodrome. He had been greatly impressed by our conversation and told me that he had learnt more in a short time from it than he had done in years before. He said he was keen on coming out to India to spend some months with me 'as my disciple'. I told him he was very welcome. His name is Mohammed Selim-el-Higazi. (This is the correct spelling of el-Higazi and not what I wrote previously to you.)

We saw the pyramids in the distance and then the desert, and soon we were over the Suez Canal. It looked absurdly small from up above. Skirting the Mediterranean, we reached Gaza in Palestine and stopped there for forty-five minutes. The journey from then onwards was very rapid. There was a following wind and we flew high – about 4400 metres. Our speed touched 350 kilometres an hour (over 200 miles an hour) which is very good going indeed. My last journey over the West Asian

----

1. Should one promote or curb the instinct for property?

deserts had been very hot and uncomfortable, when I came in September last. This time it was cool. Partly this was due to the weather, but chiefly, I think, to the great height we were flying. We were 14,000 feet high and few mountains are so high. A slight frost collected on our window-panes – a curious experience to have over the Dead Sea and the desert. We did not see much of the Dead Sea owing to clouds. We covered the 600 miles from Gaza to Baghdad in three and a quarter hours and were here early in the afternoon. We are making quite a long stay here – the greater part of the day and night. We start very early tomorrow – before four – and we are going to be called at two forty-five a.m. Tomorrow's run is a very long one. It will take us to the heart of India. We pass Karachi at tea-time and reach Jodhpur in the evening. There we spend the night and another two hours day after tomorrow morning will bring us to Allahabad – the end of my journey.

I went out for a drive with a fellow passenger round Baghdad. It is a dreary enough place with nothing to commend it. The buildings are drab and muddy, the people very undistinguished-looking. I dislike their clothes and it is seldom that one sees a really intelligent and sensitive type. Such types were rarer among the men than among the women. The women almost invariably had long black cloaks covering them from head to ankle, usually with their faces exposed. Sometimes the faces also were veiled. There were plenty of women about. Most of them seemed to wear short skirts under their cloaks and high-heeled shoes. Some had slippers without heels or back, like they do in India. In the outskirts of Baghdad we saw the quarters of the very poor – they lived in huts covered with palm-leaves. Poverty indeed was visible all over the town. There were plenty of cafés of various kinds and degrees of respectability and all of them seemed to be crowded with people (men) drinking coffee or smoking hookahs. I almost shuddered at the thought of having to sit there.

Our hotel is a bit of a change after the luxury hotels we have so far had. This is a very mediocre affair, and yet it is the best in the town.

During my drive round the town I stopped at an Indian shop and went & introduced myself to the owner. He was a Sindhi. He became quite excited and later on he and a crowd of other Indians trooped up to my hotel and we talked for about two hours.

It appears that I have quite a reputation in Iraq. The newspapers often refer to me and one of their promising young men – who is now the Iraqi minister in Rome – has been nicknamed 'the Jawaharlal of Iraq'. Fortunately none knew of my coming and I escaped interviews and the like. I was glad and I was tired and in no mood for this kind of thing.

I learnt today here that yesterday was *Holi.* How we forget our festivals! Not that I would have done anything even if I had remembered. And today is Dol Amma's birthday. It must have been a cheerless one.

This is my last letter to you from the way. My next will be probably from Anand Bhawan.

And now to bed for a short while, for I have to be up soon after two.

My love to you, my dear.

Your loving,
Papu

145.

[Anand Bhawan]
Allahabad,
12th March, 1936

Darling,

Yesterday the *Perkoetet* brought me to Bamrauli soon after eight in the morning. There were many friends there, sad-looking and silent. At home Dol Amma sat looking terribly shrivelled up. The shock had been very great for her.

All day people came and hundreds of telegrams. In the afternoon there was a huge procession carrying the ashes to the *Sangam*. For three hours we walked silently right through the city and across a long stretch of sand, and then at the *Sangam* I put the ashes in the Ganga to be borne away to the sea.

I have been feeling very tired and weary but I may not rest. The Congress session is very near and I must see people before then and then sit down to write my address.[1] Day after tomorrow I go to Lucknow and then to Sitapur (to visit Nani). From there I go to Delhi to Bapu . . .

Write to Dol Amma. She has been hard hit and a line from you will cheer her.

Love,
Papu

146.

La Pelouse,
Bex,
19th March [1936]

Darling Papu,

I was waiting for your promised telegram and – when it did not come – for a letter on your arrival. As yet there is no news. However I realise you must be terribly busy, so please don't bother about writing.

1. Jawaharlal Nehru was President of the forty-ninth session of the Indian National Congress held at Lucknow in April 1936.

As for me, I am as I told you in my last letter, working very hard. There is such an awful lot to do in Latin and the texts, though they look small, contain quite a lot of matter in their thin pages & small type. Whenever I get a free moment I turn to the enormous pile of newspapers and periodicals in my room. By the way, how will they come? At present I receive them all, the daily *Times* & the Indian papers included. If the subscription has been paid for a long time, don't you think it's better to ask them to send the things direct instead of to Lausanne. And you do not want any of them to be sent to you, do you? I have sent you a *Time & Tide* in which there was an article of yours.

Mlle H. is sweetness itself and I am being terribly spoilt. Princess Aristarchi writes almost twice a week & is very kind & charming.

I have a letter from Nanu. He says Prof. Lesny[1] was very pleased to get my letter & was showing it to his friends.

Did you leave a small mirror at the Lausanne watchmaker's? They have sent it to me.

> With lots of love,
> Indu

147.

La Pelouse,
Bex,
22nd March [1936]

Darling Papu,

I have your letters. I do not know where or when you will get this as you are travelling about.

How time flies. In less than two weeks the holidays begin. In two weeks I shall be admiring the masterpieces of the Ancient Romans and the beauties of Grecian culture in Sicily. And in the odd free moments – Latin! Somehow I am not excited at the prospect: it is queer, for it is the sort of thing I have always liked & it is all the more a wonderful opportunity because the teachers with us are experts (almost!) in the history of Roman & Grecian art. But somehow I feel I would be happier in a tiny cottage all by myself and books. And yet when I am alone it is not good for me for I mope. And 'books', says Mlle H. are depressing for me. The exam is coming nearer and nearer and I am not at all prepared for it. What's to be done? I can hardly spend more time on my books than I do now, unless of course I was allowed to stay up later than eight thirty which everybody thinks is an unthinkable idea.

The spring has definitely arrived. We feel it in the Foehn that blows &

---

1. Professor Lesny: Czech scholar specialising in Indian studies.

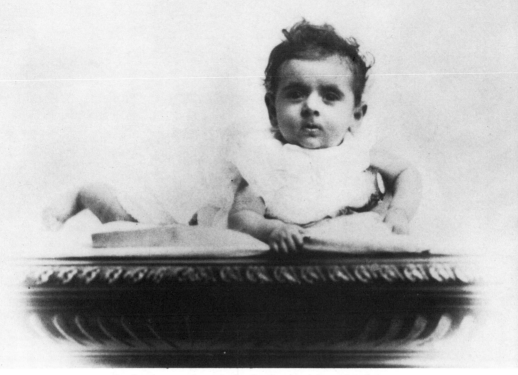

The first known photograph of Indira, at six months of age.

Indira, one year old, with her father and mother.

The old Anand Bhawan, where Indira was born; it is now called Swaraj Bhawan.

One-year-old Indira in
grandmother's arm, with other
members of the family.
Standing: Jawaharlal and Motilal
Nehru. Seated: Vijayalakshmi,
Kamala and Swarup Rani with
Krishna squatting on carpet.

Family group in Geneva in 1926. Clockwise: Kamala, Krishna, Jawaharlal, Vijayalakshmi and Indira.

*With fond love
Indu.*

Indira in a performance at
St. Cecilia's School, Allahabad.

Indira in Geneva in 1926.

Indira — profile.

Indira with two school friends in Switzerland.

Geneva
6-6-26

My dear mummie and papu
I am sorry that I was'nt good. But from to-day I am going to be good. And if I am not good do not speak to me. And I will try my best to be good. And I will do what ever you tell me to do.

Love from your
Indu

Indira's letter to her parents from Geneva in 1926.

At the Lahore session of the Congress in 1929. Jawaharlal Nehru, the President of the session, is on a stand. Behind him on the right are Motilal and Indira. On the left are J. M. Sen Gupta (with glasses), Abul Kalam Azad (with his hand shading his brow) and M. A. Ansari.

Indira with parents, in 1931.

Group at the Vakils, "Pupils' Own School", Poona. Indira is first from left in the third row.

A holiday in Kashmir, 1934.

Indira and Kamala in the porch at Anand Bhawan.

Kamala and Indira at Panchagani, 1932.

Indira with Mahatma Gandhi in Bombay before sailing to Europe with her mother.

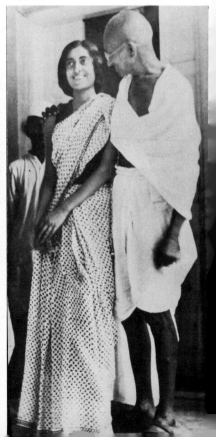

With Rabindranath Tagore in Santiniketan.

Indira and two friends in Santiniketan.

Excursion to Italy, 1936.

Indira with Feroze and Madan Atal in Switzerland.

Group photograph, Somerville College, Oxford. Indira is in the fourth row.

With her father, during a visit to Malaya, 1937.

Skiing holiday in 1939.

Portrait of Indira taken by Feroze Gandhi.

With friends at a sanatorium in Switzerland, 1939.

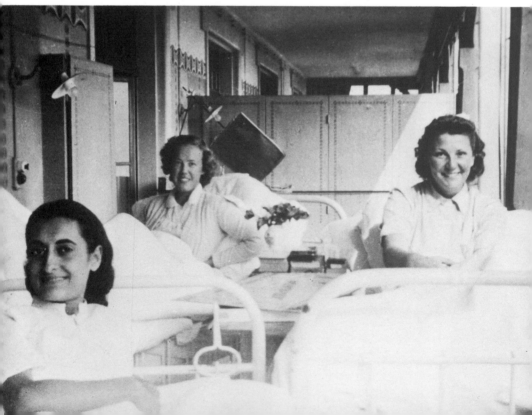

howls as in winter and yet its warmth & gentleness seem to bring a new message to us and to the tiny violets that peep above the grass shyly and coyly, to the swaying cowslips and the lovely anemones. The sun shines brightly every morning and with every sunset we can see a little bit more of the rocks of the Dent du Midi.

Your letters are always welcome & I look forward to them but please don't write if you don't have the time – I feel awfully guilty. And please do try to snatch a little rest whenever you can – instead of writing to me.

My love to Bapu & *namaskars* to everybody I know.

With lots of love,
Indu

I am writing to Dol Amma.

━━━━━━━◆■━━━━━━

148.   Harijan Colony,
Delhi,
22nd March, 1936

Darling,

Your letter[1] with the cheque from Vendredi has reached me here. I am still carrying on here but as the days go by I get more and more tired. Probably I shall be here for another three days & then I return to Allahabad. I shall have very little time to write my Congress address. I am afraid the next three weeks are going to tax me rather heavily.

Gurudev passed this way two nights ago and I went to see him at the station. He made all manner of enquiries after you. He was travelling with his troupe to Lahore to give some performances and collect funds. It is scandalous that at his age he should have to tour about in this way. He is very weak and it seemed to me that his mind was giving way – that is, he forgets things very rapidly. On his way here he paid a visit to Allahabad. Bapu told me that Gurudev paid a very beautiful tribute to Mummie. I have not seen it but as soon as I get it I shall send it to you.

In Rome I found soon after my arrival that an engagement had been fixed up with Mussolini – in spite of my repeated requests that no such thing should be done. However I stuck to my decision not to see him; with great politeness & firmness I declined. It was a very difficult and trying time for me.

Padmaja is here, or rather in New Delhi. She has grown much thinner and is very weak and frail. Fory also came to see me. And of course there are innumerable people here whom I know.

---

1. Letter not published.

I enclose three snapshots taken at the Karachi aerodrome on my return. You will notice Girdhari Lal very much in the picture.

Love,

Your loving,
Papu

Today I saw an exceedingly beautiful picture. It was by a Bulgarian artist, Boris Georgiev. The picture represented the Indian peasant with all his misery and resignation and devotion. I looked at it for long and was greatly moved by it. On it the artist had written (for he has learnt a little Hindi): *Daridra Nārāyan ko Namaskār.*[1] He travels about in a motor caravan which he has himself built. He made a sketch of me today. It was a strain for me to pose for some time. The sketch was not bad but he was not satisfied and he is going to have another shot soon.

P.

149.   [Anand Bhawan]

Allahabad,
26th March, 1936

Darling,

I returned from Delhi today after an absence of twelve days. An enormous pile of letters – about 300 – awaited me here and in this mountain were hidden three from you. I spotted them immediately.

I have returned to Allahabad for two days only. Then I go to Lucknow to attend the opening ceremony of the Swadeshi exhibition by Bapu. I return to Allahabad and have just under a week to write my presidential address. Bapu is also coming here and so I am not going to have an easy time. And then the Congress. There is a devil of a lot of trouble and much pulling different ways and the strain of all this is great.

Mridula [Sarabhai] is here. She is a dear and is just the same as ever. How different she is from her sister, Bharati!

This letter is going to be a short one. Dol Amma asks me to send her love to you.

Love,

Your loving,
Papu

---

1. Salutations to God as manifested in the poor.

150.   [Anand Bhawan]
Allahabad,
30th March, 1936

Sweetheart,

Two days ago I got your letter of the 19th.[1] I read with surprise that you had not received my cable which I had sent on arrival here. That cable was sent within a quarter of an hour of my reaching Anand Bhawan. It contained just two words: 'Love – Papu' – what more could I say. I have enquired into the matter and the receipt for the cable is here. What has happened to it?

So you are being overwhelmed with newspapers. The daily *Times* must have stopped for my subscription to it expired about the 17th March. As for the Indian papers I shall stop them at this end. But if you want any particular paper, I shall arrange to have it sent. Daily papers from this distance are such a nuisance and unfortunately there are no decent weeklies. I shall try to send you with my letters press cuttings that might interest you.

I did not leave any mirror at the Lausanne watchmakers. Perhaps Madan Bhai did. He seems to be still undecided as to what he should do. His last letter is from Vienna where his address is c/o the American Express Co.

Perhaps you know that the British Govt. has informed Subhas Bose that if he returns to India he is liable to be arrested and sent to prison. This news upset me and made me very angry. On arrival here from Delhi I had a letter from Subhas asking me what he should do. A difficult question for me to answer. All my inclination was that he should come back in spite of the Govt.'s intimation to him. And yet it is not easy to send another to prison. So at first I cabled to him to postpone his departure. But on further consideration and after consulting colleagues I cabled again suggesting to him to return immediately. I have thus made myself responsible for his return to prison.[2]

I have been to Lucknow for a few hours to be present at the opening of the khadi & village craft exhibition by Bapu. Bapu is staying on in Lucknow and will come here on 4th April to be followed two days later by the whole Working Committee. We shall be pretty full up then. On the 8th we go to Lucknow for the Congress.

Mridula has gone back to Ahmedabad. It was rather silly of her to go back for a few days and then return for the Congress. But she is no slacker

1. Refers to letter No. 146.
2. Subhas Chandra Bose did in fact return and was imprisoned. He was elected President of the Congress in 1938 and 1939.

and she felt she could do some useful work there in between. She is now organising the women there.

I enclose some resolutions that have been passed by the Working Committee at Delhi. These will be placed before the Congress. Of course there will be other resolutions also.

Don't send me any of the newspapers you get. Destroy them.

So you are very busy and working hard. I hope you will have some relief from work and a pleasant holiday soon in Italy. That will be just the time when we are meeting in Congress and there will be little relief for me. Even now time presses. I started yesterday writing my presidential address. It is hard job and I have only four or five days for it.

Did I tell you that I had a short note from the secretary of Miss Darbyshire, the principal of Somerville? There was nothing much in it.

By ordinary post I am sending you some photographs. They were taken at the Karachi aerodrome in September when I went to Europe and again in March on my return. Also at Delhi. Perhaps you might stick them in your album as a record of past events.

All my love,

> Your loving,
> Papu

---

151.   [La Pelouse]
                                                              Bex,
                                                    1st April, 1936

Darling Papu,

Your letter[1] from Delhi arrived a few days ago. Thank you for the snapshots.

I long to come to you to help you in some way so that you may get a few moments of rest. But what can I do from here or even if I were in India? And if I were there beside you it would be more painful to see your dear face so tired and your eyes closing with weariness and I so close by but unable to prevent its being so or to help in any way. Please try and snatch a little rest every free moment – I know it is not easy for there is such [an] immense lot to be done, but you must try for it will help you to do more the next day.

Mlle H. received a letter from Rome this morning that rooms were not available until Easter Monday at our pension – so we will spend two days at Florence. Mlle herself is rather delighted at this, for Florence is a beautiful place and she loves it.

---

1. Refers to letter No. 148.

Did you know Madan Bhai was in Vienna? I was surprised to get a letter from him from that place yesterday. He asks me to go there too if I have the time after the trip to Sicily! What a crazy notion!

I received a perfectly lovely letter from Christiane Trancaux. I can't tell how sweet it was. The poor thing has been run over by a motorbike and is lying at a clinique.

Spring is so beautiful here and this year it has come earlier than usual. I miss you so much – I should like to lead you through the garden, show you the magnolias that are opening, to take you through fields of swaying daffodils and the woods full of heather – the bonny purple heather about which so many poets have sung.

With all my love,
Indu

---

152.   Anand Bhawan,

Allahabad,
1st April, 1936

Darling mine,
Your letter of the 22nd March[1] came today. What awful things examinations are to worry and harass us! I remember reading once a comparison made by a Professor of the Sorbonne, many hundreds of years ago, of examinations with the torments of purgatory and he came to the decision that the former were worse. They are evil things, these examinations. Yet somehow they pursue us and we cannot quite get rid of them. But do not worry over much. I am sure you will do well. And if you think in June that you are not strong enough in Latin, and your teacher agrees with you, why [not] drop it for the time and appear in it later? But you have two months more and that is a fair period.

I hope you are already in Italy and feeling the charm and magic of that beautiful country. How I wish I was with you. My own visits to Italy have been too brief and I have always hungered for a closer acquaintance. To Sicily I have never been and all I know of it is from the distant glimpses from on board ship as we passed the Straits of Messina.

You have the spring. Here the brief spring is passing, though it is pleasant enough still, and the trees have dropped their leaves. Fans sometimes are necessary and the sun is hot.

Do not worry about my having time or not to write to you. I always have time for that. I like writing to you and it is a relief to me from care and work. It is true that I am well occupied and likely to be more so. Today I

---

1. Refers to letter No. 147.

feel quite light and free. I had reserved five or six days for writing my presidential address for the Congress. For three days I laboured hard at it all day and late last night I finished it. Suddenly, as I finished it, I felt as if a burden was off my shoulders. It is not finally done with for I am likely to change it, but the first draft is off my hands. I do not usually change my original drafts but others might induce me to make changes. It is being typed now and I hope to send you a copy separately tomorrow by air.

I wrote to you about Gurudev's tribute to Mummie. I saw it a little while ago and it moved me greatly. I am enclosing it. It is really a wonderful thing how Mummie's personality has impressed millions of people. Nothing like it has happened to my knowledge in India. The tributes that have come from the most unexpected quarters have not been formal ones; they have been full of affection and sorrow and admiration. Character and dignity and quiet restraint, together with inner fire, have a way of stealing into the hearts of millions.

Many poems in English and Hindi & Urdu and other languages have been written. They are not good as poetry, often they are silly, but they give some expression to the universal love which vast numbers felt for Mummie. I enclose two such poems for you to see.

I am enclosing also a copy of some resolutions passed by the Working Committee at Delhi.

My Longines wristwatch, of which I have been so proud and which has given me uninterrupted service for nine years, suddenly stopped the other day, to my astonishment. I had no other and I could not do without one, so I rushed to a local watch dealer and purchased a cheap West End one – an *incassable*.[1] Three days later the Longines changed its mind and started functioning again, but I am a little doubtful of it now. It was curious that after returning from the home of watches I should have to buy one in Allahabad.

Your letter reached Dol Amma today. She was greatly affected when she had it read out to her.

I have a fairly light day tomorrow – mostly letters. But from tomorrow night a stream of guests are coming. First Kamaladevi Chattopadhyaya[2] for a day or so. Then Bapu with his entourage and soon after the whole Working Committee crowd. We shall have a busy time and Anand Bhawan will be very full.

Love,

Your loving,
Papu

1. Unbreakable.
2. Kamaladevi Chattopadhyaya: socialist and pioneering leader of the women's movement in India.

Would you like me to send you unusual foreign stamps? I get them pretty often. I have been giving many, which I received on condolence letters, to Chand.

———————————

153.   [Original in Hindi]   [Anand Bhawan]
Allahabad,
2nd April, 1936

Dear daughter,
A letter for you has come from Bapu. I am sending it. He has not written neatly therefore I am writing it again so that you can read it easily.

Lucknow,
30th March, 1936

Chi.[1] Indu,
Kamala's passing away has added to your responsibilities but I have no misgivings about you. You have grown so wise that you understand your *dharma* fully well. Kamala possessed some qualities rarely found in other women. I am entertaining the hope that all the qualities of Kamala will be manifested in you in equal measure. May God give you long life and strength to emulate her virtues.

This time I have been able to have heart-to-heart talks with Jawaharlal. I shall leave here for Allahabad on the 3rd April. It has been decided that I should stay on till the Congress session but you should address your reply to Wardha.[2]

Blessings from,
Bapu

———————————

154.   Roma,
6th April, 1936

Darling Papu,
Here I am in Rome. We arrived at about 6 o'clock and walked about here & there & in the Piazza Venezia. Somehow I am disappointed in Rome – it is not what I expected – though of course it is too early to judge yet, without seeing anything.

Florence was a most charming place. The narrow streets and quaint

---

1. *Chiranjīv*: May you live long. This term is often used in Hindi when an elder writes in an affectionate tone to a younger person.

2. Town in the Central Provinces, now called Madhya Pradesh. In 1930 Mahatma Gandhi moved from Ahmedabad to a village called Segaon, near Wardha. This village was renamed Sevagram, the Village of Service.

houses were delightful and the churches were so beautiful. And there were the incomparable works of Michelangelo. At Florence there were even a few rickshaws.

Here everybody talks of the great Italian victories. I do not care for the roads & the huge structure on the Piazza Venezia is positively ugly. Il Duce's photographs are very much in evidence.

Katyar just phoned. We are rushing so much I don't know if I shall be able to meet him or not. I am telephoning to him tomorrow morning.

7th April
7.30 p.m.

It has been a lovely day.
We went to the Museum of the Vatican, St Peter's & inside the Vatican.

8th April
9 p.m.

Your letter has just arrived. We have been looking at the most beautiful things. It is a pity we have not more time to admire. We have seen most of the churches & this morning had an audience with the Pope.[1] He looked very tired but seemed sympathetic.

Tomorrow Dr Katyar is coming early in the morning and he might bring a private car with him to put at our disposal for the day. It's awfully good of him.

We are leaving Rome tomorrow evening for Naples and from there we go to Palermo.

I do miss you so & want to write long letters but here we have no time. We leave the pension at eight fifteen a.m. and return at nine p.m. Yesterday we went to see some dances (which were very beautiful). I am generally very tired after supper and go straight to bed.

All my love,
Indu

---

155.   [Anand Bhawan]
Allahabad,
6th April, 1936

Darling Indu,
You must be in Italy having some rest I hope, and filling your eyes with the sight of beautiful things. I think of you wandering through that beautiful country and some of the joy that you must experience passes on to me.

We are full up here in Anand Bhawan, overfull with guests. There is

1. Pope Pius XI, born 1875, Pope 1922–39.

Bapu and Ba[1] and Mahadeva and four others of their party. And Vallabhbhai and his daughter. And Mrs Naidu and Padmaja. Betty & Raja are here also with their two kids. Tomorrow morning Bul and Perin are arriving. Swaraj Bhawan contains a crowd of Working Committee members. All day today we have sat in committee and talked and argued till most of us were worn out. We repeat the process tomorrow and at night proceed to Lucknow. It is all very exhausting and the prospect is not an easy one.

My presidential address is ready now. It is being sent to you by ordinary post. Some changes have been made from the typed copy I sent you by airmail.

I wanted to send you a bunch of photographs taken at Karachi. But somehow I have mislaid them. I enclose some of them.

You will have brief letters from me from Lucknow.

Love,

> Your loving,
> Papu

---

156.   Palermo,
14th April [1936]

Darling Papu,

I wonder if you got my letter[2] from Rome. In our rushing about it is awfully difficult to post letters by airmail.

You must be very busy with the Congress. Here there is such a lot to see and hardly enough time. We have to rush through museums & churches with the most beautiful mosaics & frescos.

I met Katyar at Rome. For a whole day he obtained a car for us. Then when we left for Naples – he said he had holidays & would come also for a day. At Naples we again obtained his friend's car & went to Pompeii, etc. The same evening we came by boat to Palermo – imagine my surprise on seeing Katyar on the boat at breakfast. He said he missed his train from Naples & so came to the boat. If one misses a train it seems more natural to wait for the next one instead of going off in the opposite direction – but still. He left Palermo for Rome last evening.

Sicily is beautiful but except for the Greek temples, museums & churches, nothing very marvellous. Everybody in our group is in ecstasy at the scenery & flowers. But it is the same in many parts of India, where I have been. The people are poor and the roads dirty & full of creaking carts

1. Kasturba Gandhi: wife of Mahatma Gandhi who was active in social work. She was affectionately called Ba (mother) by the people.
2. Refers to letter No. 154.

& victorias. There are many beggars and a lot of singing and shouting in the streets. The people are dark and stare at us as at strange objects in a museum – in the villages the sight of a car seems to be rare, for as we are passing through everybody shouts to each other & rushes out to see the marvel. It reminds me so much of India – I feel terribly homesick.

Mussolini's sayings are printed in huge letters on village walls & at almost every street corner there is printed a rectangle with '18 NOVEMBER' printed inside. These words are also formed by plants & stones in the parks and every Italian carries in his purse a piece of paper with the notice – Do Not Forget 18th November. This is the date sanctions[1] were applied.

Sicilians are very proud of their little island & especially Palermo. The first question anybody in the street asks is how do you like our city.

The sea is lovely – we have been bathing three times; it was wonderful.

The weather has so far been favourable – not too hot and not cold. I do hope it continues so.

With tons of love,
Indu

157.   Lucknow,
                                                    14th April, 1936
                                                         1.30 a.m.

Darling mine,
Just to send you my love. I think of you in Sicily now and the thought gives me pleasure. It must be beautiful there with the spring flowers out, nestling in the remains of an ancient civilisation.

The Congress ended its second day's session today at seven a.m. I have just come back from it. We sat continuously for nearly eight hours. The *pandal*[2] is an open one and so we can only sit in the evening after sun has set. All day we spend in committees.

And so my love.

Your loving,
Papu

I send you some odd press cuttings. Send them to Madan Bhai when you have seen them.

---

1. In an attempt to stop the war which broke out in 1935 between Italy and Abyssinia, the League of Nations declared Italy the aggressor and adopted sanctions against her.
2. A large temporary structure of bamboo, thatch and cloth, meant for holding meetings or wedding receptions.

158.   Taormina,
                19th April, 1936

Darling Papu,
Sorry there is no more ink in my pen. I received three letters of yours in Palermo – all on the same day. Thank you for the cuttings & snaps.

We arrived here last evening. It is a very lovely spot. We are staying at a small hotel just out of town on the seashore. In many ways it resembles India. The town is one of the most adorable ones I have ever seen. It is situated on the top of a hill & [the] view from all sides is wonderful. And in the far distance we have a glimpse of the snow-covered Etna.

It has however its bad points – the drinking water is not good, there are innumerable mosquitoes & flies and we have to sleep with mosquito nets.

Yesterday [when] we went into a tiny restaurant for tea, a little boy of six came to sell cards – we offered him something to eat & asked him about his family. He at once gave us a long lecture on sanctions & said that his father was out of work because of sanctions & the wicked people of foreign countries. In the streets we are invariably taken for Germans. Queer, isn't it? But the Italians seem to like the Germans more than any other people & the Germans in their turn crowd all the hotels here.

I enclose a letter for you that was redirected from Bex & which I found waiting here.
       Au revoir & lots of love,
        Indu

---

159.   La Pelouse,
                Bex,
            26th April [1936]

Darling Papu,
Back at La Pelouse the trip to Sicily seems just a beautiful dream. We arrived here only this morning but already the journey seems to be a thing of the long past.

The trip was lovely and we saw things of wondrous beauty. But my thoughts were ever with you. Standing before the gorgeous Mediterranean and admiring its wonderful colours, a face tired & sad would float on it and I hated myself for being there among such loveliness while you had such hard work and were so tired. It was a lovely trip – everything was worth seeing but of all Agrigento was the most magnificent, with its ancient Greek temples – the ruins, of course. But to live in, Florence & Taormina are simply paradise.

The journey from Syracuse was awful – we left at two o'clock on Friday and reached Bex on Sunday morning at five thirty a.m. – specially as the trains were crowded & we could not stretch out at all.

I found your letter of the 14th[1] & the cuttings as well as your presidential address.

I enclose a cheque from the *Time & Tide*. I am afraid this letter is terrible but I'm so sleepy still that it's impossible to continue or to write better.

All my love,
Indu

I shall send the cuttings to M.B. c/o the bank for I have no idea of his whereabouts.

---

160. Nagpur,
27th April, 1936

Darling Indu,

I have had a very strenuous three days in Nagpur – huge meetings and speeches one after the other, and the Hindustani literary conference. I have even ventured to hold forth on the development of Hindi literature, not knowing much about it! I am afraid I must live up, or try to do so, to the literary reputation I am acquiring. That will be a hard job. I feel I must improve my Urdu also. That will be even harder. But something of this kind must be done if we are to live in touch with developments of thought in our country.

We are just off to Wardha by car. There I intend remaining for two days and then I go back to Allahabad.

All my love.

Your loving,
Papu

It has been very hot here, hotter than at Allahabad.

---

161. [La Pelouse]
Bex,
7th May, 1936

Darling Papu,

I did not write to you last Sunday. I have such an enormous lot to do that it is terrible. Apart from meals & other compulsory things such as walks, etc., there is not a moment when I am not buried in my textbooks. I receive

---

    1. Refers to letter No. 157.

letters every day and I do not know when to write replies. I am feeling tired and the worst of it is that being tired I cannot work as fast as I might have, nor as well. The trip to Sicily was beautiful & I enjoyed it but now I am regretting it. I would much rather have worked a little throughout the vacations than to have enjoyed myself then and to have to rush myself now. I work all day and every day – even on Sundays – except when there is something to prevent it.

Princess Aristarchi came over last Sunday. She had some business in Lucerne & Zurich & Lausanne. So she came here for lunch and tea. It was nice having her. The more I see of her, the better I like her. Besides she is so awfully kind. She writes regularly and each time she comes she brings some little present. Last time it was a tiny book of short stories by a Czech. This time a lovely vase from Freiburg. I have filled it with a golden bunch of buttercups and it brings in so much colour and charm to my little room. I gave [her] a copy of the *Letters*[1] – for she had not seen that book before. I wonder if you have asked John Lane to send her your new book.[2]

Sunday next I am going to lunch with Mlle Rolland. I am not feeling like it at all but did not know how to refuse.

Perhaps you know that there is an Indian doctor at Leysin. He phoned several times for me asking for an appointment just to have *darshan*,[3] more or less. That was before the holidays. Mlle received the messages & told him I had no time & was soon leaving for Italy, which was quite true. Then he phoned when the Princess was here. At last I received a letter from him a few days ago. He wanted to come on Sunday but I am going out. I have however fixed next Thursday.

Agatha Harrison[4] has sent me Thompson's[5] review of your book. I wonder if you have seen it. Will the publishers send you all the reviews or do you have to fish for yourself?

When I go to London, where shall I stay? I can take advantage of Agatha Harrison for two or three days but hardly more. The same difficulty presents itself if I go to the Continent for some time or, as you advise, 'make Paris my headquarters'. At Oxford of course I shall put up at Somerville.

It might interest you to hear that all the frocks I had last summer and which fitted me to perfection are now a bit too short and so narrow that I can hardly breathe in them and, mind you, they have *not* shrunk! But don't

---

1. *Letters from a Father to his Daughter*, Allahabad Law Journal Press, Allahabad, 1930. See p. 154.

2. The *Autobiography* was published by John Lane, the Bodley Head, in 1936.

3. Seeing a person with feelings of regard.

4. Agatha Harrison: British Quaker activist who supported the national movement in India. She was close to Mahatma Gandhi and Jawaharlal Nehru.

5. Edward Thompson: missionary and writer who supported the cause of Indian freedom. He was a close friend of Jawaharlal Nehru.

be alarmed, I shall not rush into the nearest shop and buy a set – I have had them all arranged and all's well now. I eat enormously and am much better at gym.

On the 1st May it was still cloudy and cold but we stopped the central heating as a protest against the weather. And a few days later the sun at last gave way and since we have wonderful sunshine. It is not too hot, for a breeze blows all the time. Many of the early spring flowers have disappeared. The fields are now quite golden with the stretches & stretches of buttercups and the apple trees are in flower. Higher up there are daffodils & narcissus.

We have put away our winter things and the light many-coloured summer frocks add so much colour & beauty. We have been feeding outside in the garden – it's marvellous. If this continues the older girls will go for an excursion to pick flowers & for the pleasure of walking. The neighbourhood's so lovely. I don't think I'll go.

All my love,
Indu

I am sending you '*des chics timbres*'![1]

---

162.   Lahore,
                                                        2nd June, 1936

Darling Indu,

I have not been able to survive the six days of my Punjab tour. Four days of it have laid me low and today, the fifth day, I am spending largely in bed. Punjabi popular welcomes are formidable affairs. In my case they have been truly terrific. Both in towns and villages, vast crowds have collected and have overwhelmed me. The programme has been a terribly heavy one, involving long motor journeys. The heat was bad but it was finally the dust that proved too much for me. My throat is all swollen and I can hardly speak without difficulty.

All this great popular affection, though trying enough, is also moving. Among a wilderness of excited compliments the most charming and pleasing was one from a young man who objected to much that was said, but added: *tusi pyare ho te change ho.*[2]

Tomorrow night I go back to Allahabad.
Love,

Your loving,
Papu

---

1. Some pretty stamps.
2. You are dear and good.

163.   In train to Wardha,
29th June, 1936

Darling,

My thoughts go to you today especially and I think of the burden of your examination. It will begin today and you will have your seven hours of it, and again tomorrow and the day after. I remember reading somewhere what a famous Professor of the Sorbonne said once during the Middle Ages.[1] He compared examinations to the sufferings in purgatory and came to the conclusion that the former were far worse. Not knowing much about purgatory I cannot say but I am sure that examinations are a nuisance. All that can be said for them is that they do push us on a little and bring some tension in our minds and thus help in making them sharp and clean. But there is too much of this tension and sometimes this results in blurring and confusing our minds instead of clearing them. Especially so in India where far too much importance is attached to the passing of exams and failure is considered a terrible disgrace. As a matter of fact, examinations as they are conducted today are no real test of anything worthwhile. Often those who do well in examinations are failures subsequently in life, and vice versa. So it is absurd to take them too seriously or to grow enthusiastic or depressed over them. We try to succeed of course in whatever we put our hands and minds to but we must not lose our sense of proportion.

Anyway your examination troubles will be over, for some time at least, when this letter reaches you and I hope you feel pleasantly relaxed. Last week I sent my letter[2] to you c/o the Principal of Somerville, Oxford. I hope it caught you there . . .

Some time I wrote to you that Mummie's big blanket & her table clock were missing from the baggage we had received from Suisse. I asked you if you had kept them. I did this because Dol Amma wrote to me that they were missing. But later she found them in one of the boxes. So don't worry about them.

I am on my way to Wardha for the Working Committee meeting. I shall be there for two or three days and then I intend going to Bombay for a day for some business – also to see Padmaja after her operation.

Love,
Papu

Wardha,
30th June

This letter was too late for the airmail yesterday & so I kept it back. As usual I have had a very tiring and distressing time with all-day debate and

1. See letter No. 152.
2. Letter not published.

argument, my colleagues in the Working Committee are greatly irritated with me as they think that my talking about socialism puts them in a false position. It frightens the rich folk, and so they have almost come to the conclusion that we should part company. This may result in my resigning from the Congress presidentship. I am not sure yet. Anyway I doubt if I can carry on in this way for long. It is a depressing business.

I wrote to you once about Vera Brittain's *Testament of Youth*. I have been reading bits of it here to try to get my mind off politics. I think it is a book you will like, especially as it contains a lot about Somerville. Shall I send it to you?

P.

---

164.   Badminton School,[1]
                                                        Westbury-on-Trym,
                                                                Bristol,
                                                        11th July, 1936

Darling Papu,
I wrote a very hurried letter[2] to you for Saturday's airmail – I have a very vague idea of its contents so please excuse any repetitions . . .

Sometime ago Efy (the Princess) told me a great secret of hers & asked me to write to you about it as she was sure you would not misunderstand. I don't know what you can do about it, but still. She has an idea, in fact she is quite sure, that Mira Behn[3] has done & is doing everything to prevent Efy's coming to India & has tried to prevent her coming near Bapu. For this reason Efy does not see the Rollands – for they are great friends of Mira's. Efy does not want Bapu or the Ashram people to know about this or indeed anybody at all – Andrews[4] knows & sympathises.

I had lunch with Menon[5] at a Chinese restaurant; he seems to be much better & certainly sounded more cheerful. At Oxford I lunched one day with Chakravarty. He will soon be going to India for good . . .

I have a nice room to myself here with a beautiful view – the early morning & late evening sky is specially lovely. The sunsets are gorgeous. But it is raining incessantly since my arrival & it is very cold & windy.

1. Indira went to Badminton School in order to learn Latin.
2. Letter not published.
3. Madeleine Slade: Englishwoman who became a disciple of Mahatma Gandhi. She was known as Mira Behn.
4. Charles F. Andrews: Cambridge missionary who supported the nationalist movement in India. He was a close friend of Mahatma Gandhi and Jawaharlal Nehru.
5. V. K. Krishna Menon: radical nationalist who promoted the cause of Indian freedom in Great Britain. He was very close to the Nehrus.

From the papers I gather what an awful time you are having and how difficult is your position. I enclose a letter for Dol Amma . . . [incomplete].

165.   [Badminton School]
Bristol,
18th July, 1936

Darling Papu,
You must have received my letter[1] after my arrival here . . .

Raj Chachi & perhaps Chacha are coming over from London to-morrow. They arrived in London on the 27th, having crossed from New York on the much talked about *Queen Mary*. They will reach Bristol at 12.25 o'clock & will stay on until seven p.m.

Agatha might come over for the day on the 27th. School closes on the 29th.

It is difficult to avoid Mrs Rama Rau[2] – specially as she phoned lots of times & I had at last to promise her I would drop in for a day or two.

I wrote to you that I met Sherwood Eddy[3] in London & liked him awfully.

Your rest must be just over but I do wonder how much of a rest it was & how you really are now. Do please take care of yourself.

As regards the immediate future – when school closes on the 29th I shall go up to London – stay there perhaps a day or two & then go to Bex. I shall spend a week or so, pack up my belongings, meet Madan Bhai & return for good – at least for sometime.

19th July

During the holidays I shall probably take tuition. And afterwards perhaps I might return here.

Raj Chachi & Shridhar Chacha came to see me today. They arrived at twelve thirty & stayed till five. They will be in [London] up till the 31st, when they leave for Berlin. And they want to have me the whole of the 30th & 31st with them.

Nanu writes that Prof. Lesny had arranged a room for me in Praha & a cottage in the country with tennis court & a swimming pool complete and lots of lovely tours. And all on the strength of a letter I wrote in March

---

1. Letter not published.
2. Wife of Benegal Rama Rau, a member of the Indian Civil Service, who was India's Agent-General in South Africa and later Governor of the Reserve Bank of India. Mrs Rama Rau was prominent in social work.
3. Sherwood Eddy: member of the American branch of the Y.M.C.A.

saying that my holidays were in July & August & I would like to go to Praha but I did not know if I would be able to.

I must end now. With lots & lots of love to you & to Dol Amma.

Indu

Chacha & Chachi looked far from well.

Madan Bhai is still very excited about my returning to Switzerland. He says it is very important but will not give me a hint as to what it is. He is going or has been probably to Prague for a few days. Nanu was in Vienna & stayed with M.B. He wrote that M.B. has very nice rooms. Nanu tells me that Eva [Geissler] is about to go through a fake marriage – if you know what that means.

Did I tell you that we saw Ruth Draper in London? She is an American impersonator & does original character sketches. She was simply marvellous. Without any make-up or change of dress except for putting on a shawl or a cardigan on her evening dress, she made herself look young or old, fat or thin, tall or short, according to the part she was acting and when she was on the stage, although there is no furniture & she is quite alone, so perfect was her acting & speaking in every detail that one imagined all the other people present. I loved her.

I wish you had met Miss Baker.[1] She is very nice. She is very interested in the League of Nations & is the Vice-President of the League of Nations Union in Bristol. She is a pacifist. The History teacher is also very interesting.

I am getting more used to the place now & have begun to distinguish a few names & faces of the 200 people that surround me. I like this place. The great difference between this school & that at Bex is that apart from the bigness I am in the VIth form. In this form everybody is preparing for a College entrance or the School of Economics. One girl is waiting to take a teachers' training. So we have interesting lectures on post-war history & such things. There is a newspaper hour in which we discuss with Miss Baker the chief events of the week & various articles & developments. In the *New Statesman* there was an interesting little paragraph about the Emperor of Abyssinia – did you see it? Some of the girls of the VI & Miss Baker & the History teacher are going to Geneva for ten days immediately after school closes to a summer course or something – they get a very interesting programme & lectures. Miss Baker wants me to come. It will not be difficult as I have to go to Bex to collect my things – I have a return ticket. But I have not decided yet. Last evening I went to a L. of N. [League of Nations] youth group meeting to hear a lecture on pacifism. This afternoon we went to see Will's cigarette factory – for the girls have

1. Miss B. M. Baker: Headmistress of Badminton School.

to study present-day conditions. I liked Will's place. But I hear that in England, the chocolate & tobacco [factories] are the best & that visitors are not encouraged in the others.

Lots of love,
Indu

---

166.   Badminton School,
                                                            Bristol,
                                                 25th July [1936]

Darling Papu,
Your letters. By now you must have received my letters and learned of my plans. I am afraid there will not be much of a holiday and there is not much time to spend on the Continent.

I am leaving for London on Wednesday the 29th morning. Raj Chachi and Shridhar Chacha came to Bristol last Sunday. They had lunch and tea with me. She wanted to have me for a whole day, if not more, and wished me to go up to London. But as they are not leaving for Berlin until the 31st, we decided that it was best if I spend the 29th & 30th with them in London after breaking up here.

Agatha is coming over for a couple of hours on Monday – she has a brother in Bristol. Have you heard that she is going to India on the 26th of Sept. for a short time . . .

Vidya is somewhere out of London. She has taken a fortnight's course of something which she thinks will be of great help in her work. She will sail for India some time in August or beginning of Sept. She has passed in her practical but she seemed doubtful about the theoretical. She looked very sad and depressed. Raj Chachi also remarked about it.

I am still undecided about the tuition during the holidays. Miss Baker said she would try & find out if it was possible to go out into the country which is more desirable than remaining in London. Agatha has some cousin staying with [her] & Mrs Grant Duff is spending her holiday in Prague with Shiela.[1] Mrs G.D. has however offered me a bed for a few days whenever I should be in London, even though the house will be empty with just the housekeeper. Then of course there is Mrs Rama Rau. Have you received any letter from Miss Baker? I think she wrote to you some time ago.

By the way, could you tell me from what event the Hindus count their years? What happened 1993 or 1994 years ago?

1. Shiela Grant Duff: author, journalist and friend of the Nehrus.

I heard from Parvati Kumaramangalam – Mr Subbarayan's[1] daughter, Mrs S. is in hospital in Basel. Her daughter & the rest of the family live in a village just outside & go into town everyday. She invites me to go there for a few days. I am afraid I cannot do so this summer.

26th July

I am afraid my letters to you are very much like patchwork, for I put down each thing as it comes to my mind. And the letter is seldom written at a stretch.

I am reading a number of books at the moment: André Maurois's *Disraeli* in French, *We Say No* by the Rev. Sheppard, some textbooks, historical biographies and I have just finished Edith Sitwell's *Victoria, Queen of England.* I liked it. Maurois also is good. I have a book of his, *Ariel*, which is the biography of Shelley in English and later I intend reading his *Edward VII et son temps.* I want also to read Strachey's *Victoria*.

I wonder if I have told you that Miss Baker & most of the people here are frightfully keen on the League of Nations. Perhaps you know that there exists a L. of N. Union which promotes interest in the League. Well, Miss Baker is the President of the Bristol Branch. Why I mention it is that in the school itself many girls are members of the 'Youth Group' of the L.N.U. and there are huge posters, etc., all over the place. The VIth form gave a show yesterday evening & Miss Baker persuaded them to give the money to the L.N.U. In the morning of the performance Miss B. gave a lecture in the dining room to the effect that nobody should give money or help to a cause with which they do not agree or which is against their principles – and this being so, any one who did not believe in the L.N. should not attend the performance however much they wanted to see it. This was rather hard on the little girls, for they had been looking forward to it for a long time. When the evening approached lots of them who had always maintained that the League did no good chucked aside their principles & came. But one little girl aged eleven, who had been one of the keenest about the show, stayed in the Library!

I usually post my letter on Monday so that it does not miss the Wednesday morning post airmail from London. This time I will give it to Agatha to post, adding at the last minute whatever we have talked about & what we have decided.

---

1. Dr P. Subbarayan: barrister and political leader of Tamil Nadu. Parvati Kumaramangalam was his daughter. The children took the surname Kumaramangalam which is the name of the estate of the family. Parvati later became a Communist member of the Indian Parliament.

27th July

I have a letter from Kamalnayan[1] from Egypt. He is on his way to Europe. He is with a company of Indians who are going to Berlin to demonstrate wrestling, etc. One of them is the gym teacher of Vakil's school [Pupils' Own School, Poona].

Sometime ago I had a letter from Psyche from some remote corner of Czechoslovakia. I have replied but no answer has come yet. Fouad Bey also has not replied to my letter – perhaps it has not reached him.

Miss Baker asks me to tell you that if she is cross with anyone it will be your responsibility for she is reading the 'auto' – she has no time during the day and so has to read late at night and she finds it so interesting that she gets very little sleep & is consequently tired in the morning!!

I have a letter from Muriel Lester.[2] She says there is a tiny room free in her house & I can come for a day or two. She wants me to meet the 'Socialists' of East London who back George Lansbury.[3]

27th July, 2.30 p.m.

Agatha has just had lunch & she will be leaving in a few minutes.

The decision reached is – I stay in London until the 2nd – spend the day in Paris, then go to Bex for a week. On my return to London, I shall take tuition & probably live with a family [of] somebody Agatha knows very well, just outside the city. I shall try & take the three subjects in Sept. Then come to this school for a term. It is going to be a pretty stiff fight for the Entrance. Everybody says its awfully difficult to get in & of course I have not had the courses & training required.

My next letter will be from London.

Tons of love,
Indu

---

167.   In running train,
Hyderabad to Multan,
28th July, 1936

Darling,

I did so want to write to you yesterday and catch today's airmail but in spite of every effort I could not find even a few minutes. Terrible programmes they draw up for me everywhere, as if I was a machine. It is going to be worse in the Punjab where I am going now. The next week will be a great

1. Son of Jamnalal Bajaj.
2. Muriel Lester: social worker in London, who played host to Mahatma Gandhi during his visit to Great Britain in 1931.
3. George Lansbury: Labour leader of the 1930s.

trial and I am longing to be back in Anand Bhawan. I am keeping well, however, in spite of all this and my throat is no worse if no better.

Travelling brings little rest, for at every station there is a crowd and much shouting of slogans, and big baskets of fruits and sweets, and of course garlands & flowers. These symbols of affection and good will are very welcome but they are burdens and often a nuisance. In the cities, caskets and addresses accumulate and I have now two packing cases full of them with me – all probably to go to the Allahabad municipal museum, and later I hope to the national museum we shall establish at Swaraj Bhawan.

This reminds me. Vyas of the Allahabad municipality has for many months been pressing me to give him for his museum the manuscript of the *Glimpses of World History*. I have told him that this is your property as they are letters addressed to you. He then asked me to refer the matter to you and get your permission. These manuscripts have some value and I should like to keep them for our future national museum. But, if you agree, I could let Vyas have them on condition that he is to return them whenever wanted by us.

Yesterday I was in Hyderabad, an attractive city. It was a day of continuous activity and yet I liked many of the functions, especially those connected with the children and girls. They have a good children's organisation in Sind. I went also to a new and very big girls' school which seemed very up-to-date and efficient. The procession in Hyderabad was unique of its kind. Across the narrow bazaar, where the rich shops were situated, hung all manner of articles. Each shop put its own goods on the strings that stretched across the street. There were silks and caps & hats & curtains and lanterns, brushes, biscuits & sweets, *lotas*[1] & vessels, & even false beards! You know that wherever you may go to in foreign countries, and especially at the great ports, there is always a Sindhi shop of silks & curios & oriental goods. All these Sindhis come from Hyderabad and have their headquarters there.

Two or three days ago I had a longish camel ride – the first I have had. It was across a sandy plain in South Sind. I liked it and found it fairly comfortable and I am sure now that I could ride a camel for hours without much difficulty. It is a question of swinging your body with the camel's motion and a person used to horse-riding should have no difficulty in doing so. But I did not like the smell of the camel.

In a remote Sind village, as we went in procession, I saw that one of the gates that had been created was named 'Indira Gate'. I thought of your heritage of storm and trouble and how, whether you liked it or not, you could not rid yourself of it. None of us, in this present age, can have an

1. Brass pitchers.

easy time or freedom from storm & trouble. But to some of us fall a greater share of them and it is your lot, because of your family and other reasons, to have to bear this heavier burden. May you be ready for it when the time comes and accept it willingly and take joy in it. Those who seek to do higher things must also face bigger difficulties.

In Karachi and Hyderabad I met a delightful little girl, who is just a year younger than you. She is Premi, the daughter of Jairamdas Doulatram, whom you must remember. She is a very bright and intelligent girl and we have become friends. She told me that her ambition was to become a Joan of Arc and I remembered your admiration for Jeanne d'Arc many years ago. Does that endure still? . . .

And now our train is approaching Multan and I must end. Processions, speeches, interviews, arguments without end – it is a tiring business.

I am glad you saw Ruth Draper. I have read about her and have long wanted to see her.

Love,

              Your loving,
              Papu

---

168.   London,
                         1st August, 1936

Darling Papu,

I am sorry I missed today's airmail – this will have to wait until Wednesday. Please excuse my wobbly writing – I have managed to do something to my right arm & shoulder & it is rather painful.

The news about Dhan Gopal[1] was a great shock. He was such a charming personality – so very lovable. He always did have his moods, but I never thought it would end like this. I heard in Bex that he was far from well. He was also having a lot of financial trouble – poor soul.

Since my arrival in London I have been mostly with Raj Chachi & Chacha and I have been rather bored. Most of the time has been spent in shopping – once Chachi spent fifteen minutes in Woolworths deciding whether to buy a green or a red pencil! The rest of the time goes in eating – huge lunches & dinners at Princes [restaurant] or some such place. There is little to talk about, for Chacha is a bit narrow minded, I am afraid. If one disagrees with him on the slightest point he gets angry & nervous and one does not know what to do. He is very proud of the fact that he has not spent a penny on books for the last eight years and that he has read very v. few! I am afraid this is something I simply cannot understand. So many good

1. Dhan Gopal Mukherjee committed suicide.

books come out every week – it just makes one's mouth water to have a peep at the bookseller's windows. I daren't walk in for I am sure I would spend a fortune before I walked out again – however I did walk in & I did spend quite a lot. This is the only money I have spent in England this time except for food, etc. I am sending you a book of Low's[1] – some of the cartoons are really good. Agatha thought you would like it & that anyway it would do you good to get in a laugh amidst all the worry and the work. I have also bought a book of Schweitzer's[2] & *Inside Europe* by Gunther.[3] Also *Edward VII* by Maurois.

I have been putting up at Mrs Grant Duffs the three days that I have been in London. There is nobody at home except the housekeeper & a friend of hers. I only sleep & have breakfast here. The other meals I have been having with Chachi or somewhere alone. At Chachi's place I met Anand Haksar, also Dr Katyial[4] (or whatever his name is) this morning.

Agatha & I have been room-hunting. We have found quite a nice quiet place in Golders Green. It is a very healthy part of London & yet not too far from town. I have made arrangements about coaching. In my next letter, which will probably be from Bex, I shall give my future address in London. I shall be at this place for just a month. Then I shall go to Oxford for the exam & then Badminton in Bristol. By the way, there was something in the *Star* dated 31st July '36 which might amuse you. I wanted to send it to you but Raj Chachi has the cutting. She will send it to you from Berlin. Chhoti Puphi might like to see it, so will you send it to her.

From Bex I will send some books which I have read – it is expensive & troublesome to cart them about from place to place.

By the time you get this letter I shall be on my way back to London so you had better write to London – c/o Agatha H.

Darling Papu, please take as much care of yourself as possible and please don't worry about me. I shall be all right & well.

With very much love,
Indu

Love from Raj Chachi. Love to Dol Amma.
I am anxious about Padmaja.

———————————————

1. David Alexander Cecil Low: British cartoonist.
2. Albert Schweitzer: Alsatian physician, missionary and humanist, awarded the Nobel Prize in 1952.
3. John Gunther: American journalist and writer.
4. Dr Chuni Lal Katyial: Indian doctor who practised in Great Britain.

169.   Bex,
8th August, 1936

Darling Papu,
Your nice long letter[1] from the running train was a very welcome & pleasant surprise this morning. I had written to you to keep on writing to London because I thought you would not get my letter in time – hence I did not expect anything here.

However many beautiful sights and places I may see, I return here to find that Switzerland is the most beautiful of all. As I write under the shade of an enormous chestnut tree, on one side the Dent du Midi (my favourite peak apart from the Matterhorn) peeps from above thin wisps of clouds and on the other in the far distance shines the Lac Leman in this glorious sunshine and the clouds make strange patterns of light and shade on the dark, almost awe-inspiring mountains beyond. It is beautiful and so peaceful & quiet. An ideal spot for a holiday, however short. I was looking forward to a week of it. But now it is even less. I arrived here on the 5th morning and am leaving early on the 10th for Zurich. And in the few days that I have had, there has been an enormous amount of packing, making parcels & packets, replying to an ever-increasing pile of letters, reading & then one has to be social & converse charmingly. Phew! What a holiday & what peaceful rest! On the 10th I go to Zurich. I wanted to see Lu & Eva [Geissler] and perhaps Nanu will also be there. This is a good opportunity – I do not know when I will next be in Suisse. I have to be back in London on the 13th, which means leaving Zurich on the 12th or late on the 11th – I shall go direct via Bâle.

On my way to Bex I spent two days in Paris. Feroze was there and he showed me round. We walked & walked & saw everything the American tourist sees. I was not a bit tired, although we must have walked miles & miles. But now my leg muscles feel awfully stiff. That's good for them, is it not? It was cold in Bristol & I had just begun a cold in the head. I am afraid I did not take much notice of it. In Paris the first night Mme Morin[2] took us to Versailles to see the *fête de nuit*[3] which only takes place thrice a year. I liked it very much, but it was cold & raining & we got quite drenched and my cold got awful. But it is all right now.

It is ages since I first saw Paris but many of the sights & old corners were very clear in my mind and several streets & boulevards had a vague familiarity. I liked the Arc de Triomphe & the Boulevard Foch which leads from it to the Bois de Boulogne, specially.

   1. Refers to letter No. 167.
   2. Louise Morin: French journalist who was later to be in charge of the French unit of the All India Radio. She was a friend of the Nehrus.
   3. Pageant of the night, a show of light, music, fountains and fireworks.

I am afraid the idea of putting the manuscript of *Glimpses* in the museum does not appeal to me. I do not know how much care is taken of these things and I should hate anything to happen to them. However if you think that they will be quite safe and that it is advisable to put them in the municipal museum let Vyas have them. I leave it to you.

When I go to London I shall spend the 13th night with Agatha & then move the next day to a room we have arranged in Hampstead. The address according to the telephone book is: 29, The Grove, N.W.11. I am not sure if this is quite sufficient for letters – it ought to be. You had better write there – if this is not enough I shall send you the complete address as soon as I can get it. I shall be there for a month [till] 20th September. Then I shall go to Oxford for a few days. Then from the 24th September to Badminton School, Westbury-on-Trym, Bristol – until Christmas.

I see from the *Bombay C* [Chronicle] that you are now touring the U.P. I do hope the programme is not a very heavy one. How is your throat now? Do try & take as much care as possible and snatch a little rest whenever you get the occasion to . . .

Tons of love,
Indu

170.   Anand Bhawan,
                                                              Allahabad,
                                                       10th August, 1936

Darling Indu,
The light has failed not only in Anand Bhawan but apparently in a good part of the city. So I sit in semi-darkness with a little candle, trying to write in the gloom. Worse than the failure of the light is the stoppage of the fans, for it is stuffy and warm. Probably this failure is due to the incessant rains we are having. For days we have had almost continuous rain, and not only we here but a great part of the province. Lucknow city is flooded and the Gomti rushes down Hazratganj and the main roads. In Gorakhpur the floods have washed away large numbers of villages.

11th August
I could not carry on last night. And so I have got up early to add a few lines before the airmail goes. This evening I am going to Lucknow.

Ernst Toller[1] has written to me. His wife, it appears, has been acting in a play in London with great success. This is Toller's own play – *No More Peace*. He writes that he & his wife have been 'waiting so much' to hear

---

1. Ernst Toller: German poet and playwright who was friendly with the Nehrus.

from you and see you. So if you are round about London you might try to
see them or write to them.

The Sarabhai family seemed to have arrived in India and soon there will
be the marriage celebrations in Ahmedabad – Suhrid with Manorama.

The sun has come out today for a change –

Love,

Your loving,
Papu

Toller's postal address is c/o John Lane,
9 Galen Place,
Bury Street,
London w.c.1.

<hr>

171.   Anand Bhawan,
Allahabad,
14th August, 1936

Darling Indu,

I missed this morning's airmail as I was travelling. The next mail day is
four days hence, but I am writing today as I am leaving Allahabad again
tomorrow.

Your letter of the 1st August[1] has reached me, also your postcard[2] from
Paris.

I have just been to some of the flooded areas in this province. Lucknow
was not so bad as I thought and my description of the Gomti rushing down
Hazratganj proved to be entirely fanciful. But round about the city and
near the riverbank many parts are flooded. Motimahal was partly under
water. The villages with their mud huts have suffered greatly, for the
whole village melts away and disappears when the waters invade it. The
district of Gorakhpur looks almost like a vast ocean. I went about in a boat
and it was a pleasing sight to see the treetops coming out of the waters. But
underneath the waters lay tragedy. Over a thousand villages had disappeared and the crops had been completely ruined. It was over these
fields that I went boating. It is a problem to feed and clothe the tens of
thousands of refugees. And a greater problem will be what to do with them
later on. The waters are going down now, leaving a scene of destruction
behind and a stench of dead and rotting fish.

1. Refers to letter No. 168.
2. Postcard not published.

I am going tomorrow to Wardha and from there to Bombay for the Working Committee and All India Congress Committee meetings. I am going to Wardha chiefly to see Khan Abdul Ghaffar Khan who has recently been discharged from prison. Puphi was going to accompany me to Wardha and Bombay but now she can't do so as Dol Amma is not at all well. We can't both leave her. For this last week she has been poorly and her blood pressure has been high. She is so weak now that even a little carelessness about food, etc., upsets her completely. She has been slightly better today and her blood pressure is coming down.

You mention reading a book by Gunther. I do not know the book but I have read many articles by him and found them very interesting. I met him in London last February . . .

Love,

Your loving,
Papu

---

172.   24 Fairfax Road,
                                                    N.W.6,
                                            27th August, 1936

Darling Papu,

I am ever so sorry to have missed the airmail last week.

Your letter of the 14th[1] arrived this morning, forwarded by Agatha. It has pink & blue spots all over for it has had a dip in the sea on its way. That also accounts for the slight delay, I suppose.

Thank you for the cheque of £17 – it is not looking its best and the sea bath was not a success, but still.

From the above address you will see that I have changed my digs. This is a great experiment in economising. I hope it will be all right. (I had to change from Hampstead because my landlady was going away for a holiday – otherwise I liked that part very much and would have liked to stay on.) Agatha had addresses & I had some from my tutors but we could not find anything below two guineas a week – even then I would have had to take lunch & tea outside. This is a nuisance & a waste of time – none of the places were near any restaurant. Agatha decided upon a [place] overlooking Regents Park (not a nice part of it). When I went to look at the rooms I did not like them – I thought them gloomy. Besides it was expensive – two and a half guineas without lunch. So I hunted on my own and this is the result. (I'm afraid Agatha did not like the idea of my giving up the Regents Park place & if she saw this place she would be wilder still.) I live up on the third floor in a sort of attic. It is a tiny room but I have a

1. Refers to letter No. 171.

good window, which catches every little wisp of breeze passing by. There is plenty of light and air. But all I can see from the window are a few treetops and the sky & the clouds. It costs £18-6-0, four meals a day, baths, etc., all complete. Besides as it is much nearer town than Hampstead (Fairfax Rd is next to Swiss Cottage, if you still remember where that is) I save 6d a day on the bus! Don't you think it's a good bargain – the room is not exactly beautiful but it is not by any means ugly & a few flowers improve it a lot.

Psyche Captain was here a few days ago and took me to see Chekhov's *The Seagull*. The heroine was Peggy Ashcroft – do you remember the girl we saw as Juliet and liked so much. The acting was not bad. Then I once went to the cinema & saw *Mutiny on the Bounty* – it was quite hopeless.

I had lunch with Mrs Toller – she is perfectly charming. I liked her enormously. I was sorry to miss Toller. Unfortunately he had to go to the American Consul for a visa & could not return in time. They are both going to France for a short holiday & then to America. If I am here when one of his plays is on I shall certainly go & see it.

I keep in touch with Menon but have not seen him this time. I had lunch with him once before going to Switzerland. He looked better . . .

Raj Chachi will be back in London in a few days.

I have not seen Vidya nor do I know her whereabouts. She is returning home in September, I hear.

When I was in Paris I just told Mme Morin that the French teacher at Badminton School had told me to read modern authors to improve my style in French and I asked her what authors she would suggest & I should read. Since then I am receiving piles of French books. I feel so embarrassed – I don't know how to keep on thanking her. I have little time to read – though there are such heaps of books I should like to read. I have not finished Gunther's *Inside Europe* yet. It is interesting, though a bit old already (it was first published in January 1936). Such a lot has happened since then. It is difficult to keep pace. I shall send the book to you when I have finished – shall I?

A Mr Mehrotra[1] or Mitra or some such person came to see me the other day. He said you sent him my address. His face seemed vaguely familiar but otherwise I did not recognise him.

I was sorry not to be able to meet Mme Edib. She had to leave London soon – and I had tuition on the day she asked me to lunch. But we had a short conversation on the phone & whenever I am next in Paris I shall go & see her.

With very much love,
Indu

---

1. Lalji Mehrotra: businessman and political activist.

173.

Anand Bhawan,
Allahabad,
28th August, 1936

Darling Indu,

I am typing this letter for a change and for some practice. I get into bad habits by relying too much on others. Upadhyaya has fallen ill and so I have to fall back on my own resources. He was ill for most of the time in Bombay and I have got so used to him that I am greatly inconvenienced if I have not got him with me. As a matter of fact, even apart from him, I require a competent secretary very badly. But so far I have not succeeded in discovering him or her. I think I wrote to you that Janak Zutshi was working for me as such. I was just beginning to hope that she would suit me and fit in with my work. She is competent enough but she did not take very great interest in my work, and now she has got a job in a college in Delhi. So I am left to carry on by myself. Of course I get a great deal of help from the A.I.C.C. [All India Congress Committee] office but I cannot take my private correspondence there and this is prodigious. Besides even in the office there is no really efficient person to do the kind of work I want done for myself. It is extraordinary how rare efficient persons are who can be relied upon to do a job thoroughly and well. I shall have to wait till you come back and help me!

I returned to Allahabad this morning from Bombay via Lucknow, which is a roundabout route. But I had to attend meetings in Lucknow. Bombay was as usual an exhausting place with heavy demands on my time and energy. Fortunately the Working Committee and All India Committee meetings passed off well and without any friction and we all met and parted in peace and harmony. We produced a big election manifesto which has had a very favourable reception. I wrote out the draft of it, after a tiring day, from midnight to four thirty a.m. I could hardly keep my eyes open but with an effort I carried on.

Apart from our political work, we made some progress with the Kamala Memorial Hospital scheme. We have so far made no real effort to collect money for it, but we have got about Rs. 50,000 already. But really we want ten *lakhs*[1] and that is a fat sum which is very difficult to collect. I would be satisfied if we could get half that for the present at least. Quite a number of anonymous donations have come. Bul received the other day a big dirty looking bundle. It was a towel carelessly pinned together and it contained a thousand five-rupee notes!

In Bombay we visited two talkie shows. This was not just for the pleasure of it but to encourage Indian Talkies which were dealing with

---

1. 100,000 rupees.

village life. One of these, called *Achhut Kanya*, was the story of an untouchable girl. It was quite a good film and Devika Rani[1] made a charming heroine.

In Bombay I had a novel experience. I made two records, one in English, the other in Hindustani. These were the first two records of a new Indian gramophone company which has just been started. I gave a kind of a message in both to the Indian people. It was a trying ordeal and I was quite exhausted by it. The actual recording business did not take much time but the tests and trials were long and tiring. Then we had to sit in a room which was closed up all round and the fans were stopped to prevent any extraneous noise from spoiling the record.

The airmail went this morning and I just missed it. But I have decided to write, or rather type, this letter today before I get involved in other work. Piles of letters await me and [the] day after tomorrow I am going to Cawnpore on an 'official' visit as Congress President. Cawnpore wants to make a big thing of it and I shall have a hard time . . .

Thank you for your delightful gift – Low's *Political Parade*. I found it waiting for me on my arrival this morning and I could not resist the temptation to look into it even at the cost of other work which was waiting for me.

The news from Spain[2] troubles me a great deal. It affects me almost as much as if all this was happening in India. Indeed what is happening in Spain will have a tremendous effect on Europe and the world, including of course India. So my interest in it cannot be theoretical.

I found Dol Amma a little better. She is of course very weak but she moves about slowly.

Harsha has come here from Bombay with Nan [Bari Puphi]. He was losing weight and not keeping well in Bombay and so he has been sent for a change. Allahabad is hardly the place for a change at present and Bombay was definitely pleasanter. But perhaps the change will do him good. He is a jolly kid. It was a great effort for Betty and Raja to part from him.

Love,

Your loving,
Papu

---

1. Devika Rani: film actress, grandniece of Rabindranath Tagore.
2. The Spanish Civil War between Republicans and Nationalists broke out in July 1936.

174.   Anand Bhawan,
                                                Allahabad,
                                        3rd September, 1936

Indu darling,
I have not had any letter from you since I wrote to you last. It is possible
that your letter has had a dip in the Mediterranean. There have been quite
a number of air disasters and I have got rather mixed up about them. More
probably you were busy fixing yourself up in your new abode.

I have had letters, however, from Agatha and she tells me that you were
looking after some Indian girl, a new arrival. I do not know who she is.

I have been to Cawnpore and back – three days there with monster
processions and innumerable meetings. Day after tomorrow I am off
again to other parts of the U.P.

I wonder if you ever meet Vidya. When you have the time you might see
her. She has been rather cut up about her failure and she has few friends.
A little company and friendship will be soothing for her.

Dol Amma is keeping fairly well now. Harsha is prospering and he is
making demands on my time. Mamu[1] is becoming popular.

Last week I sent you a cheque for £25. I mention this as letters might go
astray owing to the vagaries of the air service.

Love,
                            Your loving,
                            Papu

———————

175.   Anand Bhawan,
                                                Allahabad,
                                    14th September, 1936

Darling Indu,
I have not written to you for the last ten days or so. It was physically
impossible for me to do so for I have been touring incessantly and not
having a moment to myself. My usual day was an eighteen-hour one with
about five hours of sleep. I have just returned. This morning at Etawah I
had a bit of strenuous exercise. A meeting at a very out-of-the-way place
had been fixed and a car could not reach it. So I had to ride a bicycle for
ten miles, a horse for fourteen miles, and to walk two miles. All this on a
muddy road – the walking was often in ankle-deep of mud. The bicycle
ride was unusual for me as I had not ridden one for long. The kutcha[2]

1. Maternal uncle. In this case the reference is to Jawaharlal Nehru himself, since he
was Harsha's maternal uncle.
2. Rough road.

muddy road made matters worse. At one place the bicycle slipped and I had a fall, scratching myself in various places. You can imagine how tired I am feeling at present, not only after today's jaunt but after these nine days of wandering . . .

Dol Amma is well and sends you her love.
Love,

Your loving,
Papu

176.   Anand Bhawan,
Allahabad,
24th September, 1936

Darling Indu,

For the last five or six hours I have been busy arranging some of Mummie's and your things. So far I have not had time to look through the luggage that came from Switzerland. Today I had a good look at it. What memories it brought me! I seem to live on memories now so much. Whenever activity in the present ceases I go back to some incident of the past. And sometimes in the middle of some activity my mind wanders away to other times.

Your examination must be over – mine goes on and on and there are no holidays. But you must have good rest and a change. This insomnia business is a bad sign. It shows that you must be run down. I suppose your real holiday will come at Christmas time. Why not go to Switzerland then and have a little skiing? That will make you fit.

I had a nice letter from Mrs Toller in which she told me about meeting you. I am glad you liked each other. I have many other friends in England who are worth meeting. I should like you to meet Mrs Huxley, Aldous Huxley's[1] wife. Would you care, to go to her? I can write to her about you or you can write directly, mentioning that I have suggested it to you. Her address is: The Albany E-2, Savile Row, London. These rooms or flats in the Albany are famous and many well-known writers and politicians have lived there in the past. They are a relic of old London. The Albany is near Piccadilly.

The Huxleys often go abroad during the summer so perhaps they are not in London now. Mrs Huxley is a Belgian.

Do send me a good photograph of yours. Go to a decent photographer and send me a dozen copies as other people will want them also.

I do not suppose you will be living in London now except for odd days.

1. Aldous Leonard Huxley: English novelist and essayist who was a friend of Jawaharlal Nehru.

But if you do have to live there do not choose digs in unwholesome surroundings just to save a little money. It is not worth it.

Nan has gone to Delhi to attend Zohra's[1] wedding and from there she goes to Mussoorie to see the children.

Love,

Your loving,
Papu

Let me know to what address I am to write to you in future.

177.

Anand Bhawan,
Allahabad,
28th September, 1936

Darling Indu,

Life's dull routine was interrupted two days ago for me. We had a police visitation, armed with a search warrant, in Swaraj Bhawan. It seemed just like old times! We have been issuing cyclostyled newsletters for abroad and objection was taken to this. This incident has in some ways added to my work, for the present at least.

For some months now I have been addressing my letters to you c/o Agatha. This seems to me very unsatisfactory and I hope you will give me your own address for the future. Other people ask me for your address and I do not know what to say. I have now given them your bank address: – the one in Haymarket. So you had better keep your bank informed of your movements. Usually it is a good thing to have the bank address as the permanent one.

Nan will not be going to Madras with me now as Tara & Rita are unwell in Mussoorie and she is with them. This is a pity. Tomorrow Betty is coming here from Bombay . . .

Love,

Your loving,
Papu

178.

24 Fairfax Road,
London N.W.6,
29th September, 1936

Darling Papu,

My thoughts are with you every moment – your tours must be tiring affairs and you must be so weary. And then all the secretarial work to do as well –

---

1. Zohra Ansari: daughter of M. A. Ansari, the eminent nationalist leader.

I hope Upadhyaya is well by now. It is not a bad habit depending on others for a little help when you have such a tremendous lot to do. You could do with much more help, I think. It is strange that there should be so few efficient secretaries among the hundreds of educated Indians who are out of work.

Forgive me for missing the last mail – and almost missing this one. I ought to have posted this letter this evening (it is twelve midnight). But it will still catch tomorrow's plane if I go to post it at the Imperial Airways office at Victoria before ten a.m. tomorrow.

I have been having a pretty tiring time (nothing compared to yours). I have been going out a lot since the exam – I [meet] so very many people here; I go to them one after the other and the list seems endless. However I am going to Bristol in a few days. It will be quiet there – no people, no shows or invitations for three months, so a little fatigue does not matter. Anyhow I am not getting thinner or weaker. I have begun to laugh (not giggle) rather a lot – that ought to be a good thing but I am not sure that it is – I never know whether I laugh because I am amused, or to hide some other feeling or just like that for nothing. Some people remarked that I have become younger & gayer – but I don't know that I feel it. And that 'laughing business' I do not like. However.

I do not know how I drifted on to this subject – or what I was going to say. Oh yes, the exam – I thought – was pretty beastly and in my opinion I did the papers much worse than last time. But the examiners probably thought otherwise – fortunately for me – and they have declared that they are satisfied with my work. In other words I have passed Responsions – all but Latin, the toughest subject. I did not appear for it this time. I think I will do it in March, along with the Entrance exam. Do you think it is wise to apply to another college – other than Somerville, I mean – just in case there is no vacancy there? Lots of people here advise that.

In one letter[1] of yours you ask me about the girl I am taking care of or some such thing. I am not taking care of anyone. Shanta Gandhi, a Gujerati, was at the Vakils with me and we were rather good friends. She comes from Kathiawar (but is in no way related to Bapu). Her father is the State Engineer there. Shanta took her I.Sc.[2] in India and wants to study medicine here. She has just appeared for her College Entrance & a University exam – about the same time as I had my Responsions. We thought it would be nice to stay near or together.

I had lunch with Agatha on the 25th and the next day she sailed for India. I met Psyche Captain also.

---

1. Refers to letter No. 174.
2. I.Sc: Intermediate Science. The Intermediate examination had to be passed after finishing school, before a student could be admitted to a degree course.

I think you had best send your next letter to Bristol. You know the address, do you not? Badminton School, Westbury-on-Trym, Bristol. I shall be there up till the Xmas holidays. Somehow I do not fancy the idea of Bristol much. But I have settled everything now. Besides I think it will do me good in many ways. I can't possibly stay in London to study. Miss Darbyshire does not want me to stay in Oxford before I come up to College. So why not Bristol?

It has become very chilly and damp. The weather experts prophesy a hard severe winter. It is going to be awful, I am sure.

I am looking forward to next summer. For I will come to India – I do so want to come for several reasons but chiefly because of you. I do miss you terribly. At times there is a terrible desire to fly to you.

With all all my love,
Indu

I enclose some snaps taken in Regent's Park.

---

179.   Badminton School,
                                          Westbury-on-Trym,
                                                    Bristol,
                                   Sunday, 4th October [1936]

Darling,

Do excuse this paper. I have just arrived & my suitcase has not been brought up yet.

The exam was over on the 25th. On the 30th I received a letter from the Principal of this school – Miss Baker – saying that they all realised I needed a holiday & are sorry it cannot be a longer one but they are anxious about my work & are wondering when I would feel inclined to begin work again! So here I am. I am afraid I am far from happy at coming back here. But that is what I usually feel coming to a new institution and I dare say the feeling will wear off. But I can never feel as one with the others – for I hate the continuous noise – the sound of loud voices – eternal chattering & pattering and all the stupid rules & regulations that must be in a big public school. However I shall have to work terribly hard and that will make time fly. March and the dreaded exam will arrive only too soon. But I will be glad when it is over and how!

Anyway I do not propose staying here later than Christmas, unless the tuition goes on so marvellously that it will be best to stay on . . .

It is funny how living in a city by oneself, exploring the roads & thoroughfares, one grows to love it. Such is my feeling for London. I got to love the crowds, the parks & everything. Perhaps because it was the first time I was entirely on my own. A tiny little room to sleep in – the whole city to live in and no one to bother about you – to go & come & do whatever you want to and just when & how you want to. Sometimes it was lonely but I liked it. If only one would not miss some people so much.

In London I saw several shows. The last one *The Insect Play* was rather unusual & interesting. A good film I saw was *Anthony Adverse* – the novel was sold like hot cakes last year in spite of the bulk.

I went into the Kohinoor restaurant the other day. Krishna Vir turned up & scolded me for not having informed him of my arrival. He invited me to lunch. Needless to say we had such an enormous meal that I almost felt sick. Talking of meals – Psyche Captain invited me & two other people to supper & the theatre. We went to the Cumberland and had a nine course supper & champagne!! (I don't know how I survived it.) We arrived half an hour late for the show, which was rather stupid anyway – *Storm in a Tea Cup*.

All my love,
Indu

Do take rest whenever you get the opportunity & take care of yourself.

———————

180.   In train – Grand Trunk Express
to Madras,
5th October, 1936

Darling Indu,
Where are you now, I wonder? What are you doing? Are you having some rest after your examinations? These thoughts come to me as I rush along to the south. I reach Madras soon and later on, after three days, I go further south to Madura and beyond, almost to Cape Comorin which we visited, Mummie and you and I, more than five years ago. This journey makes me feel that I am going further away from you. And so I am, but it is not so much the actual distance that counts but the fact that news of you does not reach me regularly and it is delayed. In Allahabad I have a sense of nearness to you – letters come more or less regularly – and there are so many things belonging to you which give me a feeling that you are not far. But when I travel away I seem to lose touch with you and I feel a little bit lonelier than I usually do. Lonely in the midst of crowds, vast and friendly crowds, overwhelming one with their affection.

Yesterday I was in Wardha and saw Bapu and then I took train and at most stations since then, night and day-time, there have been crowds. A tiring business. I am a little frightened of this Madras tour, for I fear it might almost prove too much for me. Because I have hardly been this way at all, the crowds are all the more eager to see me.

I am being promoted. I came to Wardha from Allahabad in a third-class compartment. From Wardha I was asked to travel second and so now I am sitting and writing in lordly fashion. But as we near Madras, I am told that we shall be transferred to a small special train which will take us to Madras. Pomp and circumstance! And then a procession – and then meetings, addresses, parties, and everywhere speeches.

During my tour I shall be taken to Pondicherry also – French India. I am rather looking forward to it. I have never been to any of the French spots in India. It was a little unusual for me to receive telegrams in French from Pondicherry.

I wish Nan had come with me. This would have been a new experience for her.

Keep fit, my dear. The mind functions well only when the body is well.

I have no idea when the airmail goes from Madras. Probably I have just missed it. And then airmails are so irregular now. Imperial Airways have had a bunch of disasters.

Love,

Your loving
Papu

This letter was too late for the airmail. So I kept it. I am just adding some pictures from the papers here.

Love,
P.

181.   [Badminton School]
                                             Bristol,
                                             6th October, 1936

Darling Papuli,
Your letter of the 24th[1] arrived this morning.

Yes, everything awakens old memories – snaps, stray letters, clothes, ordinary conversation. Somehow all thoughts drift back to the past. I thought one forgot with time but I find it is otherwise. At first I had not realised what had happened but with time – each day – that realisation presses deeper into the heart. It almost pushes out all else. Sometimes I do not know what to do. People say one gets used to everything. Of course

---

1. Refers to letter No. 176.

one does – even to torture & sorrow, but as long as it continues, does it help to be used to it?

But why do you have to look at the luggage & other domestic affairs when you have such a lot to do? Surely someone could manage that – even Hari.

I should love to meet Mrs Huxley. What does she do – I mean apart from managing the house? And before her marriage?

I am afraid you will have to wait for a good photograph until I return to London. I sent you lots of snapshots last week. How did you like them?

9th October

Nearly a week since I arrived and still in bed. The rest has done me a tremendous lot of good but now I'm getting fed up and anxious to begin work. What is more, the cold shows no signs of going away in spite of my swallowing all sorts of disagreeable stuff & gargling & what not. But if the sun comes out I will be allowed to get up at about midday today – no signs of it yet!

Your letter of the 28th[1] arrived yesterday. I read about the search or rather was told about it by Krishna Vir, the other day when I went to lunch with him.

I am sorry about Mini for I am terribly fond of animals – especially dogs. But this was the first I heard of her and I suppose will be the last. Personally I think pets should not be kept in Anand Bhawan. No one looks after them properly – no one has the time. No wonder the poor little things die – it is a shock to everyone and then they forget & it happens all over again and again.

10th October

Excuse this many-dated affair.

I got up in time for tea yesterday and attended a lecture on Europe in the sixteenth century . . .

I am thinking of becoming a member of the Left Book Club. Have you heard of it? Its aim is to help in the terribly urgent struggle for World Peace & a better social & economic order & against Fascism by spreading knowledge. All a member has to do is to buy a book – the book of the month – from them every month. This book costs 2/6 in their special edition, whereas to the general public it may be sold for any price up to 12/6. They publish worthwhile books – selected by Laski,[2] Strachey[3] & Gollancz.[4]

1. Refers to letter No. 177.
2. Harold Joseph Laski: political scientist and Labour leader.
3. John Strachey: British Labour leader.
4. Victor Gollancz: left-wing author and publisher.

In the *Manchester Guardian* I read a rather comic statement – considering the circumstances – of Lessona, the Italian Colonial Secretary. He says that experiments in settling the Italians will first be made in the area around Addis Ababa & that land belonging to natives will be respected!

Tons of love,
Indu

Have you read *Arabia Felix*?[1] If not, do you want to?

---

182.   Somewhere in Tamil Nad
(my geography is not strong enough
to remember their odd names)
15th October, 1936

Darling Indu,

For some days I have been attempting to write to you – in vain. I am carried along in a rush from early morning to midnight and it is not easy to write after a twenty-hour stretch of speaking and motoring alternately. The way the people have come to meet us everywhere has been astounding. Yesterday I was within hail of Kanya Kumari and I did so want to go there. I like this place and especially the feeling that I am on the uttermost tip of India. But it was sixty miles away and that meant 120 miles there and back on an indifferent road. This could not possibly be fitted in to my terribly heavy programme.

Today I was at Madura and I made a point of going to the famous temple there. It was a private visit. Hardly anyone was told of it. But, lo and behold, a great crowd surrounded the temple and followed me into its vast corridors. A strange way to see a place, with a mass of seething humanity! My ideas of the temple are consequently vague. But the vast size was impressive and sometimes oppressive. The corridors were enormous, and huge statuary, some of which [was] very good. I was taken to the inner sanctum, the holy of holies, the shrine of Menakshi, an incarnation of Parvati. A great honour. I was struck by the curious way of the Hindu faith which refuses to part with any born within its fold. Here I am accused of irreligion and yet treated as one who is a devout follower. A present of a silk scarf was also given to me – a special gift of the goddess. I realised in this vast temple with its innumerable corridors and inner chambers, faintly lighted up, the great psychological influence of these religious edifices. How they must impress and rather frighten the multitudes and increase the power of the priesthood. That temple put me in mind of the

---

1. *Arabia Felix: Across the Empty Quarter of Arabia* by Bertram Thomas.

days when the priests were triumphant and ruled over the minds of men, of the great temples of Egypt and Mesopotamia and, to some extent, of the great cathedrals. There are not many people who can resist this numbing effect.

I have never seen so many roses in my life as here. Everywhere there are enormous garlands of roses, fat, heavy things, each containing a thousand to two thousand roses. In the course of the day I might get 200 of such garlands! They are not specially good roses but even so their very number is overwhelming. It seems such a pity to waste them, and what am I to do with these quantities? The car gets filled up and then I distribute them to girls and women and children by the roadside.

Sometimes very artistic decorations are made for our meetings, festoons of flowers, roses and chrysanthemums, the meeting area shaded with a bamboo network covered with green leaves.

But I must not go on. I am due to be back in Allahabad on the 22nd.

I have had no news of you for ages. No doubt you must have written and your letter is following me about.

Love,

Your loving,
Papu

---

183.   Badminton School,
                                                              Bristol,
                                                    21st October, 1936

Darling Papu,

I'm breaking school regulations by writing on a weekday – especially as I have four essays & heaps of other work waiting. However it cannot be helped.

I woke up this morning with rather a wretched feeling – a strange emptiness and a desperate loneliness. As the day goes on the feeling grows. I attended a couple of lectures but don't know what they were about and it was impossible to read or do any work. To make matters worse B.M.B. (the headmistress) said that I must not go to London during the holidays but go to Cornwall. I agree that London is not a healthy place but it is the only place where I have friends. When one's so dreadfully lonely is that not worth a tremendous lot? I suggested Switzerland. She said it was a long, tiring & cold journey & wondered whether it was worth it. I don't want to go to Cornwall among strangers – especially after spending three months in a school and going to spend another two months. For I have decided to return here after the hols and stay up till the exam in March. I don't feel too happy about it but I think it's best for my work and, after all, one ought to have some discipline – brave words! I only wish one's heart always agreed with the head.

In going to Switzerland one consideration is the cost, though it is cheaper than it was.

Please write about this to me & also to B.M.B. She said she has written to you. Personally I should like to be at least a week in London & the rest of the hols on the Continent somewhere – we will probably get a month's vacation. I promise to take care of myself.

Someone told me this morning that from next year airmail to India will leave six times a week & will only cost 1½d for ¼oz. (She says she saw it in the *Times*.) That's lovely, isn't it?

With tons of love,
Indu

Agatha must have reached India by now.

184.
Anand Bhawan,
Allahabad,
29th October, 1936

Darling,

I have just returned after a hundred mile drive in a car from Fatehpur district where I had a number of meetings today. It is eleven p.m. . . .

I do not think I have thanked you for the snaps you sent me – those taken in Regent's Park. Some of them are quite good. But you should have a decent photograph taken when you go to London.

Lu [Louise Geissler] wrote to me that you have to put up with a large correspondence and this troubles you a lot. Then you tell me of your numerous engagements when in London. This kind of thing is terribly boring after a while. One can escape the engagements by going out of London, but what can one do with the letters one gets? Having myself to deal with an enormous pile of them, I know how troublesome they are. I have learnt by long practice how to deal with them. Some – the useless ones – I destroy, many others I pass on to someone else to answer with brief notes on the margin. Still a large number remain and I try to deal with them personally. I do it rapidly enough. You cannot adopt these dodges and you cannot have other's help. So you had better discourage most of the writers who are not worthwhile. Gladstone used to say that most letters answer themselves after some time if you simply leave them alone. I am not passing on this advice to you. Still one must choose worthwhile persons to see and correspond with, or else one is snowed under by the wrong sort of people.

About Mrs Huxley, I shall write to her about you one of these days. And then when you go to London you can drop her a line. She is certainly worth meeting and so is her husband. I know nothing about her or her work except that she is Belgian and is Aldous's wife. Many interesting persons go to her house. A frequent visitor is Gerald Heard[1] whom I liked very much.

Certainly join the Left Book Club. I have myself been thinking of doing so. *Arabia Felix* I have not read, though I have heard of the book. It is I believe a book worth reading though I am not likely to have the time for it.

Your decision about your subjects is probably right. Anyway you are in the best position to decide. Personally I do not think you will have any real difficulty about your Entrance exam because the subjects are interesting and they require general intelligence, clear thinking and a capacity to write, and not mugging. The only difficulty you might have is in the Latin and even there you have considerable time now. There seems to me to be no reason whatever for pessimism. I often think how absurd it is for me to be pessimistic about anything. When I think of the horror in Spain everything else seems trivial in comparison . . .

I am writing to Krishna Menon today, suggesting to him to come to India soon for a few months at least. If he agrees to do so, he might start by the end of November.

I am feeling sleepy now . . .

I enclose a letter from Dol Amma.

Love,

Your loving,
Papu

---

185.   [Badminton School]
Bristol,
31st October [1936]

Papu darling

Thanks terrifically for your letters.

Dr Katju[2] & his son Ramji are coming over tomorrow, probably by car. I shall be glad to see him for he will have first-hand news of you & the rest of the family. Somehow you seem very near these days and this little interview will bring you nearer still and so I look forward to it.

A friend of mine, Shanta, is coming over from London. She will soon be

---

1. Gerald Heard: British author.
2. Dr Kailash Nath Katju: lawyer and nationalist leader who later held ministerial office in the Government of India.

arriving – I shall go to the station to fetch her & we will have lunch out. She will stay the night & leave on Sunday. This is half-term & almost all the girls have gone home – the ones who are staying here are going to a picnic. In the evening everybody is going to the opera – *Cavalleria Rusticana* & *Pagliacci*. I think I shall go too.

Sunday, 1st November

Dr Katju has just been. His train was forty-five minutes late – so he had to do without tea: he left in half an hour. He forgot to bring the presents. But I expect they will reach me tomorrow or the day after by post. Dr K. will tell you that I am quite unchanged & as thin as ever! By the way, so far I have been gaining ¼ lb per week!! My weight is 89 lbs. I gained 3 lbs in London in spite of the fatigue & the exam in 1 month. In 1 ½ months here I gained ½ lb!

Shanta has also left. She seemed to bring a bit of London with her. We went to the Bristol Opera. It was nothing extraordinary – but not at all bad.

The weather is miserable. If it's sunny and warm in the morning it is sure to end up by being cold & rainy and vice versa. Because of these sudden changes almost everyone has caught colds – not me, touch wood!

The rain it raineth every day.

The unjust hath the just's umbrella!

Is it not stupid? Some bishop sent it to the *Times* as a comment on their article on umbrellas. But at the moment I feel its truth for my umbrella is lying in the Lost Property Office! I cannot fetch it till Monday.

I find it rather difficult to concentrate on my work, these days. And I have a great desire to read books other than textbooks. If I do, I cannot get my work done. I have just read Macartney's *Walls have Mouths*. Perhaps you saw its reviews in English papers. It is an account of Macartney's ten years' penal servitude – describing everything in English prisons.

Through the Left Book Club I get two of the latest books per month. If you like I could send them to you. There is a lot of difference between the Club & the general public prices. Of the Left Book Club books – I have also *World Politics 1918–1936* by Palme Dutt[1] and *Under the Axe of Fascism* by Prof. Salvemini. In a few days I will receive John Strachey's *The Theory & Practice of Socialism* & Horrabin's *An Atlas of Current Affairs*.

In French we are doing some poems of Victor Hugo. I think he's grand.

---

1. Rajani Palme Dutt: Marxist leader.

We have just finished 'L'expiation' – an extract from the bigger poem, 'Les Châtiments'! Have you read it, I wonder. It is about the retreat from Moscow. Isn't this beautiful?

> *Quel dieu, quel moissonneur de*
> *l'éternel été*
> *avait, en s'en allant, négligemment jeté*
> *cette faucille d'or dans le champs*
> *des étoiles*[1]

It is from another of his poems. This reminds me how very lovely the sky is nowadays, except when it is hidden by the clouds. The moon was gorgeous last night. I see the Big Bear very well from my bed and the old old habit – asleep for so many years – of watching the stars has awakened. It makes me think of the days when we used to look at them together & when you used to point out each one to me & tell me its name. I remember how thrilled I was as you thus solved part of the mystery of the heavens and first awakened a new sort of interest for them in me.

When I get up in the mornings, I see an ocean of soft white with just a couple of lonely tree-tops peeping above it. It is beautiful to watch it gradually thinning – very slowly one sees vague shapes and then they get more & more distinct and one is surprised that after all the beautiful picture was only the dreary and rather ugly-looking group of houses that one sees every day. The autumn tint of the leaves on the trees and strewn all over the place is exquisite.

I am still rather puzzled about the hols. I have more or less made up my mind about going to Switzerland. But the trouble is, I do not want to go to Bex. I'm so fed up of rules that I could not bear them during the hols. And at Bex they are worse than here in some ways, though in other ways I was much freer. I want to go somewhere not 'chic', with crowds of fashionable, painted-up people & very expensive, but a quiet place with good walks & nice slopes & nice people! I am not at all sure if such a place is available because the place must not be too far away, like Les Voeltes which had one grocer shop with a telephone – the only shopping centre & no post-office!

I have done no work at all during this weekend & so will have to rush during the week. Life here is mostly made of essays – of all descriptions but mainly historical.

With lots of love,
Indu

---

1. For English translation see Appendix C, III.

B.M.B. (the headmistress) sends her regards and wants you to pay a flying visit to Bristol! Wouldn't that be marvellous – but like most v. marvellous things impossible. And far too good to come true.

---

186.   1st November [1936]

Papu darling,

I have just posted a letter[1] to you. In it I quoted a Bishop – but not being quite sure of the lines I left a blank & forgot to fill it up. The thing is:

> The rain it raineth every day,
> upon the just & unjust fellow
> But chiefly on the just, because
> the unjust hath the just's umbrella.[2]

You will probably get this P.C. & the letter together.

My love to Dol Amma and the rest of the family.

Always your loving,
Indu

I am sending you by ordinary post – Left Book Club news-sheet & a snapshot.

---

187.   In train to Calcutta,
                                                   5th November, 1936

Darling,

Yesterday I was in Santiniketan and it was peaceful and quiet there. It was vacation time; the Puja holidays were not over, but still there was a considerable colony resident in Santiniketan and Sriniketan. I stayed at Sriniketan as Gurudev was living there and I had a long long talk with him about many things. My affection for him grows. I found him a little better than he was when I saw him last in Delhi in March, soon after my return from Europe. He was more wide-awake, though age steals over him. And yet he still thinks of travelling abroad and visiting China next summer! But I doubt if he will be able to go. Fortunately some big donations have relieved him of financial anxiety for Santiniketan.

1. Refers to letter No. 185.
2. The actual verse is by Lord Bowen (1835–94):

> The rain it raineth on the just
>   And also on the unjust fella:
> But chiefly on the just because
>   The unjust steals the just's umbrella.

We talked of you and he told me what a good influence you had been for others in Santiniketan. And I fell to wondering what influences had shaped you – how good they were or otherwise – and how you were reacting to your present environment. It is eight months since I saw you, my dear, and I wonder how you are growing and changing. Perhaps in another six months' time we might meet again.

There was Krishna Kripalani there and his wife Nandita[1] and Anil Chanda and one or two others whom I recognised and many whom I did not know.

And now I am off to Calcutta.

Love,

Your loving,
Papu

188.   [Badminton School]
                                                 Bristol,
                             7th November, 1936

Papu darling,

I have your letter of the 29th.[2] Thank you.

My cold is more or less all right. I almost felt like sending news of it to the *Bombay Chronicle*! I have been reading (it is in such big letters that one reads it whether one wants to or not) for the last week, news of Queen Mary's cold, on the top of page 12, beside the Spanish news, in the *Times*! . . .

Meanwhile the rebels get nearer & nearer Madrid. Yesterday was the first attack on the town itself. What is going to happen?* If they win it will be a great help to the Croix de Feu in France & other such organisations in other countries. As it is, Fascism seems to be spreading almost like flames, while the various Labour parties fold their arms & vote for non-intervention. The Fascists in Belgium, Croix de Feu in France, in Switzerland, everywhere Fascist parties are working underground and overground whenever they can. Here in England by many – one could even say most – newspapers the rebels are called 'patriots'. One bright person wrote a letter to a paper, when Moscow first wanted to intervene in Spain, suggesting that the best thing for Eng. to do was to recognise Franco's govt. Then if anyone intervened on behalf of the socialists they'd be against the recognised govt!

Most school debates are on war, peace, the League of Nations & such

1. Nandita Kripalani: granddaughter of Rabindranath Tagore, wife of Krishna Kripalani.
2. Refers to letter No. 184.

subjects. There [is] great talk of Christianity and God – these two arguments are shoved into every possible subject. And Duff Cooper[1] the Secretary for War says, 'It is not a beautiful thing or a desirable thing to kill one's fellow men – it is a hateful thing and a damnable thing – but as it has to be done, it had better be done well.'

Thank you for the things you sent. Dr Katju forgot to bring them with him when he came last Sunday. He sent them by post & I received them yesterday. The bags are beautiful & the sandalwood smells wonderful and they both are so typically Indian. I felt almost at home when I saw them.

I forgot to send you the Left Book Club News last week. I wish to do so this Thursday. I am sending the Oct. & the Nov. ones . . .

With very much love,

Your loving,
Indu

Sunday, 8th November

The result of my swab was negative. I think its awfully lucky for the school. Out of 200 people, only two were 'carriers'. And those two were not boarders but local Bristol ones so they were sent home at once. But we all have to stay in quarantine for a week. If nobody gets it in that time, it means we are quite safe.

Dr Katju told me that Ballo had chucked the silk factory and had taken up aviation and might come over to England. Katju wasn't quite sure, though. Is it true? From what people said of him I shouldn't have thought he would have the guts to do that.

The atmosphere at school is terribly anti-Fascist & very pacifist. B.M.B. is a socialist & so are most of the other teachers – the history one has great tendencies towards Communism. It is interesting to hear them affirm again and again that they are not Communist – in almost every class we are told that. But on the whole, imperialism seems to be inherent in the bones of the girls. But they hate to hear you say so. They worship the King, admire Baldwin[2] & although Eden's[3] popularity is waning off, he is still considered by some as the last word in cherubic innocence!

With very much love,
Indu

*Franco has since entered Madrid.

---

1. Alfred Duff Cooper: a leading member of the British Conservative Party, Secretary of War, 1935–7.

2. Stanley Baldwin: British Prime Minister, 1935–7.

3. Anthony Eden (later Lord Avon): Minister for League of Nations 1935, British Foreign Minister, 1935–8.

189.   14th November, 1936

[Papu darling]
Many happy returns of the day and very best love & kisses to Papu darling.
                              From Indu

This is Kodak's latest. A friend who took this snap in Regent's Park sent me a number of these 'greeting cards'.

———————————◆◆———————————

190.   [Badminton School]
                                        Bristol,
                                        15th November, 1936

Papu darling,
Thanks most awfully much for the cheque. Do you mind if I keep it till the holidays and then buy something in London? For some time I have wanted to buy a gramophone or a wireless. The latter, though a little more expensive (anyway for the gramophone, records will be necessary), seems more worthwhile. Going to piano recitals, etc., means a lot of money and time. And music is a great help to work – indeed sometimes it almost seems a necessity. A gorgeous small radio is available for £5. But you must not spoil me so. Am I not spoilt enough, wherever I go? The more one gets, the more one seems to demand – things that were once a luxury to be dreamt of, become a necessity and so on.
   It is difficult to fit in with the usual English schoolgirl. I have had quite a different life – an entirely different background. Everybody seems to talk for the sake of talking. I hate chatting – unless I have something to say. But I can get used to it, as one does to everything. Though having settled down to a regular school life I feel – dead. (That is the only word which approaches the meaning I wish to convey.)
   Strangely enough, in spite of the 'thick rich cream' I seem to be losing weight regularly. And have almost lost the 4 lbs I gained in London during the last holidays.
   I wrote to the Swiss Travel Bureau and now I am surrounded by bits of hotels, timetables & hundreds of pamphlets & leaflets with the most tempting pictures. I might go to Grindelwald in the Bernese Oberland. I do not wish to go to Bex or to any family – for it will not be possible to study.
   I enclose an article from the *News Chronicle*. I wonder if you have heard of a book called *The English: Are They Human?* I read it years ago in India. It amused me then but I did not think much of it. Now when I came into closer contact with the English, my mind goes back to that book. I am

afraid a lot of the admiration I had for the English has vanished – I mean for the people as a whole. There are many many exceptions – which, as it were, go to prove the general rule. On the other hand, some of the working class – the unemployed are really decent & sympathetic. One meets them often sitting on a roadside bench in the evening, with little clothing in the cold unfriendly darkness. They welcome anything to eat or to cover themselves with; for even the morning's paper their gratitude is infinite. I am afraid the numerous boxes of chocolate given me by Raj Chachi & Psyche and others have helped to bring smiles on several haggard faces. It is so pathetic to see them admire the . . . gaily coloured lids.

I feel I have changed tremendously since you last saw me – I cannot describe it to you and I do not know if you will notice it for it is not expressed outwardly.

I was glad of my stay in Santiniketan – chiefly because of Gurudev. In the very atmosphere there, his spirit seemed to roam and hover over one & follow one with a loving though deep watchfulness. And this spirit, I feel, has greatly influenced my life and thought . . .

You must be back from Calcutta & off to some other place. I get vague news about you through the *B.C.* [Bombay Chronicle] – about three or four weeks late.

With very much love,
Indu

191.

Anand Bhawan,
Allahabad,
19th November, 1936

Darling Indu,

I am back again here – for a day and a half only! Kailash Nath Katju has just been and has told us of his visit to you. He could not tell me anything that was new but still a personal account is pleasing.

On arrival here I found a letter from you and the card with your picture and two books: [Peter] Fleming's *News from Tartary* and Peers's *The Spanish Tragedy*. These two books came from Bristol so I presume you sent them. But why Fleming's book should be a 'Left' book I do not understand. Anyway both books are good and the kind I like. I accepted them as birthday presents. I had a rather unusual birthday this year. I spent it in motoring from place to place and addressing about twenty-five meetings. I travelled 200 miles by car in the course of the day. The people in the villages and small towns I visited got scent of the fact that it was my birthday and I had many little gifts and blessings from Brahmans reciting Vedic verses.

The verses about 'the rain it raineth every day', etc., are not frightfully new. I remember repeating them to people when I was at Cambridge. Perhaps the old Bishop heard them about the same time!

About the 'Left' books, send me any you do not want to keep. But if you want to keep any, then you had better do so. I can usually get copies here. I have got Dutt's *World Politics* – also Horrabin's Atlas.

About your Christmas holidays a bright idea has just struck me. Why not go to Praha? *En route* you may stop in Suisse for a while. Praha or some other place in C.S.R. [Czechoslovak Republic] will be new & interesting and your dear friend Prof. Lesny will be there. Nanu I suppose will be available. In Suisse Bex will certainly not be exciting, and if you go all by yourself to some place that will be dull and boring. So C.S.R. seems to be indicated. It may cost you a little more in travelling expenses and the like but not much more, and it will be worthwhile. During my student days I was disinclined to go to new places during my hols and I have regretted that ever since. Chances do not repeat themselves. So take such as come your way.

In Praha you might meet Shiela Grant Duff unless she comes home for Christmas.

I do not remember anything about Harold Bing though the name seems vaguely familiar.

Ballo is carrying on with his silk factory though I think his heart is in flying and he occasionally indulges in it. He is a very nice, clean-limbed boy but his parents, I am afraid, are terribly keen on looking after him and deciding everything for him . . .

I have been sending you by the ordinary post bundles of newspaper clippings – chiefly my pictures! I am treated almost like a movie star.

I enclose a card which came here addressed to you. Do you remember the name? The couple who were with us in the pension at Badenweiler – the blond man & his young bride – have had a son.

All my love,

Your loving,
Papu

Today is your birthday! We have celebrated it by having *Khir*.[1] What will be your address during the hols?

---

1. A sweet dish made of rice and milk.

192.　　　　　　　　　　　　　　　　　　[Badminton School]
　　　　　　　　　　　　　　　　　　　　　　Bristol,
　　　　　　　　　　　　　　　　　21st November [1936]

Darlingest Papu,
There wasn't a letter from you this week but probably you are awfully
busy.

I am busy too – is it not strange, the more one does the more one is able
to do. But whatever one is doing, one is busy. I have a lot to do & it takes all
my time and yet I feel that if I had to do a few more things I could manage
them, without feeling busier than I do now.

I have been trying to analyse my loneliness. It is I think due to my not
having any real friend. I have got friends but none who really understand
me, none to whom I can speak what I feel – most people think I am gone
off my head slightly. There are people who understand one side of me &
others, who sympathise with other parts but no one can realise what the
whole is. However.

It is beginning to get cold & foggy. Today we had frost for the first time
this year. But the cold does not stimulate one & freshen one as it does in
Suisse – here it just gets into one's very bones and somehow makes one
feel old & it gives one a desire to rush to the fire & sleep.

During the holidays, I am going to Switzerland with friends – probably
to Grindelwald in the Bernese Oberland. I have never been in that part of
Suisse before – it ought to be fun if there is enough snow. I shall go for
eighteen days, most probably & stay the rest of the holidays in London. I
promise to be good. Our hols begin on the 18th of Dec. How time flies!
The vacations are almost here & will as soon be over. And then will come
the exam – I am dreading it – and then the visit to India, to which I am
looking forward, oh, so eagerly!
　　　　　　　　　　　With very much love,
　　　　　　　　　　　　　　Indu

　　　　　　　　　　　　　　　　　　　　　23rd November
Meghaduta[1] has just arrived. What a beautiful gift. It is like you to think of
the right thing. You cannot imagine what joy it brought to me – the
sunshine and the warmth of India in this damp & dreary land.
　　　　　　　　　　　Love,
　　　　　　　　　　　　Indu

---

1. A well-known poem by the Sanskrit poet Kalidasa.

193.   Dugadda–Garhwal,
                                                  25th November, 1936

My darling one,
I am sitting in the mountains again, or rather the outer fringe of them. The
morning I reached Kotdwar, which, as its name implies, is the gate, the
gate of Garhwal. This mountain district of our province is singularly cut
off from the outside world. Except to Lansdowne,[1] which is a military
centre, there are hardly any roads, and so the outsider seldom comes. I
never entered it properly before, although I have skirted the fringe. It is a
huge district, 200 miles long, sprawling over the Himalayan foothills &
mountains.

Dugadda means the two rivers. How uncouth is *gaddhā* for river –
compare it to the melodious, flowing *nadi, jharra, dariya*![2] Poor, poverty
stricken areas, with fine human material, as we often find in the mountains. But Garhwal has become famous for the Garhwali regiment which
refused to fire in Peshawar during the Civil Disobedience movement of
1930. Even now two of the Indian officers – Chandra Singh and Narayan
Singh – are in prison for that offence.

It is chilly here even at midday. At night it must be very cold. I am here
for a few hours only and this evening I return. I would like to go in the
interior but I may not. There has been one great disappointment. Did I
write to you that I intended going to Badrinath, the famous place of
pilgrimage high up in the Himalayas? I was so looking forward to it. I could
not of course go on a fortnight's journey over the mountains. But for some
time past an air service functions from Hardwar and goes about two-
thirds of the way. I cannot go to Badrinath because of the difficulty of
landing there. But I had hoped to be able to fly over Badrinath without
alighting there and have a good look at the vast expanses of snow and ice.
All this has gone as I find that the service stopped because of the coming
winter. I feel deprived of a pleasure I had been looking forward to so
greatly.

I was at Bareilly for three days for the Provincial Conference. M. N.
Roy[3] came there, just discharged after five years of prison, broken in
health, his fine straight body rather bent and the signs of age on him. I

---

1. A hill station in the Punjab.
2. Hindi equivalent for river or rivulet.
3. Manabendra Nath Roy: prominent Marxist thinker and activist, who was associated
with Lenin in the shaping of Comintern policy towards the colonies. He founded the
Radical Humanist Movement in the 1930s.

have sent him to Lucknow to consult doctors. Then he will come to Allahabad and stay with us for a few days early in December. Agatha Harrison is also coming and Charlie Andrews. So we shall have a mixed lot in Anand Bhawan.

The Garhwalis are gathering for the meeting. Many have tramped fifty miles over the mountains. Simple people, I like them. But then I like mountain folk for we have also some mountain blood in our veins. I am going now to the meeting and I shall speak standing under a big precipice – a noble background.

Love,

Your loving,
Papu

194.   [Badminton School]
Bristol,
6th December [1936]

Darling Papu,

Thanks most frightfully for your letter of the 25th.[1] Anand Bhawan has always been a meeting place of all types of people. Somehow it is difficult to imagine Agatha with Roy.

I am so sorry you could not go to Badrinath. It would have been a break from your endless meeting & speechifying – a brief holiday. In two weeks' time I shall be on a holiday among the snows of La Suisse. I feel very guilty for having so many holidays, when those who need them most can't get them.

I shall miss you in Wengen – I hear the view of the Jungfraujoch & other ranges is magnificent.

The excitement over the constitutional crises has overshadowed foreign affairs. There are pages about the King[2] & the Cabinet & extracts from other pages about the same subject – the war in Spain has receded into the background. Hitler might use the opportunity for another of his dramatic coups. Personally, my sympathies are with the King. Although I do agree with most of the newspapers which have long articles about the duties of a king-emperor – only the *News Chronicle* & the *Star* show any consideration for the man's feelings. *Bombay* [*Chronicle?*] thinks that he will give in this time and wait for public opinion to help him. As it is, large crowds gathered outside the Palace, shouting that they were with him.

---

1. Refers to letter No. 193.
2. British newspapers first printed stories about the relationship between Mrs Simpson and King Edward VIII on 3rd December 1936. The King abdicated on 10th December.

Yesterday, I believe, there was another crowd outside the Duke of York's place saying, 'We want Edward – We won't have the Duke of York', with huge posters, 'Come & shout for the King', etc. But perhaps this is the beginning of the end of the monarchy in England.

The Secretary of the Students' Career Association came and gave us two lectures on careers needing a university degree & otherwise. Of course she talked from the practical & material side.

How are you keeping?

Tons of love,
Indu

I expect you've heard of the poor old Crystal Palace being burned down. It wasn't particularly beautiful but the fireworks were jolly good. I hear you've been re-elected President. This will mean more work and I do wish you'd take a holiday.

195.　　　　　　　　　　　　　　　　　Anand Bhawan,
　　　　　　　　　　　　　　　　　　　　　　Allahabad,
　　　　　　　　　　　　　　　　　8th December, 1936

Darling,
I have been wanting to write to you at some leisure and some length – perilous thought for [it] results in my waiting for this leisure. Four days ago I was rushed and so I did not write. Today I have been reduced to this, that I have to scribble these lines in the early morning, just before catching the mail to Bombay. It is difficult to develop a mood for writing under these circumstances, and yet my mind has been full of odd ideas and fancies seeking to clothe themselves with ink and appear bravely on the written page. They have no great importance and I suppose they will retire and be for the moment forgotten, cropping up at odd times from some odd corner of my brain.

You must be in London or may be in Switzerland when this letter reaches you. Have a good time and enjoy your holidays and come back refreshed in body and mind. For me Christmas Week will be the heaviest of all. For it is practically certain now that I shall be President again of the Congress, and the burden is a heavy one. I feel rather flat and stale already and my capacity for work seems to be less than it was. Even a week's change would put an end to this but I shall have no such week till the end of February.

Agatha has been here – she spent only a day and a half with us but it was good to have some first-hand information and impressions of you. She has gone back to Wardha.

I enclose a snap taken at Sriniketan. Nandita is standing near me.
The train calls me now – I must go away.
Love,

Your loving,
Papu

196.

Anand Bhawan,
Allahabad,
14th December, 1936

Darling,
You must be leaving school for the Christmas holidays. After a period of
hard work a holiday is pleasant and I hope you will enjoy it. And through
you I shall also have my share of joy. The present is rather a heavy time for
me. The Congress is coming and I am again to be its President. The
presidential address is the next job for me – a difficult one, for my mind is
tired and stale. Ten days in the Himalayas would freshen me but I could
not possibly manage them. Within a week we go to Faizpur and so far I
have not given even thought to the address. There are so many other
things to do, urgent matters which cannot be overlooked. After tomorrow
I think I shall lock myself in.

So you have changed![1] Of course you have and you should at your age. I
find myself growing and changing even at my age. Strangers may not
notice such changes for they see the surface only, but when there is
an emotional bond between two persons even slight moods become
apparent. A gesture, a word, a way of looking or speaking betrays the
change. So you are not likely to pass unnoticed by me, or rather the change
in you. Only the dull and self-centred ones remain more or less static. And
we are not dull and too narrow, are we?

Edward Thompson, whose article you sent me, has paid us a rather nice
compliment. 'You Nehrus,' he writes to me, 'have been very lucky in many
ways, and lucky most of all in your charming and splendid women.' He
was thinking of Mummie perhaps, about whom he had read in my book,
and he had recently met Nan. He goes on to say: 'Your Letters to Indira
are an altogether charming record. If she will regard my wife and myself as
friends we shall feel honoured; and she will find we are friends.' They live
at Oxford. So when you go there you might meet them. They will help you
to form your ideas about the English as a race. He writes a very stupid
article (the one you sent me) and yet in his own way he is perfectly straight
and honest and keen on doing the right thing.

1. See letter No. 190.

I was amused to read about your reactions to the English. They are a curious people. I must say I like many of their qualities – most of all their restraint. It impresses one. It is an aristocratic quality. But when the aristocrat becomes afraid of losing his special privileges he comes down the scale immediately. And so the English people, fearful now of losing their special position, are losing the good qualities they possessed. Yet some remain. Unhappily we have always come into touch with the wrong side of them. That was inevitable as our relationship was all wrong.

I suppose the change of kings and all that lay behind it has excited people a lot in England. Yet I must say that everybody behaved rather decently. The human element in the drama was powerful and when kings behave as simple humans, people are gripped by the story. On the whole Edward came out rather well. Not as a very great person, but at any rate as one who refused to behave as an automaton and who could decide for himself in spite of all the pressure that was brought to bear on him. I listened to his farewell speech on the wireless.

All my love,

Your loving,
Papu

197.   Anand Bhawan,
Allahabad,
21st December, 1936

Darling,

I am packing up to go to Faizpur, for I go tomorrow morning. Hurriedly I have written my address,[1] a very scrappy affair. It is being sent to you by air.

Feroze [Gandhi] has sent me a picture of Mummie's done by a French artist. I wonder if you have seen it. It is a remarkably fine thing. The eyes are bubbling over with laughter and the whole face is so alive.

As I write I am waiting for news by phone and telegram of the result of nominations for elections. Today is nomination day. Nan is in Cawnpore, Ranjit is in the District Court here, Uma Bhabi is in Farukhabad. Finding it difficult to defeat us in open contest, our opponents are trying their level best to get our candidates disqualified on some technical plea. The attack on Nan is the fiercest, as she is opposing Lady Kailash Srivastava.[2] Very

1. Jawaharlal Nehru was President of the fiftieth session of the Indian National Congress held at Faizpur in December 1936.

2. Lady Kailash Srivastava: wife of Sir J. P. Srivastava. She stood for election to the U.P. Legislative Assembly from Kanpur in 1937 against Vijaya Lakshmi Pandit.

soon people will be coming here in crowds for the court so I had better end this.

Love,

Your loving,
Papu

A multitude of good wishes for the New Year – and may we meet soon!

---

198.   Y.W.C.A.,
                                                        London,
                                           22nd December [1936]

Darling Papu,

Your letter of the 14th[1] has just come. London again! Compared to Bristol it is very warm – indeed it is like autumn still. The stuffiness tires one even when one does nothing. Yesterday morning I went shopping – just two or three odds & ends. And I had tea with Agatha's sister, Ruth.

I love Christmas – at least the few days before Christmas: the shops are lovely, the people's faces are lighted up, the whole atmosphere is such a happy one.

Two days ago I was taken to see a film called – *Green Pastures*. You must have heard of it. It was banned a year or so ago for it shows Heaven, paradise & 'De Lawd' as the Negroes see them, that is, as they are themselves. Heaven, by the way, is full of 'fish fries' & 6d cigars can be had free for the asking. The whole cast is Negro. It was a very unusual picture & very charming. What struck me most was the utter simplicity of the whole thing. European actors could never have had that effect. The film was worth seeing.

There was a great deal of excitement over Edward's abdication for many reasons & Mrs Simpson was not the most important one. It had been well known for some time that the King & Parliament, or rather Cabinet, did not get on at all well together. Two or three times he openly spoke against their policy. And now Liberal and other papers as well as people 'in the know' say that there has been a 'lot of dirty work' behind the scenes.

With lots of love,
Indu

I shall be in Wengen till Jan. 2nd. I do hope the Congress will not be too tiring.

---

1. Refers to letter No. 196.

PART III

Indira Comes into Her Own
(1937–9)

199.   In train,
                                                    4th January, 1937

Darling,
I wrote to you[1] before going to Faizpur, two weeks ago, and there has been
this big gap since. The Congress is over now with all its huge crowds and
stress of work and you will read about it in the papers. Compared to
Lucknow it was a peaceful affair and there was not so much mental strain
on me. We did our work rapidly and in a businesslike way and ended
sooner than was expected. Indeed we had to, for the very success of this
village[2] was more than we had bargained or arranged for. Nearly 200,000
persons are said to have poured into Faizpur and to feed them itself was a
terrible problem. In a big city there are shops and large stocks of food but
not so in a village. So I hurried through the business and finished the
Congress on the 28th night. The next day there was a committee meeting
and then I stole a day for Ajanta, which was not far. Quite a crowd went
with us. I would much rather have gone quietly with a few friends. But that
was not to be and I can seldom go anywhere now quietly.
    How beautiful are the painted Bodhisattvas[3] and the women of Ajanta!
After more than a thousand years of decay and covering over with dirt, and
scratching by man and beast, still they live on those walls and fill one with
longing for this beauty of mind and body, so far so unattainable. So they
look today. What must they have been long years ago when the paint was
fresher and the legends they embody vivid in people's minds. And what of
the unknown artists who created them with all love and reverence. And
what of that culture which flourished in this old land of ours in the dim
past, how rich its content was, how splendid its imagining, how titanic its
conception!
    One looks at those lovely and graceful figures almost with pain. They
have a dreamlike quality, far removed from the vulgarity and cheapness of
the life we see. There is no haste about them, only a slumberous ease and
peace.
    You and I must go there together one day and feast our eyes on this
beauty that our forefathers created.
    After this dream of the past, the present claimed my attention. Im-
mediately I started on my election tour from the Central Provinces. Then
two days in Allahabad and now I am on the move again. In seven weeks
now, till the 22nd February, I shall be rushing about, not remaining in one

    1. Refers to letter No. 197.
    2. The annual session of the Congress was generally held in some large town.
However, in December 1936 it was held for the first time in a village called Faizpur.
    3. One who is on the way to the attainment of perfect knowledge. Hence – 'a future
Buddha.'

place for two days. But the seven weeks will pass and another month or two and then we shall meet each other, my dear, and I shall seek a little rest from politics, if only for a short while. Among other things, I have a visit to Burma in mind in summer. There is some work to be done there and I want to make of this an excuse for a visit. We might go together, might we not?

You wrote to me some time back that you had sent me some of the Left Book Club books. I have not received any. Which books did you send?

I suppose by the time this reaches you, you will be back in England. I hope you had good sport at Wengen and are returning full of freshness and energy.

I am sending you by ocean mail some pictures of Ajanta.

Love,

Your loving,
Papu

———

200.   43, Belsize Park,
London N.W. 3,
9th January, 1937

Papu darling,

I am afraid I have been awfully irregular with my airmail these last weeks.

Well, here is 1937 and half the holiday is over. When I got off the train at Victoria I had not the vaguest idea where I was going to stay – I hated bothering any friends such as Miss Harrison or Mrs Grant Duff for I shall be in London quite a few days. I went into the nearest phone box & rang up various likely places with no success. There is a rush of foreigners to London because of various conferences & of course the holidays. The Y.W.C.A. & all such places are quite full up. The only thing to do was to leave my luggage somewhere & find a room. So I tramped & tramped. It was a good idea coming to Swiss Cottage for most of the houses in this locality have rooms to let. But no such luck, every house was full. Just as I had given up hope, I decided to have one more try. I knocked at No. 43, Belsize Park, and here I am in an awfully nice room. There is not much view but it is very nicely furnished and is cheerful and fairly big.

Outside the West End, London looked awfully dull and dark & gloomy. It seems so strange after the bright whiteness & sunshine of Switzerland.

C.F.A.[1] is in England and if he comes to London before I leave for Bristol I shall see him. He will have first-hand news of you. I hear he is not very well.

---

1. C.F.A.: C. F. Andrews.

The English papers were quite enthusiastic over Bapu's speech at the Congress. I wonder if you could let me have the full text of it sometime.

I was perfectly all right all the time I was in Switzerland – pink cheeks, etc., all complete. (They were caused more by the sun than anything else, probably & became quite painful at times – for instance when I tried to grin from ear to ear!) But no sooner had I set foot on English soil, everyone on the train, the buses, restaurants & tubes had a cold or a cough or a slight attack of the flu. I have managed to get rather a nasty cough. Otherwise I'm flourishing. I am glad you liked Mummie's picture done by the German artist. I have not seen it, although it is a copy of a snap I have. There are so very few good pictures of Mummie.

I wonder if I told you that Mrs Margarita Barns[1] – I think Puphi knows her – asked me for a good photograph or a snap of yours, not a studio one. I sent her the only one I had – the one in which you are examining a sketch of yours. I hear it is being put in some book or magazine or something.

It is amazing the way you are carrying on. Only I do wish you would try to squeeze in some rest in between – I am sure it would help you tremendously.

With very much love,
Indu

I have not met Vidya – I do not know where she is. I hear she has passed in her exam. I had lunch with Mrs Grant Duff yesterday. She sends you her best wishes. Shiela is, I believe, still in Prague. At Mrs G.D.'s I met rather an interesting Prof. Maulik. He does something about insects at the London University & has just written a fat book on Indian Beetles. He is a great admirer of yours.

Indu

11th January
I am sending you two snaps taken in Wengen. Am leaving for Bristol on the 18th. What shall I do if I fail in the exam? Try again next year?

---

201.   In train,
                                         14th January, 1937

Darling Indu,
It is long since I have written to you. I live in a kind of moving cyclone – in trains and motors and vast gatherings. In trains one might occasionally write but in a car that is impossible, and I have spent my time chiefly in

---

1. Margarita Barns: British journalist closely associated with Indian politics.

cars, swallowing large quantities of dust. It is a race between my completing my programme or breaking down in health for the time being at least. I shall win the race I hope, though two days ago I seemed to be on the point of losing it. But I have recovered. The aeroplane is going to be called in to save time by speeding my journeys. So I am afraid I cannot write to you as I would like to. But I think of you often and my love goes to you.

Your loving,
Papu

---

202.   43, Belsize Park,
                                                      N.W. 3,
                                              18th January, 1937

Darling Papu,
I have your lovely letter of the 4th,[1] written soon after the Faizpur Congress.

Before your letter came I was wondering if Faizpur was anywhere near the Ajanta Caves and whether you would be able to pay them a brief visit, if it was. I am so glad you could. Have you ever been there before? I should love to go there with you. There are so many things we must do together – but will they ever come off? Time flies so rapidly and a lifetime is all too short for the millions of things one would like to do. I have never been to Ajanta or Ellora. Three times I prepared for the journey with the Vakils but luck was against us. Once Kaka fell seriously ill, another time there was a severe storm & we could not go because a big bridge broke down and the third time I forget what happened.

I have not sent you any Left Club books. I asked you if you wanted any. All I sent was their monthly review. Menon tells me that the review is banned in India & so are most of the books. I hear that Feroze has sent you some, though probably the books are held up at Bombay.

Your programme of tours, etc., seems terrific. I don't know how you can manage it. I do so wish you could take a little rest now and then – a few days even would be such a help to you. I am looking forward very very much indeed to the summer holidays, for with it will come India & you. It will be lovely going to Burma with you. I do hope it will be possible. Do you think there is any chance of your going to jail?

But before the holiday there is work to be done – yours is so stupendous & strenuous and weighs so heavily on you; mine is nothing really but at the moment seems bad enough to me. My mind feels suddenly tired and anxious. I do not know if I shall be able to pass & be admitted to college.

1. Refers to letter No. 199.

What will happen if I don't? Will it mean another year of just this or what shall I do?

I am leaving for Bristol tomorrow and shall stay there till my exam which is in March – probably about the 15th or 16th. Do you think I had better leave for India immediately afterwards or wait some time? In July or September or perhaps March, if I can manage it, I have to take the Latin part of Responsions.

With very much love,
Indu

Mrs Grant Duff sends you her best wishes. Shiela is still in Prague.

Mrs Rama Rau came for ten mins the other day. She has just returned from India & she brought me a parcel of saris from the two Puphis & Dol Amma.

---

203.   Roorkee,
23rd January, 1937

Darling,

I am stealing a few minutes from the night to write these lines to you. I am on the move still, continuously so, and time and I rush along and I cannot attend to letters. I had a card from you the other day. I have lost count of days and hours as my mind lives in a whirl of crowds and speeches and rushing about. If only I could have a little more sleep. I shall plenty of it later – how I look forward to it. The continuous changes in climate as I move about rapidly and expose myself to sun and dust have made me look terribly weather-beaten. But I am getting very conceited about my vitality. In spite of all, I am keeping good health.

You must be back at the Badminton School. My love to you – and though I do not write to you as often as I wish, I think of you so often.

Your loving,
Papu

---

204.   [Badminton School]
Bristol,
29th January, 1937

Darling Papu,

This is going to be a hurried note for I have a lecture in a few minutes and after that there is little time before the post leaves & I do want you to get this as soon as possible. But I am afraid even so it will be too late.

I do hope all this has not alarmed you for nothing serious or alarming has happened.

I have just received the sailing lists of all the lines going to India. I think you would like me to come by the French Messagerie Maritime. That is the cheapest, but takes the longest time and calls at Colombo, not Bombay. If I come by this line I shall have to take the *Andre Lebon* leaving Marseilles on 2nd April & reaching Colombo on the 19th April.

An alternative is the *Strathmore* (the P & O steamer) leaving London 10th April & arriving Bombay on 22nd April. Travelling tourist class this will cost anything from £30 to £54 single fare & £52 to £97 return fare – the price depends on the cabin.

The Messagerie Maritime single fare is third class £21 & I will get a twenty-five per cent reduction on the return fare, second class single fare: £34.

The Lloyd Triestino, I suppose, is out of the question.

I don't think you will get this in time but which do you suggest I come by. However I shall have to book pretty soon & as you are travelling about, I do not know if your advice will come in time. Personally I am inclined towards the French line.

At the moment I have about £66 at the bank. I have just received a bill from Badminton School for about that amount. I shall try & have it reduced, for I am only staying here till half-term. But even then, there is hardly enough to get to Allahabad with.

By the end of February I shall have another £20 – I had lent it to Madan Bhai & he has given me a cheque dated 25th February.

So could you please arrange for some money to be sent to me. I am sorry to be bothering you, but I am not at all sure if Bachhraj will be able to send some or not – they have just sent £50.

The last two days have been very cold & since last evening it is snowing.

April seems very near & need I say how very much I am looking forward to seeing you.

With very very much love,
Indu

If I came by the Messagerie Maritime, shall I let the American Express make arrangements for me at Colombo, or do you know anybody there who could help? I should like to spend as little time there as possible. And from Colombo, I suppose I had better go to Bombay? Where will you be?

205.
Anand Bhawan,
Allahabad,
7th February, 1937

Darling,

I fell asleep as I was writing to you in the train. Suddenly I was woken up at Barabanki and dragged out of the train. There were meetings by the roadside on the way to Lucknow. From Lucknow I went north to Bareilly, etc., and then came back here. Today I am off to Maharashtra. On the 18th I take a plane to Cannanore in Malabar. And so on and on till the 20th when I hope to have a brief respite in Anand Bhawan.

On arrival here I received your two letters. I suppose there is no doubt about your success in the Somerville exam. Don't worry. But suppose you do not succeed – what then? It seems rather absurd for you to spend another year in preparing for it. That would be precious time wasted. It may be desirable for us to change your plans completely and leave out Oxford and revert to the Continent – Paris. But there is no point in our thinking of this now. But in any event you should get through the full Responsions as this is recognised on the Continent & everywhere. For the moment do not bother about all this. Carry on with your exam. After the exam you will know where you are and you should then consult the Somerville head (I have forgotten her name – I have got it – Darbyshire) and Agatha and any others. Then when you come here we can decide.

You had better come here as soon as you can or rather as soon as you have fixed up your plans with Darbyshire, etc. About your passage, I do not fancy your going to Colombo. This will mean a lot of time wasted and no great saving in money. I am inclined to think that an air journey by K.L.M. is indicated. This is very expensive it is true but it has its advantages. I should like to have you here as long as possible and Dol Amma's health is so precarious that I want you here soon. Perhaps you have heard that she has had another attack of paralysis. This was a mild one and she is slowly recovering but still she is very weak and I am afraid she has not a long span of life in front of her. She is very keen on seeing you. Naturally. So I think you had better come by air early in April. You will like the experience. You will pass through Cairo. Mind you inform Fouad Bey (he has become a Pasha now). He will be happy to meet you and will show you round Cairo. You will thus arrive at Bamrauli near Allahabad. I hope to be here then but one never knows.

About money I shall arrange to send you funds sufficient to cover your air trip. I am so busy now that I may not be able to make arrangements soon. But in any event you will get them by the end of February or beginning March. Meanwhile I enclose a cheque for £20. Unfortunately John Lane has bust up and so my royalties have gone in the air.

You will have no difficulty in getting a passage by K.L.M. as during this season few people come East. The traffic is the other way. Don't fix up your passage too soon for if you have to change the date you will lose some money.

You will only be able to bring two small valises with you, which K.L.M. supply. The rest of your luggage will have to come by steamer. The K.L.M. people will take charge of this. Have it sent to Bombay to Jal (J. A. D. Naoroji, 78, Nepean Sea Road, Bombay).

Let me know how much money you are likely to require for your various expenses, including air trip, etc.

Yesterday I sent you a cable.

When booking your passage by the K.L.M. take a single passage, not return. A return saves money but it is not worthwhile under the circumstances as we do not yet know how you will go back.

Fouad Bey's address is:

> Fouad Selim Pasha el-Higazi
> 33, Sharia Dawawine
> Cairo

You had better write to him in good time and send a cable a little before starting. En route you will have no difficulty and you need not carry much money as the K.L.M. pays for hotels, etc. These hotels are of the luxury type. Remember, it will be hot after you leave Europe and it will be very hot over Western Asia. Keep a pair of sunglasses. Better travel in European dress. You can take to the sari at Karachi! In Baghdad go to any Indian (Sindhi) shop and tell them who you are and they will be happy to take you round if you feel in the mood for it. But there is little to see in Baghdad.

I am likely to miss your letters for the next twelve days as I shall be in South India – and I may not be able to write to you. But I shall remember to send you money at the latest on my return to Allahabad, about the 20th.

All my love,

Your loving,
Papu

---

206.   Badminton School,
                                                          Bristol,
                                                   8th February, 1937

Darlingest Papu,
Your wire has just arrived – at least it was given to me this morning. It came by post from London! Isn't it strange, something told me to wait for

your letter long before the telegram came. In fact, [the] day before yesterday Miss Baker asked me to hurry up & book my passage and I told her that I would rather wait and see what you thought about it. There isn't any hurry really, because very few people go East at this time of the year, specially as the Coronation is taking place in May.

I should love to go by air and it does save time. But it's awfully expensive. As it is, I hate asking for money beyond the £50 every other month. However, let's see what you have to say about it.

I have been following the elections in the *Times* – it is surprising how much more news of India appears in the *Times* than in the *Manchester Guardian.* These days, there is something about the election or the Congress every morning in the *Times* and in spite of the propaganda one can get at what's happening out there.

I was awfully excited over the victories in Sind & Bihar. I do hope we get a majority everywhere.[1]

It is curious also how the *Times* justifies Stalin for the Moscow Trials while the *M. G.* is giving a lot of airing to the idea of having an international trial for Trotsky . . .

I am looking forward so very very much – it is quite impossible to express in words, just how much – to seeing you. But I do hope I shall be able to be with you & that you will [not] have to go rushing all over the place all the time . . .

With all my love.

Ever your loving,
Indu

---

207.   Badminton School,
Bristol,
13th February, 1937

Darling Papu,

Please do excuse my writing in pencil: my pen is downstairs in the classroom and some sort of a meeting is being held there.

I have not had news from you for some time. Usually I do not mind as I

---

1. Indian Elections: Although the Congress rejected the new Constitution imposed upon India by the Government of India Act of 1935, it later decided to participate in the provincial elections held under this Constitution. The Congress emerged victorious in Bombay, Madras, the United Provinces, the Central Provinces, Orissa, Assam, Bihar, Sind and the North-West Frontier Province. The election results demonstrated the hold of the Congress over the people. The Party then proceeded to form Governments in these provinces. In two provinces – Bengal and Punjab – the Congress failed to secure absolute majorities; non-Congress coalition governments were formed there.

know how busy you are but this time it is annoying for since I received your telegram I know that you have written and the letter is on its way to England. I know it cannot get here before a certain date and yet I look for it in the post every morning!

There is not much news to give, I am going on with my work, feeling more & more disgusted with Latin and the English climate!

A Spanish lady – Dr Komas – lecturer in Biology at the University of Barcelona, has come to England, I don't quite know why. She came to Bristol and stayed with Miss Baker. I think she spoke at the University here. We also had a small meeting: some of the staff, the VI form, some of the other older girls in the school and a few outsiders. Dr Komas said little about the war itself, apart from briefly sketching its background. She spoke of what interested her most: children and education. She told us of the groups of people who were trying to shield the children of Spain from the horrors of war, to give them as calm an education and as healthy a life as possible in the circumstances. Big colonies have been founded in Barcelona and Valencia for children and here the littlest ones are sent by train from Madrid and the surrounding villages in the hands of the government. In these colonies there are schools; the children are clothed and fed. Many of them wear new clothes for the first time in their lives. The Barcelona booksellers told Dr Komas that they had never before sold so many children's books. Food is scarce but the grown-ups manage with biscuits and anything else that they can get whilst all the milk and bread available is sent to the colonies for the children. The main difficulty so far is the transport of the children, for the trains are very slow & the journey is made much longer by the necessity of having to avoid the fighting fronts. One would hardly expect Madrid to rejoice during Christmas or New Year, but the government said that the children should not be disappointed. A 'children's week' was organised: everybody gave voluntary help and during that week the children had their cinema shows and games. Every child received a toy – many for the first time. 'We tried to make them happy,' said Dr Komas, 'and their smiling faces gave us renewed courage and strength; they made us happy and we were glad that all that was possible was being done for their safety and welfare.' But this was only in the daytime. At night they woke up at the sound of bombs – the little ones cried and the older ones remembered the terrible scenes of war. Dr Komas showed us the children's week posters and other pictures.

Dr Komas, I found, was very charming. She spoke quietly but without any sign of emotion. Her English was very broken but it was surprising how well she chose her words. When she had left Miss Baker told us that her family was in Majorca when the war broke out. Majorca as you know was one of the first places taken by Franco. For six months she had no news of her people, then she had a brief note; of course they cannot write about conditions nor are they allowed to leave the island. With Dr Komas was the Prof. of English of the Barcelona University. His home is in Majorca & he told us how the island was taken by Franco.

Meanwhile the non-intervention committee is deciding whether 'other European countries' should intervene in the war!!

I wonder if you have ever been to Hyde Park on a Sunday – it's priceless. The other day, when I was in London, I was passing through & overheard the following: 'And why do we want a foreign policy and foreign relations? Aren't the ones at home good enough?'

Did you know Agatha used to live in Bristol? Her brother still does & this morning I had a cup of coffee with the sister-in-law.

> With very very much love,
> Indu

---

208.   Anand Bhawan,
                                                    Allahabad,
                                            22nd February, 1937

Darling,

For a change I have actually been in one place for four days and I have not held forth at a public meeting during all this long period! This is a change for me, for previously for months I have been addressing a dozen or more big meetings daily.

I have been rereading your old letters – those that have come during the last two or three months. I had not been able to answer them properly and I wondered if anything still required an answer. I was so glad to read of your skiing experiences and how you took to this fascinating sport. I do think that there is nothing to beat it. I suppose you are pretty good at it now. You had better keep it up, which means going to Suisse or Norway next winter.

You say that you read my Faizpur address in the *Chronicle*. I sent you a copy by air mail to Wengen. Evidently you did not get it. And perhaps you did not get a letter of mine also sent there.

Do not send me any Left Book Club publications. Feroze sent me some and they never reached me.

You want me to send you Bapu's address at Faizpur. I have no copy of it. You must have seen it in the *Chronicle*.

And now about your plans. I understand that you will finish with your exam on 22nd March – a month today. After that you will naturally require a few days to meet people and do odd jobs. You should also, as far as you can, fix up about your plans on your return to England from India. When you are supposed to be back and what you are supposed to do. I should like you to stay in India as long as you can conveniently do so without interfering with your work. There is a very very faint possibility of my going to Europe in autumn, perhaps September. If this comes off, I should like to accompany you back. But my going is very doubtful.

I expect you to start for India as soon as you can easily manage it – probably at the beginning of April. Don't arrive here on the 1st of April! It is going to be a big *hartal* day for us – an anti-Constitution demonstration. But you can come as soon after that as possible. I have made no programme for April and after. I want to wait for your arrival. There is of course the Burma trip to be undertaken some time. Unfortunately May and later are rainy months. But we must put up with that, as you will have to put up with the summer heat of Allahabad.

After your arrival here you will of course stay for some time in Anand Bhawan with Dol Amma. Chand, Tara and Rita will not be here. They will be at Woodstock.[1] They have a fortnight off during the summer and the idea is that they and you & I might spend this at Khali. Betty is thinking of going to Ceylon for part of the summer. Later she might come up here.

I am quite clear that you should come here by air – K.L.M. So you had better book your passage. Mind you get the two valises from them. Send your heavy luggage ahead to Bombay or Allahabad through K.L.M. or, if it is more convenient, through American Express. I suggested to you in a previous letter[2] that if you wanted to go to Paris on the way back, you had better take the K.L.M. plane at Marseilles. That is for you to decide. Take a single passage.

About finances. I have sent you a cheque for £20. I now enclose a cheque for £80. The passage will cost you just £100, I think. Early in March you will get another £50 from Bachhraj. Probably this will be enough for your other expenses before starting. But do not rely on getting the £20 from Madan Bhai. He is frightfully forgetful about money matters. His casualness surprises me. It is just possible that you may require some more money. If so, do not hesitate to write or cable to me. I can easily send you another £20 or more – I have got some such balance in my London bank.

Before you return, see Agatha and Krishna Menon. They might want to send something to me.

I am giving you below my provisional programme in case you wish to communicate with me by cable. I go to Wardha on the 25th – return on 1st March. I shall be in Lucknow on 6th & 7th March. Then Allahabad till the 16th or 17th. In Delhi probably from the 18th to the 24th or 25th. This

1. A co-educational school at Mussoorie, founded by missionaries from the United States.
2. Letter not published.

really means that you should write or cable to Allahabad except during the week when I am in Delhi. You can time your letters so as to reach me in Delhi. My address in Delhi: 1 Daryaganj, Delhi. I shall let you know more definitely about these dates later.

Bring two or three small soft leather purses with you – the kind with the zip attachment, which are meant for loose silver. They used to cost a mark or so in Germany.

This will reach you on the eve of your exam. Good luck to you. Do not worry or work too hard. Keep fresh. That is the best way to face an exam – another few hours' work will not make much difference but tiredness and freshness do make a tremendous difference.

Love,

Your loving,
Papu

Don't forget to write to Fouad Bey about the date of your passing through Cairo.

---

209.   [Badminton School]
Bristol,
23rd February, 1937

Darling Papu,

. . . Krishna Menon phoned to me on Saturday night asking me if I could go up to London on Friday, 5th March & in connection with some entertainment or other, in which I would have to make an appeal for Spain. Just before the call, I had been reading the *Times*'s account of Madrid and the description of the town, the queues of hungry people – shops which did not want to seem empty & so had decorated their windows with multi-coloured boxes and tins, and had a little printed notice on one side saying that these boxes contain nothing but sawdust! (This is not entirely true, says the *Times* correspondent, they had plenty of toothpicks!) It was all so vivid in my mind that I said I would if I could. I have asked Miss Baker and she has given me permission to go up to London for the weekend just after my exam. I shall probably come back here afterwards, though.

With lots of love,
Indu

Shall probably reach Allahabad sometime in the first week of April!

---

210.   Anand Bhawan,
                                                          Allahabad,
                                                   25th February, 1937

Indu darling,
Your letter of 13th February[1] (in pencil) came two days ago. I liked your
account of Dr Komas's lecture on Spain so much that I have sent it to the
press!

I was a little surprised to find that you had not received my letter[2] &
cheque at the time of writing. Perhaps it reached you soon after. Two or
three days ago I sent you a cheque for £80. Previously I sent £20 and soon
(early in March) you will receive £50 from Bachhraj. I imagine this will
meet your journey and other expenses. However I enclose another cheque
for £10. It is possible of course that my calculations are wrong and you
may want more. If so, send me a brief cable mentioning the amount. Or in
case of emergency I suppose you could ask Agatha or Krishna Menon for
a few pounds which I could immediately send them.

When coming here you will of course leave most of your luggage
behind. Or at any rate part of it. You had better get this stored in
London . . .

I am just off to Wardha.

My love,
                                                    Your loving,
                                                        Papu

As soon as you have definitely fixed up your sailing date by K.L.M. you
might send me a brief cable: Sailing . . . (mention date). I shall presume
that it is K.L.M. and calculate accordingly.

———————— ▪ ————————

211.   Badminton School,
                                                            Bristol,
                                                      5th March, 1937

Darling Papu,
Your letter of the 25th[3] came this morning. Thank you for the cheque of
£10 and the one for £80 which came a few days ago. I think I have already
written to you about receiving the £20 cheque.

I admit I was rather startled about part of that pencil scribble going

1. Refers to letter No. 207.
2. Refers to letter No. 205.
3. Refers to letter No. 210.

to the press! I was not frightfully well then and it was written in a great hurry – the style, I know, was perfectly incredible! However.

As I wrote to you in my last letter, Menon has persuaded me to speak at an 'Indian Evening' arranged by Mrs Saklatvala[1] and the India–Spain League. I thought it was going to be a tiny affair but alas! I was sadly mistaken. Strachey is also speaking & the public will consist of people like the London School of Economics students! However, one must make the best of a bad job. I propose busying myself for at least two days in pamphlets and books on Spain. But I think I shall speak on the lines of Dr Komas's lecture, for that is a side of the question that interests me. Besides it has been given little publicity, whilst hundreds of pamphlets and books and lectures have dealt with the various political aspects and the effect of the war on the outside world. There will also be dancing – Indian – and other such entertainment at the 'evening'. It is on Friday, the 12th. This date was specially fixed for my benefit – I told Menon I would not be able to go to London on the 5th.

I shall go to London on Thursday, the 11th, & return to Bristol on the 13th. Then I have to wait here & see if Somerville wants me. If it does, I shall have to go up to Oxford, if not I shall go to London at the end of the week – that is on the 21st.

Agatha thinks the 11th is too far off, so she is coming to Bristol today to see me. She will leave tomorrow. I shall probably stay with her in London for the weekend, but later I might stay at the Y.W.C.A. or some such place.

I have not definitely booked my seat to India. But I intend leaving Croydon on the 31st or perhaps it is the 30th – we leave Amsterdam on the 31st morning and go via the winter route, i.e. Marseilles and Rome. The plane stops at Alexandria but not at Cairo. Hence there is not much point in bothering Fouad Bey. By the way, I wrote to him some time ago but have received no reply.

Anyhow if I can get a seat on the plane leaving Amsterdam on the 31st March I shall be in Allahabad on the 3rd April morning – less than a month from today! If there is no vacant seat, I shall take the next plane which leaves Amsterdam on the 3rd of April & reaches Allahabad on the 7th . . .

I intend leaving most of my luggage in London. I shall only bring what I need on the journey and perhaps in India and also those things which I do not need here and which are therefore a nuisance . . .

---

1. Sehri Saklatvala: wife of Shapurji Saklatvala, a radical leader of the Indian community in Great Britain.

Hari must have got in – the *B.C.* says he is a 'hot-favourite'. He must be thrilled.

All my love to you – *Au revoir, À bientôt.*[1]

Indu

212.

Anand Bhawan,
Allahabad,
8th March, 1937

Darling Indu,

You must be in London now, I suppose, far from the burden of your examination. But I do not know your address, so this letter goes to Bristol. There won't be many more letters to you before you leave for India.

I hope all your arrangements for your air voyage have now been fixed up and that you do not lack funds or anything else. Remember to cable to me on what date you are sailing and wherefrom. I returned from Lucknow today and I shall remain here till I go to Delhi on the 14th evening for the A.I.C.C. meeting and the Convention. My address from the 15th to the 21st will be Daryaganj, Delhi. After that I return to Allahabad.

I see that you have written to Fouad Bey or rather Fouad Pasha. But he is not good at replying, partly because he does not trust his English. So you had better inform him again about the time of your arrival in Cairo. Better send a telegram.

Dol Amma is still bedridden but I think she is just a little better.

Love,

Your loving
Papu

213.

[Badminton School]
Bristol,
8th March [1937]

Papu darling,

In my last letter,[2] I believe I said that I would reach Allahabad on the 3rd April if I got a seat on the plane leaving Amsterdam on the 31st March. This is not correct. I shall reach Bamrauli on the 4th April – a day later. I do hope I get accommodation on that aeroplane. If I don't, I hope to reach home on the 7th.

Miss Harrison came down to Bristol on Friday. It was lovely seeing her

1. See you soon.
2. Refers to letter No. 211.

for she brought me first-hand news of you and all the other people I wished to know about. For a few minutes her talk transported me across the sea and land and even days to the Faizpur Congress and Bapu's little hut and then to Anand Bhawan. She increased my longing for seeing you & India. However, there is not long to wait . . .

Last week I came across a most startling theory of the Russian trials in a London paper called the *Leader.* It is an article by Vivian Meik. He says that some people think that the executions never took place at all and that the trials were part of a great game of bluff which Stalin & Trotsky are playing to secure world power for Communism. He says that while to the outside world Stalin & Trotsky seem enemies, it will be easier for them to work together towards the 'culmination of the greatest plot in History'. The so-called executed men will be free to work unhindered for this common aim for 'What,' says Meik, 'more perfect hiding place than the grave?'!

Do you ever see the *World Review* – a monthly magazine edited by Vernon Bartlett. I happened to pick up the February number from somewhere the other day. It is almost full of articles on India: there are extracts from various speeches of yours and from the Congress Manifesto – also from Lord Linlithgow's[1] address to the members of the Indian legislatures. There is an interesting article by Edward Thompson – it is from a broadcast talk he gave from Delhi. It is called 'Mae West Goes East' or 'The Little Boy Who Threatens India'. He says that American films as well as Indian ones are going to destroy all Indian culture.

The weather continues to be most tricky. It snowed a bit this morning and is very cold.

With very much love from,
Your loving,
Indu

I am looking forward to seeing you tremendously.

———————

214.   Anand Bhawan,
                                                  Allahabad,
                                            11th March, 1937

Darling Indu,
Your card[2] has just come, informing me that you have decided to start by K.L.M. from London and that you are not going to pass Marseilles or Cairo. I do not quite know what the summer route of the K.L.M. is. I had

1. Lord Linlithgow: Viceroy of India, 1936–43.
2. Postcard not traceable.

an idea that it omitted Rome also and went via Budapest. Remember to cable to me as soon as you have fixed up the date of departure.

I shall probably write to you again but I am not quite sure. Day after tomorrow I am going to Delhi and there will be a succession of meetings there: Working Committee, A.I.C.C., and then the Convention. I shall be in Delhi till the 21st. I imagine I shall be able to send you brief letters.

By the way, you might bring your rucksack with you if it is not too much trouble – not with you on the plane but with your heavy luggage. If we go on the mountains it would be useful.

Love,

> Your loving,
> Papu

---

215.   [Badminton School]
                                                        Bristol,
                                              14th March, 1937

Papu darling,

I am so sorry for having missed the last airmail.

I went to London for the weekend. It was nice to get away from the monotonous routine of school and to meet new and interesting people but it was dreadfully tiring – my programme was almost as bad as yours when you came here! Though of course my appointments were not half as strenuous. I arrived at Paddington on Thursday morning and from then till Saturday evening when I got into the train for Bristol at Paddington it was one tremendous rush. I have come to the conclusion that weekends in London are not desirable – specially when people know that I am coming there. Anyhow it was all in a good cause. We collected nearly £60 on the platform at the 'Indian Evening' for Spain. And we must have got over £20 from the seats – even though admission was free.

Another good outcome of the meeting was that I met John Strachey. He only said a few words to me but I liked him awfully. Another speaker at the 'evening' was Mrs Isobel Brown.

I have definitely booked my seat on the plane leaving Amsterdam on the 31st morning. This means leaving London on the 30th. I shall go by air to Amsterdam, for the difference in price between the air & train journeys is only about £2.

I shall be in India early on the 4th April.

I met Madan Bhai in London and also Vidya. M. Bhai was awfully excited about Russia and could talk of nothing else. He will be in London till the 25th or 26th and will then go to the Continent – he intends sailing for India some time in April.

I was surprised to see Vidya at the meeting – I had an idea that she was in India. I was glad to meet her, though we had only a few minutes together – I shall try to get her when I next go to London. She also wants to sail in April.

Mr Hannington – the travelling agency man – is arranging everything for me – all that I shall have to do is to be at Croydon with my two K.L.M. suitcases before twelve o'clock on the 30th.

The money from Bachhraj has arrived – thanks awfully.

I am terribly tired so I shall stop now.

I do hope you won't get arrested on 1st April! People here seem to think there is a possibility.

With very much love & kisses,
Indu

15th March

It has just struck me that if anything happens on 1st April I shall not hear of it until I reach India on the 3rd. So could you please arrange for a short wire to be sent if you are arrested. I shall be spending the night at Basra. I enclose the timetable. Otherwise somebody could meet me at Karachi & give me the news – just as you think best.

A Mrs Bondfield[1] is staying with Miss Baker. She was England's first woman Cabinet Minister – she is very strongly Labour. But we had a nice talk.

Love,
Indu

16th March

Have just heard from Oxford. I have to go up tomorrow for an interview!

---

216. Badminton School,
Bristol,
20th March [1937]

Papu darling,

I have your two letters of the 8th[2] and the 11th.[3]

I have sent you a telegram telling you of my departure from Amsterdam, to your Delhi address. Leaving Amsterdam on the 31st means reaching Allahabad on the morning of the 4th. In a previous letter I sent you the

---

1. Margaret Grace Bondfield: British politician, Labour M.P., 1923–4, 1926–31; Minister of Labour, 1929–31.
2. Refers to letter No. 212.
3. Refers to letter No. 214.

timetable. You will see that I go by the winter route, after all. But we do not pass Cairo at all – so I am not informing Fouad Pasha. At least I shall write a letter to him saying that I do not pass Cairo.

I do not possess a rucksack – do you think it is worthwhile buying one?

In my last letter[1] I told you that I had been sent for, for an interview. I was rather terrified but it was not half as bad as I had expected. I had three interviews – one with the Principal and the other two with my future dons. They asked very general questions – I was told that my history papers were very interesting and my style of writing was so nice that it was a pleasure to read whatever I wrote! I got very good marks for French and my Latin was abominable!! I was asked if I would be able to work at it between now and October, if I came to College in October! Of course I said that I would try to!

I shall know the final result on Wednesday. The same day I am going to Oxford for Latin Responsion. Latin however is – I think – far below the standard, but still –

From Oxford I shall go straight on to London.

Lu, Mlle Hemmerlin, Mme Morin, Mrs Grant Duff, Mlle Rolland and Miss Baker (what a strange mixture!) all send you their very best wishes. We are having a 'Peace Week' here. We have invited all the nearby schools and youth groups, etc., to participate. Every evening there is either a lecture or lectures or some kind of entertainment. Yesterday I spoke on India – a very general sort of affair.

Since I spoke at the Spain–India meeting I received an invitation from Edinburgh to go there during the Easter vac. and speak to the Indians. This person writes that he has made several attempts at getting help for Spain but many of the Indians say 'why shouldn't the money go to India?' Hence he has not been frightfully successful. Of course I am unable to go.

Then Fenner Brockway[2] asked me to write an article for the *New Leader* on what is going to happen in India on April 1st and why.[3] At that time I had exams going on, so I could not. Besides I am not very sure if I could write such an article.

I wonder if I told you that I met Vidya in London. She is not sailing till next month, about the same time as Madan Bhai – so that they might go together.

I have been following your activities with interest – but I do not like writing to you about such affairs for I think you have an overdose as it is.

With heaps of love,
Indu

1. Refers to letter No. 215.
2. Archibald Fenner Brockway: leading member of the Independent Labour Party who took a sympathetic interest in the national movement in India.
3. See letter No. 208, p. 318.

I do not know what I wrote to you in my last letter about sending me a wire on 2nd April. Don't send any if you are not arrested and somehow I have a feeling you won't be.

———————◆———————

217.   Wardha,
                                        2nd July, 1937

Darling Indu,
I felt rather sorry at not having you here. I should have liked you to see the village work & Bapu's surroundings here. But this time when we had to return from Bapu it was raining hard and it was not possible for a car to go to the village. So we came back in a tiny bullock-cart – Maulana Abul Kalam Azad[1] and I wedged in and being bumped and shaken for over an hour, I decided then that you were well out of it.
    Love,
                        Your loving,
                            Papu

Give the enclosed to Puphi.

———————◆———————

218.   P & O Steam Navigation Co.,
                                        SS *Viceroy of India*,
                                   18th September, 1937

Darling Papu,
We are nearing Suez – will probably reach it at four a.m. tomorrow. Up till Aden it was fairly cool but rather rough. The Red Sea till this morning was unbearably hot & stuffy and very calm. But this morning it is difficult to keep on one's feet and the sea is feeling more energetic.
    I spend over two hours every day in the swimming bath. It is the most marvellous bath I have ever seen on a ship – Pompeiian, they call it. I wish the colours were more subdued – glaring red pillars & light green tiles that don't like the red! And in the water me in a bright orange bathing suit! The water is cool & the swim is very enjoyable when there are not too many people.
    The rest of the time goes in doing work for Somerville & walking. In the evenings there is always something on. Yesterday there was the cinema & the night before a race meeting. I won ten shillings and sixpence! Not bad for a first go, was it?

    1. A leader of the struggle for freedom in India.

Either just before or just after Aden I sent you a letter-telegram.[1] It cost only four shillings and it was lovely to know that you would get it within the week . . .

Lots of love & kisses,
Indu

21st September

I meant to post this in Port Said but somehow it got left behind on the ship.

A most awful man has come on board at Port Said. And as luck would have it – he sits next to me at table! Almost the first thing he said to me was that Gurudev – Tagore – had died on the 16th.[2] I read the wireless news every morning but had not noticed anything except that he was seriously ill. I looked through all the piles but could find nothing & nobody on board could help me. I am feeling so upset – it is awful to be in such uncertainty. And I do hope that the news is a false alarm.

We have only three more days to reach Marseilles. Tonight we pass through the Straits of Messina. The last time I saw Messina was in Easter 1936!

Lots of love,
Indu

---

219.   Ajmer,
                                              19th September, 1937

Darling,

You must be ploughing your way through the Red Sea – or perhaps you are in the Suez Canal or round about Cairo. I have spent the last week in ploughing through crowds of men and women. Gujarat gave me an overwhelming welcome and I had a pretty hard time. Now I am in Ajmer for a day and by tomorrow evening I ought to be in Lucknow. My voice is threatening to subside but from tomorrow it will have some rest from public speaking.

Probably I shall hear from you from Paris first by air and later from Aden & Port Said, unless you send your letters from Port Said by air. I doubt if you had much peace on board with the crowd accompanying you. Still, you ought to feel better after your voyage. I hope you will take care of your health and put in a few stretching exercises every day, especially the *Sarvangasan* which is extraordinarily good.

I cannot write more – an engagement awaits me. Remember me to

1. Letter not published.
2. Rabindranath Tagore actually died on 7th August 1941.

Louise Morin & Jean-Jacques[1] and give my love to them. I have not written to her for a long time, although I have had several letters from her. I shall write from Allahabad. Remember to see Mr Shah in Paris.

All my love, my darling one.

Your loving,
Papu

220.

P & O Steam Navigation Co.,
SS Viceroy of India,
23rd September, 1937

Darlingest Papu,

Yesterday was the most marvellous day we have ever had on such a voyage. First – a little before lunch – we saw a submarine emerge out of the waters & come towards us very suspiciously. When it discovered who we were it turned back – rather contemptuously! We saluted it by dipping our flag & it returned the salute. It was an Italian one. (It was only that very morning that we had learnt that Italy too had agreed to the Nyon Pact.)[2] This was probably one of the first patrols. Already we were nearing the shores of Sicily – soon Italy too appeared. We had a most gorgeous view of the two coasts for we passed through the Straits of Messina. Do you remember how enthusiastic I was about Taormina when I was there with the École Nouvelle in Easter 1936? I had no idea I would see it again so soon – so when Sir C.V.[3] showed it me through his binoculars I got so excited! I jumped up on the railings until somebody behind said, 'Hey now Miss be careful!' Unfortunately it was cloudy & it was not possible to see Stromboli.

At about five p.m. we passed the volcano Stromboli. It was absolutely grand. At first we saw just the steam coming out but as we came closer, there was a grand explosion – a column of fire and then quiet. Magnificent isn't the word for it. Sir C.V. was wildly excited & so was I, so much so that the whole ship stared at us instead of at the Stromboli.

During this voyage I have seen innumerable 'optical illusions' – because Sir C.V. is always there to point them out. As we were entering the St. of Messina, this is what it looked like.

NOTE: See sketch at foot of letter shown overleaf.

1. Jean-Jacques: son of Louise Morin, who worked in the International Labour Organisation.

2. Nyon Pact: treaty signed by Great Britain and France at Nyon, Switzerland, in 1937 to extend protection to the Spanish Navy.

3. C. V. Raman: Indian physicist who was awarded the Nobel Prize in 1930.

P & O. S. N. Co.

S.S.

At first we saw just the steam coming out but as we came close, there was a grand explosion — a column of fire and then quiet. Magnificent isn't the word for it. Sir C. V. was wildly excited & so was I. So much so that the whole ship stared at us instead of at the Stromboli.

During this voyage I have seen innumerable "optical illusions" — because Sir C. V. is always there to point them out. As we were entering the St. of Messina, this is what it looked like.

This afternoon we pass between Corsica & Sardinia. I was sorry we did not stop at Malta – but this was exciting enough & lovely.

Tons of love & kisses,

Indu

P.S.

I have not yet decided how long I am staying in Paris. Write to London c/o Agatha.

Two days ago something happened to break the monotony of the ship life. The P & O Co. booked two berths for four passengers – or so they say. Two of them – Indian students – occupied the berths in Bombay. In Aden they were told that they would have to move to a four-berthed cabin. They refused & the purser said it was all right. The students wanted to go to Cairo so they disembarked in Suez. When they came on board again at Port Said they found that their luggage had been moved. They complained to the purser who said that he was very sorry but that now what had been done could not be undone – sort of thing. The real reason for doing this was that the two passengers who now occupy the two-berthed cabin are Europeans – and how could they be put in a four-berthed cabin with an Indian. Of course nobody will ever admit this. The treatment given to Indian students, particularly those travelling second, is appalling. This is not the first time such an incident has taken place – nor will it be the last. But on this particular ship when there are people such as Mohan Kumaramangalam[1] & myself on board, we cannot take it lying down. First we decided to demand an explanation from the Commander but now we are writing to the P & O board of directors & are issuing a press statement, the whole idea being to get Lloyd Triestino & other lines to give concession rates to Indian students. I think we will succeed to some extent at least. I have also been doing a great deal of propaganda towards that end with the Italian journalist. He seemed very impressed with the idea, so it might come to something. What a blow it would be to the P & O if they lost the student passengers. We must show them that they cannot treat us anyhow just because we are going half price! We are not introducing any racial element in the statements and I am glad to say that more students are also taking an interest!

This letter seems to go on & on. And reading it over I find it is most boring. But it just means so much time spent with you. And that is so precious to me. Besides it is so difficult to write from Paris & London. Life is rather a rush there because somehow I never seem to be there for long

---

1. Surendra Mohan Kumaramangalam: contemporary of Indira Gandhi in Great Britain, prominent in student politics. He was later a leading member of the Indian Government.

enough at a stretch. But you know & I know that wherever I am, whatever I am doing, a corner of my mind is thinking of you – accompanying you on your journeys & watching you at home. I do miss you so much, darling – and I do so love you – much more than I ever did before.

Please do take care of yourself and come to Europe in the summer. I shall be looking forward to it.

All my love,
Indu

❖

221.   Lucknow,
                                                    23rd September, 1937

My darling one,

I have not yet got back to Allahabad. Two days ago I reached here on my way back from Gujarat and Ajmer, and immediately I got involved in the Cawnpore labour situation, which is very grave, and in many other local and provincial troubles. I have stayed on here longer than I intended, partly because Dol Amma has not kept well, partly because I felt tired. I was not keen on going back to Allahabad and to Anand Bhawan empty and rather desolate.

Your ocean letter[1] has reached me only today. It came by messenger from Allahabad with other letters. I was happy to receive it.

Tonight I go to Allahabad but for a day only. Then to Cawnpore for two days to harangue the workers there. Afterwards I hope to spend a week or more in Allahabad.

You must be in France now – how far you are from me! I am afraid I shall not come soon to you, for I am tied up by the strong ropes of circumstance and responsibility. They are of my own seeking and hence all the more difficult to get rid of. I should love to go over to see you and perhaps I may do so next year. But I think it is as well that we meet infrequently, for you should grow up unhampered by my presence and ideas. Each one of us has to find anchorage and to lean on others is not helpful. For over five months we were together – a long enough time – and no doubt we influenced each other as we were bound to do. And yet, is it not curious that during all these months we hardly had a proper conversation, apart from our brief talks about our day-to-day activities. I felt the gulf between two generations and I could not bridge it. No doubt you must have felt this way also.

I am very glad you were with me during these months, for personal

---

1. Letter not published.

reasons of course, but also because they enabled you to have some glimpses of present-day India and of the kind of life I lead. I am tired of this life but I must carry on till February next when the Congress meets at Haripura. Not much relief will come even then for the burden of responsibility will continue but still I shall feel free. Already people are beginning to talk of my continuing as President for another year – an absurd proposition to which I cannot agree. But somehow I have come to occupy a curious position in Indian politics and people are afraid that another person as President may not be able to hold the balance between various forces and tendencies as I have done. But I am quite sure that I must not continue.

Nani is here and I met her today.

In London you might try to get into touch with Jal. I have just had a letter from him and he wants you to see him. His address is: c/o Tata Limited, Thames House, Millbank, London s.w.1 Telephone – Victoria 3462. You can send some of your superfluous luggage back with him to India, if you so desire it. But not if he is coming back by air.

Also don't forget to visit Edward Thompson & his wife at Oxford (Boar's Hill). He has written to me so many times about this and if you do not see him he will not forgive me.

The lions in the zoo roar away here and I listen to them at night.

All my love,

Your loving,
Papu

---

222.   Anand Bhawan,
                                            Allahabad,
                                    30th September, 1937

Darling Indu,

I have had no news from you or of you since you left, except the ocean-letter-radio[1] that you sent. I suppose however that you reached Marseilles safely and proceeded to Paris, and saw the Exhibition, and had an enjoyable time generally in that most attractive city. Perhaps you are on your way to London or are already there. And in another week you will be going to Oxford. My next letter will be sent to Oxford.

I have been living here in Anand Bhawan, a solitary individual, feeding by myself, working alone except when I am in [the] office. I sit here in my room and the door connecting it with your room is usually open. And at night, and sometimes in the daytime too, I go to your room and have a look

---

1. Letter not published.

round and say goodnight to it. Your presence seems to hover round the room and I have not liked the idea of disturbing anything in it. Various oddments lie about, as you left them, and one has a feeling that the room has been recently occupied.

I find it difficult to keep pace with my work. My absence for three weeks has piled it up and I struggle vainly with it. But there is another disadvantage. I am not quite as efficient as I ought to be and usually am. I feel a little stale. Three days ago, when I returned to Allahabad from Lucknow, I did an extraordinary thing. On coming from [the] office at teatime I fell asleep and slept on till dinner time.

Apart from my usual work, I have foolishly agreed to write articles for various foreign periodicals. This is weighing on me. I like to write and I want to write – all manner of ideas and words and phrases float in my mind. But it is difficult to do so in odd moments when one is tired out. However I shall have to keep my promise. I have another week here – of this two days at Lucknow – and then I am off on my journeys again – to the Punjab and the Frontier. Early in November I am keen on going to Assam where I have never been. These Frontier Provinces attract me. The Kashmiri blood, I suppose, has a border tinge.

And so we carry on, and meanwhile you explore Oxford and gradually fall into the life there, and the Japanese bomb and kill the Chinese.[1]

I suppose you will meet Jal Naoroji and he will give you a fancy lunch or dinner. If you have news of Madan Bhai pass it on to me. Write to him if you know the address. Or you can write c/o Lloyds Bank.

I am asking the *Bombay Chronicle* people to send a separate copy to you direct. I think this will be best. After seeing it, you can pass it on to the Oxford Indian Majlis.[2] I do not want to put the burden of having to forward it weekly on you or Efy Aristarchi. She will get her copy separately. For the present I am having the paper sent to you for six months only.

What am I to write to you, my dear? There is so much to write and yet so little – it just depends on how you look at it. But I am terribly busy and you must be pretty well occupied and so I shall restrain myself.

Tell Agatha that I had her letter with the cuttings. She must forgive me for not writing to her. There is nothing special that demands writing just at present.

Love,

Your loving,
Papu

1. The Sino-Japanese War of 1937–45 started as a skirmish between Japanese and Chinese troops on the outskirts of Peking, but within three weeks had developed into an all-out Japanese offensive.
2. Society of Indian Students.

I am getting any number of letters protesting against my sending my daughter to a foreign country, especially England, for her education. This is supposed to be an offence against nationalism.

223.

Somerville College,
Oxford,
10th October, 1937

Darlingest Papu

So I am in College at last! I came up on the 7th from London, feeling terribly nervous and agitated. I do not know why it is that the little things upset me so much more than the bigger ones. Well, I arrived here at about two on Thursday with piles of luggage and everything was so strange, so new and so terrifying. There were innumerable interviews & the seemingly endless dark corridors of Somerville did much to augment the existing confusion. The next two days were pretty full: more interviews and lectures on the tradition of Somerville and rules and regulations. Then there was the unpacking and the trying to get an air of comfort and beauty into my little room. I am afraid I am not very thrilled by the aesthetic sense of the English. The rooms – except a few in the newest part of the building – are terribly uncomfortable and ugly.

Fortunately for me, I had met quite a number of 'Freshers' when we all came up for our viva last March. That made the first few days here considerably more bearable. I have made friends with a charming Arab girl. She has lived mostly in England, having left Syria when she was about eight, but her features are unmistakable. Then there is a lovely Parsi girl who looks & is completely English. I have friends in other women's colleges too. I have also become the secretary of the Indian Majlis & a member of the executive of the China–India Committee. It is so difficult to collect funds these days. I have persuaded Uday Shankar – who is in London – to give a performance for China. It is to be on the 31st Oct. I want to go down to London for it but I do not think I will be allowed to.

I have not yet become a master of the art of lighting a fire which is a nuisance for there is no central heating and it is awfully cold sometimes, especially at night.

This term is going to be very very busy, we are told & already we have been given work for next week. In December we have our Pass Mods exam.

On Tuesday is the Matriculation ceremony, when we shall have to march in crocodile fashion down the chief street of Oxford in our caps & gowns. I rather like the cap but the gown is idiotic.

Lots of love,
Indu

---

224.   Somerville College,
Oxford,
14th October, 1937

Darlingest Papu,

I do so wish you would shut yourself up in a tiny cottage up on a hilltop & not [write] any articles or give press interviews – just for a week or so. I am sure your work would not suffer, for you would be so much fresher to do it. Do please seriously consider the proposal.

I am quite settled down now and feel that I have lived in Somerville all my life. My little room is looking considerably cosier and nicer and by the end of the term I hope it will improve tremendously. At the moment I am terribly in need of a good armchair – a really comfortable one. I have two chairs in my room: one is for the writing table, the other is a rocking chair which, besides being terribly ugly and uncomfortable, falls backwards when you sit on it!

Life here is terribly full. They work us like slaves. Then there are tea parties & coffee parties and all kinds of meetings and concerts & what nots. I think I shall enjoy it very much – somehow just before I came I had my doubts about that!

Now I am a fully pledged member of the University of Oxford. We were matriculated on Tuesday – a most tedious & boring ceremony.

I have written to Edward Thompson. I wasn't sure of his address but I suppose 'Boar's Hill' will reach him.

The Warden of New College has asked me to tea – I believe you wrote to him. I am afraid I cannot decipher his signature. Is it the Fisher[1] who wrote the history books? . . .

I have decided not to go anywhere for the vacs. I shall stay in London most of the time & really & truly work hard. For a few days I might go to Dartington Hall.[2] I expect you know all about that.

I went to a meeting on China last evening. One of the speakers was Prof. Chang Feng-Chun of Nanhai University. He was awfully good: very dignified & restrained. Gilbert Murray[3] also said a few words.

Menon is coming up to speak at one of the Labour Club meetings on the 29th.

With lots & lots of love & great hopes of your taking a good rest,

Indu

---

1. H. A. L. Fisher: British historian and politician.

2. An institution based on a new system of education with emphasis on creative work. Its founder, Leonard K. Elmhirst, was a friend of Rabindranath Tagore. Indira met him in Visva-Bharati.

3. Gilbert Murray: British classical scholar.

225.

Somerville College,
Oxford,
17th October, 1937

Darling Papu,

I have had a lovely day today. I worked solidly from nine thirty to one. After lunch I went out for a long walk in the fields – got back home by three thirty. Went to tea with H. A. L. Fisher. He is awfully nice and his wife is perfectly charming – I wonder if you have met her. There were a number of New College Freshers there and two or three other people too. I had a marvellous time. Then I had dinner with Mrs Rhys-Davis[1] & the Majlis executive – afterwards was the Majlis meeting at which Mrs Rhys-Davis spoke. By the way, I do not remember whether in my last letter I told you that I have become the Women's Secretary of the Majlis. Fortunately I have to do nothing at all – the proper Secretary does all the work.

I am having rather a terrible time trying to sell tickets for the Uday Shankar performance. Undergrads can't run down to London for the night whenever they feel like it – and the tickets I have are quite expensive.

I love Oxford. The so-called 'relaxing' atmosphere has so far had no effect on me – probably because I have much too much to do all the time. But somehow & when I am rushing about it does annoy me to see somebody strolling along the streets quite leisurely, with his hands in his pockets.

I am feeling so worried about you. Must you keep rushing about all the time?

Lots & lots of love,
Indu

———————————

226.

Anand Bhawan,
Allahabad,
20th October, 1937

Darling,

Your first letter[2] from England has come, full of the excitement of going to College. I am afraid my memory of the day when I first went to Cambridge as a Fresher has rather faded, but still I remember something of the excitement and self-importance that accompanied it. But the novelty fades soon enough and we fall into the old rut.

---

1. Caroline Augusta Foley Rhys-Davis: Buddhist scholar and wife of the orientalist, Thomas William Rhys-Davis.
2. Refers to letter No. 223.

My visit to the Frontier was most interesting and even exhilarating. The pleasant and crisp climate contributed to this, but it was the psychological background that appealed to me. I liked the Frontier people – simple, childlike, brave and rather primitive. It was heartening to see their enthusiasm for the Congress and Indian freedom, and their discipline was astonishing. I spent only three days over there – three full days. One day in Peshawar, the second in Utmanzai, where Khan Abdul Ghaffar Khan has his home, and the third was largely taken up by a visit to the Khyber Pass. I loved standing on a hillock overlooking the pass, with Afghanistan stretching on one side beyond the pass, and on the other the wide plains of Hindustan. Facing me on a hilltop stood the remains of an ancient fortress built by Asoka.[1] And all around were dotted pickets and fortifications built by the British. The whole pageant of Indian history seemed to pass before my eyes, conquerors and invaders, pilgrims and traders and students; how many caravans had passed through that narrow defile into the plains of Hindustan right through the ages! What a wonderful gateway to India it was, how easy to defend against almost a world in arms. Surely there is no other country whose land frontier is so secure and difficult of passage. The Himalayas make it impassable except for two or three difficult passes and the most frequented was the Khyber. And even this could be made a terror to the hostile intruder. Yet invading armies have passed through it again and again. But that was not nature's fault. We suffered for our own weakness.

An Afridi would pass us on the road, a rifle strung loosely from the shoulder. He would give the Pushto greeting which means: may you never be tired – a beautiful wish, whether you apply it to the journey through the mountains or to the far more difficult journey through life. The answer was: may good fortune attend you.

Villagers gave us gram *chanā* and *gur*[2] also an enormous loaf of bread which was good enough for half a dozen persons. It was excellent bread, rather like *shirmal*.[3] I was told that this was a small loaf and the big ones were a yard in diameter and two to three inches thick.

We skirted the Frontier for many miles and I was sorely tempted to cross over into the tribal territory. But this might have brought political complications and I wanted to avoid these. We saw the tribal villages, all surrounded by high mud walls and turrets with gun holes. They were like little fortresses.

And so I returned, but before I did so I had already promised to go back

1. Asoka: one of the greatest emperors of India, he lived in the third century B.C. and consolidated the subcontinent of India into a single polity. He was inspired by Buddhism and is specially known for his renunciation of war.

2. Lumps of unrefined sugar.

3. Sweet bread prepared on festive occasions.

as soon as ever I could. Probably I shall visit the Frontier again early in December. It will be cold then, very cold, but I shall enjoy that. I hope to spend a fortnight there. Perhaps, if I have the time, I might dash across to Kashmir for a few days. It will be delightful there in December. But all these are idle fancies and I shan't have the time.

I am going tomorrow to Bijnor for an important election – a Muslim by-election. The Muslim League[1] has been misbehaving and acting generally in a hysterical manner. It is a nuisance. If we win this election as we hope to, it will be an effective damper for these communalists.

On my return from Bijnor I go off immediately to Calcutta for the A.I.C.C. meetings. These will last a week. Then beautiful Assam and the Surma Valley – another frontier of India, the north-eastern. So I shall be on the move till the middle of November – my letters to you will be irregular.

I have brought back from Peshawar two lovely pairs of *chappals* [sandals]. They are strong and comfortable and quite smart looking. No one dare criticise my footwear now!

Feroze has sent me a cable asking for a message for Uday Shankar's performance. I am sending something for him by airmail.

Bibi Amma has been unwell.

Love,
Papu

227.

Somerville College,
Oxford,
21st October, 1937

Papu darling,

It is strange that you did not get my letter from Paris.[2] I wrote it in Old Man Shah's villa and gave it to him to post. I had a lovely time in Paris and Mme Morin introduced me to some very nice girls. I was five days in Paris & most of them were spent in the Exhibition. Louise Morin had to speak at a colonial conference so she could not be with me a lot. I was not frightfully impressed by the pavilions of [the] various nations. The only part I really enjoyed was the various art exhibitions and something which will make you very envious – The Palace of Discovery. It was absolutely marvellous. They have every scientific discovery & invention ever made & there are five guides who explain whatsoever you ask them. The first time I went to the P. of D. I was terribly impressed & interested but I am afraid

---

1. Muslim League: political party which, under the leadership of Mohamed Ali Jinnah, believed that the Muslims of India constituted a distinct nation. This led to the partition of India in 1947.
2. Letter not traceable.

there were so very many things that I did not understand. So in the afternoon I went again – this time having persuaded Sir C. V. Raman to come with us. And he made all the difference.

In London I did nothing much except seeing people and rushing about for the China–India Committee.

I have fallen completely in love with Oxford. It was so difficult to take work seriously after years of not doing anything like this – but I am settling down now & find it easier to spend a whole morning solidly working.

This evening I am going to supper with the Thompsons & on Sunday week to tea with the Mathews.[1]

My tutors & the other dons who have anything to do with me are awfully nice. The Latin one, I hear, is an iceberg. But thank goodness I don't go to her. I do Latin separately with a Mr Luce, who used to teach at Eton. He is as ancient as the Sphinx and terribly deaf! But explains things quite well, in spite of his false teeth. I go to him once a week. Somebody said the other day that Miss Darbyshire looked like a tea-cosy. I think the description suits her perfectly.

My love to Dol Amma & the rest of the family.

All my love,
Indu

---

228.   Somerville College,

Oxford,
29th October [1937]

Darling Papu,

Your letter of the 20th[2] has just come.

I am so very glad that you went to the Frontier and were able to snatch a few hours out of your crowded programme to go to the Khyber Pass. How I wish you could have stayed there longer and how I wish that I were with you! Your letter took me across the land and sea and the many miles that lie between us and for a few flying moments I was with you, gazing down upon the plains of Hindustan – and then I realised that you were already far from the Frontier and had begun your wanderings anew and I was here in Oxford entrapped in the routine of College life. I seem to be in a terrific rush always. One struggles and sits up at night to finish a series of essays and as soon as they are done, it is time for the next series to begin. And, in between, there are innumerable meetings and other engagements.

I think I have told you that I have joined only two societies in Oxford.

1. Basil Joseph Mathews: scholar in the field of missionary movements, and his wife.
2. Refers to letter No. 226.

The Indian Majlis and the University Labour Club. There are all shades of opinions in the Labour Club & it is not affiliated to the Labour Party. But in two days is the County Council election and we want the Labour candidate to get in. I went out canvassing one night and spent a good hour yesterday folding and filling in blanks in election addresses.

The Uday Shankar performance is tomorrow night. I have got late leave & am going down to London. I shall have to go out early from the show as I have to catch the 9.50 train back. It is a nuisance.

The library here is very inadequate. There are so very many of us wanting the same books. I was just wondering that if we have got Stubbs's[1] *Constitutional History* at home, could you have it sent? I couldn't find a second-hand one and the new ones are terribly expensive.

Good luck in the election and in all you do – and as the Afridis say: May you never get tired.

All my love,
Indu

---

229.   Calcutta,
30th October, 1937

Darling,

I have not written to you for many days. The Working Committee and A.I.C.C. absorb all my time. We are in the thick of them. Bapu is here. Nan arrived today. We shall carry on for another three days here and then I go off to the far east of India – Assam & Surma Valley. There will be many river journeys on the Brahmaputra.

I am so glad you like Oxford and feel at home there. The place grows on one. I remember having tea with the Fishers – they are a delightful couple.

You wrote to me something about your financial affairs. I forget what the exact position was but if you are in need of money let me know and I shall send you a cheque on my return to Allahabad, that is about the 16th Nov. Your reply should come about that time.

Love,

Your loving,
Papu

Gurudev is here. I met him four days ago. He is fairly well now but his fine beard has gone – only a tuft remains. His hair also has been cut short.

---

1. William Stubbs: British constitutional historian.

230.   Somerville College,
                                                                Oxford,
                                                    8th November [1937]

Darling Papu,
The post is just leaving so this is just a very hurried line to send you all my love.

Your letter of the 30th,[1] written from Calcutta, arrived this morning. I also had one from Puphi. She says that you are not behaving at all – that is rushing about at a hurricane rate, same as usual.

I am getting on fine. But I am afraid I am acquiring some of your bad habits. Yesterday I had a terribly full day. I had to go out in the morning – then at two there was a Labour study group. At three fifteen Basil Mathews and his wife came & took me to their house on Boar's Hill for tea. I got back at six forty-five – at seven I was having supper with 'The Darb', [Miss Darbyshire] and at eight thirty I had to go to a Majlis meeting – for Krishna Menon was speaking. After that I had coffee with Krishna and got home at eleven fifteen p.m. – just in time not to be locked out! My essay on the Evolution of Parliament had to be read at a class at ten a.m. this morning and until eleven fifteen last evening I had not even read about it! Well, I read until twelve forty-five and then wrote until three fifteen a.m. It was a job getting up this morning – I missed signing the register, as well as my breakfast, for I was ready only just in time for a lecture at ten a.m.! However I got Very Good for the essay! I spent a delightful afternoon with Basil Mathews but did not like his wife much.

Oh, and did I tell you – I went up to town last Thursday & lunched with Julian Huxley[2] & his wife – they are both absolutely charming. She is Swiss.

Meanwhile P. Mods is rearing its ugly head in the not so distant future. I do hope I get through – otherwise it will be such a nuisance.

The best of luck & please do try to rest once in a while.
                                                           Love,
                                                           Indu

———————— ▬▬

231.   Anand Bhawan,
                                                               Allahabad,
                                                    10th November, 1937

My darling,
I rejoice in your letters which tell me of your life full of activity and work and joy. Your written word brings innumerable pictures to my mind, a

1. Refers to letter No. 229.
2. Julian Huxley: British biologist, brother of the novelist Aldous Huxley.

crowd of memories and visions of days gone by, and the sense of emptiness in this silent deserted house goes from me. For otherwise it is

> a lone house filled
> with the cricket's call;
> and the scampering mouse
> in the hollow wall.

The sudden change of my programme, the postponement of my Assam tour, has left me high and dry here. I have enough work of course, more than enough, and I am glad of the opportunity to finish off arrears. But the silence of Anand Bhawan is sometimes quite oppressive and reminds me of my days in prison. I am now planning to go to Assam earlier – perhaps in a fortnight's time. Meanwhile I shall potter about between Allahabad and Lucknow and Mirzapur and a few other nearby places.

Feroze has sent me the programme of the Uday Shankar show. Uday Shankar has also written to me. He wants me to be a patron of his proposed centre for dancing and music in India. I have agreed though I am about the unfittest person for the job.

I am afraid I cannot find Stubbs's *Constitutional History*. It used to be here. Anyway an old edition is not much good. You had better buy a new copy, in spite of its exorbitant price, and not rely too much on the Somerville library. It is better to own textbooks so that you can mark them and use them when you like. I am sending you another book which is pretty well known. This is Taswell-Langmead's[1] *Constitutional History*. You might like to refer to it occasionally.

Last week I sent you one of Tagore's latest pictures, or rather a reproduction of it. This is somewhat remarkable in its own way. When he was recovering from his severe illness, one day he suddenly got up and started painting. He was hardly supposed to be fully conscious at that time. This was the picture he dashed off and it seems to be symbolical of his return to light from the shadows. You see the light breaking through the dark forest of trees. On the back of the picture I have put the date – 15th Sept, 1937.

I enclose an article which has appeared in the current number the *Modern Review*. It is well written and will interest you. I think it is very largely true. Don't you? Do you get the *Modern Review*? If not, I shall arrange to have it sent. The Majlis would at any rate profit by it. Satish Kalelkar[2] has written to me how the Majlis people appreciate your *Chronicle*.

1. Thomas Pitts Taswell-Langmead: scholar in the field of constitutional history and law.

2. Satish Kalelkar: son of Kakasaheb Kalelkar, who was a prominent associate of Mahatma Gandhi; contemporary of Indira Nehru in Great Britain, later served in the Indian Foreign Service.

I am glad you have had some experience of canvassing. It is a useful experience to have and one learns much of human nature from it. But it is often a disheartening process. I am no good at it and anyhow I can't do it now, at any rate, on the individual basis. I canvass *en bloc*, taking a few thousands at a time.

Have you ever eaten persimmons? Have you even heard of them? This is a delightful fruit – a cross between a tomato and an apricot. Some kind-hearted individual whom I don't know has been sending me parcels of it from the Kulu Valley.

Love,

> Your loving,
> Papu

232.

> Somerville College,
> Oxford,
> 14th November [1937]

Darling Papu,

It is your birthday today and I do not know where you will be rushing about. Here in Oxford it is a lovely day, cold and frosty but with the sun smiling down on us. I am going to have a busy day – I usually do on a Sunday.

Most people go to church on Sunday morning and this place is quite deserted and so quiet – a very welcome state of affairs – and so different from the almost maddening noise of weekdays.

I am glad I have taken the History schools. The only other possibility, of course, was Modern Greats – in other words Politics, Philosophy & Economics. But the general opinion seems to be that the P.P.E. schools are very superficial and therefore unintellectual! Besides I enjoy History immensely & I shall enjoy it still more when I don't have to do any Latin or French. The French is easy enough but I hate doing 'reference-to-the-context' questions, they are so uninteresting.

16th November

As usual I forgot to post this letter last night & consequently missed this morning's airmail.

Lord Zetland[1] came to the Majlis last night and spoke on 'Please try to understand us'. What a subject to have! He is not a good speaker & in any case there wasn't much to say. There were some questions at the end – he dared not reply – so sat down after saying a couple of inaudible words.

1. Lord Zetland: Secretary of State for India, 1935–40.

And all the time he looked so superior & smug – I could have done I don't know what to him. Ach – the man makes me mad. It was a stupid idea to have him up, anyway. I knew what it would be like.

Do you remember that bump I got on my head in Singapore.[1] Well, the bump itself has more or less disappeared but the pain hasn't. I suddenly become aware of it when I am doing my hair or sleeping on that side. I don't know whether it is worthwhile going to a doctor.

Lots of love,
Indu

233.   Somerville College,
                                                            Oxford,
                                             21st November [1937]

Darling Papu,
Thanks a lot for your charming letter.[2]

And thank you for sending Gurudev's latest picture – Krishna Kripalani of Santiniketan had told me about it when I wrote to ask him about Gurudev's health.

This is going to be a wretched letter. My head is in such a muddle & my hand is aching as well!

People who live in digs have a lot to be thankful for. At what seemed to be the middle of the night – when I was sleeping peacefully last night – I heard a weird noise. I swore at the girl next door, thinking that she was carrying out an experiment or something – she is a science student! The noise persisted & someone barged into my room & said, 'Fire-drill!' At that time of day on a cold and frosty morning!

It is getting really cold now – the parks were quite white with frost all day & the little stream had layers of thin ice . . .

22nd November

I have just come from a most interesting lunch. It was at the home of a Mr & Mrs Spalding. I don't quite know who they are except that they are connected with the dear old 'Varsity'. He is terrifically interested in history & I have promised to show him the *Glimpses*. Then there was Prof. Wang, the lecturer in Chinese. I liked him awfully. He isn't attached to any special College yet for he is very busy learning English. But he is a great scholar & comes from a family of scholars and is very interesting to talk to. Like most Chinese, he seemed to me very simple and straight-

1. Indira visited Singapore in the course of a trip to Burma and Malaya taken with her father in 1937.
2. Refers to letter No. 231.

forward but with an immensity of depth – I don't know why people say that Orientals have intricate & complicated natures.

I also met somebody who had tea with you some time ago in Simla. He is a don at University College & one of our college governors.

Gurudev's painting – or rather the copy of it – has just arrived. It is beautiful and so very expressive. Thank you for sending it . . .

My exam is drawing nearer & nearer. I am quite terrified. There is a great agitation for reforming it, supported by several dons and most undergrads. And the matter is being taken up by various societies such as the Faculty of History Society & the Political & Economic Society. Nothing will come of it for quite some time, I am sure, and we will certainly not benefit by the reform – whatever shape it takes. But it's worth fighting for, for the sake of future generations. We are jolly grateful to the undergrads of the last generation, who secured the deletion of the clause in the Mods syllabus which made Greek as well as Latin compulsory.

Next Sunday at the Majlis we are having Palme Dutt. He is going to speak on 'Why we understand the British Govt. too well'. It is going to be a sort of answer to Lord Zetland. I am told that P. Dutt is not a very good speaker.

I have to rush off to a Latin Tute now – so cheerio, and do keep well & fit & fresh.

All my love,
Indu

234.   Somerville College,
                                                  Oxford,
                                     25th November [1937]

Darling Papu,
I am afraid this is going to be another of my 'rush' notes. The post is just going.

And anyway nothing seems to have happened this week – at least nothing special. I have met a number of quite interesting undergrads – in fact the rate at which people are introduced to me is so terrific that I can't possibly remember any names at all.

Then, one evening, I went round the shops and restaurants in connection with [the] Japanese Boycott. We have asked all the restaurants to put up a petition signed by ten dons – including Gilbert Murray. And at the shops we want to put up enormous posters saying, 'WE SELL NO JAPANESE GOODS'. Of course it is terribly difficult. Jap goods are so dashed cheap. In fact if the boycott were at all successful, Woolworth's would have to close down altogether and other cheap shops, such as Marks & Spencer, would lose terrifically.

Laski is speaking at the Labour Club tonight. I should have liked to go but in a moment of forgetfulness I accepted an invitation to go to a concert tonight – I shouldn't really grumble because it is a very good concert – Roy Henderson – and good concerts are much rarer than speakers like Laski!

Meanwhile P. Mods comes ever nearer and I am all 'a-tremble'.

Tons of love,
Indu

235.

Somewhere in Assam,
Kamrup district,
27th November, 1937

Darling Indu,

I am far away from you, even further away than usual, for I am wandering in the north-east corner of India. Within a few days I shall almost touch the frontiers of Burma and Tibet. After a day and two nights' journey from Allahabad I entered Assam last night. Today I have skirted the Brahma-putra and rushed through two districts and looked at large numbers of faintly mongoloid Assamese people. We have now arrived at the end of the day's journey and are staying at a Harijan Ashram. The man in charge and his wife – a Mahratta couple – evidently know their job and the hut I am staying in is most efficiently and artistically made – all bamboo and thatch. The bed is pure bamboo and an ideal garden seat it would make. As a bed it is just like a plank of wood, hard and resistant.

I have been worried about one thing. You wrote to me[1] that you intended spending the Christmas holidays in London. This does not seem to me a frightfully attractive proposition. I suppose your Mods will be over then and even if they are not, you deserve a more health-giving holiday. I am sure a spell of winter sports will do you more good than anything else. Good health is of tremendous help in intellectual work. Your experience last year proved that much to you. I hope therefore that you will try to put in some days in a winter resort. Even if you don't go far or on the Continent, try to take some real rest in good surroundings. London won't give you much rest and you will return to Oxford in a tired condition. Do not mind a little extra cost . . .

Love,
Papu

1. Refers to letter No. 224.

236.   Somerville College,
                                                                 Oxford,
                                                        3rd December [1937]

Darling Papu,
Nearer and nearer comes P. Mods and I am in the throes of revision. At
last the timetable has been put up – the exam begins on Monday, 6th Dec.,
and will be over, at least as far as I am concerned, on the 9th morning. I
shall go to London on the 10th.

I don't yet know what I am doing in the vac. There is a terrific lot of
reading to do, so I should stay in London for sometime. Agatha came up
here last Sunday and was horrified at the idea – this winter is much colder
& foggier than usual, I believe! Personally I don't mind the fog or the cold
– but perhaps I might go to the Tyrol or some such place and squeeze in a
week or ten days of skiing. I also want to learn to skate. I have never done it
& it is so very graceful.

I am feeling rather drawn towards the Honour School of P.P.E. –
Politics, Philosophy & Economics – but being also tremendously interested in History, I just don't know what to do. The work in P.P.E. will
probably be too heavy for me. This is our History work: the whole of
English History to 1914, including of course the history of the colonies,
dependencies and the like. Then a General History paper – we can
choose one period:

     i)   285–604
    ii)   476–919
   iii)   919–1273
    iv)   1273–1494
     v)   1414–1559
    vi)   1559–1715
   vii)   1715–1815
  viii)   1789–1871
    ix)   1815–1914

Next there are general questions related to History & Political Thought.
The fourth paper will be on Political Science. Then there is French (or
any other modern language) translation. We have also to choose a special
subject from among the following:

    1) St Augustine
    2) The Third Crusade
    3) Medieval English Boroughs
    4) The Period of Edward I

5) The Italian Renaissance
6) The Protectorate and Restoration
7) British India, 1772–1805
8) The American Revolution
9) The French Revolution
10) British Colonial Policy, 1830–1860
11) Political Economy
12) Industrial Relations
13) Principles of Modern English Government, 1867–1931
14) Military History and Strategy

For my special subject I want to do No. 5, the Italian Renaissance – it will mean learning Italian & perhaps doing some Latin as well, but I think it is worth it. Do tell me what you think about it all – and the General History paper.

The cheque you sent me for my birthday has been returned by your bank with 'no advice' written on it. I am sending it to you . . .

Lots of love,
Indu

---

237.   Assam-Bengal Railway,

On the way to Sylhet,
4th December, 1937

Darling Indu,
I have had no letter from you since I left Allahabad. Probably your letters await me in Anand Bhawan and no one has taken the trouble to forward them. It was a risky business as I was moving about.

My eight days' tour of the valley of the Brahmaputra ended today and now I am going to the Surma Valley – Sylhet and Cachar. I have liked my visit to Assam. The uncommon mixture of semi-tropical scenery with a background of snow-covered mountains and a noble river is attractive. Much of my journeying has been done on the Brahmaputra and I have especially enjoyed sailing in a country boat.

There are any number of backward tribal people near the frontier and some of them looked intelligent. I wish I had more time to give to them. The Assamese people . . . are pleasant and likable. Gauhati, Tezpur, Silghat, Goalpara, North Lakhimpur, Jorhat, Goalhat, Dibrugarh, Tinsukhia, Digboi, Dum Duma – these are a few of the places I visited. Have you heard of them? A number of them were well situated on the banks of the Brahmaputra, and Tezpur, in addition, nestled at the foot of the hills.

I am travelling in style – first class! This is the same railway by which we came from Chittagong. There is no second class. I tried to travel Inter[1] but the railway authorities have cleared that whatever ticket I might hold I should be accommodated in a first-class compartment. I put up with this during a short journey once with an inter ticket. But it is embarrassing and this time, on a longer journey, I had to decide to buy a first ticket. It is as well, as I am tired and the inter is crowded. But I get little rest, as at every station – we stop at every station! – crowds come and fill the air with their slogans. They are mostly tea-garden coolies. In their poverty they give us some money for 'Swaraj' or for the Kamala Memorial Fund.[2] I feel terribly small when these gifts are offered. At the last station some owner of a tea garden presented me with a case of the best Assam tea – enough to last us for a year or two. Also a dozen huge pineapples grown here. Some weavers gave me a piece of *endi*, the strong coarse Assam silk. So my luggage is increasing.

I read in a Calcutta paper the other day a full report of the Majlis' debate where Zetland came. It must have been an interesting function.

Love,

Your loving,
Papu

---

238.   In train,
                                                    5th December [1937]

[Darling Indu]

At an odd station called Lumding a packet of letters from Allahabad reached me and in this I found a letter[3] from you.

I had all along thought that you were taking Modern Greats but now I learn that you have chosen the History schools. If you like this better then you have done well. After all, these different schools are more or less pegs on which to hang your reading and thinking.

I am concerned about your headache. I think it would be as well to consult a doctor. I don't suppose any medication will do much good but still expert advice is always desirable. You might consult the local doctor

---

1. Indian railways at that time had four classes of compartments, First, Second, Inter(mediate) and Third.

2. After Kamala Nehru's death, it was decided to open a hospital in her name in Anand Bhawan, with subscriptions from the public.

3. Refers to letter No. 232.

and later, when you go to London, a specialist, who will no doubt relieve you of a few guineas.

Have you news of Madan Bhai?

Papu

———————————

239.   Garmisch,
                                                28th December [1937]

Darling Papu,
There hasn't been any news from you or anybody else from India for simply ages. I expect most airmail letters are still lying at the bottom of the sea. Your letter dated 27th Nov.[1] reached me on 18th Dec. in a big envelope marked 'On His Majesty's Service' and 'Damaged by sea water'. The letter was all smudged but I managed to decipher most of it without difficulty.

After Mods were over, I was feeling so dreadfully tired and worn out – almost ill – and a few days' stay in London did me no good. So I packed up a rucksack, slung it on to my back, got into my ski trousers and big boots and here I am.

The only reason for choosing Garmisch was that the snow here is said to be the most marvellous in all Europe – that is why Garmisch was chosen for the Winter Olympics.

When I first arrived the snow was not too good but then it snowed all day & night over Christmas and Gosh what snow! I have never enjoyed skiing so much. I left London with the intention of trying skating as well as skiing – but skiing leaves no time for anything else. (Though I manage to get in a little reading in the evenings.)

It is cold but so fresh and beautiful and perfectly glorious. I eat enormously and have gone up six pounds in the eight days that I have been here! Good work, isn't it?

30th December

... I went down to Innsbruck in the Austrian Tyrol yesterday. I must confess I was terribly disappointed. I did not find it half as beautiful as I had expected to do. The people were terribly grim looking – one somehow felt that it was a crime to laugh out aloud in the streets. But the surrounding mountain ranges were indeed lovely and I believe there are some marvellous slopes for skiing. I paid a brief visit to the museum of folk art. It was interesting.

Tomorrow morning – 31st Dec. – I leave Garmisch. I shall spend the

1. Refers to letter No. 235.

day in Munich – specially to see the famous Deutsches Museum. Do you remember how hard we tried to see it together? Unfortunately that was not possible. But tomorrow, when I am walking through the museum, I shall think of you & shall try to tell you about it or to send you pictures of it.

Last night there was ski jumping on the small Olympic Jump. It was marvellous. The biggest jump was fifty-eight metres – that is jolly good considering the size of the jump. And the night before last I went to watch an ice hockey match between Budapest & Riessersee. It was very exciting – otherwise I do not think anyone could have borne the cold. The stadium is quite open and it was snowing quite hard. All the Germans were naturally backing Riessersee so I backed Budapest which won by two goals to nil. There were three games of hockey and in between there was figure skating. There were some quite famous skaters and among them a little girl aged about eight from Vienna. She was awfully good. I think she won some championship at the Olympic games last year. I love watching skating – it is the most graceful of sports, don't you think? I want to learn it some time soon.

My skiing has improved considerably since last year. I do wish you could see me coming down one of these terrific slopes or, better still, if you could be coming down it too with me.

Garmisch has been a dream of beauty and fun. But like all dreams it must end. Tomorrow I say goodbye to it and then back to London and hard work with the noise & the crowds & the rain! Term begins on the 15th. So on the 14th I shall be back in Oxford.

Lots of love – I wish so much I could pay you a flying visit and have a glimpse of you and say a few words.

Ever your loving,
Indu

240.   London,
                                    4th January, 1938

Darlingest Papu,

I don't know what has come over me – I haven't written to you for ages and I now find that even my last letter[1] was not posted in Garmisch. I am ever so sorry – I arrived in London on the 2nd evening. It was raining hard and most miserably cold. It has not yet stopped drizzling. It is so dark even in the mornings & afternoons and a very grim sort of atmosphere prevails over the town. Garmisch seems so very far away. I wonder if I ever actually went there or whether I just dreamt it.

---

1. Refers to letter No. 239.

Munich was a terrific rush and very tiring. I arrived there at about eleven a.m. on the 31st Dec. All museums were closed! So I just walked around the town – it's not very big but it has a certain charm about it. The German police are terribly strict about people crossing the road at the wrong time – I was in eternal terror of being fined several marks every time I crossed, as it was my supply of marks was very limited for my stay in Germany was drawing to an end! On the 1st Jan. the Deutsches Museum was open only from one o'clock to six. So in the morning I went to the Alte Pinakotheke in which there is a most marvellous collection of paintings, of Rubens, Van Dyck and Murillo – also Durer and many others. I wanted to leave for London the same evening so there was not very much time left for the museum. I was there punctually at one when the gate opened and I stayed there until five o'clock – when I had to leave if I did not wish to miss my train. In these four hours all I could do was to rush through the ground floor! But it did give me an idea of what the whole museum is like. It's tremendous. Everything is explained in detail – take coal for instance. It began with how mines were made and so on, with every stage until we came up to coal ready to be sold & then all the three products that are made from coal. For this there was an actual underground mine with wax figures doing the work. Opposite the museum is the museum library and in it was being held an anti-Jew exhibition. The entrance was free. It was widely advertised in every German city & we saw crowds going in to see it. At the entrance & in most of the advertisements were enormous pictures of a very ugly Jew holding a bag of money in one hand and the map of the U.S.S.R. & hammer & sickle in the other. The very sight of the picture made me sick. It was absolutely revolting.

At the museum & other places also people like guides & postmen were very friendly and asked about Bapu & talked of how my ancestors & their own were the same – both being Aryans!

The train journey back was very tiring, for the train was packed.

All my love,
Indu

241.

London,
7th January, 1938

Darling Papu,
Thank you ever so much for the cheque of £15. You do spoil me terribly. It's not good, you know – although of course I love it! . . .

There's nothing very exciting happening in London. I have rather a lot of work to do and so don't go out much. But the other day I went to a film called *The Life of Emile Zola.* I don't know how far the story is historically correct but the film is great. Emile Zola is acted by Paul Muni – who was Wang the Farmer in *The Good Earth.* His acting in this film is much better – he is really stupendous in some scenes.

There is tremendous agitation going on amongst the London Indians on the subject of Subhas Bose's proposed visit to England. There are endless committee meetings at which nothing is ever decided. The reception committee itself has about fifty members and almost every one of them wanted to speak at the Bose meeting! With great difficulty it was decided that only three people should speak. This caused great discontent, for the names could not be decided upon – at last it was passed that there should be no speakers except Bose & Palme Dutt, who is to be chairman of the meeting! Meanwhile the English papers insist on printing the news that Bose has been seeing Mussolini and the Duke of Windsor. Bose says he has not but does not contradict the news publicly – as a result some students believe that he did have these interviews and this causes unnecessary opposition to Bose & the plans of the reception committee.

Lots of love,
Indu

What is Shammie's name & address?

P.S.
There is going to be another exhibition of Chinese painting – probably the best of the pictures that were exhibited last time. The proceeds will be sent to the China Medical Aid Committee. I hope to be able to see it.

Another exhibition that I am keen on going to is the XVII Century Art in Europe one. I hear it is very wonderful.

---

242.   Anand Bhawan,

Allahabad,
9th January, 1938

Darling Indu,
News from Europe tells us that almost the whole Continent is in the grip of a cold wave. I have been wondering how you fared in South Germany where it must have been terribly cold. Probably this was good for winter sports. Here the cold has suddenly retreated and we are having a fairly warm spell.

I was in Bombay last week for five days for the Working Committee meeting. It was warm there of course. Bapu was recuperating at Juhu and I went there twice. The beach was delightful and I was sorely tempted to have a dip in the sea. But no such luck.

In Bombay I met Somerset Maugham,[1] the writer. Also Gunther, the author of *Inside Europe*, and his wife.[2] Last year Gunther published his diaries in *Nash's* magazine – perhaps you saw them. He had met me two years ago in London and he had said in his diary that I had a rich chocolate complexion exactly like Josephine Baker's! The poor man was repeatedly reminded of this, much to his embarrassment. I presided over a meeting he addressed in Bombay and our speeches were broadcast. I think this was the first time I have been broadcast in this way.

The house is full at present. There is Nan and her children, and Betty and her kids. But soon Anand Bhawan will be empty again. Nan is going to Lucknow tonight and Chand & Co. will go back to Woodstock. Betty will be going to Bombay. I shall go to Lucknow and from there to Lahore and the Frontier. On my return at the end of the month I shall have to go to Wardha for another Working Committee meeting. Soon after this will be the Haripura Congress. I am so tired of this moving about. But constant travelling is an unavoidable routine in this vast country for a politician.

What is far worse is the conflict that is rapidly developing within the Congress. I am worried about this and I do not know what I shall do after Haripura. I want to be free from all burden of office and to devote myself to special departments of Congress work as well as reading and writing. But it is not always possible to do what one wants to do. And when a serious situation arises, one cannot shirk responsibility. So I am in a tangle.

You will let me know, will you not, if you want more money? I have a small balance at Lloyd's now and I can let you have a cheque if you are in need of it. I suppose you received £50 on January 1st through Lloyd's.

Love,
Papu

I suppose you have met Subhas Bose in London. He will be declared elected to the Congress Presidentship in another week or ten days.

243.

Anand Bhawan,
Allahabad,
10th January, 1938

Indu dear,
Last night I wrote to you.[3] Within an hour or two of that Dol Amma had an unexpected paralytic attack. It was severe and after heavy breathing all

1. Somerset Maugham: English writer.
2. Frances Gunther: American journalist, wife of John Gunther.
3. Refers to letter No. 242.

night, she expired early this morning. Fortunately she was not conscious all this time and so probably did not suffer. By a curious chance we were all with her when the attack came – Nan, Betty, Ranjit & myself. Nan was going to Lucknow & she was just bidding goodbye to Mother. Even the children were all in the house.

Papu

---

244.   London,
12th January [1938]

Darling Papu,
You will forgive me, I know, if I write only a few lines. What can one say on such occasions? I have never been able to speak or to write when I feel deeply. But [with] these few lines I send you all my love and you know that my thoughts are with you.

College does not open until the 15th – and till then I am in London. Your telegram was therefore redirected from Oxford and reached London late in the evening of the 10th. I learnt the news from the evening papers on Victoria Station, where I had gone to meet Subhas Bose. She was so very frail – perhaps we all expected this to happen in the very near future & yet sometimes one is not prepared even for the expected and the inevitable. The house will be empty without her and how we shall all miss that tiny figure silently sitting in the dining room or fussing around about the food and how much or rather how little everyone ate.

How did it happen? And were you near her?

All my love, Papu darling, and if thoughts mean anything at all, you will know that I am thinking of you all the time – I only wish I could be with you.

Indu

---

245.   Anand Bhawan,
Allahabad,
14th January, 1938

Darling Indu,
Four days ago I wrote to you a brief note.[1] But that day was not to end before death again hovered over Anand Bhawan. Before we had recovered from one shock, another came and numbed us. Death is almost always an unwelcome visitor and yet it came as it should come – suddenly

---

1. Refers to letter No. 243.

and in the fullness of time. I was always afraid that Dol Amma might be paralysed and linger on in pain and torment. Fortunately there was the briefest of pain, if any, and she fainted and became wholly unconscious right at the beginning. For nearly six hours she remained in this state, breathing heavily, and then quietly and peacefully passed away in the early morning at four forty-five a.m.

We had spent a busy bustling day. Nan was going that night to Lucknow and Chand, Tara & Rita were following in the car the next morning. Betty & her children were leaving soon for Bombay. And so there was packing and arranging and talking, and I felt too tired to go to [the] office and remained at home most of the time. I played with the children. And then there were several big packing cases containing caskets and addresses from Assam and these had been opened. I sent for Vyas to take them away for the museum. There was more of a family atmosphere than I had experienced for a long time. Dol Amma was more active than usual and I noticed particularly that she was better than she had been. We sat down to dinner, a large family party, and Dol Amma and Bibi also sat there. We talked of old times and family affairs and told stories of each other. Then Nan went away to pack and prepare for departure. We all adjourned to Dol Amma's room. She asked me about you – how you were – if I had heard from you recently – if I had written to you. I told her that I had written that very evening. 'Did you send my love to her?' she asked. I confessed that I had not specifically mentioned it but it was there of course, taken for granted. But she was not satisfied. She said she could not write herself and so I must not forget to send you always her love. I promised to do so.

We all moved to Nan's dressing room and sat there for a few minutes. It was about ten forty-five p.m. Nan said it was time for her to go and we all got up. Dol Amma got up with some difficulty, from a stool on which she had been sitting. She bent forward to embrace Nan and suddenly fell towards Nan. Nan and I took hold of her. We saw that all was not well and that something had happened. I asked her what the matter was but there was no answer. I took her gently to her bedroom, partly leading her, partly almost carrying her. She tried to walk but was not very successful. We put her in bed and soon she was wholly unconscious. She started breathing hard. The doctor came and said it was a bad attack of paralysis and the brain was probably affected – cerebral haemorrhage. If so there was little hope. Anyway there was nothing to be done except to wait and see for the next few hours. Bibi and I were in her room all night and Nan and Betty were next door in Nan's room, coming in frequently to see how Mother was. At about four thirty a.m. the hard breathing became slower and quieter. At four forty-five it was all over. That was exactly the time seven years ago when Dadu died.

After the first shock Bibi worked hard at various arrangements. There were crowds of people coming. All business was suspended in the city and at midday the funeral procession started. On the insistence of people this took a long route, right through Katra and Chowk, on to the embankment and then to the *Sangam.* A vast, more or less silent crowd followed.

We returned about four-thirty p.m. I learnt on return that Bibi, after finishing up the cleaning, etc., had felt unwell and had fainted. She was lying unconscious and was breathing in exactly the same way as Mother had done the night before. Still we thought that she was merely tired out. The doctor came and disillusioned us, telling us that Bibi was suffering from exactly the same trouble as Dol Amma. She did not regain consciousness. At four forty-five a.m. exactly, on 11th January she passed away.

So within twenty-four hours we had two deaths in Anand Bhawan and though Death had triumphed, it seemed almost that it came at Bibi's bidding. It was strange how peaceful both the faces were after death, especially Bibi's.

People have come to us in large numbers. And thousands of messages. And incessant activity has kept us moving and occupied during these three days. But this house feels strange and odd, and I find myself going unconsciously to Mother's room to say goodnight to her or to ask her about something.

Anand Bhawan has been full. It will be completely deserted day after tomorrow. Nan has just gone to Lucknow, Betty and Raja (he rushed up to Allahabad on learning of Mother's death) are leaving after a few hours. So am I and Ranjit. I do not like the idea of living here all by myself.

We shall have to seek fresh adjustments and to settle down to new ways. That always happens as one generation passes off, leaving the stage to another. One generation in our family has now gone completely, and I have become an elder, gradually fading off. It is going to be lonely in Anand Bhawan. For the next fortnight I shall be away and then I shall come back.

It is *melá* [fair] time and crowds of pilgrims are streaming into Anand Bhawan. The house remains but more and more it becomes a hollow shell. So it will remain till a new spirit fills its empty rooms and verandahs.

And so I shall keep my last promise to your grandmother and send you her love. But how can I convey in words the abundance and intensity of that love of hers for you? Or her love for her son which enveloped her and filled her. I know well that whatever love and affection may be in store for us in the future, and we have been fortunate in that respect in the past, neither of us will ever experience that full flood of unselfish and enveloping love that only a mother or a grandmother can give.

But we must not be sorrowful for she died at the right time and as she

should have done. For years now she was almost a wraith, weary of life.
Death must have been a release to her.

Love,
Papu

***

246.   Somerville College,
                                                                        Oxford,
                                                      18th January [1938]

Darling Papu,
Term has begun – and what a term. It is going to be most terribly heavy.
And I have made good resolutions which, for a change, I am going to stick
to very strictly. To begin with I shall go to bed every night before ten
fifteen p.m. – exception to this rule is only to be made (at the most) once a
week. I shall not accept more invitations than one a week! And I am not
going to take any part in the Majlis or the Labour Club activities. This, in
short, is my curriculum for Hilary term. After the Easter holidays I hope to
lead a more healthy life!

I wonder if I have ever told you of Mr & Mrs Lieftinck. They are a
charming couple with whom I stayed in Amsterdam for about twenty-four
hours just before flying to India. I have a letter from Mrs Lieftinck today.
It is mainly about Kagawa of Japan[1] and his cooperative movement. Here
is an extract from her letter.

Kagawa has organised his people in cooperatives because he believes
that the economic [problems] must be solved before we come to
real unity and happiness. I had many talks with Miss Topping (K's
secretary) and she feels v. strongly that this coop movt. can only be of
value when it is international and gets trade into its hands. This will be a
strong power to overcome imperialistic forces, as money is the thing
everybody needs. What I want to ask you is this: Do you believe that
your father would like to come into touch with this idea & to organise in
India, cooperatives so that Kagawa in Japan & your father could
become stronger in an unbloody way?

Well! What do you think of that? I shall reply to Mrs Lieftinck – as I can
guess more or less how you feel about the whole question.

The thrill of Oxford has worn off I am afraid and Oxford life as it really
is, is not a very attractive spectacle. Of course in Oxford one can lead just

1. Toyohiko Kagawa: Japanese social reformer and evangelist.

the kind of life one wants to but it is depressing to know to what use about fifty per cent of the students put that freedom and then all the time are grumbling and asking for more. I wonder if you have heard of Keith Bryant's (who was up at Oxford until 1936) book *Oxford Limited*. It caused quite a scandal in England & the daily newspapers made much of it – it contains a great deal of truth, but not all the truth, for if it had done it could not have been published.

Lots and lots of love, darling, and keep fit.

Indu

247.

Somerville College,
Oxford,
21st January [1938]

Darling Papu,
Day before yesterday came your two letters of the 9th[1] & 10th.[2]

I realise what a terrific strain the present situation in the Congress must be on you – and how very worried you must be about recent developments. A couple of days ago I saw the news in some London paper that the ban on the Congress ministers' participation in official functions has been lifted[3] – and worse still, that the wording of the Independence Pledge[4] has been modified 'to suit times of peace' (such as we have at present?). Pathetic, isn't it? And yet – perfectly logical sequence to acceptance of office. I admit I felt quite wild when I read the tiny paragraph and am still feeling terribly 'hot and bothered'. What do you think will happen next – where is all this leading us to?

Subhas Bose has been in England as you know. He met very many people – specially MPs of the Labour Party and other left-wingers. But I am afraid – from what I have gathered – nothing much came of it, and the 'firebrands' of London politics were not much impressed. Like so many of our Indian political leaders, he hardly attempts to understand the world situation or how India as well as the rest of the colonies is an integral part of world politics.

But I do hope that you will be able to get some time to yourself, once you lay down this heavy burden of presidentship. There is such a lot that is

1. Refers to letter No. 242.
2. Refers to letter No. 243.
3. When the Congress Party formed governments in the provinces in 1937, Congress ministers had initially decided not to take part in formal official functions.
4. Independence Pledge was taken after the Lahore session of the Congress (December 1929) every year on 26th January reiterating the demand for complete independence by the people of India.

waiting to be done by people like you – work that cannot be done by anybody else . . .

  With lots & lots of love – darling Papu,
Indu

P.S.
The old old problem is bothering me again – History or P.P.E.? I am still tremendously interested in History – but in Modern History. And in working for the History schools we spend half our time over the ancient and medieval stuff. Somehow Roman Britain, fascinating as it is in many ways, does not attract me enough to take it for final schools. It is the kind of thing I would like to read when I am old and grey and am sitting by the fire! On the other hand – there is a terrific lot of history in P.P.E. (Politics, Philosophy & Economics). The only thing that bothers me about P.P.E. is that it means a terrible lot of work & jolly hard work too. And also I am not very good friends with Economics. However, if it is not already too late to change over I shall consult Miss Darbyshire & my tutor. The only trouble is that nobody here treats one as if one were a person at all – one is just a machine that gives in essays on time.

  I am sorry to bother you with my trivial troubles but there isn't another soul I can talk to like this or to take my little bothers to – and it is such a relief sometimes to have one's say.
Indu

248.
Kohat,
North-West Frontier Province,
24th January, 1938

Darling,
A letter came from you yesterday reaching me at Peshawar. I feel like writing to you, although I am tired after a very heavy day and it is late. A more serious difficulty is the lack of a suitable pen to write. My three fountain-pens have suddenly and most unaccountably failed me – including my close companion of seven or eight years which wrote the *Glimpses* and the *Auto*. Almost there seems to have been a conspiracy in the pen world. I have to use Upadhyaya's pen and this is utterly bad.

  These four days in the Frontier have been full of interest and even some excitement. The weather has been ideal – cold and sunny. In the daytime the sun is hot and almost scorching but the wind is cold. In the shade one shivers. I would love to sunbathe in this climate. I find my appetite going up.

  At Abbottabad a welcome gate consisting of pillars of snow was erected.

I have had tremendous welcomes everywhere, including the welcome of the tribal people in the independent areas. One old Khan – (the wretched pen has failed me!) who had lost everything during the Civil Disobedience Movement and had his house burnt down by the military, gave me his warm Chitral[1] coat. It was an ancient, well-worn garment, not even clean – but it was the most precious thing he had and he gave it to me. It is no use to me, but the graciousness of the gift has made it very valuable.

Today we motored from Peshawar to Kohat. On the way we passed through many miles of tribal territory inhabited by the Afridi. At every village they had turned out in force to welcome us, almost everyone with a gun carelessly hanging round his shoulder. There are no restrictions on the keeping of arms in this tribal area and dearer than wife or child is the gun of the Afridi. They make them themselves in primitive fashion but astonishingly good and cheap.

The Afridis gave us a welcoming salvo of gunfire before each village. We had to get down and speak to them and have tea and hard-boiled eggs. It was difficult to consume eggs every two hundred yards or so, yet one had to do it. Then came a refugee banquet *dumba* (roast lamb) and fine thick bread. Both were well cooked. At one place a lamb and a goat were presented to us alive. We could not carry them about and so we gave them back and I suppose they were slaughtered later.

One of my Pathan hosts has presented me with some handspun & handwoven pieces of cloth done by his womenfolk. One piece was for me, the other and the finer one for 'Indira'! It is a fine piece of work, though done somewhat crudely. I thought of you at Oxford and how, whether you willed it or not, the burden of notoriety was already yours. And with that notoriety an abundance of affection and goodwill from numberless persons unknown to you. You cannot escape it or the responsibility that it entails, even as I am a prisoner bound down by cords harder than those of steel.

What a magnificent people are these men and women of the North. And the border tribes, about whom we read so much and perhaps imagine to be fierce savages, how profitable and likeable they are.

Writing in pencil is a tiring business. So goodbye, my darling.

Papu

---

1. A princely state in North-West Frontier Province, known for its picturesque scenery.

249.   Lucknow,
                                                29th January, 1938

Darling Indu,
I have just come back from the Frontier – a few hours at Lahore *en route*
and now a few hours in Lucknow before I proceed to Allahabad. As I have
come here rather unexpectedly, I have a little leisure and how can I
employ it to better advantage than by writing to you? I shall be in Allahabad
for two days only, tomorrow and the day after, and they will be very full
days. So I am writing now but I shall post this letter from Allahabad where
I expect to find your letters awaiting me.

The week in the Frontier Province has been full of new and worthwhile
experiences and, if I had the time, I could write a lot about it. It has been a
heartening time and I have had a peep at an aspect of India which few of us
know much about. I might have written to you again from the train or from
some halting place but the tragedy of my fountainpens came in the way. At
last someone took pity on me and presented me with his own pen. The nib
does not suit but it functions anyway.

The cold wind and the hot sun have left their marks on my face. It is
sunburnt and the skin is peeling off. But I feel fit and well, except for a
slight lack of sufficient sleep. My appetite, as I wrote to you, went up
markedly and I consumed more meat than I have ever done. There was
little help for it, as meat was the chief diet. One of the most satisfying
meals I have had was with the Afridis in the tribal territory. It consisted of
dumba – lamb – roasted and thick bread somewhat resembling *shirmal*.
Even Upadhyaya relished it.

My visit to the Frontier was fairly well reported and people are full of it
here, especially the great welcome I had from the tribal people, particularly the Afridis and Waziris. I was presented with a lamb and a goat and
one Afridi Khan even presented his son to Khan Saheb and me. A bit of a
handful! We told him to join the Khudai Khidmatgars (the Redshirts) and
thus serve the country. These Redshirts were all over the place and
sometimes lined the road for miles. Each group had its pipers and
drummers, and often bag-pipes. In the tribal territory almost everyone
seemed to have a gun – not the Redshirts, who were confined to the
Frontier Province. We noticed even a donkey boy in the tribal area
carrying a gun. Every group of villages had a primitive gun factory.

Fine upstanding men and women they were all over the Frontier and
bonny children but all very poor and shabby. There was no cringing about
them but an open-hearted welcome and hospitality. There was a
tremendous shaking of hands with them and *salam-aleikum* and *starey
mashey* and *Pa Khan aglai*. The first you know – it is the universal Islamic
greeting meaning 'peace be upon you' to which the answer is *waleikum-as-*

salam – 'and on you be peace'. *Starey mashey* is a beautiful greeting. I think I wrote to you about it. It means 'may you not get tired'. How suitable it is, not only for travellers on the road but for all pilgrims through life. The third greeting *Pa Khan aglai* means something to the effect that you hope the person addressed has come in safety and well-being.

I am so fascinated by these people that I want to get nearer to them and that can only be through their language – Pushtu. I have brought back primers & books in this. I wonder if I shall ever have time to read them. But I have little doubt that I shall be drawn back to the Frontier. And next time I go that way I shall certainly try to cross over to Kashmir. I was within a dozen miles of Kashmir this time and quite a number of Kashmiris came over to one of my meetings.

Abdul Ghaffar Khan was always addressed as *Fakhr-e-Afghan* – the pride of the Afghans. Sometimes they addressed me as *Fakhr-e-Hind* – the pride of India. Once there was 'Jawaharlal Khan *Zindabad*'[1].

The Redshirts used to dance sometimes and I was struck by the resemblance to Russian dancing. I realised the common origin from Central Asia. The Russian men's dancing is, I believe, derived from Cossack dancing. And this made me realise that in effect, geographically and partly culturally, I was in Central Asia. There is a vast difference between the Frontier people and the Punjabis. And yet there was definitely that link, that something, which binds the whole of India together. My mind wandered repeatedly to past times and to the great events that the Frontier had seen. To the caravans that had come through and across it through countless ages – to the Aryans and Scythians and Turks and Huns and Mughals who had marched into India and been largely absorbed by India. To the coming of Alexander and the Macedonians. I crossed the Indus almost at the very spot where Alexander is supposed to have crossed.

I thought of the ancient times of the Mahabharat when Afghanistan was called Gandhara (from which Gandhari the mother of the Kauravas); of Asoka who has innumerable memorials all over the Frontier; of the Kushan Empire with its seat at Peshawar, the meeting place of the these great cultures; the Indians, the Chinese and the Western Asian mixed with Graeco-Romans. The cultural intercourse of ages came to my mind – how India gave her religion and art to the Far East, her science and mathematics to the Arab world. But I cannot go on adding to this list!

---

1. May you live long.

Allahabad,
30th January

I could not continue this letter in Lucknow. My night journey was an exciting one as vast numbers of pilgrims were travelling here for Mauni Amavasya *melá* which takes place tomorrow. The platform was crowded with them and the third-class carriages were crammed. I have never seen so many people jammed in a railway carriage. They were so tightly packed that it was literally impossible for a person to move or lift up his hand. Many of them were partly hanging out of the windows. I had an intermediate ticket but even the inter was over full. A number of special trains had preceded us but still the rush continued. At the last moment some additional carriages were added and there was an empty Second-Class compartment. So I promoted myself to Second. Within half an hour, at a wayside station, my compartment was suddenly invaded by about twenty or twenty-five persons. They were all Third-Class passengers but I did not have the heart to ask them to go. They were decent folk and we made friends and travelled together for the rest of the night. They did everything in their power not to disturb me, and I, selfish creature, spread out on my berth and tried to sleep while the others were closely seated on all the berths as well as the floor of the compartment. The train was greatly delayed and arrived over two hours late.

On arrival here I saw a sheaf of letters waiting for me, among them three from you. But before dealing with them I shall carry on with my old theme – with intervening distractions. For I hear the *jais* of the pilgrims who come to visit Anand Bhawan in crowds and I have to go to see them every few minutes. They are swarming all over Anand Bhawan and Swaraj Bhawan, and I am the only person here to meet and welcome them.

Do you remember, when you were here, there was much excitement over the abduction of Hindu women by the Waziris? I issued a statement to the press also – 'Bombing and kidnapping on the Frontier'. When I was in Bannu in the Frontier Province recently I referred to these incidents. Unfortunate as they were, it was obvious that the motive behind was economic. These dwellers of the lone mountains have little to sustain them and for generations their chief occupation has been fighting each other or the British Govt. They try to make both ends meet by occasional raids and abductions of persons whom they hold up for ransom. They treat their captives courteously and well. They look upon the whole transaction as a purely business proposition. The policy of the British Govt. has kept them [backward] economically, educationally & culturally and has at the same time roused all their warlike instincts. A friendly approach and some planned attempt to meet their economic difficulties would go a long way to solve these problems. They are extraordinarily hospitable and susceptible to friendly overtures.

As I was speaking to a vast audience at Bannu, which included many tribesmen, suddenly you crept into my mind and I began talking of you. I have a daughter, I said, an only child, young in years, whom I have sent abroad for her education. From her childhood upwards I have tried to make her self-reliant, so that she might be able to take care of herself wherever she might be and face every contingency with courage and confidence. I sent her to distant schools in various parts of India to enable her to get to know our countrymen better and have some knowledge of their languages. For I wanted her, as I want all others, to realise the diversity and at the same time the unity of this land of ours. I have sent her abroad so that she may get to know something of the wide world and its problems and so fit herself for the service of India and her people. I should like all young men and women in India to train themselves in some such way and thus become true and efficient soldiers of freedom. So I spoke. And then I said that if she happened to come to the Frontier Territory, as I hoped she would, I would unhesitatingly and willingly agree to her going to Waziristan unaccompanied, for I was confident that she could look after herself and I was equally confident that the Waziris would welcome her and treat her as a friend and a guest.

After the meeting a man from Waziristan came to me, apparently thinking that you were on the point of starting for that country, and offered his services to accompany you and serve you during your journey.

From Bannu we went to Dera Ismail Khan, passing on the way big hills of solid rock salt. We saw the mining and brought away some beautiful crystals of salt. These salt hills, nature's gift to man, are closely guarded by the Govt. of India so as to preserve their salt monopoly. And the poor people round about even lack for salt. Such is the modern world.

I have just come back from my fourth or fifth visit to the verandahs & portico to meet the crowds that are pouring in. There is a hum all over this empty house. But the affection of these simple folk fills this emptiness.

I now come to your letters.[1] About the suggestion made by the Lieftincks, what do you expect me to say? Of course the cooperative movement is good and should be pushed, but to be a success it must have an economic & social basis of the right kind. Just at present it is difficult even to push it far. Kagawa with all his earnestness and following has not been able to affect Japan's policy.

Do not bother about the complexities of the present situation in India. They are inevitable and no country can escape them. We must go through all these stages. Personally I keep well in spite of everything – I wish you had my health and vitality.

1. Refers to letters No. 246 and 247.

About the Independence Pledge I think you are under some mis-apprehension. The new pledge is not a toning down of the old one; it is a shortening of it and a leaving out of the last part calling for an immediate campaign of civil disobedience. This was necessary in 1930 but does not fit in with present circumstances. Otherwise the pledge is the same, minus some details.

The ban on Congress ministers participating in official functions has not been lifted, though some ministers have misbehaved. Of course it is difficult to draw the line often as the ministers themselves being high officials have to meet others on business.

About your schools it is difficult for me to suggest anything worthwhile. Personally for myself I would prefer P.P.E. But that does not help as the choice has to be made by you. Miss Darbyshire & your tutor should certainly be consulted.

You must remember that these schools are really pegs on which you hang your general reading and training. Whichever peg is helpful should be taken, but the really important thing is something besides the peg. And this leads me to your health. It is not right that you should be tired out.

Later

I could not write on because of numerous interruptions. And then I went to the *mela* by the riverbank and spent some time there. I have just returned.

Why should you suffer from malaise? Your father seems to flourish under almost any conceivable circumstances and the ordinary ailments do not touch him. Do you worry about anything? I suppose I ought to worry about various matters but as a matter of fact I seldom do, and if I do get hot and bothered, it is only for a short while. I recover soon. It is really not worthwhile and is certainly not helpful. Even worrying about one's health is not good enough. If you sleep enough and take some exercise, then you can work as hard as you like. Do not overdo the exercise if you feel at all tired. I think one or two simple *asans* are definitely good, especially the *Sarvangasan*. Try doing this two or three times a day for a couple of minutes each time. It has an extraordinarily refreshing effect. Try also some simple breathing exercises – if you can remember what I used to do. All this takes very little time and it tones one up.

Probably we shall meet next summer – in June or thereabouts. I intend going to Europe but if that is not possible then you will have to come here. But I do not like the idea of your coming here in summer and I feel definitely that I want a mental change from India. So, unless the unforeseen occurs, I shall go West. After the Haripura Congress is over I shall sit down and fashion out a programme. Just at present I am in a state of flux.

You ask for some money. Of course you should let me know when you want it, or you can always write to Bachhraj direct. As a matter of fact the money that is paid to you two-monthly cannot be enough for you. This amounts to £300 a year. When I was at Cambridge I used to get about £400 a year, but then my father was richer than yours! At the same time prices and costs of everything have gone up considerably since then. So it is quite natural that you should want to supplement your fixed allowance. It was meant to be supplemented. I enclose a cheque for £30. If you want more you will let me know.

Today I received two rather unusual pictures of me. I do not remember when they were taken – probably in Calcutta recently. I am sending them to you.

I enclose a translation of an interesting letter I received last October from the Faqir of Ipi,[1] the Waziri leader. I am issuing it to the press today.

Do you remember my sending you a cutting of an article from the *Modern Review*, called the Rashtrapati?[2] I have a confession to make. I wrote that article! It gave me some amusement and the idea of watching other people's reactions to it was also entertaining. One evening after dinner I was in the mood to write and so I sat down to it and finished it off. I did not want anyone here to know and so did not even give it to Upadhyaya to type. I sent the mss. in original to Padmaja and asked her to send a typed copy to the *Modern Review*. Nobody found out. I have now taken a number of persons into the secret, and indeed it will not remain much of a secret for long.

This letter has become scandalously long, and with its enclosures will make a bulky packet. But perhaps I shall not write to you a long letter again till after the Haripura Congress. So I have devoted a good part of today to you.

Love,
Papu

250.

Somerville College,
Oxford,
1st February [1938]

Darling Papu,

There is no news from you or of you. Even the *Bombay Chronicle* has been delayed.

Of myself there is little news to give – the routine of work continues. As soon as the work for one week is over that for next week begins – time

1. Haji Mirza Ali Khan (Faqir of Ipi): Pathan leader who led his people against the British Government.
2. See letter No. 231.

doesn't seem to be flying and yet one by one the weeks go – already a whole month of the new year has passed.

Outside it is cold and moaningly windy and dark. The world goes on as usual and in spite of the wars and so very many happenings – the papers can still devote columns to the birth of a royal baby.[1] I am glad it has arrived – if only because I was sick of seeing – whichever paper I opened – how Juliana went for a walk in the garden or for a drive in the storm.

The problem of the Basque children is a serious one. Unless something can be done about them, they will be sent back to Spain, for the government is not helping in any way. We – that is Somerville College – have adopted two children – this means that each one of us has to pay 3d a week – about 2 sh a term.

Malaviyaji's rejuvenation[2] is most amusing. I'm longing to see what he looks like – how did he get such a marvellous idea anyway?

The Labour Club & the Oxford University Peace Council are doing all they can for the boycott of Japanese goods. But I am afraid they are not meeting with any success. It is so difficult when the govt. continues to import or allows the importation of Japanese goods. Then the Jap products are so very much cheaper. Shops like Woolworth's & Marks & Spencers are full of them. One great triumph that we have secured is to get an undertaking from Woolworth that they will not import any more goods from Japan – but they insist on selling off all their remaining stock, which will last for about a year.

The recent raid on Valencia has made me very anxious about Madan Bhai.[3] I had a letter from him some time ago. He says he is coming to London at the end of spring.

With lots of love,
Indu

251.   Somerville College,
                                                       Oxford,
                                          4th February, 1938

Darling Papu,
The morning after I had posted my letter to you, arrived two of yours: one from Haripura[4] and the other from Kohat[5].

1. Princess Beatrix, eldest daughter of the then Princess Juliana (later Queen) and Prince Bernhard of the Netherlands, now Queen Beatrix of the Netherlands.
2. Madan Mohan Malaviya: nationalist leader and educationalist. He underwent the *Kaya Kalpa*, an Ayurvedic method of rejuvenation lasting forty days in January 1938.
3. Dr Madan Atal was on a medical mission in Spain.
4. Letter not traceable.
5. Refers to letter No. 248.

I am so glad that you were able to spend a few days in the N.W.F.P. They must have been strenuous days but – may I hope – not more strenuous than they would have been elsewhere in India. The change of climate and surroundings, the sunshine in the dry and bracing cold must have done you good. The very sight of snow is always refreshing. How vast and interesting and how very beautiful is our country. How different is the climate, the scenery, how very different the people and their customs in each part. Yet so few of us have the time or the means to break through the narrow walls of daily routine that enclose our lives, to get to know this immense space of land that is India, to enjoy her loveliness and to make friends with our fellow countrymen who speak a tongue and think thoughts that are not our own. And those who have the means and could make the time – they have not the inclination for such 'useless' things! How I wish I were with you as you spread the magic message of freedom from one distant corner to another.

But here I am in Oxford – where many would doubtless love to be. I am definitely doing the History schools. Life is on the whole rather monotonous. From time to time there is an interesting lecture or an especially wonderful concert. Last week all England & most of Europe saw the most gorgeous sight of a lifetime 'the Aurora Borealis'. But we poor souls working in the library drew the curtains against that lovely sight and never guessed what we were missing until the next morning's papers came! Some scientists have expressed the hope that it might be seen – though perhaps not so brilliantly – some time during the next week. I do hope it is.

On Sunday the Majlis programme promises to be worth listening to. Palme Dutt and Prof. Sir Alfred Zimmern[1] are speaking on the international situation. I heard Palme Dutt last term – he is a marvellous speaker and what he has to say is always worthwhile.

Last Wednesday I went to supper with the Thompsons. Mrs Thompson was brought up in Syria, where she still owns a house and often goes there. She was very interested in an Arab girl at Somerville and wanted me to bring her to her house. We had quite an interesting evening although Edward Thompson and I almost came to a quarrel several times. He is so dreadfully pessimistic.

Well, Papu darling – *Au revoir* (whenever will it be?) and lots and lots of love.

Your loving,
Indu

---

1. Professor Alfred Zimmern (later Sir Alfred): Montague Burton Professor of International Relations in the University of Oxford; joined the Research Department of the British Foreign Office in 1939.

252.   Jarakhar,
                                        Dist Hamirpur U.P.,
                                        7th February, 1938

Darling,

Here I am in a remote rural area in the U.P. I have come here from Wardha by car and train, and I intended finishing up the journey by plane. But the plans fell through owing to the non-receipt of my telegram by the people here in time. An express telegram that I sent [the] day before yesterday reached here this afternoon. And so when I reached Jhansi, confidently expecting a plane to be waiting for me, I found to my surprise that there was not a soul expecting me. I did not feel very bright or happy about it as these few days before the Congress are full of work and I had only consented to come here after much persuasion. I betook myself to the waiting room, had a bath, and sat down to read Aldous Huxley's *Ends and Means*. For some time I have been carrying this about with me unread. And now I was suddenly at a loose end, an unusual experience. After my irritation toned down, I rather liked this experience. I found the book very interesting in the real sense of the word, that is thought-provoking. One was repeatedly compelled to examine one's own public activities by some of the tests suggested.

But I was found out soon enough and taken away from my refuge. There was nothing special to be done and so I went out for a drive. I saw (from outside) Rani Lakshmi Bai's[1] palace, where now – a scandalous state of affairs – a Kotwali flourishes. Later in the evening I took a slow train and after the train journey a long thirty-mile drive by car.

A district conference is being held here. It is now all the fashion to hold our conferences in villages and this experiment, started at Faizpur last year, has succeeded wonderfully. Vast crowds roll up and the whole atmosphere is that of rural India, so different from our towns. In the towns the villagers come of course but they feel out of place and ill at ease. About a month ago we had our U.P. Provincial Conference at Harduaganj, a village near Aligarh. About a hundred thousand persons turned up – it was an astonishing sight.

Successful as these conferences are, they are not unmixed blessings for the villagers. A large area is occupied, crops have to be cut down (with compensation), and, what is worse, their neighbouring fields get spoilt. Thousands of people come by bullock-cart and the bullocks graze about & consume the crops.

I have just been for a midnight stroll in the grounds here. Thousands of

---

1. Rani Lakshmi Bai (Ruler of Jhansi): an outstanding leader of the Uprising of 1857, more familiar to Europeans as the Indian Mutiny.

people sleeping on the ground in the open – some with quilts *lihaf*, most with cotton sheets only to cover them. Bullock-carts parked all over the place. Scores of new shops put up temporarily. Some amusements – a theatre, even a cinema! The little village blossoms out as a town almost.

Haripura of course is going to do this on a grand scale. Under Nandalal Bose's direction an artistic town of huts is growing up, with many of the modern conveniences – water supply, proper roads, electric lighting, sanitation, organised food supply, etc.

I must go to bed now. I have not had a decent night's rest for a week. Because of this I have agreed to fly back to Allahabad tomorrow. This will save me another tiring journey and a bad night.

8th February

I have been wandering about this village and the camps of the numerous village folk who have come here. This is Bundelkhand and the Bundel-khandis are a sturdy lot of people. It is a poor country, hilly and stony and lacking water. Consequently the people are poor and backward. The women here wear huge rings round their ankles – silver or of cheaper stuff, usually the latter. These vary in weight from a pound to ten pounds each. Imagine having to wear these and having to walk and run about with them! They are not only heavy but also broad so that the feet have to be kept fairly wide apart. They tinkle when the women walk; it is a pleasant sound.

The more I see of village women the more I like their figures as compared to town women. Perhaps this is so because they work hard. But the ideal exercise for learning poise and the way to walk is to walk with a jar of water on the head. Almost every woman in the villages here has to do this daily and often several times a day. I have seen women with three earthen pots – *ghare* – one on top of the other, balanced on the head, walking unconcernedly along. Occasionally they would take an additional one under the arm.

Anand Bhawan,
8th February

I have come here by plane. It took an hour and twenty minutes and saved me a long and very tiring railway journey. The house is empty and very silent. As I returned rather unexpectedly no one has been to see me.

Sarojini Naidu suggested that I might send you the enclosed cutting of my speech at Dera Ismail Khan. She gave me the cutting. So I enclose it.

A brief note from you has met me here.

Love,

Your loving,
Papu

253.

Somerville College,
Oxford,
8th February, 1938

Darling Papu,

Your letter of the 29th & 30th[1] – half of it written in Lucknow and half in Allahabad – came this morning. I can't express in words how very welcome it was – and how very happy it made me. I got so excited I couldn't do any work. In fact I am still very elated and excited. In moments such as these one truly feels that it is worthwhile being alive, that the world is bound to extricate itself from all the troubles that entangle it. Gosh! it's good to get a letter from you – a real letter and not just a hurried note. It is the best time ever for one's spirits. But what made me happier was that the note of tiredness and weariness that occurred so often in your letters lately, was absent in this last one.

And of course the most marvellous news of all was about the long vacation. I am thrilled – I do hope you can manage to come. It will do you good and it will do me good, in fact it will do everybody good. The West needs people to come over occasionally and remind it of India & the Congress. And India needs people who are refreshed, with outside contacts. And most of all I need you – so it is good to know that if you can't come over I shall still be able to cross the seas and come to you. I don't really mind the summer and anyway it's about time I got used to it. My holidays begin on the 20th June and I have to be back in College on the 7th October – that gives me just three and a half months' vacation. And whoopee! Am I looking forward to it! (Excuse this American language – but I find it is so much more expressive when one is feeling like I am.)

Thanks enormously for the cheque for £30. I don't know why you spoil me so much – I'm sure I don't deserve it. I don't know how I manage to spend such a lot either – for I don't seem to buy anything except books and they are rather an expensive item. Then it is so difficult not to contribute to the fund for Spanish medical relief & for the Chinese one, the fund for the International Brigade in Spain and for the upkeep of the Basque children! However £30 might last me ages.

My darling Papu – I am afraid I shall have to disappoint you. I was not at all surprised to hear about the *Modern Review* article.[2] In fact I had almost guessed it and wanted to ask you. The style of it and the English is so typically yours. But it was the viewpoint – that special way of looking at things and people – that first gave me the idea of the true author. And who else but you could have or would have put in those quotations? They betrayed you completely. But I admit there was a doubt in my mind about

1. Refers to letter No. 249.
2. See letters No. 231 and 249.

the whole thing, although I was sure that whosoever had written it was not an Indian – or else he was of a type that I have never come across. So you see you cannot keep such secrets from me!

You make the Frontier people sound so attractive and through your description I felt – almost – as if I had accompanied you on your tour and had met these brave people and had enjoyed their dancing and their beautiful scenery. I hope some time, some day, we shall be able to go there together. I was very interested to read the Faqir of Ipi's letter to you. I am afraid you forgot to enclose the two unusual pictures of yourself.

In one of my letters, I think, I mentioned a Mr Radice who was a commissioner or some such thing in the U.P. His sister – a very charming person – is up at Somerville. I had tea with her one day and then she said that her people would like to meet me. So last Saturday we took the train to her home – it is in a tiny village quite near Oxford. This was my first visit to a proper English home and I loved it. Mr & Mrs Radice were out in India for the twenty-five years necessary in the Civil Service. Then they wandered round the Continent and about three years ago they settled in Coomb Halt – it isn't big enough to have a real station. They have a very typically English house – rather old with cobbled pavement floor, etc., and a tiny garden which had little snowdrops scattered all over the place. I had lunch there and then came back to Oxford. They have rather an interesting ancestor. Mr Radice's grandfather was an Italian (hence the name) who was one of the leaders of the Italian revolt of 1820. With five others he was sentenced to death – three of them managed to escape and came and settled in England. And in the corridor of the Radices' home they have a copy of the death warrant framed and hanging on the wall! The present Mr Radice Senior is an enthusiastic pacifist! He is very proud of this fact – in the whole of his twenty-five years' service in India he never once had to use the police or the military in any riot or other disorder. He says he just went and sat down and talked and everything was all right. His brother also adopted the same policy with great success.

The only other thing of interest that I did since I last wrote to you was the Majlis' meeting on Sunday night. It was about 'The International Situation'. The speakers were Prof. Alfred Zimmern and the Hon. Frank Pakenham[1] – or as he prefers to be known, Commander Pakenham. They are both lecturers here. Pakenham is very young and a great admirer of yours. He is very brilliant and was wonderful at the meeting, which turned out into a debate, for there were very few things that Pakenham and Zimmern agreed about except that they wanted peace. Satish Kalelkar

---

1. Frank Pakenham (later Lord Longford): became prospective parliamentary Labour candidate for Oxford City in 1938.

(Kaka Kalelkar's son) was good too – he asked Zimmern some very awkward questions. After the meeting Zimmern says to me, 'I love a good argument, don't you?'!! Pakenham was the Labour candidate for the County Council election last term – he got in with a thumping majority partly because lots of Conservatives voted for his 'Hon'!

Some time last week I had a letter from a Mr Vaidya, written on behalf of the *News Chronicle*. He said that India was celebrating 7th Feb. as Gaidilu Rani[1] day and that on that date he was issuing an appeal for the release of Indian women political prisoners in the *News Chronicle*. The *N. Chronicle* was also publishing Gaidilu's story. And would I please send them a few lines? Well, I did – but there is no sign of anything about India or her political prisoners in the *News Chronicle* of the 7th or in the *Star* which is the *N.C.*'s evening paper. Nor have I heard any more from the mysterious Mr Vaidya. I don't know what has happened or is going to happen.

Well – I suppose I had better stop rambling on and on –

'*Starey Mashey*' and *au revoir*. How I am longing to see you!

With my love,
Indu

---

254.   Somerville College,
Oxford,
11th February, 1938

Darling Papu,

I went to hear Kreisler, the famous violinist, the other day. He was glorious. The hall was packed full – all Oxford was there and I'm so glad I didn't miss it. He played two great favourites of mine, a piece of Bach's and Mozart's Rondo in G Major. I just shut my eyes and forgot everything except that heavenly music – even the memory of it thrills me. It seemed almost an insult to clap after his playing but if we hadn't, he would not have given us any encores. I didn't know I liked music – like is hardly the word, but still. In fact he inspired me so much that I felt like starting my violin all over again. But of course there isn't any time.

If the world can still produce such harmony and melody, there must be some hope for us!

This morning a rumour, that poor old Adolf H. had been murdered, spread round like fire. I had just begun an essay which had to be finished by the end of the morning but I couldn't resist wasting over twenty minutes of very precious time to rush out for a special edition of the *Oxford*

---

1. Rani Gaidilu: Naga freedom fighter who was inspired by Mahatma Gandhi.

Mail – there was no special edition but early in the afternoon the ordinary edition contained two inconspicuous lines saying that Herr Hitler was feeling extremely well!

It has been most freezingly cold today – I'm sure we are having a cold wave or something, but it's a lovely day – fairly dry and clear with some sun. In fact a real spring day.

Lots of love,

Ever your own,
Indu

255.

Somerville College,
Oxford,
22nd February, 1938

Darling Papu,

Two very good photographs of you – probably the ones you spoke about – arrived yesterday. This morning came your letter of the 12th[1] – just before you left for Haripura.

The crisis you speak of has come and – from what the papers here say – seems to be cooling down. It came as rather a surprise that the other ministers were not asked to resign – or was it that they were asked and refused? All this must be a terrible strain on you. I realise that Congress must, above all, keep up a united front in the face of the enemy and yet the right wing seems to grow stronger & stronger and seems to do its best to crush the left wing. How long can the left afford to give in thus on every issue? And if it breaks away, is it strong enough to stand on its own legs? I shouldn't think so – for a people need getting used to new names and new parties. And Congress has won a great name for itself in the country & outside and all the good that it has done in the past cannot easily be forgotten – nor should it be. A division in the ranks always means a weakening but at this critical point it would be disastrous. But something must be done for if things continue as they have been, a split is bound to come sooner or later.

Madan Bhai is back from Spain. He came up to Oxford last Saturday. On Sunday I took him to our Majlis study group, when he spoke of his experiences in Spain and in the afternoon he left for he had to address the London Majlis. He has grown considerably thinner & his old clothes hardly fit him. It was interesting talking to him – and some of his stories were too horrible to hear. He badly needs a rest, for his nerves are shaken – he would get a start almost every time a car made a certain kind of noise

---

1. Letter not published.

and he couldn't quite forget the air raids. He is not at all definite about his plans – he wants to stay in England for four or five months & then go back to India. But he isn't sure. He is completely out of touch with Indian affairs for he hasn't seen a single paper for the past year – the letters he got were few and far between. And as he proposed starting work as soon as he got back, I suggested that he should first get his knowledge of Indian affairs more up-to-date while he was resting here.

At the Majlis Ben Bradley[1] spoke on the 'Problems before the Congress'. He is a very good speaker. Unfortunately I could not stay until the end of his speech.

Every day something sensational seems to happen – what a strange atmosphere we live in – anything may happen at any time anywhere. The great news last week was the Indian crisis & Hitler's demands in Austria. This week Anthony Eden is front-page news.[2] His resignation was the best thing that has happened in the National Govt. for some time. And it has increased his popularity immensely. As for the government, heaven knows what will happen with Halifax[3] as Foreign Secretary. He seems to me to be too much the perfect English country gentleman, firmly believing in the tragedy that must accompany socialism, to realise the real harm that Hitler & Mussolini can do & will do to England – as for the rest of the world, he doesn't care about it!

Lots of love, darling,
Indu

256.   Somerville College,
                Oxford,
            24th February [1938]

Darling Papu,

Most associations which hold their meetings on Wednesday evenings, cancelled them on account of the 'present crisis'. And instead we had a joint meeting of the Labour & Liberal Clubs & the British Universities League of Nations Union. It was a tremendous success. The Union Debating Hall was packed full and the speakers were good. The audience consisted of three kinds of people – those who were Conservatives & admirers of Eden and thought that the Cabinet would be badly off without him; those who were against the govt. and the Conservatives but admired Eden 'for sticking to his principles'; and those who while applauding Eden

---

1. Benjamin F. Bradley: British radical who came to India in the 1920s.
2. Anthony Eden resigned as Foreign Secretary in protest at Neville Chamberlain's appeasement policies.
3. Lord Halifax (later Earl): Viceroy of India, 1926–31, Foreign Secretary, 1938–40.

for resigning thought he was no better than any other Tory and in fact that he was better out of the Cabinet, for now at least we know where we stand and 'the velvet glove is off the iron hand'! Personally I agree with the third lot: after all, if Eden does have any principles, he has thought of this rather late – in fact too late – in the day. Abyssinia, Spain, China, where were his principles then? Frank Pakenham (I believe I mentioned him in one of my letters) compared Mr Eden with Jenkins – but of course you don't know him: there was an attempted murder case which occupied many headlines for over a week: 'The Mayfair case'. Jenkins & three other Mayfair men occupied a suite in a big hotel & lured a jeweller there, saying they wished to buy some jewellery & later tried to dispose of him! 'Eden,' said Pakenham, 'took a suite in the League of Nations & tried to dispose of collective security.' Another case that is causing a great stir is the 'Torso case': a body has been found – whose it is or who put it there is unknown. The chairman startled us by suddenly saying that he knew all about it: the corpse was that of the League of Nations & Chamberlain put it there! However it was a good meeting & we all felt inspired to do something about it. Many telegrams were sent to Halifax saying 'Oxford says Resign'. What good that will do I don't know – not that it is likely to happen, but still. Labour wants a General Election – the recent Ipswich by-election, in which the Labour candidate got in by a thumping majority on an anti-rearmament programme, has inspired them with confidence. And today the students of London, Cambridge & Oxford are going to 'lobby' the House of Commons & to ask their respective M.P.s questions about their Election pledges. I wish I could have gone but I haven't the time. Apart from that, we want to stir public opinion up and I am sure that if we are successful in that we are bound to get some results. And then this crisis, which the *Times* says is almost forgotten, will prove a real crisis for the National Govt.

Besides sending telegrams of support to Eden & of condemnation to Halifax, Oxford is busy with a China Week. We have opened a tiny China shop, where students & other helpers sell things – Chinese and otherwise – in aid of China. Various meetings are being held and on Saturday there will be a procession. We are doing tremendous propaganda for the boycott of Japanese goods but I am afraid it has not been very successful in this town. The town people and the pacifists are great hindrances. Visitors to our College will be startled this week – on the outside of almost every door is an enormous poster saying 'Boycott Japanese Goods. Save China. Save Peace', etc., etc. There is an absolute craze for China posters these days & some of them are remarkably good. I have one which I want to hang up in my room but it is a bit too big. It shows a very beautiful peasant foot clad in a string sandal about to tread on a swastika, which is already cracking. Then I have another poster on my wall – it is a most wonderful photograph

– three men skiing down a slope with the light behind them. It is really lovely. A friend of mine managed to get it for me from a travelling agency!

In London today the China–India committee is observing China Day. In the afternoon there is to be a poster parade & meeting.

The English papers are silent on Indian affairs. I haven't the vaguest idea what is happening. Menon sent me copies of the telegram that you & Bose sent to the India League & of your statement, or report as you call it, to the Subjects Committee[1].

I do hope all this trouble won't come in the way of your trip to Europe in the summer. I am so looking forward to it. Chhoti Puphi writes that she & Raja Bhai might also turn up if they can possibly produce enough cash and deposit the children somewhere!

25th February

Agatha is coming up next Sunday for tea –
                With lots & lots of love,
                        Indu

---

257.   Somerville College,
                                                                Oxford,
                                                        1st March, 1938

Darling Papu,

How fast time does go! In two more weeks the term will end and the gown population will desert the townsmen, who I daresay will be only too glad. The Easter vac is just as long as the Christmas one. I haven't the vaguest idea of what I shall do – I want to stay in England – I don't know it at all except London, Bristol & Oxford!

Last Sunday was one of the best evenings in the history of the Majlis – at least as far as I have known it. Prof. C. E. M. Joad[2] & Prof. Radhakrishnan[3] spoke on 'Religion in the West'. They are both really good speakers and it was absolutely grand. I had never heard or read Joad before but I hear from others that he had made his speech several times before & that it has also appeared in several magazines almost verbatim! Joad quoted a lot from *Ends and Means*. However, it was very interesting to me & I enjoyed the evening. I am going to tea with Prof. Radhakrishnan on Sunday.

The weather is very treacherous these days. But on the whole I think

1. Two days before every plenary session of the Congress, the members of the All-India Congress Committee met as the Subjects Committee to frame the session's agenda.

2. C. E. M. Joad: British philosopher and author.

3. Dr S. Radhakrishnan: philosopher, later President of India, 1962–7.

that spring has come to stay. It was a glorious day today. I have discovered a new flower, 'Forsythia', named after a Scotchman Forsyth[1] who first found it. It is one of the first spring flowers and perfectly lovely.

With lots of love,
Indu

---

258.   Lucknow,
                                            2nd March, 1938

Darling Indu,

Your letters await me, I suppose, in Allahabad and so for long I have not received any. I am still on my way and Lucknow is a halting place only. For two days I have been here, resting partly and attending some committee meetings. I am gradually getting over my cold and tiredness. For a while I feared that something like last year's illness might be repeated but I am sure now that this will not happen. The doctor has thumped and patted me all over and pronounced me generally fit. What is more to the point, I feel much better already. I intend having my fortnight at Khali[2] soon – probably from the 10th to the 25th March – and I expect to return to the plains bursting with energy.

About my going to Europe everything is vague and uncertain, except my desire to go there and see you. But the story has gone round and everyone asks me about it. It is a tiring business to have to answer the same question over and over again. By the time I have decided finally there will probably be no berth left! But that is a minor matter and is not likely to keep me back. It may perhaps delay my departure and make me take the full taste of the monsoon.

When in Bombay I spent a morning with Jamnalalji at Juhu. He arranged for horses and I had a gallop on the sands – so did Raja but with little success as he had a fall. Then we all had a swim in the sea, or at least those who could swim, the others not venturing far. I managed to get hold of a Lilo air bed and it was delightful to float about on it. I remembered that the last sea bath I had was at Port Dickson with you.

Another unusual experience in Bombay was a visit to Elephanta.[3] Long long ago I had gone there when I was a child and I had forgotten all about it. Always when I go to Bombay my days are so crowded that I find no time for excursions. This time I was luckier. Taken as a whole I was dis-

1. William Forsyth: British botanist and gardener.
2. A place in the Almora Hills in Uttar Pradesh where Ranjit Pandit owned a house.
3. Elephanta is an island near Bombay. It contains cave temples belonging to the ninth century. One of the most famous sculptures there is the Trimurti (meaning the three images), depicting the three-headed Shiva.

appointed in the caves – I expected a greater richness and variety. There were three or four fine figures – a bashful Parvati on her wedding day and some *dwarpals*.[1] But the Trimurti was magnificent and overpowering. That head with the wisdom and thought of ages behind it, ascetic and yet so sophisticated and full of the knowledge of life, unattached and unentangled and yet enveloping all that came within its ken, calm and with an astonishing strength. I thought of the Rock of Ages, how appropriate in a way it was; but that too only described one aspect of it. My mind wandered to the sculptors who had wrought this wondrous thing in ages past, seemingly with their hands but really with the genius which filled their minds. How long did it take them? Was it the work of one generation or more? As I stood there gazing in wonderment I felt very trivial and commonplace before this majesty in stone. Silent and contemplative, I returned to my launch.

Tara & Rita have had their tonsils taken out. They came back from hospital yesterday and are still in the quiet icy stage. In Bombay Dr Shah asked me about your throat and I discovered what a careless father I was. I had never asked you about it? Have you had any throat trouble? Colds or sore-throats or anything else which might be traceable to the removal of the tonsils?

Love,

Your loving,
Papu

259.   [Anand Bhawan]

Allahabad,
8th March, 1938

Darling,
I am writing in some haste as I am leaving for Lucknow and Khali soon and I do not want to go away without sending you a few lines. These few days in Allahabad after a long absence have been busy. And now I am going again and looking forward so much to Khali and the snow.

I found three letters from you when I came and another has just come. I hope you will have good rest during the Easter vac and go back to Oxford refreshed. Allahabad is warming up, though it is still pleasant.

I toy with the idea of going to Europe and make no arrangements. I suppose I shall go on doing so. I am getting used to a hand-to-mouth existence and hesitate to make distant programmes. But the idea of going abroad has taken possession of me and only something big will prevent

---

1. Gatekeepers.

me. I want to see how things shape themselves during the next month. Let me know when your next term ends. Perhaps you could meet me on the Continent. If you are hard up for money at any time let me know also.

Love,
Papu

---

260.   Lucknow,
                                                    9th March, 1938

Darling Indu,

I arrived here this morning to find Mehr Taj[1] ill in bed. The poor girl has a thin time in school and is not properly looked after. She came to Nan a few days ago looking ghastly. When her temperature was taken it was found that she had fairly high fever. She had also hurt her knee running. She is now getting better. It has been a great thing for her that she could come to visit Nan and the children every Sunday during the past few months. Otherwise she would have been completely isolated. Her people seldom write to her. The Pathan does not believe in reading or writing.

The ministerial crisis ended on the very terms that we had been asking.[2] It was a complete come-down for the British Govt. Of course the language used was roundabout and diplomatic, as is always the case. We had decided that if the crisis continued we would ask the other ministries to resign also. To do so right at the beginning would have been unwise and it would have made it impossible for the Viceroy [Lord Linlithgow] to climb down as he did eventually.

I met Joad in London. His writings are interesting but he seemed to me one of those persons who are so ineffective and disillusioned with everything and everybody.

Some people have come to see me & so I must go off.

Love,
Papu

---

1. Mehr Taj: daughter of Abdul Ghaffar Khan.
2. Congress ministries in the United Provinces and Bihar resigned on 15th February 1938 on the issue of release of political prisoners. The ministries resumed office after reaching an understanding with the British Government.

261.

Khali,
Almora U.P.,
Kumaon Hills,
11th March, 1938

Darling Indu,

So at last I have come to Khali. For more than two years there has been talk about it and during this period I have wandered a good deal all over India. But Khali, in my own province and not difficult of access, still remained outside my track. I remember just three years ago when Ranjit and I discussed the proposal of acquiring Khali in Almora Jail. He had come to pay me a visit. At that time I was thinking of some such place where Mummie might be able to live during the summer, for it was obvious that she could not stay in the plains even if she recovered.

I have been here just a day and a night and the weather has not been as good as it might be. I have not seen the snows yet from Khali because of the clouds and there has been some rain. But already I am enchanted with the place. I like the situation of the house on a hilltop. To the east and west there are deep valleys winding away with streaks of water shining in the sunlight. To the north-east there is Binsar Hill dominating the neighbourhood. To the north there is the snow range which I have not seen yet. The house itself is a solid, neatly built structure, not very big but big enough for half a dozen persons to live in comfort. There are plenty of small cottages and outhouses. Round about are stately deodars and pines and oak trees and two magnificent eucalyptus trees. I had never seen such huge eucalyptus trees before. Among the trees the pines predominate and they give the peculiar and pleasant pine smell. But for stateliness it is difficult to beat the deodar and the whisper of the wind as it passes through them is extraordinarily soothing.

Ranjit has worked hard here during the past two years and more. It was jungle when he came and the house was full of bats and hardly habitable. There was lack of water. The sole use that Jamnalalji, who owned the place previously, found for the trees was to cut them down. The cut stump of [a] fine old deodar bears mute witness to the tragedy, so also other stumps here and there.

Now the jungle has been cleared off and a farm and orchard have taken their place. There is prospect of green fields with the growing crops swaying gracefully in the wind. Hundreds of fruit trees are dotted about and there must be dozens of varieties of good fruits. Just at present many of these trees are bare for they have not wholly recovered from the winter. But already some are full of bloom, notably the peach trees and apricots. The peach flowers are a mass of purple or rather mauve. Little buds are peeping out of the other fruit trees and probably within two or three weeks they will also be in full bloom. And in the summer they will have ripe rich fruit hanging in abundance from their branches. There will be apples and pears, peaches and apricots, oranges and tangerines, grapes and cherries, plums & mulberries, strawberries and raspberries, pomeloes and pomegranates, walnuts and almonds, chestnuts and persimmons – what a list! Imagine living in this abundance and I have not exhausted the list – for instance there are greengages & nectarines also and probably some others I cannot remember. All their fruits will not appear this year but a good number will. Many of these trees have been obtained from Kashmir & even foreign countries and are specially selected varieties.

The farm contains wheat, barley, oats, rice, Indian corn, bajra, peanuts, *mōong phali* [groundnuts] and some varieties of local grains.

Of the flowers I shall not give a list. It would be far too long. Just at present it is too early for most of them. But in April they will be in all their glory and will form brilliant and vivid patches of colour all round the house. Apart from the ordinary annuals there are special varieties of rose creepers, wistarias, Kashmir varieties of lilac and dahlias and gladioli and iris and daffodils & wallflowers. There are innumerable other varieties. The daffodils are out now and put up a brave show. The acacias are also in full bloom. I imagine that before I go down in a fortnight many more flowers will come out.

Among the new trees Ranjit has planted Kashmir chenars and poplars.

It is fascinating to go round the garden and farm with Ranjit. He takes a personal and individual interest in almost each tree and flowering plant. He tends it and watches it grow like a child. I remembered what vast difference it makes if one personally takes this interest in a garden. In Almora prison every plant was a friend of mine whose fortunes I followed with a certain degree of excitement. It was a great thing to see the new buds shoot forth and peep out into a new world. They had their own way of looking round, just as human babies have. Some were bright and alert, some quite impish, some dull. Every morning and evening I visited every plant and noted the changes that were taking place and I knew exactly the number of flowers even that each plant had. I had a small garden of course and Ranjit has a fine expanse. But his love for flowers and trees is fascinating and delightful.

The lack of water here has been remedied by hard labour and simple contrivance which pumps up the little water which trickles from a spring below. There is now thus a good water supply in the house. Soon there will be other improvements – electric light from a small motor or perhaps generated from power taken from the wind. And so on & so forth.

There is another aspect of Khali which Ranjit has developed. Wool-spinning has been organised and a number of persons sit here all day, spinning away. About a hundred of them in the surrounding villages take the wool to their homes to spin and bring it back. There is fine spinning and I see no reason why good *pashminas*[1] should not be made here. Soon weaving will begin. The local govt. has taken over charge of this spinning & weaving.

A school for children is in prospect.

Then there is bee-keeping and we get good honey, and cattle and a poultry farm.

Altogether this is an enchanting place with any number of pleasant walks under the pines and excursions to places nearby – Binsar is a famous place for its view of the snows and this is only two and a half miles from here. A longer excursion is to the Pindari glacier – six days' easy march. Even Kailas and Mansarovar seem easy of access. The journey can be done in two weeks one way, though this would be hard going. Three weeks is the usual time taken.

I have told you all about Khali now – or a great deal about it. Enough at least to make you want to come here. Of course we shall come together some day.

Perhaps your Easter vacations will be soon upon you. You told me that you intended seeing England. Certainly do so. But I would suggest that as a rule it would be worthwhile to go to the Continent for the vacations. You will anyhow get quite enough of the English atmosphere and try to become unawares rather insular, as I did. It is desirable to see the world from others' spectacles and others' points of view. Also that is the only time you will have to keep up foreign languages. Easter is not a bad time for the tour of France.

Love,

Your loving,
Papu

---

262.   Khali,
Almora U.P.,
15th March, 1938

Darling Indu,

Lying in the sun here, imbibing warmth and energy, I allow my mind to wander. For the moment I am far from the daily work and worry, although some of it pursues me here. I can afford to think of other matters and to dream a little. So I evolved plans of your meeting me at my landing place – Venice or Genoa. From there we might go to Vienna and then, why not? Budapest. Having gone thus far it seemed a pity not to go a few steps

---

1. A superior variety of woollen cloth made from the hair of a species of Himalayan goat.

further to Istanbul. But it was rather far. Anyway Prague was indicated and from there to Munich to have another look at the Deutsches Museum. To Switzerland then & Paris & England. That was one route. Others vaguely impressed themselves on my mind. It was pleasant to form these airy programmes. Another bright idea struck me. Why should I not return to India via Russia, Tadjikistan and Afghanistan!

Foolish fancies! Even in this remote place news has reached of Hitler's coup in Austria[1] and all my peace and quiet have vanished and the relaxation given place to tension. Is it war? Or if not right now, when will it begin and drown the world in blood and ruins? What will happen to you and me when this comes? Will I have news of you? We do not get newspapers here regularly. They come irregularly two or three days after issue. For aught I know the fatal step might have been taken. But whether it has been taken already or not, we live on the brink of it, and the making of programmes seems folly. I suppose I shall not know till the last few days definitely whether I am going to Europe. But I will go unless some insuperable obstacle intervenes.

Meanwhile I take the sun and have my fill of the snows and the mountains.

I find from one of your letters that your term ends on 20th June. When is it possible to meet me, at the earliest, in Paris or in Venice? This will give me some idea and I can draw up my programme accordingly.

I do not know how you have been keeping. I think you ought to take yourself in hand scientifically and get rid of your minor ailments. They are not inevitable and it is foolish to become a slave to them. There is nothing radically wrong with you, as the doctors have frequently said. But you are not strong enough and this means that your powers of resistance to disease and infection are not adequate. Perhaps you have inherited this lack of resisting power from Mummie. Let us recognise it and provide for it.

Do you know that my grandfather died young probably of T.B. So also one of my aunts (father's sister). When Dadu was born there was fear of his getting T.B. He never got it, largely because he made up his mind not to. From boyhood up he looked after his health, took exercise, etc. And so he developed a remarkably fine constitution. He suffered a great deal from asthma but this did not touch his strong constitution and almost to the last he was strong and generally healthy. I was a weak and rather sickly child and had numerous ailments during my infancy and childhood. Later I kept good health and for a long term of years I was not seriously ill. All the time I was at Harrow, Cambridge and London I never had occasion to consult a doctor except once when I was hurt at football and another time

1. On 11th March, 1938 Hitler ordered German troops to cross the Austrian border and two days later the Austrian Government declared Austria part of the German Reich.

for my baldness! This was partly due, I suppose, to my having inherited a good constitution from Dadu, but partly also to my care of myself. By care I do not mean a morbid interest in my body. I never had that. But I did follow some simple rules of health – exercise, good sleep, simple food; for the rest as much work as I liked. Some people imagine that I am neglectful of myself and are full of good advice. As a matter of fact I have stood the strain of heavy work, jail, etc., of these last eighteen years remarkably well and I am far fitter today than many of my old friends who have lived an easy and comfortable life and have swallowed innumerable pills and concoctions. I have kept well because I continued to follow my simple rules – they became a habit – and never worried about myself or took to medicine. Also I can adapt myself to changing circumstances, like jail, etc. I have worked very hard but, curiously enough, I have succeeded in benefiting both mentally and physically from the changes that have come my way. I suppose there is a psychological reason for this, as they fitted in with my mood and so did not oppress me as they might have done. But there is the simpler and somewhat disciplined life also.

All this long account may bore you. But I want you to think about the matter and lay the foundations for good health and vitality. Do not rely too much on medicines, etc. Of course sometimes one has to take them. Do not bother about your body. But just get into the habit of following some rules . . .

What a curious place Europe is getting! There is hardly room for a decent person in large parts of it. Gunther, when he was here, asked me if I had selected a quiet corner for myself to provide for the day when the world was overrun by Fascism! I thought of Khali immediately. But there are no safe refuges for the likes of us.

I enclose a small note for Madan Bhai. Please send it to him. I do not know his address.

All my love,

Your loving,
Papu

Mridula and Bharati are coming here tomorrow. After spending a few days here they will take a house in Almora for a month or so. Mridula has overworked herself at the Haripura Congress and is unwell. She was the head of the women volunteers – 800 strong.

263.   1 Chalcot Crescent,
                                                Regents Park Road,
                                                        N.W. 1.,
                                                2nd April, 1938

Darling Papu,
I am told that some Indian papers have printed the date of your departure
from India as 1st June. I do not know how far this is true, for you have not
written anything definite either to me or to Krishna Menon. I met Krishna
yesterday and we talked mostly of your visit. I don't think you have written
to Krishna whether or not you want him to make the arrangements for
your stay in England. There are so many groups and parties here and
Krishna is not popular with any of them. But still I think he is the best man
to take charge of your visit. When Bose came there were terrific to-dos &
quarrels amongst the local Indians, and we don't want that to happen
again. From the point of view of meeting people in England, the summer
is quite useless, for everyone goes off to the seaside or some such place. So
it would be a good thing if you came here first – in June. Krishna thinks
you ought to stay in England at least three weeks. It is important that you
do not get tired – and it would be an excellent idea if you could go to
Manchester or Lancaster or some such place for a day or two. From
England we could go to the Continent & have a real good holiday. I agree
with Krishna that it would be much better not to have innumerable small
meetings as you had when you came in 1935 and as Bose had. Your visit
must be better planned – just one really big show preferably in the Albert
Hall, if we can possibly afford [it]. Albert Hall is terrific – by far the biggest
hall in London. Then you could speak privately to associations & have
interviews, etc. Nothing after ten p.m.! Write & let me know what further
plans you have made & what you think of the above suggestions. Gosh! I
am looking forward to seeing you.
    Today was the great Varsity Boat Race. What tremendous excitement
there is over such events! I had thought of staying at home and just
listening on the radio – for the progress of the crews is broadcast by a man
following the boats in a motor boat. But the Mitchisons[1] live right on the
river & have one of the best views of the race from their roof. They asked
me to come & have a look – and tonight I am going there to dinner with
Krishna. I met quite a lot of interesting people there. The race was
exciting – in spite of losing the toss we won by two and a half lengths! And
tonight London will run wild – it always does after the race & the
Twickenham Football finals! Barricades have been put up around the

---

1. Naomi Mitchison and her husband. She was a sister of J. B. S. Haldane, and an
author in her own right.

Eros at Piccadilly Circus, for he, being in the very centre of the West End, always suffers the most from the gaiety of Londoners.

Poor Agatha has been down with flu & is feeling rather poorly – she has gone to Broadstairs for a couple of days to 'recover'.

How is Jal Naoroji? We are all very anxious about him.

From Mrs Lankasta I hear that Puphi is thinking of accompanying you to Europe. Is there any truth in this?

With lots of love,

Your loving,
Indu

How are you getting on with the revision of *The Glimpses*?

---

264.   Somerville College,
                                                          Oxford,
                                                 23rd April, 1938

Darling Papu,

I haven't been able to write to you for sometime because my eyes had been giving trouble. I went to an oculist and got them tested and have now landed myself with specs. Fortunately I have only to wear them for reading & other close work & not all the time . . .

I have been seeing Krishna about your trip. Both Krishna & Agatha are looking for suitable flats where we can stay. Krishna will write & tell you about all the arrangements that he is making. The only thing that is worrying me is your intention of staying with Lothian[1] – and please don't think that it has anything to do with what Krishna thinks of him – Lothian is not just another Conservative. He is a very prominent member of the 'Cliveden Set',[2] the set that forced Eden to resign and the set that is commonly known as 'Hitler's friends in Britain'. He is a thorough Fascist & doesn't make any bones about it. He even praised Hitler on the Austrian affair. And just now he is a very important personage in England and very much in the public eye. Your staying with him would amount to the same as if you spent a weekend with Hitler himself or with Mussolini. It would create a terrifically bad impression on all people in this country who are even slightly 'left' & who sympathise with India & the Congress. So please do think it over. After all, Lothian is against all that you stand for and believe in and the people that you are likely to meet in his house will be the

1. Philip Henry, 11th Marquis of Lothian: British diplomat and statesman.

2. An influential British group, including Lord Lothian, which supported the policy of appeasement of Nazi Germany in the late 1930s. This group used to meet at Cliveden, the country home of Lord and Lady Astor.

same – die-hard Tories and Fascists. I am afraid I feel very strongly on the point and even if you do go – Lord Lothian will have to excuse me. It is not only I or Krishna Menon who feel this way but every student – Indian or English – who believes in an independent & socialist India, and the whole Left element. I do hope you will reconsider the matter and change your mind about it.

In Mods I failed in Latin – this means taking just the Latin at the end of the term – on the 20th or the 21st June. So I shall not be able to get away before that date . . .

With lots of love,
Indu

---

265.   Lucknow,
                                              24th April, 1938

Darling Indu,

I have not written to you for a few days. This communal business in Allahabad has taken up a lot of my time. I came here today for meetings of the Provincial Congress.

I have now decided to sail from Bombay on 2nd June by the Lloyd Triestino *Biancamano*, which should reach Genoa about the 12th June or thereabouts. I have not actually booked my passage yet but I suppose there will be no great difficulty about it. There is a faint possibility of Betty accompanying me. I have suggested this to her as she has not been feeling very happy about various matters and requires a change. But I doubt if she will agree. If she comes she will leave the children behind.

When I arrive I suppose you will be still at Oxford. You need not trouble to come to the Continent to meet me. If you can manage it, you can come to London. I should like to go to Oxford before your term ends to see your rooms, etc., meet Miss Darbyshire & perhaps some others. So my first few days after arrival in London should be kept free for this. I have asked Krishna Menon to draw up my programme in consultation with you. Please see that this is not too heavy. It should not go beyond three weeks in England. We shall see to the rest when I reach there. There may be some weekend visits – Stafford Cripps,[1] Lothians. I think both of them should be accepted.

I have not got too much time left here now – just about five weeks. Out of this two weeks or so will be taken up by Working Committee meetings next month. A week is going to be spent in Garhwal and I am looking forward to this. I shall go via Hardwar, probably by plane over the

---

1. Sir (Richard) Stafford Cripps: British Labour leader.

Himalayas. We shall fly over Badrinath and then go to Srinagar (of Garhwal, not of Kashmir). Nan intends accompanying me.

For some days past I had Bee Batlivala[1] staying at Anand Bhawan. Do you know her? She says she met you at lunch with Jal. Her younger sister went with you last year on board the P & O.

Love,

Your loving,
Papu

I am writing to Lothian referring him to you & Krishna. I think we should accept his weekend invitations.

———————

266.   Anand Bhawan,
                                            Allahabad,
                                 30th April, 1938

Indu darling,

Your letter of the 23rd[2] has just come.

Latin seems to be your weak spot. It is a nuisance to have to carry on with it and I hope that after Mods are done with finally you will have no more Latin examinations. Your failing to pass does not matter much as you can easily get through it at the end of term. But I am sorry for it as this means an additional burden on you this term. Fortunately the term is a short one and you will soon be rid of the burden.

Your Latin exam might affect my programme. Agatha suggests that I should loiter somewhere on the Continent till you are free. She further suggests that you might come over to Paris after your exam and meet me there and spend two or three days quietly in Paris. Agatha is optimistic if she imagines that I shall have much quiet in Paris. Still, the idea is not bad if you approve of it. I seem to remember however that Stafford Cripps wanted me to go for a weekend to his country house about the 25th June. Nothing was fixed up as my programme was uncertain. Now that I am going by the earlier boat Krishna will probably want me to accept Stafford Cripps's invitation. Anyway it is for you & Krishna to decide when I am to reach London – I shall loiter about on the Continent if that is required of me. From Genoa I can go to the Riviera or to Paris. You will let me know.

I am not surprised at your feeling strongly about Lothian. I feel more or less the same way. I know about the Cliveden Set and Lothian's pro-

---

1. Mrs Mansell née Bee Batlivala: contemporary of Indira Gandhi who practised law in London for some time.
2. Refers to letter No. 264.

Fascist and pro-Hitler activities. I think they are dangerous. But still after careful consideration I decided to accept his invitation. In effect I had done so over two years ago and I had repeated my acceptance later. It is a long-standing promise and I do not want to break it. But I would have refused in spite of that old promise if I had been convinced that it was the wrong thing for me to do. I happen to be something more than a prominent leader of a group or party. I have a special position in India and a certain international status. I have to function as such whatever my personal likes or dislikes might be. If anybody thinks that by my visiting Lothian I am betraying my cause, or adding to Lothian's prestige, or tarnishing my own reputation, I cannot help it. I happen to know something about my work and I am not unacquainted with international affairs. I have to judge what I should do and should not do, after consulting others of course. And I am quite clear in my own mind that I cannot say no to Lothian so far as accepting his invitation is concerned. If I am so weak as to be influenced by him then I am not much good anyway. It may be that I am in a stronger position to counter him later. I feel therefore that I should accept. Indeed I have done so already. I shall be sorry if you are unable to accompany me.

It is quite possible that Linlithgow might want to meet me in England. I am not keen on seeing him but if he expresses a wish to see me I shall not refuse. Last time when I was in London I made it clear that I was not seeking any interview with anybody but I was prepared to meet anyone who wished to see me, regardless of his political affiliations, whether he was diehard Conservative or Communist. I made only one exception – that I would not meet people connected with the government, because the government was responsible for what was happening in India then. I did not make any exceptions about individuals. So I met Conservatives & diehards who were not in the govt. But I refused to meet Cabinet ministers, such as Halifax and Zetland. Generally speaking, my attitude will be the same this time but I might relax over members of the govt. as the position in India is slightly different.

I have hastened to answer your letter as I wanted to tell you how I felt about this matter.

Love,

> Your loving,
> Papu

267.   Srinagar (Garhwal),
                                   4th May, 1938

Darling Indu,

Here we are – Nan, Raja and I – not far, so far as the map goes, from the rest of the world and yet cut off from it to an extraordinary degree. This letter is supposed to go by air and yet it will be taken first by runners and then by motor bus and then by trains till it reaches the airline. We have had two unusual days. Yesterday morning we reached Hardwar. As usual there was no proper staff work and we did not know what our programme was going to be except that an aeroplane was waiting for us. Our luggage could not go by it, nor Upadhyaya, and I did not relish the idea of being stranded in the mountains without any luggage. Nan also was not well and I did not want to add to her troubles. So I decided to fly to Badrinath & Kedarnath and come back to Hardwar and then start afresh for Garhwal.

We had a good flight following the course of the Ganga and the Alaknanda. We went to Kedarnath first and went fairly near to the snowy peaks and then returned. Then Badrinath which was grander. We did not and could not descend, nor did we actually see the temples. I was not very interested in them. The high peaks going up to 23,000 feet attracted me. We returned to a place called Gochar which is the nearest landing ground to Badrinath – it is five or six days' journey by road. The whole trip so far had taken us two and three quarter hours and we had covered nearly 200 miles, or somewhat less. At Gochar we had a meeting and addresses and food, spending nearly three hours there. And then back by plane to Hardwar. In the course of a few hours we had flown about 270 miles and done a journey which on foot (and there is no other way) takes five weeks. The difference was a measure of the gap between the new world and the old.

The flying was good but we had a few good bumps when we suddenly came across air pockets or currents in the valleys. Once I shot up and banged my head against the roof of the cabin. Nan, however, did not have a happy time and was thoroughly sick on both journeys.

On return to Hardwar we drew up our programme afresh and left by cars for Devaprayag, a journey of fifty-seven miles by a very tortuous mountain road. We reached there at dusk and spent the night there in a *panda*'s[1] house, which was not bad and was beautifully situated on a high precipice overhanging the Alaknanda. What is the Alaknanda? You will ask, ignorant one. I was myself rather vague on the subject till a day or two ago. Well I shall tell you. At Devaprayag two rivers meet – the Bhagirathi and the Alaknanda – and both together are then called Ganga. The real

1. Temple priest.

Ganga so named, starts from Devaprayag from where it goes down to Rishikesh and Hardwar and beyond. Both are thus the Ganga in a sense, but usually the Bhagirathi is considered the Ganga proper and this comes from Gangotri, the source of the Ganga. I have not been to Gangotri, nor did we fly that way yesterday although I saw the Gangotri winding away between the hills above Devaprayag. The Alaknanda we followed by air right up to its sources, Badrinath & Kedarnath.

This morning I had a dip in the Alaknanda at Devaprayag. The right place was the junction with the Bhagirathi but this was a mile away and I wanted to save time. The current of the Alaknanda (and even more so of the Bhagirathi) was so strong and the stones so slippery that it was not possible to go more than a few feet from the bank. But even so the water was delightfully cold and refreshing.

This morning we started from Devaprayag on ponies and rode about nineteen miles. It was fairly hot going and we were rather tired at the end of it. Almost right through we followed the course of the Alaknanda. Many pilgrims, looking tired and footsore, were trudging away to Badrinath, with the prospect of another month's journey before them. It seemed strange that we had done this very journey by air in a few hours the day before. Our bridle path was a good one and a pleasant and sometimes heavy scent of jasmine hung along it.

We reached here soon after noon, long before our luggage. This eventually arrived after seven in the evening. This (Srinagar) is a pleasant little place, rather warm (we are only about 2000 ft high or perhaps 2500) and with an atmosphere of isolation surrounding it. Everybody here has got one major desire – to have a motor road connecting Srinagar with the outside world, a very legitimate wish. Another wish, rapidly taking form and entirely right, is to develop electric power. In a hill country with numerous rivers and waterfalls this is the obvious thing but our governments have never thought along these lines. They only make roads and think of electricity for the hill stations where the officials go to. And because officials seldom come this way this poor spread-out district of the U.P., bordering on Tibet, has been grossly neglected.

We shall remain here two days and then go to Pauri, a hill station 6000 ft high, which is the headquarters of the district and is eight miles away from here. From there we shall go to Devaprayag and Hardwar and back to the better-known but more drab world.

It is very pleasant here in the late evening. Just cool enough. Some of the hillsides have fires on them, intentionally caused as this is supposed to improve the soil. The burnt grass and shrubs make good manure when the rains come. It is a poor country and there are few forests, the hillsides are almost bare. In spite of the abundance of rivers, there is lack of water for the fields, although simple pumps could give enough for the fields. When

I go back from here I shall add yet another picture to the long gallery in my mind – that of Garhwal, poor and neglected but full of great possibilities, if scientifically tackled. What an enormous number of things we have to do in India when once we get going.

The Alaknanda runs some distance down below us. Early tomorrow morning I hope to have a good dip in it. The current is not so strong here and it will be easier to sprawl about. I am looking forward to it.

Love,

Your loving,
Papu

_____

268.   Somerville College,
                                                        Oxford,
                                                        6th May, 1938

Darling Papu,
. . . Darling, I did not for a moment presume to advise you on what to do or to suggest that you had not been following Lothian's tactics – of course you are the only person who can decide what is the best thing to do. I was only stating my own opinion on the matter. And, I am afraid, it is still unchanged. I shall hate being away from you for even a couple of days but I don't think I could bear to stay with Lothian. On the other hand I don't want to seem rude to Lothian so I think the best thing for me to do in the circumstances would be to get myself invited by some friends for the very weekend on which you will be at Lothian's. I do not know when this will be – nor am I sure of Lothian's address. I have written to Krishna for further illumination.

Has anything definite been decided about Choti Puphi? Is she accompanying you? Of course that won't make a difference in your programme. But I should like to know because of getting a larger flat.

Krishna says that he has written to you about your visiting Spain. Again it is a matter entirely for you to decide. I admit it would be good propaganda for Spain & for India. And I know that the element of risk & danger will appeal to you. But I admit I am feeling very worried about it – in fact the more I think of it the less I like it. And if you are coming for a rest, Spain will hardly provide any. However.

I hope this reaches you in Bombay & doesn't have to follow you around.

All my love,
Indu

269.   Bombay,
                                                   15th May, 1938

Darling Indu,
Just a few lines from a very tired person late at night. Your letter of the 6th[1]
has just come.

    In a moment of weakness I have decided to travel first by steamer. The
cabins of the second class did not frighten me (except for the possibility of
having an unwelcome companion) but the little deck space and want of
other places where I could work in peace and relative comfort was
unpleasant to contemplate. I want to do a good deal of revising and writing
on board. Everybody conspired to induce me to change over to first and I
have succumbed. So I shall travel in style.

    I think I have written to you that Betty is not coming with me to Europe,
nor is she coming later.

    I cabled to Krishna that I was prepared to go to Spain. Of course I must
go if there is a chance to do so. I am surprised that you should grow soft
over the idea. I am thick-skinned and hard-headed enough and it seems to
me quite absurd . . . not to go because there is some slight risk. There was
an equal or greater risk in the streets of Allahabad some days ago when I
might conceivably have been stabbed during the days of communal
trouble.

    About Lothian I have already written to you fully. You will of course do
just what you think best.

    Love,
                            Your loving,
                            Papu

                    ━━━━━━■ ▬━━━━━━

270.   Lucknow,
                                                   21st May, 1938

Darling Indu,
The days are slipping by and very soon I shall be on board, speeding away
to the West. I have just come here from Bombay. Three days in Lucknow
– three days in Allahabad – a day in Panchgani to see Jal – three days in
Bombay, and then I sail.

    I went to see Jal day before yesterday. I flew from Bombay to Poona and
from there to Panchgani by car. Our plane did not function well and so
after flying for fifteen or twenty minutes we returned to the Juhu
aerodrome and changed over to another plane.

    1. Refers to letter No. 268.

I was shocked to see Jal. He was thin and emaciated and in continuous pain. I am afraid there is not much chance of his recovering. And yet there is just one chance and probably one shall know within two or three weeks. Jal's case is a very sad one. He really is one of the very few men who could and were likely to play an important role in India. There are hardly any important industrialists who think like him or have big ideas. Just before his illness he had been made a director of Tata's Steel Works – a big position. And then he is so straight and fundamentally solid. I am very depressed about him. In spite of the shortness of time at my disposal I have decided to pay him another visit before I leave. Poor Malati's case is pitiable.

I am getting the endorsement for Spain. There has been no difficulty. Congress govts. are useful at times. What will happen to me after I land at Genoa I do not know. I await Mishra's instructions. If I have an odd day or so I should like to go to the Riviera. I have told you – have I not? – that I am travelling first in great luxury on the Lloyd Triestino boat – the *Biancamano.*

When will I see you, my dear? On the 22nd just after your exam is over? If it is to be later you might join me in Paris.

Nan is in Mussoorie. She is bringing Chand to Bombay to have her eyes attended to. We shall meet before I sail.

Love,
Papu

271.
Somerville College,
Oxford,
10th June, 1938

Darling Papu,

This is just a hurried line to welcome you. I am feeling so excited about seeing you that I can hardly think of anything to say.

Life here is very 'end-of-term'-ish and exhausting. Then there is my Latin. Between all this I am feeling like going to bed for weeks. That is why I decided it was best not to meet you in Paris. I shall go to London on Tuesday the 21st morning & spend the whole day in Agatha's most comfortable bed, so as to be first & energetic to greet you.

Meanwhile this little note brings you all my love & good wishes. Oh, I am so looking forward to the 23rd! I do hope your English programme – or any programme for that matter – is [not] too heavy. So very many people want to see you & meet you. I ran into the Thompsons this morning & they said would I arrange an interview for them. This afternoon I had tea with

Prof. Sir Radhakrishnan & the University lecturer in Chinese philosophy & they are both very eager too. I tell everyone to approach Krishna.

With all my love – À Bientôt,
Indu

---

272.   Marseilles,
                                                      14th June, 1938

Darling,

So we have arrived at last.[1] This morning we reached Genoa – met Krishna Menon there – took the plane to Marseilles and spent the whole day without food or drink in search for various visas and endorsements for Spain. I have never had quite such a painful experience of how bureaucracy works. At last we got them all and returned worn out in the evening. We leave at four thirty a.m. tomorrow for Barcelona. How I wish you were with me.

Bee Batlivala was with me on board and functioned as my secretary. She was quite helpful. She wanted to go to Spain and is accompanying Krishna and me.

I have so much to tell you but I must not write much now. A bath is immediately indicated and then a brief three hours' sleep.

These few lines are just to send you my love. Don't worry about your examination. You will do well in it.

All my love,

Your loving,
Papu

---

273.   London,
                                                    15th September, 1938

Darling,

Here are some postcards.

I am writing this after midnight. The morning papers are out already telling us of Chamberlain's flight[2] to Hitler. His first flight! Well I shall stick to my flight to Geneva and watch events take shape from the air & from the land.

---

1. In 1938 Jawaharlal travelled to Europe and Great Britain on an extended visit. Indira joined her father after his arrival in England.

2. Neville Chamberlain flew to Berchtesgaden on 15th September, 1938 to discuss a peace settlement with Hitler.

Look after yourself and get strong & well soon. Only the fit in mind &
body can do much and there is big work ahead.

Love,
Papu

---

274.   Brentford Hospital,[1]

Brentford,
Middlesex,
15th September, 1938

Darling Papu,
Thank you for the postcards. One by one they will be finding their way to
you soon.

I hope you had a good flight. And I wonder what sort of a journey that
other eastbound traveller – Chamberlain – had; it might have an effect on
how he talks to Hitler! I can't help thinking that he is up to no good and
will make a mess anyway as far as Czechoslovakia is concerned. I missed
the first part of the news and the evening paper has not been delivered so I
am completely in the dark about the latest developments.

I am more or less the same – have been feeling terribly tired all day. In
the afternoon I was weighed – 85 lbs.

Up till lunch time my luggage had not arrived at Bhandari's[2] . . .

I am going to miss you no end – Geneva seems so far away from my view
of green apples and a church spire.

Here is a letter which came night before last –

Lots of love,
Indu

---

275.   [Brentford Hospital

Middlesex]
21st September [1938]

Darling Papu,
Your telegram has just arrived addressed to Indiro Nehro!

I wrote you a postcard[3] yesterday morning but it is so difficult to get

---

   1. While travelling in Europe with her father, Indira was taken ill in Hungary in the
autumn of 1938. The ailment was diagnosed as pleurisy, which troubled her for several
months.

   2. Dr P. C. Bhandari: Indian doctor practising in England who was consulted by Indira.

   3. Postcard not published.

things posted – especially as I have been out of stamps for some days. I do not know when you will receive it.

I am feeling much better today. In the afternoon I shall sit up in the armchair for an hour or so. By Saturday I shall be up & about, for on Friday week I leave the hospital! . . .

Isn't the European situation perfectly sickening? What can one say about it? Words seem so superfluous. I knew Chamberlain couldn't be up to any good when he flew to Germany & I shouldn't be surprised if our friend Nancy [Astor] was the originator of the bright idea. Meanwhile all that is being done is sending in mild 'protests' to the Prime Minister! And even then the only papers that publish them are the *News Chronicle* & the *Manchester Guardian*! Czech propaganda in this country has been seriously neglected and it is taking time for the people to realise what actually has happened. But surely even now public opinion could force Chamberlain to call Parliament – it depends largely on Labour. But what can the British Parliament now do to save Czechoslovakia? Whether the proposals be accepted or not, whether there is war or not, there can be no peace for Czechoslovakia.

Good lord, I've started on a lecture! Bhandari is wondering where I should go after Brentford. He suggests the Grand Hotel in some place in Devon, where 'palms grow'. But Agatha & Puphi are full of praises for Castlemere, Broadstairs.

I am looking forward to seeing you. It seems such ages since you left.
All my love,
Indu

276.
[Brentford Hospital,
Middlesex]
22nd September [1938]

Darling Papu,

Today I'm feeling as near 'a million dollars' as one can when one is in bed. Last evening I sat for an hour and a half – three thirty to five. Except for the first ten minutes or so I did not feel at all tired . . . I had quite a crowd of visitors: Agatha came in the morning and in the afternoon Dr & Mrs Mahomedi (the Swiss one) came with the most enormous & gorgeous white chrysanthemums that I have ever seen, too enormous & expensive looking to suit my little room, I think, for they seem to dominate over everything else. Marion Robey, a friend of mine who is a teacher, also came.

I was weighed again this morning. My weight is the same as last week: 6 stone 1 lb.

It's a lovely day. But the droning of the aeroplanes is not a pleasant sound & it goes on from morn till evening. Agatha was right: Heston Aerodrome is only two miles away from here . . .

Meanwhile I suppose all that can be done is to hope for the best and to mobilise public opinion so that it may be effective in guarding the interests (as far as possible) of the rump Czechoslovakia! Have you news of Nanu? What is he going to do – is he staying on in Prague? Gosh, I feel so sick at heart when I think of the people we met: the dear Prof. Lesny and the little smiling Hertzkova.[1] What are they doing & what are they thinking? And there are millions like them.

All my love,
Indu

277.

Wardha,
10th December, 1938

Darling Indu,

I hope your packing has been completed without fatiguing you too much. I am afraid you have not had as much rest in Allahabad as we had hoped. You realise of course that you have undertaken a biggish job – to build up your health on an unshakeable foundation. This is not easy unless tackled in a businesslike way. You have got an excellent chance to do so. The real difficulty is that you might slacken your vigilance because you feel a little better. This getting tired easily must be conquered. It is not good enough to go through life in a physically tired condition with occasional illnesses. I hope therefore that you will apply your will and determination to get fit rapidly and carry out a regime of rest, etc., in Almora. Probably it will be desirable to spend the first two days almost completely in bed. Then three days of small walks, on the level – in the morning and evening with long rests – for the rest of the time in bed or on an easy chair. Do not go in for walking up & down hill. For these days you had better walk in your garden, which I presume you will have. Later, when you feel better, you can venture out. But remember in any event to

(1) Take your temperature morning & evening.
(2) Three hours' rest in the afternoon and some rest before and after meals.
(3) If you feel tired increase your rest. Also if there is any rise in temperature.

---

1. Gertrud Hertzka-Loew: A German, who acted as guide to Jawaharlal Nehru when he visited Prague in 1938.

You had better take a new supply of your tonics with you from Allahabad as you may not get them in Almora.

So far as I can remember, your house is beautifully situated on the Khali Road, with a gorgeous view of the snows. I am convinced that you will prosper there. Take care not to catch chills. Be well clad & covered.

When you go Anand Bhawan will be unoccupied and all our mail will go to Swaraj Bhawan. Inform the A.I.C.C. office to forward *your* letters to Almora. No other address is necessary but if you find out from Girish Chandra Joshi the name of the house, you can give this, and also write it to me. On arrival at Almora write to the Post Office & Telegraph Office telling them of your existence & address.

I do not know how long I shall be here. In any event I am here till the 14th evening, perhaps till the 15th. Then Bombay. I shall try to reach Allahabad on the 21st night.

I picked up the December *Lilliput* at the Nagpur Station. I am posting it to you.

Take your weight before you leave Allahabad.

Love,
Papu

---

278.   In train,
                                                           Bombay–Allahabad,
                                                           22nd December, 1938

Darling Indu,

It is long since I wrote to you – ten long days or even more. And yet every day I felt the urge as I thought of you, and words and phrases tumbled over each other in my mind. Several times I took pen in hand and was on the point of beginning, but bodily weariness overcame me and I said to myself: let it be tomorrow when I am fresher in body and spirit. I have not been keeping as well as I ought to be and some kind of a chill or cold, or perhaps a mild dose of flu, has pursued me from Wardha onwards, resulting in a bad throat and occasional fever. A day's full rest in bed would have suppressed this distemper, but instead of this I sat for long weary hours in committee, with aching limbs and fevered brow. Gradually I conquered over this passing trouble and I am much better now. Friends pressed me to stay another day or two in Bombay to rest and get fitter for the journey. They did not realise that I can get better rest in a railway train during a long journey when no one knows that I am travelling and hence there is no interference – provided of course I travel in a higher class than usual. And so I am seated now in lordly fashion in a second-class coupé, all by myself, after having had a long and restful sleep.

But I am writing about myself when my mind hungers for news of you. I have had none for many days, except a brief reference in Betty's letter to Raja. I was glad of this morsel though I wish there was more of it. I hope it is well with you, and the sight and cold air of the snow-covered mountains is filling you with vitality and strength. Vicariously I take joy in that prospect and I plan a visit when I can be with you and the mountains. I have refused so many engagements but the web of life encircles me and makes me prisoner. I had hoped to keep the first half of January free. It is no longer so. The Working Committee meets again in January – on the 7th, 8th and 9th – in remote Bardoli. In the second half of January other demands are made on me but so far I have resisted them. I still hope to reach Khali, or wherever you might be, about the middle of January. I must have this respite for body and mind before the Congress session, and yet I dare not feel certain about it, lest the mocking gods trap me up again, and entangle me in their snares.

From now to the middle of January my days are terribly full. Three days in Allahabad (December 23rd to 25th) with an important conference of Congress Muslims and numerous other activities and a hundred letters clamouring for answer. There will be many guests in Anand Bhawan. On the 25th night I go to Lucknow for a day, on the 27th to Fyzabad for the Provincial Conference over which I am presiding. I shall be in Fyzabad for five days and I am not looking forward to this visit. It will mean a great strain.

On 1st January I go from Fyzabad to Calcutta direct. Two days there attending All India Students' Conference and Keshub Chandra Sen's[1] centenary gathering. Probably on 4th Jan. Santiniketan if Gurudev is there. Leave that evening for Bombay, travelling right across India. Reach Bombay 6th Jan. morning – various meetings there. Leave same night for Bardoli where I stay for three days: 7th, 8th, 9th Jan. Back in Allahabad, 11th Jan. night. Some important meetings there on 12th Jan. Probably leave Allahabad on 13th Jan. night for Lucknow, spend a day there and proceed to Kathgodam and beyond. If all this works out I should reach Khali on 15th January evening. I should like to spend two weeks there or at least ten days.

Please write to me so as to catch me in various places where I go to. Address in Fyzabad c/o Provincial Conference. In Calcutta c/o Dr B. C. Roy,[2] 36 Wellington Street, Calcutta.

In Bombay I have been having a novel experience in presiding over the Planning Committee. It is a very mixed crew – big business, professors, economists, scientists, govt. ministers, and odd people. Rather out of my

1. Keshub Chandra Sen: social and religious reformer in India in the 19th century.
2. Dr Bidhan Chandra Roy: physician and Congress leader, later Chief Minister of Bengal.

line and therefore more fatiguing than other activities, but full of interest and instruction for me. Whatever the Planning Committee might achieve, it will certainly add to my education, and though I grow old I have not lost the knack of learning and filling the enormous gaps in my mind. By the time I grow decrepit with age and weary of this business of life, when I am even more querulous and intolerant than I am now, and have lost all the strength and vitality that I still possess, and bent-backed stumble forward painfully, supported by you, my dear, by that time, perhaps, I shall be full of wisdom. But what will it avail me then when the power to act has gone? *Si jeunesse savait; si vieillesse pouvait!*[1]

Many years ago I used to dream that when you grew up, you also would play a brave part in what is called public life in India, to shoulder this heavy burden, to help in putting brick upon brick in the building of the India of our dreams. And I wanted you to train and fit yourself in body and mind for this engrossing task. But I am not sure that I desire you to do this now, and to experience the heartache and the crushing of the spirit that this involves. Each one of us has enough of burden to carry, do we do much good by shouldering the burdens of others? Yet we may not and cannot escape them. But perhaps it is better for us to function in a limited sphere that we understand and to serve India in that restricted field, rather than presume to enter the wide expanse of Indian humanity. For me there is no escape, no refuge, till the inevitable escape that comes to us all. But why should I encourage others who are dear to me to enter into the heart-breaking business?

What am I writing to you? Instead of cheering you, I am writing depressing stuff, the outcome of a slightly disordered and fevered mind. But this will pass soon enough and I shall write to you more cheerful letters.

How do you stand as regards money? You have not got much. Let me know how much you require for the next three weeks or so till I come up.

Tell Betty that I have given heavy work to Raja. This will keep him fully occupied for the next fortnight. After that he will have a brief respite but not for long. I have suggested to him to accompany me to Khali when I go up in mid-January.

Give my love to Betty and the children, and for yourself, my dear, what more can I give you than what you have already?

Your loving,
Papu

———————— ◆◆ ————————

1. If only the young knew; if only the old could.

279.

Almora,
New Year's Day, 1939

Darling Papu,
Your telegram from Allahabad has just come. Ours is awaiting you in Calcutta, for we were not sure of your changed programme until just after we had despatched the telegram on New Year's Eve.

I have got more or less used to the little discomforts and like Snow View much better than I did at first sight. I do hope you will be able to come up.

It is probably snowing on Nanda Devi and the other peaks, for they are completely enveloped in cloud. Even here it has suddenly become considerably colder. You probably know by now that we had to send Shukru down. His temperature was continuing – he had bronchitis. Also we heard that he had been very very ill a short while before my arrival in India.

Otherwise life goes on much as usual. My cold is more or less the same. It is impossible not to catch a cold when the only heating is a wood fire, when every room has a different temperature.

The children are very sweet but naughtier than ever – they simply cannot get used to the place and give poor Puphi a lot of trouble. Every morning they wake up asking: *Kyā ham āj Bombay jāenge?*[1]

We have entered into the social life of Almora – that is we have been to some meal or other with Uday Shankar, the Sens,[2] Dr Khazan Chand, Mr Vir & the Brewsters. Tomorrow we are going on a picnic lunch to Shimtola which is a very beautiful spot about half a mile away. As the climb is stiff I shall go in a *dandi*.

Love,
Indu

280.

[Almora]
4th January, 1939

Papu darling,
Joshiji came today with news of you.

I gave him the keys of my wardrobe to give to Hari. I do not know if they are now in Lucknow or Allahabad. If they are in Allahabad & easily available, I should like you to bring some things out of my wardrobe. I shall let you know the details later on.

---

1. Will we go to Bombay today?
2. Boshi Sen and his wife Gertrude Emerson-Sen. They were friends of Jawaharlal Nehru and lived in Almora.

Gertrude Sen is anxious to read the Zakir Hussain committee's report – the one you showed me. If you could get hold of one, could you please send it to me or direct to her?

Puphi & Harsha are not feeling quite up to the mark. I am all right. But we did not go to the Shimtola picnic which I mentioned in my last letter as I wasn't feeling too bright. Afterwards we were glad we didn't go for Gertrude says they walked five or six miles!

It has gone much colder here. The snow range is completely hidden behind clouds. It snows there all day & probably night, but clears up in the mornings.

With love from us all.

Indu

P.S.
We should be glad to have the *Time & Tide* & the *New Statesman* if nobody else wants them – for you will be out of Allahabad all the time.

281.

Snow View,
[Almora]
9th January, 1939

Darling Papu,
I have your letters.

We shall expect you on the 16th. Please bring plenty of warm things – especially for the night. It rained a lot last night and has turned much colder. There is a cutting wind blowing. It might snow a little in the near future.

Is Upadhyaya coming too? Please let us know in advance. There is plenty of room as we are using only half the house – but of course we shall have to get the room ready.

I want a few things from Allahabad – I shall send a list to Allahabad as this letter might go astray.

Boshi is looking forward tremendously to your coming – Gertrude & he were here for lunch yesterday. He adores the children and they always give him a right royal welcome. Mr Elmhirst is coming up in a couple of days.

Puphi is not feeling too good – but the rest of us are all right.

Love,
Indu

282.

Bombay,
15th April [1939]

Darling Papu,
This is just to send my love. I was so glad to hear your voice, even if it [was] only on the phone.

Don't worry about me, darling. I shall be all right. Things seem to have quietened down a bit, though of course the tension persists. Most of the English Cabinet have gone off on holidays. But the war risk insurance has gone up to 400%! And the insurance companies, especially Lloyd's, generally know what they are talking about.

We don't have to be on the pier until eleven o'clock. So on our way there we are going to drop in at the Munshis'[1] place for a couple of minutes – Mrs Munshi's daughter is getting married & they are very insistent that we should look in.

Jivraj[2] came again this morning – just to say how d'you do. Bharucha & he examined me on the 13th. I enclose a small note which he wrote in the way of a report. My blood pressure & pulse seem to be better. The X-ray photograph is exactly the same as the one taken in Bombay. About future treatment they say their advice to me last time still holds good. They advise my going to Switzerland or to France, since France would be easier to get out of. But of course I shall first consult Hebert & Bhandari.

Dr Schacht[3] is still busy being entertained by the big industrialists. He is trying hard to explain to them & convince them that when Hitler called Indians 'monkeys' he did not mean Mr Ambalal Sarabhai[4] & his son! (This came out in the papers!) I have asked Upadhyaya to show a cutting from the *Chronicle* – a letter to Dr Schacht from Karaka.[5] It is the best thing – in fact the only good thing – that Karaka has so far written. Schacht is very indignant at the Gujarati papers & the *Chronicle* & *Sentinel.* He is even said to have reported to the Governor about them & especially the *Chronicle*, which sent a German Jew to interview Schacht.

I must go & feed now. So *au revoir* and all all my love.

Indu

Thank you very much for your letter. I shall write from on board. Love.

---

1. K. M. Munshi: lawyer and nationalist politician from Bombay.
2. Dr Jivraj Mehta: physician and nationalist.
3. Hjalmar Schacht: German financier.
4. Ambalal Sarabhai: industrialist and merchant of Ahmedabad.
5. D. F. Karaka: Bombay journalist.

283.   [S.S. *Strathaird*]
                                         18th April, 1939

Darling Papu,
So I have sailed after all!! I did hate leaving India & you this time. It has left
a strange sort of emptiness inside me. But here I am and there is no
turning back. And indeed the fault is entirely mine, for mine was the
decision to leave. It wouldn't be so bad if I did not keep seeing your face –
so sad, with something more than just sadness. Darling, don't be so
defeatist – no one can defeat you except yourself. You are so much above
all the pettiness that is invading Indian politics. It is distressing to watch it
taking a hold – but you mustn't let it make any real difference. These
happen the world over. And they always pass.

I miss you terribly – for the sea is so lovely and by its very beauty throws
into relief all the pettiness and hardness and egotism of men.

Travelling tourist is uncomfortable but much nicer than first. I have a
two-berth cabin, which I share with a Kashmiri-Punjabi dame who is
married to a Bengali. She is very amusing. She talks & talks & talks from
morn till night incessantly and without a break. It is fortunate that she does
not mind who she is talking to, and still more fortunate that she requires
no answers. We have no porthole, no window in our cabin. It is stuffy and
very hot. But up on deck it is nice. On the whole ship, not one berth is
vacant. The passengers are kind and friendly but not over interesting. The
only one I like is Mlle Bossenée the French superintendent of the
Santiniketan Girls' Hostel. You have met her. But perhaps you do not
remember. She is charming as only a French woman knows how. Also on
board is George Pool – we met him at the Brewsters in Almora. I have just
said how d'you do to him. He seems to be moving around all by himself & I
never see him about the decks.

We reach Marseilles on the 25th. I have let Madame Morin know.

With all all my love – darling mine.

                                              Indu

———————————————

284.   Anand Bhawan,
                                           Allahabad,
                                         18th April, 1939

Darling,
Last night, as I sat listening to the radio, I suddenly felt assured that you
would reach England safely before war came. Whether war will ultimately
come or not I do not know but it is clear that it will not descend upon us for

another ten days or more. For Hitler is going to give his answer to Roosevelt on the 28th April.

I was thinking of giving you full directions as to what you should do in case war broke out by the time you reached Egypt. That would mean your being held up there without much money. But there are plenty of friends there who would help you – Nahas Pasha[1] and other Egyptians and the Indian community in Cairo. However this is not likely now and you will plough through the Mediterranean and probably see innumerable warships and planes, but they will not trouble you.

I do not know if this letter will reach you at Port Said. And so I am not writing much. Tomorrow morning I am going to Dhanbad to see Subhas. He has asked me to visit him. We are in a hopeless tangle and there seems no way out.

When in London do not forget the Robesons[2] and convey my greetings to them.

Love,

Your loving,
Papu

285.

Anand Bhawan,
Allahabad,
26th April, 1939

Darling,

I have come to Allahabad for a few hours and am just going to Calcutta for the A.I.C.C. Upadhyaya has already gone off with my luggage to the station and I am hurriedly scribbling these few lines.

Your letter from Port Tewfeik came today. I am glad you have had a fairly good voyage. Now you must be in Paris. I hope you have looked up our old friend Shah.

You give me a lot of good advice, my dear to keep smiling, etc. Of course. But it is a little difficult. I suppose age is telling upon me and I am losing my resilience.

I must go to the station now.

Love,

Your loving,
Papu

---

1. Egyptian nationalist leader.
2. Paul Robeson and his wife.

286.   Y.W.C.A. Central Club,
                                              Great Russell Street,
                                                     W.C.I.,
                                               1st May, 1939

Darlingest,
Last night I was taking a snack somewhere in Belsize Park, when I ran into
Mohan Kumaramangalam. He told me that Kabadi[1] has just received a
telegram saying that Subhas had resigned & Rajendra Babu elected in his
stead. This is disturbing news. The possibility of Subhas resigning has
been in everyone's mind and yet the news of it came as a shock. Whatever
Subhas's actual politics, he had come to be regarded as the leader of the
'left', so that his resignation seems to be a terrific setback to the socialist
movement and great victory – one may almost call it personal – for
Vallabhbhai. Anyway, we are at last out of the deadlock and even the
wrong road may be better than not moving at all. I suppose Bengal will be
more troublesome than ever before. I was glad to hear that you brought
forward a resolution that Bose should stay. I wonder why you had to
withdraw it? We have so little news.

I arrived in London in the midst of a slight mist and pouring rain last
afternoon. The mist has cleared but the downpour has not lessened.
Much as I love London, I could never call it beautiful. But just now it is
perfectly ugly. Do you remember the little black Eros in the middle of
Piccadilly Circus? They have barricaded him and on the barricades are
stuck enormous seven-foot posters: 'We've got to be prepared.' 'National
Service – Enrol now.' 'Have you done your duty?' 'What are you doing for
your country?' You see these terrific posters everywhere – on the Nelson
Column, on walls, outside cinemas, in shop windows. There are so many
of them that soon the letters start swimming in front of one's eyes and one
sees them even in places where they are not. In every room there are
instructions for A.R.P. [Air Raid Precautions]. But I hear that the Paris
preparations have been much better carried out. While I was there they
were continually having blackouts & sirens were shrieking away even
during the day.

Today is May Day – day of demonstrations, processions and meetings.
The India League usually takes part. So the boys are all out, marching
towards Hyde Park in spite of the incessant rain. Characteristically, the
Labour Party is not taking part. People are quite agitated about compulsory conscription. The mass of the people approve of the move and the
National Govt. is even more secure in its hold of the country. Labour &
the Trade Unions are opposed – because this gives greater military

1. Sunder Kabadi: Indian journalist in Britain.

strength to the govt., which will inevitably use it to crush trade unions and such movements.

I had an enjoyable stay in Paris. The weather was none too good but I met some interesting people. Nanu is there now & so is Shankar – the *Hindustan Times* cartoonist. Shankar is going back to India this month. Have you met him? I think he is very nice. He is rather fed up with the politics of the *H.T.* but he has hardly any choice.

In spite of the weather, in spite of everything, spring is in the air. It sort of gives you an uplift. All over France & England the little wild fragrant spring flowers are covering the hillsides and the plains and the blossoms are out. Paris was full of my favourite flower – lilies of the valley – '*muguet*' in French. Do you know them? They grow wild in sheltered woods, little snow-white bells, perfect in form and delicious perfume. They are the flowers of May. And there is a custom in France to give small bunches of them to one's friends on May Day.

The best thing I did in Paris was to go to a permanent exhibition of 'The Nymphiades of Claude Monet'. I do not think you have been there. It is a pity. Had I known of them earlier I should certainly have taken you. Mlle Bossenée, who was on the *Strathaird* with me, told me that I would find them beautiful. So I asked Louise to take me to them. And now it is one of my most beautiful memories. Monet was one of the first of the Impressionist painters. He has painted only ponds and trees. The sheer beauty of them is breathtaking. His colours are perfect and he gives such an atmosphere of quiet and peaceful calm. I went there at the end of a tiring afternoon but within a few seconds my fatigue fell off me like an unwanted cloak, my eyes felt as if I had just washed them in soothing cold lotion and I came out into the outside world fresh enough to do anything. We missed you so very much. You would have found them beautiful. Unfortunately the photographs of them do not convey anything – else I should send you some. There is at Tooth's in London a small exhibition of Monet. I shall not miss it. I have got into touch with Bhandari, who will find out when Hebert can see me. When this is settled, I shall go up to Oxford for a day to see Darb. Krishna is going to Paris on the 11th. If I finish all I have to do by then, I shall accompany him and then go on to Switzerland. In spite of all these feverish preparations & scares, I still think that there will be no war. Nobody seems to agree with me!

Your letter came this morning. Thanks a lot.

All my love to you.

Your loving,
Indu

2nd May

Darling – I couldn't post this yesterday because the man at the post office said that it would not go until tomorrow in any case.

Yesterday was the most successful May Day for over ten years. The Indian contingent was one of the best and one of the most cheered. And this in spite of – or is it because of? – the rain! I did not go of course but someone stuck a May Day badge on my coat & for the rest of the day, wherever I went, in the tube stations and in buses, there were several voices, 'Greetings, Comrade.'

The rain has stopped today. But there is no sun and it is terribly cold and windy. But summer time has begun and already several establishments have stopped the central heating! It reminds me of Ogden Nash.[1]

> Then giddy up Napoleon, giddy up Gideon!
> The Sun has crossed the right meridian
> What if the blasts of winter sting?
> Officially, at least, it's spring.
> My love,
> Indu

---

287.   Lucknow,
                                                   12th May, 1939

Darling Indu,

It is a month today, is it not, since you left Allahabad and now you are many thousands of miles away. I do not quite know where you are – I suppose you are still in England, probably in London. But I hesitate to send this letter to the Y.W.C.A., and yet I suppose that is the best address. Louise Morin wrote to me of your arrival in and departure from Paris. Of your arrival in London I have so far not heard.

For the past week I have been so engrossed in Lucknow affairs that I have almost forgotten Hitler, Mussolini and all their unholy tribe. I came here specially for the Shia–Sunni trouble.[2] It has grown to enormous dimensions and nearly 8700 Shias are in prison and the bitterness between the two is something unbelievable. For this week I have spent long and exhausting hours, nearly all day and till far into the night, talking, discussing, arguing, drafting statements. Gradually we seemed to be coming nearer a settlement, or at any rate a provisional arrangement. We thought of clinching the matter today and then at the last moment

1. Ogden Nash: American humorous poet.
2. Refers to conflict between two Muslim sects, Shias and Sunnis.

everything broke down! And so here we are wondering what to do, at a loose end. Still, I suppose we have to go on trying and we shall make another effort tomorrow. Anything more distressing or irritating I can hardly imagine.

To add to my troubles I fell ill. Nothing much but I was confined to bed. I am up again and have been pushed about in the hospital for various X-rays which displayed a fairly healthy inside.

Ranjit lies in the grip of a fierce attack of malaria with his temperature running to over 106°F.

I am for the present held up here because of the Shia–Sunni affair. I do not know how long I shall have to stay on. In any event I have to be here again a few days later for various meetings.

I shall go to Bombay at the beginning of June and remain there for two weeks or more. So remember to write to me there.

Agatha has taken with her a gramophone record for you. This is the new *Bande Mataram* tune. Do you remember a doctor who travelled with us when we went to Santiniketan? He promised to send you a python skin. Well, he has sent it. I do not quite know how to send it on to you. Such things give trouble in the customs. I shall try to find someone to take it.

Love,

> Your loving,
> Papu

---

288.   Lucknow,
17th May, 1939

Darling Indu,

I have come back to Lucknow after two days in Allahabad. I received your letter[1] from London and your card[2] from Marseilles – the latter came after the letter. Bhandari also wrote to me and I was glad to know that he found a great improvement in you. He suggested that you might go to Switzerland early in June.

For the present you will have enough cash with you. But please remember that we have so far made no arrangements for remittances to go to you regularly. You will get £50 more soon – I forget the date. Bachhraj will send this. For subsequent payments please instruct Bachhraj directly. I should like you to keep the £50 I sent you apart for emergencies and not to use it for your ordinary expenditure.

---

1. Refers to letter No. 286.
2. Postcard not published.

Puphi has gone to Mussoorie. She is likely to be away for some weeks. Ranjit is better now. He will go off to Khali next week . . . [incomplete]

[Papu]

━━━━━━━━━━ ◆ ▬

289.   [Hotel Winkelried]
                                                            Stansstad,
                                                         Switzerland,
                                                       27th May, 1939

Darling Papu,

I haven't written to you for simply ages. Your letter of the 17th from Lucknow[1] came this morning.

This is my second day in Stansstad. I left London on the 24th. Stansstad was Bhandari's idea. He has spent four or five summers here in this very hotel and was ecstatic about everything: the hotel, the family who runs it, the town, the surroundings. He says its his idea of paradise. I have never been in these parts before but it is supposed to be the most beautiful part of Switzerland. Stansstad is on the Lake of Lucerne, just thirty-five minutes from Lucerne by lake steamer. I haven't done any sightseeing yet. The weather is not too good – cold & dark. I expect I shall be here for most of the summer, so I hope the sun comes out soon & stays out.

You have already had the doctors' report from Bhandari. Hebert was more cautious – I suppose Harley Street specialists have to be. He said there was still a shadow or darkening (or some such thing) on the left side & that I would have to be very careful & be examined & X-rayed every six months or so. But that I could go to Oxford in October.

I wrote to the Darb as soon as Hebert had seen me. She asked me up to Oxford to spend the night with her, adding: 'Miss Sutherland (that's my tutor) & I hope you will come prepared to stay up for the rest of this term.' Apparently she had written to me to London suggesting that I should go up to College for the remaining four weeks of the summer term – but I did not receive that letter. Anyway I rang up Bhandari at once & informed him of the Darb's wishes. He just muttered 'impossible'. I went up to Oxford for a couple of days – the Darb was very affable, kissed me on both cheeks & asked which room would I like to have in October. So I am going up definitely in October to do the 'Social Administration' Diploma. Most of my work will be outside College & in my first term I shall tute with a Mr Scoffes (or some such name). I have sent him my address and am waiting for his reply & the list of books that I have to read.

I met Agatha & Krishna just before leaving. Krishna came to the station too.

1. Refers to letter No. 288.

Things in England are much the same, except for a wave of pro-Sovietism. The Russian pact will probably be signed soon. At least that is how I feel – two days before I left, I saw Krishna & he said Chamberlain would never do it. But I am not so sure. The Labour Party are worse than ever. Duff Cooper, speaking at a large Conservative meeting, said, 'Those of you who have tendencies towards the Left should pay a visit to the headquarters of the T.U.C. to take a lesson in Conservatism'!

I didn't do very much in London in the way of seeing plays & things. But I did go one evening to the *Babes in the Wood – a pantomime with political point* at the Unity Theatre. I enjoyed it thoroughly. The hit of the show was the 'bad uncle' – i.e. Chamberlain. He was truly wonderful – in a photograph it was impossible to tell him apart from the real Chamberlain. It is said that for over two months the man hung around 10 Downing Street and walked behind the premier in St James's Park, studying his movements. Then one day, as a dress rehearsal he went to St James's Park all dressed up as Neville and was greeted as such by everyone in the park!! He was colossal. The babes-in-the-wood theme was the perfect vehicle for a satire on the events of Munich & the Chamberlain National Govt. The Wicked Uncle is a devastating caricature of the Prime Minister, the two Robbers fit in perfectly as the two European bullies, while the Babes, as two small and unprotected states, betrayed by their guardians, the Wicked Uncle, fall readily for the charming heroics of Robin Hood, the friend of the oppressed, the spirit of Democracy. This is the only Unity Theatre play which has been reviewed & praised by *The Times*! I enclose a photograph of the 'Wicked Uncle'.

In August there is a music festival in Lucerne. I hope to go to at least one concert, conducted by Bruno Walter.[1]

The other day, I was dining at the Vega with Krishna & he was trying to persuade me to go to a meeting on 'Nutrition in India' when I spotted Miss Hill, Stafford Cripps's Secretary. She sent Cripps's & her own best regards to you.

I expect Krishna has written to you about the charts of the *Glimpses*. He says they will have to be issued separately otherwise the book will be delayed until the autumn, which is not a good thing.

I got a terrible shock to suddenly read the news of Toller's suicide in New York. It is awful news. I wanted to write to his wife, but nobody seems to know where she is – probably somewhere in America, possibly Hollywood.

With much love,
Indu

---

1. Bruno Walter: opera and symphony conductor.

290.   Hotel Winkelried,
                                                           Stansstad,
                                                           Switzerland
                                                       5th June, 1939

Darling Papu,
Agatha has just forwarded your two letters[1] with the snapshots. The snaps
seem to be a bit under-exposed, though the ones of Montana & the
Marble Rocks are good.

I am so glad Mamu[2] has got the Kew Garden job – he was looking
forward to it. I shall not be in London when he arrives, for Dr Bhandari
wants me to stay on in Switzerland till the end of summer.

Since the last three days, the weather has been fine. Every morning
after breakfast I take a small flat boat – you hire them for fifty centimes –
take it out towards the middle of the lake and then let it drift while I stretch
out in my bathing costume and sunbathe as well as do some reading.
Already I have gone a deep sienna brown. It is very pleasant. I come back
to the hotel after lunch – rest a bit & then go for a walk.

Dr Bhandari knows this region pretty well and yesterday I had a letter
from him advising me what to do in the way of sightseeing. The most
important item of this list is: 'See the dawn & a sunset from the top of the
Jungfrau in the month of July'!

Have you come across a book just recently published – *Reaching for the
Stars* by Nora Waln?[3] It is selling like hot cakes in England, and is said to
be one of the most interesting publications on Germany. I haven't read it
but Agatha seems to be very keen that I should send it to you. Agatha knew
Nora Waln years ago before she married.

I have been reading and enjoying very much Auden[4] & Isherwood's[5]
Journey to a War.

I am worried about your health and wondering how you are now. Do
take care of yourself and rest a while in some place more congenial than
Allahabad or the offices of the *National Herald*.[6] I do get the *Herald*
regularly.

I believe, from what people tell me, that I am looking much better but
my weight is still being obstinate – 84 lbs. I am taking regular exercise,

---

1. Letters not published.
2. Kailas Nath Kaul: Kamala Nehru's brother. He was a botanist. ('Manu' means
'uncle')
3. Nora Waln: American writer.
4. Wystan Hugh Auden: English poet.
5. Christopher Isherwood: English playwright and novelist.
6. Jawaharlal Nehru established the *National Herald* in 1938 and frequently wrote for it.

eating enormous meals and sleeping fairly well. I don't know what more to do.

All my love,
Indu

Love to the Hutheesing 'menage'.

———————————

291.   Hotel Winkelried,
Stansstad,
Switzerland,
15th June, 1939

Darling Papu,
After a whole week of rain down here & snow slightly higher up, the sun has come up again. It feels as if it had never been behind the clouds. Otherwise everything is the same, the days come & go with a deadly routine. In the rain, I go for very short brisk walks – in the sun I walk more slowly but go further, lingering on the way and picking wild flowers for my room. This morning I had to go right in the midst of masses of stinging nettle to pick some rather lovely yellow irises and I am still feeling itchy.

If the fine weather keeps, I shall take a cheap holiday ticket & do some sightseeing. There are some fine mountains round about here – the Pilatus & the Rigi & the Stanserhorn to mention the nearest & the highest. Dr Bhandari thinks I ought to go somewhere higher than Stansstad when the hot weather really sets in. So I am looking round for a place. Perhaps I shall stay somewhere on the Rigi.

I weighed myself on Sunday last & found I was 42 kilos – which comes to 92 lbs according to Cassell's dictionary. I was quite surprised. I am looking slightly rounder too.

I enclose some cartoons which might amuse you. The French ones were sent by Louise Morin & the others are from the *Manchester Guardian*, so also are a book review & an article on German policy.

With all my love,
Indu

———————————

292.   Juhu,
20th June, 1939

Darling Indu,
I have escaped from Bombay for two or three days and am living in a spacious mansion facing the sea. At this time of the year Juhu is deserted

and the houses lie empty. Psyche fixed this house up and brought me here and I have loved the quiet – not so quiet, for the sea is roaring all the time.

For over two weeks we worked hard in the National Planning Committee and the members were thoroughly exhausted. I hardly had time to read my mail and it piled up mostly unread. I have now gone through it here in Juhu, finding that many letters have answered themselves during this period, as so often happens if there is delay in answering.

From tomorrow various meetings begin – the Working Committee, the A.I.C.C., the States People, etc. I suppose I shall be here for another week.

I hope you are having a good time and prospering at Stansstad. How long do you intend remaining there?

I am vaguely thinking of paying a brief visit to China in August–September. By air it does not take much time now. The real difficulty is the expense, as it is a costly business. I doubt if I shall go. Probably various developments – international & national – will come in the way.

Love,

Your loving,
Papu

Kailas must have reached Genoa yesterday.

---

293.   Anand Bhawan,
                                                      Allahabad,
                                                  3rd July, 1939

Darling Indu,
Early on 1st June I left Allahabad for Bombay and on the 30th night I returned after a full month's absence. I have come back for a few days only – brief visits to Allahabad and Lucknow and then back to Bombay on my way to Ceylon. For I am going to Ceylon for a week or ten days, not for pleasure or rest but on business.

It is long since I have written to you – two weeks or so since I wrote to you from Juhu.[1] My letters to you grow infrequent, or at any rate the letters I actually write and post. But other letters take shape in my mind and remain unwritten. Often I think of writing to you, for you are always in my mind, but I hesitate and put it off. A vague feeling that too frequent letters might be a nuisance and a burden to you holds me back. It is hateful to have to write because one has to. I do not want you to feel that way and so the letters I send you go at much longer intervals than they used to.

1. Refers to letter No. 292.

Perhaps I am undergoing some inner change also, due to age and a variety of experiences. I am withdrawing into myself more and more and my incursions into the outer world are being limited. They are far too many still and I am entangled in a hundred ways. One part of me pushes out, the other tries to hide itself from the world. A Jekyll & Hyde existence. Here in Allahabad the introvert prevails and I live in this big house in absolute silence with very few interruptions. A visitor might well think that the house is uninhabited. Most of the rooms are locked and no one visits them. I reach Anand Bhawan and come up to my room and pay a visit to yours and look round and see the familiar pictures and books and articles. Then back to my room where I live day and night, except for brief visits down below for food or to see an occasional visitor. I do not encourage visitors and I am glad that they respect my wishes. I am beginning to think that there is something in the old Hindu idea of *sanyasa*[1] after a certain age. There is no chance of my becoming a *sanyasi*[2] but the idea is not without attraction.

Bundles of books awaited me here, most of them sent by authors or publishers. There was Gunther's *Inside Asia* and Edward Thompson's new book – *You Have Lived Through All This*, which to my surprise I found he had dedicated to me. I have been reading these and musing on this strange world in which we live.

I have mentioned above that I am going to Ceylon. For some time past the lot of Indians in Ceylon has grown progressively worse. Indeed all over the world they are being ill-treated and, from some places, kicked out. Little Ceylon has been behaving very shabbily. Two weeks ago I had an indirect and informal invitation from some ministers of the Ceylon Govt. to go there. I sent a disdainful reply. If Indians were not good enough for Ceylon, Ceylon was not good enough for me. But when the Working Committee pressed me to go on their behalf and the A.I.C.C. passed a resolution to this effect, I had to agree. So I am going by air on the 15th. Probably I shall be in Colombo most of the time but I hope to steal a day for Kandy and a few hours for Anuradhapura where I want to see again the old statue of the seated Buddha in contemplation. For the last seven years I had a picture of this almost always with me, in prison or outside. Do you remember the sonnet I sent you long ago, I think from Almora jail?[3]

> Nay, do not mock me with those carven eyes:
>   I too might grow, beneath that gaze of thine,
> Desireless, immortal, unerringly wise,

1. Renunciation.
2. One who practises renunciation.
3. See letter No. 107.

Disdaining human dreams. Lo, by the shrine
A multitude slow-worshipping still goes
  Unsandalled, bearing perfumed offerings,
While down the avenues of time still flows
  The splendid pageant of all timeless things.
Nay, do not mock me with that ecstasy,
  Born of a peace abstracted from life's pain:
Love and its futile dream shall trouble me
  Too briefly – I shall find myself again,
And look on thee unpassioned, mute, alone,
  An agelessness invincible in stone.

Desireless I might wish to be, but not immortal or unerringly wise, and to disdain human dreams is to disdain life.

I gladly accepted the job in Ceylon although it is a difficult one and there is little hope of success. It is a matter of a week or two only at most, and it takes me away from scores of other troubles here. Although it is intensive and hard work, it does not disturb me or distress me. I was indeed thinking vaguely of going to China for a few weeks – did I write to you about it? This Ceylon visit comes in the way somewhat but I have not entirely given up the idea of a China visit. If there are no international complications and no internal bust-up, I might yet go there. If so I shall go by air about the 20th August direct to Chungking, returning if possible by the Burma Road. But all this is in the air and I shall decide on my return from Ceylon at the end of this month.

Indeed everything is in the air because of continuous talk of war, and if war comes all our little plans will be upset. How it will affect you I do not know but I do not worry, for you can well look after yourself. You will decide for yourself what to do and where to go. If you require more money you can get it directly from Bachhraj or write to me. It seems hardly possible that we shall escape war for long. I hate the prospect of war and yet I wish this tension would cease and something definite should take place to end the present instability. War of course would end so many things in India and we shall all be on the high road again.

Betty is also going to Ceylon, not exactly with me but at the same time. She has been unwell and a fortnight away will do her good.

Kailas has reached London. I suppose you have heard from him. Bijju Bhai accompanied him on the *Victoria*. In Paris he spent two days with Louise Morin and Jean-Jacques. Sheila[1] suddenly decided to follow him and has sailed by the P&O boat on 1st July. She is going all the way by sea to Tilbury.

1. Kailas Nath Kaul's wife.

The [Kamala] Memorial Hospital has at last begun to take shape. The architects and contractors are here and are digging the foundations. It should be ready and functioning within a year.

The hot summer day waves and waves and wearily passes into the brief night. It is very hot and stuffy. The monsoon clouds lessen the heat of the sun but increase the closeness of the air.

I go tonight to Lucknow for Congress Committee meetings.
Love,

Your loving,
Papu

294.   Park Hotel,
Burgenstock,
Near Lucerne,
Switzerland,
15th July, 1939

Darlingest Papu,

How can your letters ever be too frequent or nuisances? I look forward to them enormously – just the sight of your handwriting on the envelope brings so much happiness. It is not nice to write because one has to – but to you I always want to write, to share with you the things that I have seen and have enjoyed. But often I have to postpone writing because, lacking your indefatigable energy, I get tired, too tired to write. But all the while I am thinking of you – wanting to convey my thoughts to you and wanting so very very much to have news of you. So please do give up all ideas that keep you from writing to me. Already I am regretting so much that I ever left you to your solitary domain. The *sanyasi* idea was bound to come to you – I suppose all people entertain it for a while. But it passes off. In you too it has to pass off for you are needed by India and so many many people – one of them is me. I have strange moods and strange ideas come fleeting across my mind; for some time I am like one possessed, and always with disastrous results. But all this too is the outcome of being alone – for I am lonely too – terribly lonely and alone. So dependent on you.

Anyway here I am in far away Switzerland. You will notice that I have changed my address. Burgenstock (suggested by Dr Bhandari) is slightly higher than Stansstad. It has a really glorious view of Lucerne and its surroundings. Dr Bhandari wants me to stay on in Suisse until Sept. But this country is terribly expensive. Central Switzerland is a tourist centre *par excellence* & this is the 'high season'. You have to pay through the nose for everything. There doesn't seem to be any such thing as the 'cheapest hotel'. I think I shall return to England at the end of this month – July. Or maybe I shall go to Zurich & spend a week or so at Lu's [Geissler] flat. That will give me the chance of seeing the 'National Swiss Exhibition' at Zurich – it is supposed to be very wonderful. Besides the fare to Zurich is only five francs.

Feroze's [Gandhi] holidays have begun & just before I left Stansstad he came over to Switzerland. We did two trips together – to Trubsee (just above Stansstad), from whence we climbed to the 'Joch Pass' and further to 'Jochstöckli', a peak above the pass. (I enclose a snap of it.) It was a climb of 1403 feet. The Joch Pass is 7303 feet above sea-level. It was an enjoyable climb for we found many lovely Alpine spring flowers. I thought of you & wanted to send you some but they would only arrive withered. There was quite a lot of snow on the way & my shoes were drenched. The other snaps were taken on the Stanserhorn, another mountain above Stansstad.

I have never known weather like this. It rains most of the week. The afternoon I witnessed one of the biggest & loveliest storms I have ever seen. The rain came in torrents & was soon changed into enormous hail stones – so large, that for quite a while after the sun had reappeared the countryside was all white, as if there was snow . . .

For the rest, I am finding it quite a job to read & take copious notes on the two colossal volumes of Finer's *Theory & Practice of Modern Govt.*

With very much love,

From your,
Indu

P.S.
I enclose a whole heap of snaps – taken with Feroze's Leica. Aren't the enlargements good? Nine enlargements & five little ones.

——————— ■■■ ———————

295.   Anand Bhawan,
                                                                       Allahabad,
                                                                   30th July, 1939

Darling Indu,
Last night I returned from Ceylon but only for a day and a half. Tomorrow I go off to Jamshedpur where the iron and steel come from, and then to Lucknow, and Wardha. As this world seems to become more and more purposeless and futile, our activities become more strenuous. I am going by special plane to Jamshedpur to save time and from there I shall fly to Lucknow. And so we create an illusion that we are making ourselves very useful.

It was a delight to receive your letter[1] and postcard[2] and more so to find that you have benefited by your stay in Suisse. The pictures you have sent are very good and you certainly look fuller and fitter in them. Why cut short your stay in Suisse? If it is doing you good, lay by a store of energy and good health. They will stand you in good stead when you have to face the November fogs of England. An extra fortnight or month now might mean a great deal. Anyway it will be foolish to go back to save a little money.

I do not know how you stand for money. I forget what arrangements were made with Bachhraj but anyway they were for a short time only. You had better look through them and write to them directly what your needs are. Meanwhile I enclose a cheque for £20.

The Ceylon visit was strenuous but still exhilarating. We were feted by all the big guns. This was not exhilarating. Ceylon high society is singularly uninspiring. It is a pale reflex of suburbia. But the popular welcome was something immense, in spite of the ill feeling that has arisen between Indians and Ceylonese. I enclose some pictures taken with my camera. Betty is still in Ceylon. She returns to Bombay on 11th August or thereabouts.

I am still revolving in my head the idea of visiting China. It takes shape. It is frightfully difficult to disentangle myself from the odd jobs I do here. But that in itself is an inducement to go away. As a preparation for the visit I have had myself vaccinated and inoculated against cholera and I am carrying about with me some stuff which will be injected inside me for protection against typhoid. This is a new experience, for I have not had any such thing done to me since my boyhood. But I wanted to avoid difficulties with regulations. Having protected my body from disease, the only danger that remains is from man. There is no vaccine or injection for that. But the danger is not great and what there is will add a spice to the visit. I wish there was real danger, I want to know how I feel when I have to face it. I imagine that I have lost the vivid desire I had to live, but I know well that when the test comes I shall not lose grip easily.

A difficulty however has arisen. The Chinese Ambassador in London urges me not to broadcast my visit but to go quietly. This is no easy matter. If I go I shall start about the 21st August by air via Hanoi in Indo-China – from there to Kunming and Chungking – a matter of three or four days from Allahabad. I hope to be back by the first week of October, that is if war does not break out earlier.

I had a letter from Kailas. He has taken a flat near Bhandari's house and seems to be happy. Sheila had not reached there.

1. Refers to letter No. 294.
2. Postcard not published.

I do not know where to send this letter. You say that you might leave Suisse by the end of July. Still, I am sending it to your last address.
Love,

Your loving,
Papu

Here is a criticism from a fairly competent person of my pamphlet, *Where are we?*[1]: 'There the technical perfection of your style – the way you take the most difficult and subtle and complicated subject matter, and turn it into spring water flowing in the sun – it's a miracle . . .'! This 'perfect' piece of writing, you will remember, was written in a great hurry overnight just before the Tripuri Congress.

296.

The Great Eastern Hotel,
Calcutta,
20th August, 1939

Darling Indu,
Just a line to send you my love before I hop it to China. I left Allahabad this afternoon by Air France and am spending the night here. Not much of a night – it is midnight now and I am supposed to get up at three a.m. Tomorrow night we spend at Saigon.

My address will be Chungking (China).

I met Gurudev today. The rest of the time was taken up by the Chinese here . . .

Love,
Papu

297.

c/o Prof. M'millan,
Hampdens,
[Penn]
High Wycombe,
Bucks,
England,
27th August, 1939

Darling Papu,
Your letter from Calcutta[2] has just come.

What an awful time you have chosen for going to China! The European

---

1. The pamphlet *Where are we?* (Kitabistan, Allahabad, 1939), contained eight articles reviewing the then political situation in India. Jawaharlal Nehru refers here to a criticism of this pamphlet by Frances Gunther in her letter dated 6 July 1939.
2. Refers to letter No. 296.

situation is pretty bad. Strangely enough, this time there is far less panic than there was last year. People feel more calm and prepared. Of course they are more prepared but whether that is enough, I do not know. Anyway this suspense is awful – suspense without any knowledge of what is going on. We hear of notes and messages and interviews but not a hint of what was actually said. From time to time the press makes a wild guess which is immediately pronounced as 'inaccurate'. And so it goes on.

The Soviet-German Pact came as a surprise to most people. But it will give China some time to breathe.

I am here in the country, somewhere between London and Oxford in a small village called Penn. I am staying with Prof. W. Macmillan & his wife & their two children. This is the result of the combined efforts of Krishna & Ellen Wilkinson,[1] who has a cottage not far from here. The air here is decidedly better than in London, but it is no quieter for the house is on the main road. Also it is much cooler than London & there is quite a lot of mist & damp. I do not know how long I shall be here. In [the] event of war, the Macmillans want to take their children up to Scotland. If there isn't war – I feel in my bones that there won't be and yet I can't think how it can be averted – I shall probably stay on here until the middle or end of September.

The Professor is an historian and has written several books on South African history. He was in South Africa for quite a long time. Among his pupils there was Miss Sutherland who is now my tutor in Oxford!

Darling, I am sure I shan't need any more money, but thanks for letting me draw on your account, all the same. I have already signed & sent off the copy of the letter to the bank, which you sent to me.

I went to London last week & both Dr Bhandari & Hebert saw me & I was also X-rayed. Their report is quite satisfactory.

I must post this now for the direct airmail to China leaves London tomorrow.

All my love, dearest Papu,
Indu

---

298.   Near Chungking,
28th August, 1939

Darling Indu,
There is so much expectation of war that it is impossible to make any plans. If war breaks out in Europe, which seems unlikely, I shall return immediately to India. Otherwise I shall stay on here for another three weeks.

1. Ellen Wilkinson: British politician and feminist.

We had another air raid here tonight. I had a glimpse of the Japanese bombers caught in the searchlights and of a fight between them and the Chinese chaser planes. But then I was hurried into a dug-out. I am spending the evening and night at the Generalissimo's [Chiang Kai-shek] house, right out of Chungking. Madame is a delightful hostess.

Love,
Papu

299.

Hampdens,
Penn,
High Wycombe,
Bucks,
2nd September, 1939

Darling Papu,

If you are not already in India you must be rushing back to it. So this is rather a hurried note to give you my love. They say that the service to India will continue, though of course along a different route. So I do hope this will reach you sometime.

I wonder if you received my letter[1] in China. I sent it to Chungking.

I have been in Penn nearly two weeks now. It is not far from either London or Oxford, being in fact about half way between the two. And yet just now it is almost impossible to go out of it for the trains & buses are most irregular – the telephone quite impossible. Anyway I shall not be here long for the Macmillans want to take their children up to a Highland glen in Scotland, where their five-year-old daughter won't ask any questions & will therefore not have to be told anything about the war.[2] Already the small scattered village of Penn is filling up with children evacuated from London, every household has two or three. For the last three days I, who have always disliked the sight of needle & thread, have been sewing almost incessantly – blankets for the evacuated children and black curtains and blinds for the nightly blackouts. I have also volunteered for canteen duty.

A couple of days ago I received a circular from Somerville College. It began:

According to instructions received earlier the government wishes the Universities to continue to function in all their teaching activities, and the University of Oxford is told to carry on where it is. The buildings

1. Refers to letter No. 297.
2. War was officially declared on Sunday, 3rd September, 1939.

of Somerville College are requisitioned for hospital purposes, but the College will continue to function in its integrity, and suitable accommodation is provided for staff & students in a building of Lady Margaret Hall & in the New Buildings of New College. In our view, students returning should regard their academic course as their serious full-time occupation.

Term will open at the usual time – 13th October. There follows a list of things we must bring to college – such as gas masks, electric torch, lightproof material and so on. Furthermore, we have to inform the College definitely whether we are returning, before 16th Sept. – otherwise the term fees will be charged in full.

I have thought over this & think that perhaps it would be best to continue with my original plans for going to Oxford. Especially so as Agatha & Dr Bhandari would not allow me to take on any full-time war service. Still, I am going up to London tomorrow to find out what I can do in and out of Oxford. There is nothing that I would dislike more than just sitting & 'resting' in some far-off and safe corner, which is what everybody seems to want me to do.

We have been strongly 'advised' by the post office that letters should be 'short & to the point'. So I think I had better stop. We have also, as you must already have noticed, to write name and address in the letter as well as on the envelope.

You will have such a lot to do in India. Don't worry about me. I am well – and nothing can happen to me. You have been in my thoughts lately more than ever, but I am glad you are in India and not in the midst of this horrible state of affairs – the sustained suspense for weeks and now the worst.

All my love, darling, and do look after yourself. And remember that I shall be thinking of you, even if letters are not always possible.

Much love,
Indu

P.S.
If the Macmillans go to Scotland, I shall go to London – so write to me c/o Agatha.

300.   c/o Prof. Macmillan,
                                                      Hampdens,
                                                          Penn,
                                                          Bucks,
                                              7th September, 1939

Darling Papu,
Agatha telephoned your cable to me [the] day before yesterday. She
couldn't make out the date and so we were not quite sure when it was sent.
But I suppose you must be back in India now.

Life is going on more or less as usual, with gas masks and blackouts and
air raid warnings. I have decided to go back to Oxford in October. The
Darb will be pleased. She wrote & said she hoped I would be able to do so.
Meanwhile I have not been doing much work. Three million people,
mostly children, have been evacuated from London with only very little
hand luggage. They are in great need of blankets, and mattresses and I
have been helping the village women to make these. Sewing dark curtains
& fixing black papers for the blackout also take a terrible lot of time.

Agatha came down here to see me last weekend. She seemed to be in a
perfect panic, simply terrified. It was quite trying to be with her.

Letters take rather a long time these days – especially as they have to go
through the censor. So I am sending you a cable, if that is possible in this
tiny village.

                            With all my love,
                                  Indu

———————————————

301.   [Anand Bhawan
                                                      Allahabad]
                                              17th September, 1939

Darling Indu,
I have just returned to Allahabad after nearly a month's absence. I found
your letter of 7th September[1] awaiting me here. I was very happy to get it.
It seems ages since you wrote to me. I think your last letter came about two
months ago before I went to Ceylon. I returned from Ceylon and after two
or three weeks in India went to China. From there I had to hurry back
when I heard of the declaration of war. Probably I would not have been
able to come back so soon if the Chinese Government had not helped me
by getting a special [plane] to carry me direct to Burma. The ordinary air
services were suspended and the few airliners that were functioning were

_____

1. Refers to letter No. 300.

completely booked up. The Chinese Government got a fine Douglas passenger plane from Hongkong for me and this took me from Chungking to Lashio on the Burma border. Lashio is in the northern Shan States and is the railhead in Burma. I did not however wait for the next train but went on by car to Mandalay which was 180 miles away. *En route* I was stopped at several places and Burmans and Indians had gathered together to welcome me and there were small meetings. Long before I reached Mandalay, our old friend Mrs Galliara met me on the road and accompanied me from there. She was very excited at seeing me and, as usual, was full of affection. She wanted me to send you her love.

From Mandalay I went by train to Rangoon, but there were floods on the way and the railway line was covered by a foot of water. The train was stopped. I was in too much of a hurry to reach Rangoon and it was arranged that I should cross the flooded area by rail trolley. Ultimately I reached Rangoon seven hours late to find a huge crowd of about ten thousand or more persons still waiting for me. There was a great deal of pushing to reach me, and as I was coming out of the station the rush was too great and many persons were unfortunately injured as they fell down and were trampled upon. Even I in trying to save others fell down. A troop of Chinese girl-guides had come to welcome me and seven or eight of these were among the injured, one getting a fracture of the collarbone. I was very much distressed at this but fortunately no injury was really serious.

From Rangoon I hurried by K.L.M. to Calcutta. I had hoped to come to Allahabad direct but the K.L.M. stopped for the day in Calcutta, as the weather was bad. Thereupon I went by train direct to Wardha where the Working Committee was meeting. I spent several days there and have just arrived here.

The air journey from Chungking to Lashio was very interesting and over mountainous and wooded country. At times I had a feeling that we were on the point of colliding against a mountain which loomed up alarmingly near. But our Chinese pilot was good. The plane returned from Lashio to China soon after landing me and unfortunately took back with it to China a little bag of mine by mistake.

I wrote to you last from a place near Chungking, the country house of Chiang Kai-shek where I was spending a day and night. I wonder if you got that letter. I was less than two weeks in China. But these few days were full of incidents and I could write much about them to you. I must not, however, do so now.

The war has brought tremendous responsibilities to all of us and our hands are going to be full. What is going to happen in India in the near future I do not quite know. But one thing is quite clear, that we are in for a dynamic situation and big changes will take place.

I am enclosing a copy of a statement issued by the Working Committee. The Committee has also appointed a small war emergency sub-committee of which I am the chairman and the other two members are Maulana Abul Kalam Azad and Sardar Vallabhbhai Patel. I have again joined the Working Committee because of this crisis. I shall be going to Lucknow in a day or two. The All India Congress Committee will meet at Wardha on the 7th October.

I have had this typewritten as in these days of censorship this might facilitate matters. You have not acknowledged my previous letters, especially the cheque and the bank instructions I sent. As for your future programme, you will decide for yourself. You are the best judge.

All my love,

Your loving,
Papu

302.

[c/o Prof. Macmillan]
Hampdens,
Penn,
High Wycombe,
Bucks,
19th September, 1939

Darling Papu,

Nobody I know has any news from India – except for the two cables to Krishna – and, of course the usual Reuter reports of the offers of the Aga Khan & the Princes![1]

I have been writing to you very regularly – twice a week – since war began. All the letters were addressed to Allahabad. This one I am sending to Wardha. I also sent you a cable to Allahabad.

It is so difficult to write these days. A French soldier wrote a long letter to his wife, who was in the country – all she received was a large square paper in the middle of which was printed 'Madame, your husband is in perfect health but he is too talkative.' Signed, the Censor!

I am quite – indeed, very well. I am still with the Macmillans & shall stay on until they leave for Scotland; they have not yet decided just when that will be.

I went up to London at the end of last week to get me some warm clothes – for autumn has come in real earnest and Penn is cold & windy.

---

1. As loyal supporters of the British, the Aga Khan and the Princes offered their services in the war effort.

I have two letters from Madame Morin. She wants me to send her cuttings of Indian news – but of course there isn't any more here than in France. She is staying with her parents in the country – Jean-Jacques must be called up by now. She sends her good wishes to you. So do Dr Bhandari & Agatha.

Bijju Chacha is in London again. He wants me to get your permission 'to make cautious experiments with the breathing exercises'. Dr Bhandari has not told him anything but has sent me a message through Agatha – not to start any exercises, breathing or otherwise, for at least three months. Bijju Chacha wrote the above after I had conveyed the doctor's message to him. Do let me know what you think of it all.

Very much love,
Indu

303.

[c/o Prof. Macmillan]
Hampdens,
Penn,
High Wycombe,
Bucks,
28th September, 1939

Darling Papu,

I was so glad to get your letter of 17th Sept.,[1] which I received yesterday.

Some time ago I lost my old spectacles and tried to use the ones I acquired in Lucknow. These gave me a lot of trouble, so I decided to see a good oculist. Ellen Wilkinson recommended me hers and I went up to London yesterday to see him. He put drops in my eyes and examined them thoroughly, and pronounced my eyesight perfectly good and normal! He said I need not have glasses at all – and that if my eyes hurt me it just meant that I was using them too much. He illustrated this by saying: If you walk twenty-five miles a day, and gradually get more & more tired, you don't go to a doctor & ask 'what's the matter with my legs – they ache?' The only thing I can do is not to read too much, especially by artificial light. He added that part of the trouble was probably due to wearing glasses and that I would be perfectly all right when I get used to doing without them. That is good news, is it not?

There seems to be something very fishy about my letters to you. I can't remember exactly how many I have written to you or when they were posted. But I am quite positive that I wrote at least two letters, one to

1. Refers to letter No. 301.

China acknowledging your letters, the cheque & your instructions to the bank, sometime before the letter dated 7th Sept.

I am keeping very well. In the beginning of October I propose going to London and on the 13th of that month I shall go up to Somerville. Saturday – day after tomorrow – is National Register Day. Based on that register, we shall get our identity cards and food rationing coupons, without which it will not be possible to live in this country.

I am enclosing an article by Brailsford.[1] I think (but am not quite sure) that it appeared in *Reynolds News* dated 24th September.

Jean-Jacques has been called upon to join. It must be terrible for Mme Morin. I don't know if she wants to go to the front with him or what – but she writes to say that she is leaving Dieulefit with him.

Are you getting your foreign magazines, such as *Time* & the *New Statesman*, as usual? In *Time* of 4th Sept., there was rather a good photograph of you & a paragraph about your visit to China.

From Somerville, all sorts of circulars & instructions continue to arrive. I am glad to see, however, that I am to have a room in the College buildings & not miles away as was previously stated.

Letters are so irregular these days & India seems to be much further away than usual, so it was good to hear from you. My thoughts are with you all the time.

> All my love,
> Indu

304.

[Anand Bhawan,
Allahabad]
30th September, 1939

Darling Indu,

I wrote to you a week ago. Every day since then I have wanted to write to you but I have restrained myself. You have been in my thoughts so often, so near to me and yet so far. This war has increased distances and lessened contacts and all manner of barriers have grown up keeping countries and people cut off from each other. My mind goes back to the last big war, before you were born, and when I was very much younger. We were all excited of course by it but it was a distant excitement as that of an onlooker at a game. But none of us are mere onlookers today, wherever we might be. And to some of us the war means a terrible burden of

1. H. N. Brailsford: British journalist known for his sympathy for India.

responsibility. It is a difficult and terrible business to carry on a war. And yet the decision is made and all energy is concentrated to that end. But when vital decisions have to be made it is an even more painful task. And that is our fate in India today.

The last war! How gradually we grew accustomed to it as month by month and year by year it dragged on with its highlights and its long dreary periods of trench fighting. It is likely to be different this time, but who knows? Yet a month of it has brought vast changes and Poland is no more and Russia dominates the scene more and more. There was no radio at the time of the last war. Now everybody is becoming a radio fan and the people of leisure hover round it for a good part of the day. I am not one of the fans but every night after dinner I spend some time over it.

I have been going backwards and forwards between Allahabad and Lucknow and tomorrow I am going to Delhi to see the Viceroy. What will come of all this I do not know. Somehow I have lost that keen incentive that gave me vitality and drove me to action. I am not so frightfully interested as I used to be. Perhaps it is age. Yet I do not think so. It is just a sense of weariness and futility that has been stealing over me these three years or more. I tried to ignore it and to suppress it by my incessant touring and hard work. I impressed others but not myself, for I realised that I was trying to escape from an inner weakness. And now this weakness seems to grow and with it a carelessness of what happens. Probably I am not a big enough man for the job that fate has thrust upon me.

We are having moonlit nights. The moon has become an inseparable companion in my mind to bombing from the air, and crowded dugouts, and warning sirens, and searchlights playing on the sky, and the conflicts of the air. A month ago I experienced all this almost daily in Chungking. It is the bright fortnight of the moon, invitation to and signal of the bomber. I feel tense when I think of this and I am surprised at the casualness of others here.

In China I expressed a desire to get a few souvenirs. I had little time to go shopping and I was not encouraged. Some things were brought to me. They were lovely woven silks (pictures, etc.) and rich embroideries. I chose a few, thinking them to be expensive. But the exchange was very much in my favour and so the price was reasonable. I chose a few more. And then I stopped for I discovered that my Chinese hosts would not let me pay. They added a few more to the lot and insisted on presenting them to me. This kind of thing is an embarrassing business, yet I could not get out of it. I wanted particularly to get some inexpensive jades but after my first experience I desisted from further shopping.

So I brought with me a boxful of silks and woven and embroidered pictures. I went to Wardha first and started distributing them. There was Sarojini Naidu and I gave her some for herself and Bebee and Papi. Then to Amrit Kaur[1] and Psyche and Bul; to Savitri and to some of my political colleagues. I sent a packet to Betty. On coming to Allahabad I sent these silks to Rup[2] and Bappi and gave other pieces to various friends. Suddenly I discovered that I was exhausting my stock. In alarm I have removed what I had left from prying eyes and locked them in your little cupboard. I hope this will remain there when you come and you will use them in some way. There are some silver trinkets also.

My Contax camera has had a long journey. When I got on the K.L.M. in Rangoon, the camera as usual was handed to the steward and locked up by him. In Calcutta, where I got off, he did not give it to me and for the moment I did not remember to ask him. When a little later I asked him in the hotel, he said that it was not easy to get at it as the camera was in the plane at Dum Dum, many miles away. The commander of the K.L.M. plane suggested that he might carry it to Allahabad and leave it there. I agreed and went off to Wardha by train. On my return to Allahabad I was told that the sealed camera box was opened here but my camera was not found in it! Some days later I was informed that when the plane reached Amsterdam they found an extra camera in it which presumably belonged to me. They brought it back but the Karachi customs authorities took possession of it and kept it. And there it is at present. I am trying to get hold of it and I shall probably succeed, but many of the pictures I took in China and which were on the spool in the camera will be lost. Anyway I have larger numbers of Chinese pictures with me.

Madame Chiang gave me some lovely Chinese men's gowns. Some are in silk, others in very fine linen which I was told was made from some kind of grass.

I enclose a printed form from Lloyds Bank. Please sign this at the bottom and send it on to the Bank. Even apart from this form you can draw on my account there, which I think amounts to about £160. Some money – about £80 – was also due to me from Drummond, the publisher, and this might be paid in. You can draw upon this account.

Write to me whenever you can. Letters are irregular, still they will manage to reach some time or other.

Love,

Your loving
Papu

---

1. Rajkumari Amrit Kaur: member of the princely family of Kapurthala, disciple of Mahatma Gandhi.
2. Rup Koul: daughter of C. B. Koul, brother of Kamala Nehru.

305.

[c/o Prof Macmillan,
Hampdens]
Penn,
[Bucks]
30th September, 1939

Darling Papu,

I wrote to you a few days ago to Wardha. This letter also goes there, for I expect you will have to stay in Wardha for some time.

This is really an odd sort of war, to say the least! When Hitler invaded Poland & England declared war I was all excited and enthusiastic and wanted to do something and I did help a bit in the billeting & looking after of the evacuated children. But the policy of the government has been so very discouraging. One begins to doubt – as indeed many people in America and other neutral countries and also in Germany are doubting – whether England is in earnest about the war. And indeed, in the light of recent history and the recent policies of the men who are now leading the country, how can one be sure? Churchill is the only man in the ministry whose words have some force and also ring true.[1] Mr Chamberlain has never been accused of being a brilliant personality but now in the hour of Britain's greatest need of leadership – I can only quote Richard Law in the *Time & Tide*: 'We do not ask of Mr Chamberlain that he should be Pitt or Chatham – only that he should seem a little less like an alderman exposing a sewage scandal.'

The Home Front is no better – everything seems to be in a frightful mess. To some extent war makes this inevitable; industry, food supply every-day business are bound to be thrown out of gear. But what about the schemes and plans which have been ready for over a year and have been having frequent rehearsals & practices, and much praise from all round – such as the voluntary & paid A.R.P. services, the evacuation of the civil population & of the University & College of London, auxiliary forces of women and many voluntary & paid war service departments? The authorities seem to be quite unaware of the situation. There is a bitter fight between the Ministry of Information – misinformation, for short – which, in spite, or is it because, of their staff of 999 are most inefficient, & the press. And when all entertainment houses were suddenly shut down, Low's Colonel Blimp came out with a 'Gad, Sir! Sir John Anderson[2] is right; there should not be any amusements and then we shall be so blue that the Nazi aeroplanes won't be able to see us even in the daytime'!

1. Winston Churchill was First Lord of the Admiralty in Chamberlain's War Cabinet.
2. Sir John Anderson: Governor of Bengal, 1932–7, was at this time British Home Secretary and Minister for Home Security.

What a frightful hotch-potch is this letter! I'm feeling rather fed up at the moment. Also I want to find out just how much – or how little – the censor will stand for.

We have already got our identity cards which we have to keep on our person all the time.

Much love,
Indu

306.　　　　　　　　　　　　　　　　　　　　　　　　Wardha,
　　　　　　　　　　　　　　　　　　　　　　　6th October, 1939

Darling Indu,

I have just reached here from Delhi and received your letter of September 19th.[1] Airmail letters seem to take a full fortnight now. You say that you have been writing to me twice a week. Since my return from China I have received three letters from you. I have also written three letters, excluding this one. I sent you a letter also from Chiang Kai-shek's house in Chungking. I wrote to Agatha also from there, telling her that Madame Chiang made all manner of enquiries about her and wanted me to convey to her her affectionate regards. In case Agatha has not got my letter, please tell her about this.

As you are not likely to get the *Herald* by ordinary post I am stopping this and asking the people there to send you cuttings from it twice a week by airmail. I hope you will get them. You can send them on later to Louise Morin.

I do not know where you are. Probably you have gone to Oxford but I shall continue sending letters c/o Agatha.

I met Satish Kalelkar here today. He came back by the *Biancamano* and had an unusual experience. He was due to arrive in Bombay by the end of August but the prospect of war breaking out induced the Italian authorities to direct the *Biancamano* to a non-British port. So it went to Batavia in Java, not touching even at Colombo. Later it came to Singapore where the unfortunate passengers for India had to wait for many days. Then they came back by different boats via Ceylon.

In Delhi I had a long interview with the Viceroy and I also met, after three years, my old friend Mr Jinnah. The position is entirely uncertain and is likely to remain so for another two weeks or so. Probably the A.I.C.C., which is meeting on the 9th, will come to no final decision and leave this to the Working Committee. The prospects of a settlement are not hopeful. If this is the ultimate result, you will realise that events will take a rapid turn.

---

1. Refers to letter No. 302.

I am quite sure that breathing exercises will do you good. You will remember that I recommended them to you when you were here. But obviously you must not do anything which the doctors forbid. I imagine that very gentle exercises cannot possibly do you harm and Bhandari will agree to them. Why not get him to meet Bijju Bhai and find out what exercises he suggests? The point is regularity in doing these exercises, however simple they might be. Even ordinary regular breathing for a while daily is very good. I am all in favour of simple regulated breathing exercises. Let Bhandari & Bijju Chacha settle the matter between them.

Yesterday from Delhi I sent a long 850-word cable message to *News Chronicle* at their request. I wonder if it has appeared.

Is it possible for you to get Delhi on the radio? If so you will get Indian news, including my movements which are reported. Try it. They have news several times a day. Usually I tune in at six p.m. or nine p.m. (Indian time). This will mean five hours or so earlier for you. Perhaps someone could tell you if it is possible to get Delhi in England.

There is much that I would like to tell you. I have had it on my mind for long. But it is not possible to write and I do not know when we shall meet – months or years hence. And these months & years will bring great changes and perhaps so many fresh experiences to each of us. How uncertain everything is. Life has become more of a question mark than ever.

I wrote to Louise Morin & Jean-Jacques a few days ago. I wonder if my letters will reach them. Anyway write to Louise and tell her that I have written to her.

I propose to write to you at least once a week, probably oftener. If you do not get my letters regularly, the fault is someone else's.

Love,

Your loving,
Papu

307.   Wardha,
                                        10th October, 1939

Darling Indu,

This paper is too obviously handmade. I have borrowed it from Dr Bidhan Roy who is staying here also. As a matter of fact exceedingly good handmade paper is being made in India now.

I have just received your letter of the 28th Sept.[1] I am very glad to learn that your eyes are in better condition than we had imagined them to be. Take care of them however, and do not use them too much by artificial

---

1. Refers to letter No. 303.

light. If it had been summer I would have suggested your going to bed very early and getting up early. But this is not of much use during winter. Do you remember my telling you to take simple eye exercises daily? There are many such and I suppose you could find out about them. But two I have practised with advantage. Wash your eyes in a tumbler of cold water in the morning. See that the eye is fully immersed in the water, open it and roll it about – up and down, right & left, diagonally and round and round in both directions. If you like put a little boric powder in the [water] but this is not absolutely necessary. At night, before retiring, repeat this performance but with tepid water. This will soothe and clear and rest the eyes. One thing more. At night massage each eye very gently with the palm of the hand, using a little cream. The eye will of course be closed and you press the eyeball gently and move the hand in a circular direction. This massage and eyewash are good at any time of the day when your eyes feel tired. They will refresh you.

I am not surprised at your letter sent to China not reaching me there. Mails are very irregular there and then there are censorship delays. China has long been a country living under war conditions. I had a curious instance of the Chinese censorship today. One of our Chinese medical unit doctors has returned and he came to see me. He brought me a letter from Madame Sun Yat-sen[1] who lives in Hongkong. She wrote to say that she had been very keen on meeting me and, fearing that I might not be able to go to Hongkong, she intended coming to Chungking to meet me. She sent me a telegram suggesting this and waited for my answer. I never got that telegram! Evidently her coming to Chungking was not approved of by the censor or his bosses.

Madame Sun has sent me a lovely photograph of herself. Did I write to you of my losing my little bag in the plane that brought me from China? Well, this bag has turned up! Our doctor friend from China has brought it with him.

I am not getting any English or American papers. This is irritating, among other reasons because of the fact that I have paid for them for the next year. I think it will be worthwhile my asking the Times Book Club (my agents) to send all these papers to you instead of to me. Meanwhile you might send me interesting cuttings by airmail.

Today we finished the A.I.C.C. meeting after a heated debate lasting two days in which I played a prominent part, being the mover of the principal resolution. We have endorsed the Working Committee's statement which I sent you previously. We await developments but events march fast and we shall not have to wait long. I shall be here for another

---

1. Madame Sun Yat-sen: wife of the President of the Chinese Republic. She later became a Vice-President of the People's Republic of China.

two days for the Working Committee. Then Allahabad, though I might go to Bombay for a day or two for the Planning Committee.

Today is Bapu's seventieth birthday according to the Indian calendar. According to the Gregorian it was 2nd October. On the latter day I heard Kamaladevi's broadcast from London on Bapu.

I met Amma in Delhi. She is very worried about you and Kailas.
Love,

> Your loving,
> Papu

---

308.   Anand Bhawan,
                                              Allahabad,
                                      13th October, 1939

Darling Indu,

I arrived here today from Wardha. This evening I was astonished to see Edward Thompson walking into the room. I had no idea he was in India. He tells me he had written to me but the letter had not reached me. He arrived by air today.

This war inevitably makes one think of the last. I remember how we grew used to it, even to the continuous submarining and the sinking of ocean-going steamers. There were no airmails then and all letters had to go by sea. To get over the loss of mails by the sinking of ships every letter used to be sent in triplicate, or at any rate every important or business letter. I used to carry on an extensive correspondence with solicitors on my own behalf and more so on behalf of Dadu and I saw to it that three copies of each letter were dispatched, one on each successive week. This came to my mind when I thought of the letters that are not reaching me now. But so far at least the fault is not due to loss of mails by enemy attack.

When I came from China I brought hosts of photographs with me. Many have appeared in the newspapers. A copy of a Malayan paper contains a bunch of them. I am enclosing this.

Ghani is getting married to Roshan next month – so I was told by Abdul Ghaffar Khan. They will probably be married at Gola in the U.P. where Ghani works.

> Love,
> Papu,

I have just received the *New Statesman* & *Time & Tide* of 2nd & 9th Sept.

---

309.   Lucknow,
                                                    17th/18th October, 1939

Darling Indu,
I wrote to you three days ago.[1] I told you then that Edward Thompson had
suddenly arrived in Allahabad. He shifted over to Anand Bhawan and
spent two days with me and I had long talks with him. He is rather erratic
in his conversation – the quality of a poet, I suppose – but it was a pleasant
change to have him and talk to him. He helped me to form a better picture
of England today and Europe, and I helped him a little perhaps to
understand the amazing complexity of India. He went off to Delhi and I
came to Lucknow. Before he went I gave him two small pieces of Chinese
silk for you – one has a woven picture and the other is an embroidery. I
could have sent you more but I did not wish to burden him or cause him
difficulties over the customs. These are a birthday gift for you – soon that
birthday will be coming and I do not know where I shall be then. So I have
seized hold of this opportunity.
     I am writing this at midnight. I have just read the Viceroy's speech
which he has made in answer to the Congress demand. The door is
banged.[2] I suppose events will march more rapidly now and I do not know
for how long I can write to you as I have done. Anyway it does not matter.
     Look after yourself, my dear, and keep your body and mind fit and
strong. You will require all your strength in the days to come.
     Love,
                                            Your loving,
                                            Papu

310.   Bombay,
                                                      25th October, 1939

Darling Indu,
I was very glad to learn from a cable from Krishna Menon that you were
progressing rapidly. I have just had a talk with Jivraj Mehta. He thinks that
a stay in Switzerland will do you a lot of good, especially during these
winter months. It will not be so much treatment that you will require as
regulated living under medical supervision. This is difficult to fix up

     1. Refers to letter No. 308.
     2. 'The door is banged': this is a reference to a speech by the Viceroy, Lord Linlithgow,
dated 17th October, 1939 in which the Viceroy had offered unacceptable terms to the
Congress leaders in return for their extension of support to the British Government
during the Second World War.

unless there is a regular routine attached to it. I do not know what Switzerland is like now or what it will be in the future as the war progresses. But presumably it will escape the war. Jivraj suggested Dr Rollier's[1] sanatorium or hotel in Leysin. This is called Les Frênes. Dr Rollier is a very agreeable person and is a friend of Jivraj's. I have written to Bhandari about this matter and asked him to consult you and Hebert about it.

The Working Committee has decided to put an end to Congress ministries. By the end of this month they will be out. Big things are ahead in India as elsewhere, but what they will be no one can foretell.

I return to Allahabad after three days.

Love,

Your loving,
Papu

---

311.   Brentford Hospital,
                                                      Brentford,
                                                      Middlesex,
                                          26th October, 1939

Darling Papu,
What a lovely photograph of you! It is quite the best I have seen for some time.

It is such a long time since I have written to you – I have now three letters & a telegram, all unacknowledged and all unanswered. The letters are dated 30th Sept., 10th Oct. and 13th Oct.[2] The telegram is the one from Itarsi. Meanwhile Dr Bhandari has received from Bombay through the London office of the American Express £50. He hasn't the vaguest idea who has sent them – he thought perhaps it might be for me.

Darling, I am terribly ashamed of myself for falling ill all over again. It is really most exasperating when you come to think of how scrupulously careful I have been about food, regular hours & rest and so on. Anyway, I have lost all the weight gained in the last year and now weigh 77 lbs! And here I am back again. I am steadily getting better however & since yesterday my temp. has been normal. The fluid is still there & my chest is very painful.

Sitting up tires me rather easily, so I won't write anymore just yet.

Dr Bhandari came in just now with another telegram from you – about Leysin. He was wanting me to go to German Switzerland – a place just

1. Dr Auguste Rollier: Swiss physician.
2. Refers to letters No. 304, 307, 308.

near Davos called Davos-dorf. Anyway, most of these places are the same and it does not much matter where one goes. Dr says I needn't stay in a sanatorium as long as I am within reach of one and a competent doctor. It's going to be very lonely and very expensive.

By the way, before I forget, I have duly completed & sent to the bank the form you enclosed in your letter.

With very much love and all good wishes – you must be having a pretty frightful time these days.

Indu

P.S.

I enclose a cartoon by Gabriel. The poster referred to, 'Freedom is in Peril, defend it with all your might', has cost the govt. a tidy sum of money & is plastered in all sizes all over London, indeed all over the whole country! You can understand what this means when you realise that the radio, as the press, is completely in the hands of the govt. in France as well as in England. And all the Germans who fought for the Spanish Republic have been imprisoned as prisoners of war by the Fr. Govt! And here, in England, every day the govt. takes on more powers and even the shadow of democracy seems to be receding.

Darling, how thoughtful of you to think of my birthday in the midst of all crises and meetings and trouble! Thank you so much. I expect I'll have to spend the day in bed in hospital! Doctor says I have to be here for another three weeks or a month. And then a few weeks somewhere in England – I do not think I shall go to Switzerland until Christmas time.

Everybody is being perfectly sweet, so don't worry about me.

With all my love and all my thoughts,

Your loving,
Indu

1st Nov., 1939

P.S.

Darling, I'm getting a bit worried about going to Switzerland. It's going to be so frightfully expensive. I can't decide what to do. I'm feeling rather upset just now. But I shall write soon & tell you what has been decided.

Lots of love,
Indu

312.
Lucknow,
6th November, 1939

Darling,

I have not written to you for about ten days and so have broken my promise made in my last letter of writing at least once a week. But life is a hard taskmaster and these days have been particularly hard. One lives in a state of tension, not knowing what will happen, and meanwhile rushing about in railway trains – Allahabad to Wardha – to Bombay – to Lucknow – to Delhi – to Allahabad – to Lucknow again. I came here today and am staying for the last time at 6, Couper Road, the ministerial mansion. The Congress Governments are over and the ministers have reverted to humbler roles. Indeed, I would not come here at all if Puphi had not stayed on owing to illness.

A cable jointly sent by Agatha and Bhandari informed me that you were going to Switzerland and that one of them (or both?) were accompanying you. I do not exactly know when and where you are going. I presume you are going to Leysin. That is a safe and quiet corner and your friend Mlle Hemmerlin will be near you! If you go to Dr Rollier's place, as I hope you will, you will meet a Gujarati boy there who was sent by Jivraj Mehta. I forget his name.

For some time past building operations have been going next to Anand Bhawan on the Memorial Hospital. The foundations have been laid and on 19th Nov. Bapu is going to lay a cornerstone. The date was fixed to suit Bapu's convenience and then I suddenly remembered that it was your birthday. I wonder if you will get my little birthday gift in time – the Chinese pictures I have sent through Edward Thompson. He is leaving by air tomorrow morning.

I enclose two pictures recently taken in Delhi. The one of Bapu and Jinnah is very characteristic. Also two cartoons of Shankar's. Did you read Samuel Hoare's[1] speech in which he referred to my being a Harrovian and put in a good word for the old school which had produced four such distinguished persons in a generation as himself, Baldwin, Winston Churchill and me! The old school tie appeal was made to me in the crudest manner.

I do not know how you stand for money or how money can be sent to Suisse. Please let me know. Have you been getting the *Herald* cuttings? . . .

Love,
Papu

---

1. Sir Samuel Hoare (later Lord Templewood): Secretary of State for India, 1931–5, was at this time Lord Privy Seal and was in 1940 to become British Ambassador to Spain on Special Mission.

313.

[Anand Bhawan,
Allahabad]
10th November, 1939,
Diwali Day

Darling Indu,

I was so happy to get your letter[1] from the Brentford Hospital. It is of course irritating and annoying that after all the care you took of yourself, a cold should bowl you over and upset your plans. Well, we shall learn from this and put in a lot of reserves of health and strength inside you, so that you can ignore and treat with contempt any outside intrusion. Anyway, there is no point in worrying. We shape our plans according to changing circumstances and, in the world of today, circumstances change, and will change, rapidly enough.

Your going to Suisse is now more or less certain. At Jivraj Mehta's instance I had suggested Leysin because Jivraj has great faith in Dr Rollier there. You write to say that Davos or near Davos will be better. It does not much matter which of these places you choose. Do not worry about the cost. Whether you stay at a sanatorium or in a pension, the main thing is that you should be well looked after and should recover health rapidly. I do not like sanatoria as a rule but some of these Swiss sanatoria, notably Rollier's, are like good cheerful hotels. In a pension the food is not likely to be so good and personal attention will be lacking. Perhaps it might be worthwhile to go to a sanatorium to begin with and after a month move to a pension or cottage. I am just suggesting all this to you but you must decide for yourself after consulting your doctors. But you must not decide for the second best in order to save cost. That is false economy and may mean a more prolonged stay later on.

I came back to Allahabad today from Lucknow. Yesterday Nan and Ranjit returned here, bidding goodbye to their house in Lucknow and bringing all their furniture, goods and chattels with them. A long procession of *thelās*[2] brought this from the station and for the moment it lies piled up all over the place. Most of it will be auctioned off soon.

Today is Diwali day and for the first time after many years Anand Bhawan is looking gay with the *dīye*[3]. There are not too many of them but still they are a pleasing sight. What a charming festival is Diwali! I was surprised to find in the western verandah below a *takhta*[4], all decorated with earthen toys and other Diwali paraphernalia, and presided over by

1. Refers to letter No. 311.
2. Wheelbarrows.
3. Small earthen lamps.
4. Wooden platform or bed.

big earthen images of Ganesh and Lakshmi. It reminded me of the days when mother was here and fixed up these things. How old customs cling to us!

I was so tired when I arrived here this morning, I have spent a good part of the day sleeping and now I feel better, though drowsy. I propose to stay on here for about a fortnight unless something extraordinary drags me away. Ten days from now we are going to have a crowd of guests – Gandhiji & the W.C. [Working Committee] members and others.

I am enclosing a flower which someone has sent me. It will remind you of Kashmir. It is the saffron crocus – *Jāfrān ka phūl*.

The cartoon you sent me induced me to write something in the *Herald*. I am sending this to you. Whenever I am in Lucknow I write a good deal for the *Herald*. An article from the *Statesman* is also enclosed. This will interest you. The *Statesman* used to be quite friendly to me but for the last month it has been very angry and has grown quite hysterical.

I should like you to figure out your future expenses, roughly, and to tell me what arrangements you would like me to make.

All my love,

Your loving,
Papu

I am glad you liked the photographs I sent. It was taken in Colombo with a Leica camera. The photographer, an amateur turned professional, preferred using this to the big camera he had. He took dozens of poses. When I arrived there I was tired and perspiring. I had been addressing three meetings previously. I suggested washing my face. Nothing of the kind, he said. The perspiration should remain there as it brings out the texture of the skin!

---

314.   12th November, 1939

To
  Jawaharlal Nehru
  Allahabad

Happy birthday darling am much better temperature normal 19 days gained 6 lbs fluid inflammation gone still staying fortnight hospital.

Indu Nehru

---

315.   Anand Bhawan,
                                                                 Allahabad,
                                                        16th November, 1939

Darling Indu,
Your message[1] was very welcome because of the news it gave about your
progress to health. The reminder of the birthday is not a pleasant one after
one approaches or passes a certain age. In China I believe the fiftieth
birthday is a great event, for age is honoured there and everyone is keen on
appearing older than he is. My own enthusiasm for age is not so great and
the figure fifty in connection with my age frightens me. Perhaps wisdom
comes with the years, but wisdom by itself does not take one very far.
There must be the urge and capacity to act up to that wisdom. *Si jeunesse
savait, si vieillesse pouvait.* So the oncoming of age is not such a pleasant
event. I must confess that I do not feel frightfully old. It surprises me to
realise that I am fifty – why, I shall be sixty and three score and ten; a
doddering old person who is a burden and a nuisance to everybody.

Sometimes I feel very old and tired. It has nothing to do with the years.
It is mental weariness and a feeling that I am something apart from the
world I live in. My contacts lessen and grow more impersonal, and I grow
more and more a spectator in the very drama in which I take part. Life is a
curious affair and puzzles and perplexes me far more now than it used to
do when I was younger and had more assurance. That assurance fades
out. What do I know, what do I understand? Every individual is a mystery
which cannot be fathomed. We carry on in our respective spheres by old
habit or just conceit and the years pass on and we pass off.

The Gunthers sent me a cable from New York: 'Birthday greetings
second fifty years are easiest when you stand fast love.' What a horrible
prospect to think of a second fifty years! Among the other messages was
one from Mussoorie: '*Salgira Mubarak jhanda uncha rahe hamara*,[2] love
Chand Tara Rita Tangle Anna.[3]' Do you remember Tangle, the spoilt
little dog which is Rita's delight?

I have spent the last few days in comparative peace and leisure, that is I
have had very few public engagements. I have been out of Allahabad for so
long that piles of correspondence had accumulated. The more important
letters – or such as the office considered important enough – were
forwarded to me. The others remained and I faced this accumulation with
alarm. I was astonished to find a large collection which had come when I

1. Refers to letter No. 314.
2. Happy Birthday. May our flag fly high.
3. Anna Ornsholt: governess of the daughters of Vijaya Lakshmi Pandit.

was in China and had not read at all. Fortunately most letters answer themselves if one leaves them to their own fate and I had the pleasure of tearing up many basketfuls of letters and papers. I have long given up my old methodical habit of trying to answer almost all the letters that I received. This became physically impossible and perhaps I grow more slipshod in my work.

So after three or four days of intensive application, I removed large quantities of papers and even books from my room which were all lying about the floor. The room looked clean and businesslike for once – but for how long?

Birthdays are occasions for renewing one's wardrobe. Except for a new *kurta* and *dhoti*[1] I had not added to my sartorial belongings in India for many years. This time there was a regular conspiracy afoot to induce me to have a new *sherwani*[2] made and I surrendered, although my old ones were quite good enough. Hope Bros. were summoned and they reminded me of the last occasion when I had a *sherwani* made – just ten years ago before the Lahore Congress! Now I am the proud possessor of a new *sherwani* and I do not quite know what to do with it.

In another two or three days a crowd of people will descend on Anand Bhawan. There is the Working Committee and the corner-stone ceremony of the Kamala Memorial Hospital. We are having tents put up.

I was surprised to read in your letter that you did not propose to go to Switzerland till after Christmas. The climate there is quite good by the end of November and if you are going there, the sooner the better. I suppose the visa difficulty will be got over. I have had a letter from Dr Samson who visited you in Brentford Hospital. As you write, he is all for German Switzerland. We know well how people from different parts of Switzerland swear by their own particular areas. I do not think one need worry about this. They are both more or less alike from the treatment point of view. You will remember how old Stephani[3] used to say that Montana was the sunniest spot in Suisse. It really does not matter where you go to in Switzerland – the French part or the German part. Go to whichever place attracts you most.

One thing you really must not worry about: that is the question of expense. Apart from other considerations, this is a necessary investment and it is folly to economise when the result of present economy will be or might be more trouble and expense later. It is best to do things well and get the most out of them. That is why I have suggested your going to a

1. A long piece of cloth tied round the waist and wrapped around each of the legs.
2. A long coat with buttoned-up collar.
3. Dr Jacques Stephani: Swiss lung specialist who had a sanatorium at Montana.

sanatorium, to begin with, even though this might be more costly, if doctors think this will do you more good. For this may result in shortening your stay in Suisse and in helping more rapidly in your recovery.

We have never worried about money matters. Why should we do so now? We can carry on easily enough, if not on income then on capital. If capital runs out we have the capacity to add to it. In this changing world, with all manner of revolutionary possibilities, no one knows what our present money may be worth a few years or even months hence. The real capital we have is our intellectual and other capacity for work and that no one can take from us. And then we have the very useful and worthwhile capacity for reducing our expenditure and changing our mode of life when necessity demands this. That in itself will be an adventure which adds zest to life. But there is no question of that for the present or the near future. Personal money matters never worry me. I am so confident about my own capacity both to earn enough and to reduce my own expenditure that the future does not trouble me.

The little book I wrote – *Letters from a Father to his Daughter* – has become quite a goldmine, though I am not going to profit by it. It is becoming a textbook in many provinces in English, Hindi and Urdu and vast numbers have been printed. I was hardly aware of this fact when I discovered that Kitabistan had made about Rs. 20,000 out of it. Something to the tune of Rs. 2500 or so trickled to me also. But I disliked the idea of exploiting poor students and so I have made a present of my rights in the book to provincial governments and universities on condition that the book was issued at a very low price. The U.P. Govt. are selling it to students at four annas[1] and yet making a substantial profit. At my suggestion they are using this money for scholarships for poor students, to be named after Kamala.

I suppose I could have made a lot of money out of my books if I had been a businessman. But I have a knack of choosing impecunious publishers or even bankrupt ones. The Tamil edition of my *Autobiography* has sold very well but I have not profited at all by it as the publisher is half-mad and half-knave and is in addition an insolvent! I cannot even keep in touch with the numerous editions of my books in India. Still, I must not complain. Some money comes in regularly and is of great help – not in personal expenditure which is not great, but for other purposes. A great drain on me has been the *National Herald.* I do not know where this will land me. Personal expenditure, yours or mine, makes little difference.

The Calcutta *Statesman* offered me Rs. 500 a month for a column a week – four columns a month – of comments on international affairs. I reject it of course. It is easy enough for me to earn a decent livelihood by

1. There were sixteen annas in a rupee.

writing. But other matters engross my attention and even when I write, it is not for payment.

So please do not worry at all about the expenses involved in your trip to Suisse. Get well, store up health and energy, become a capitalist in health, and the rest does not matter.

You have done well to write to my bank to find out how my account stands. I do not know myself. I imagine that you should have now with you & in my bank together about £200. Probably more royalties will be due in December and this will bring up the figure to £250. This is enough for you to carry on with. Remember that you can always write or cable to Bachhraj, Bombay, for money. During war-time it is desirable to keep some money easily available to avoid difficulties. I am told that money can be sent to Suisse. All these arrangements can be made without my intervention. So long as I am there, of course I shall look after them.

It is perfectly delightful weather here now, though I would prefer it to be somewhat colder. The nights are cool, the days very pleasant.

Love,

> Your loving,
> Papu

I enclose a card that has come for you – a pre-war card from Germany. It took two months to come here. As it would not fit in my envelope I tried to cut it down! Now I have chosen another envelope.

316.

> Brentford Hospital,
> Brentford,
> Middlesex,
> 19th November, 1939

Darling Papu,

Your telegram has just come. I was thinking of you at the moment, but that is not even a coincidence for you have been in my thoughts so much these last weeks.

Nobody [knows] here that it is my birthday today and yet by a strange coincidence – or rather, series of coincidences – I am celebrating it in a fitting manner. After a most unusually unrestful and stormy night, windy and noisy with the banging of doors and the rattling of blinds, Sunday dawned one of the most beautiful days of the year: sunny, dry and very clear with just a few clouds to cast occasional shadows and to make the sky more interesting. England started the day by having an extra hour in bed, for this morning at three a.m. British Summer Time came to an end and all clocks were put back an hour. After that I was allowed to walk, even to have a real regular bath, the first since I fell ill five weeks ago. I wasn't allowed to stay in very long but it was grand all the same.

The last three days I have been sitting up for tea and in the mornings have my bed pulled right up to the window – which, thank goodness, I can keep wide open – so I can look out on more cheerful objects than the grey walls of a hospital ward.

Day before yesterday the Macmillans, the people I was staying with out in the country, in Penn, Bucks., drove along here to see me. Wasn't it sweet of them? They're both most frightfully busy people & a forty-mile drive is not very amusing in these days of petrol rationing. Moreover, they had no idea where Brentford was and got rather lost! Prof. Macmillan thought I would be interested to meet G. D. H. Cole[1] and, before he heard that I was ill, wrote to him to look me up at Somerville. Poor G.D.H. trotted up to Somerville and had to spend quite a while in the very dreary porter's lodge before he found out that I hadn't come up.

Except for a packet of cuttings from the *N.H.* at the beginning of last week, nobody seems to have had any news from India, neither letters nor papers.

Dr Samson is sailing for India on the 23rd Nov. He is coming to see me again on the day before. Dr Bhandari thinks he wants to be armed with an excuse for meeting you! I do not know if it will be possible for you or him to do so but he will be able to see Chhoti Puphi in Bombay. He is rather a charming person – a sensitive face.

You might be interested in these cuttings of Byrd's[2] expedition. Do such news creep through to the Indian papers? American magazines, such as *Life* and *Time* are having very interesting sections on the present war. Do you manage to see them, I wonder.

Here I am writing to you of fleeting, foolish things, while you at the moment must be in conference, burdened with [the] responsibility of important decisions! Good luck & all my love.

Indu

21st November

Still not posted this letter! One of the major nuisances of being ill is being completely dependent for one's everyday needs on the memory and time of other people.

Your letter of the 6th Nov. has come this morning. It is good to hear from you. By now you will have received the letters from me & Dr B. referring to the objections to Leysin.

1. G. D. H. Cole: British economist and socialist.
2. Richard Evelyn Byrd: American aviator and explorer. In 1939 he commanded the U.S. Antarctic Service, a government-sponsored expedition.

Bapu sent me a cable on the 19th, mentioning the 'ceremony'. I couldn't quite get the meaning of it until your letter came and I found that it was the ceremony of laying the corner-stone of the hospital.

The cuttings you enclose are lovely – especially the photographs. The one of Jinnah is most expressive, but I love best yours and Bapu's.

Agatha is bringing Lady Maharaj Singh[1] to see me today. Lady M. has just come from Montana – one of her sons has T.B. & is under treatment there. She is returning on the 6th Dec. & asks if I will go along with her if I am ready. Dr Bhandari is dead against Montana.

From friends in Somerville has come the birthday gift of a book on the Impressionists, with glorious colour prints of some of their paintings. It is a joy to look at & I miss you for I would share those colours and the beauty of it with you.

Much love, darling,
Indu

P.S.
I am getting the *N.H.* cuttings regularly – but it is rather extravagant, isn't it – Rs. 4–9 annas a week?

———————————————

317.

Brentford Hospital,
Brentford,
Middlesex,
24th November, 1939

Darlingest Papu,
Your letters of the 10th & 16th[2] arrived practically together. I loved your long letter – but not all of it. What's all this about getting old? No one has any right to pretend he's getting old when he's only just fifty – no one, that is, who has ever been young. The essentials of youth belong to you for as long as you like. What do the years matter? You have been young always and even now, except for occasional depressions which everybody has, you are younger in spirit than most of us. You are a case of *jeunesse qui sait*, or if you prefer – *vieillesse qui peut*.[3] As for growing into a 'doddering old person' (your words) – isn't your imagination running away with you just a little bit? I am afraid this myth of old age is vastly overdone in India and I have always held strong views on the subject. And the other day, I came across an article which said more precisely than I ever could just what I thought. Do you mind if I quote?

1. Lady Maharaj Singh: wife of Sir Maharaj Singh of the princely family of Kapurthala State.
2. Refers to letters No. 313, 315.
3. You are a case of youth that knows, or if you prefer – old age that can.

Something whispers in the ear of every person over forty, 'You are getting old. You are not so good as you used to be.' And God help him if he listens. Youth says it, believing that it needs to insist on that chance to make a place for itself. One's own lazy contemporaries say it to justify their own self-coddlings and abandonment of effort. Under our prevailing notions the first grey hair gives that magnificent excuse long sought by the indolence of our natures. We forget that what fifty years of sunshine and winter cold have done to our wrinkles means nothing as to the man or woman inside and has often added an interest and a beauty of power and character that was never there in youth.

. . . This spirit of youth is a fine thing, but far less humane [or] potentially joyous than the spirit of maturity. Glorify youth and one glorifies whatever is the moment's fashion. We are all familiar with the piddling literary attempts of most great writers in their youth. That out of such feeble cleverness finally emerges original work of authentic power is little short of miraculous. Yet we ignore such facts & idealise that one characteristic which is our weakness and danger – the imitative and sentimental restlessness of youth.

I have a letter from Edward Thompson. He writes: 'Your father was an angel to me. He is a wonderful fellow; so boyish, and so drawing every one's eyes with affection and admiration. You should have seen him at Wardha! He runs like a boy and his face lights up with a boy's smile . . .'

The Chinese silks have not arrived yet, for the Thompsons did not know my address & have written asking for it. They have sold their Boar's Hill house in Oxford and are now living in Bucks. Mrs Thompson asked me over to stay a week or so with them but Doctor thinks I better go straight to Switzerland . . .

I am allowed to walk about a bit each day, now, and sit up for tea. I am afraid my telegram to you was not quite correct. Apparently, although the inflammation is fast disappearing there is still some there. Doctor examined me again today. He said, 'There's still a rub here,' whatever that may mean!

The German blockade is certainly a thing to be reckoned with – more than twenty ships sunk this week – the mighty British Navy is fast losing her minesweepers and destroyers. 200 German mines were swept ashore last week. Hitler's secret weapon is now said to be the 'magnetic mine'. It is said to lie much deeper than the reach of a minesweeper, attached to a needle-like thing which floats on the surface but is too small to be noticed. As soon as a vessel comes into contact with this needle, it draws up the mine and causes it to explode.

They make one get up at seven fifteen a.m. here and so I usually start the day grumbling, but today I was glad of it for it was glorious – very clear, but very cold, the grass and the trees glistening white with frost and the sky bathed in the sunrise.

Lots of love, darling – keep well and forget those fifty years of yours.

Arrivederci,[1]

Indu

---

318.   [Anand Bhawan,
Allahabad]
2nd December, 1939

Darling Indu,

I returned yesterday from Muttra (what an awful way of spelling a sweet sounding word like Mathura),[2] and found your letter of the 19th/21st Nov.[3] awaiting me. I am so happy to learn that you had an enjoyable birthday with plenty of flowers and fruit and sunshine – not to mention chocolates. But in your description I missed one thing. Has not Edward Thompson given you the Chinese pictures I sent through him? He is very absent-minded and might easily forget. The pictures are in an envelope – a big one – and can be overlooked.

The problem of your going to Switzerland seems to get more and more intricate. Where to go? Leysin, Montana, Davos, or the Stunnes' place? It is absurd for me to say much about it as the decision must be made at the other end, and so far as I am concerned, it does not matter much where you go. I do feel that Montana – Lady Maharaj Singh's choice – is not very desirable for a variety of reasons. Jivraj Mehta still sticks to Leysin as he is a believer in Dr Rollier's ability and also thinks that Leysin is preferable as it is more easily accessible and probably cheaper.

I liked my visit to Muttra. On my way there I spent a few hours at Agra just to see the Taj on the night of the full moon – the *Kārtiki Purnima.*[4] I like the Taj very much, not only because of its exceeding beauty, but also because it takes me out of the present. It is something to feel detached for a while and away from this world of strife and war. Muttra again was full of the atmosphere of a bygone age with its Krishna legends and its delightful and melodious Braj-Bhasha.[5] It was extraordinary to notice how the peasantry were full of this old culture and tradition. In course of conversation, they would refer to some old story or quote a line from Tulsi

---

1. Goodbye for the present.
2. Historic place in Uttar Pradesh connected with legends of Lord Krishna.
3. Refers to letter No. 316.
4. *Kartik* is a month in the Hindu calendar. *Purnima* is the full moon.
5. Regional variety of Hindi.

Das.[1] There is something in an old culture after all, which gives poise and distinction to life.

Early one morning some of our party went to a neighbouring well for a bath. This was situated amidst the fields and the peasant owner or tenant came with his bullocks to draw out water from the well for his fields. They use a big leather bucket called a *mot*. When the first bucket came up our people wanted to start bathing. But the peasant asked them to wait as the first lot of water was dedicated to Kanhaiyaji[2] (what a sweet name this is). He said that he liked pouring out the first five *mot* fulls to Kanhaiyaji and other favourite divinities, but in any event the first one should not be touched. Sometimes, he said, people would come and use even this first lot of water, much to his dismay. But he did not want to quarrel about it and so he let them. Our people told him that they were certainly not going to interfere with his old custom. They were Congressmen and between the Congress and the peasants there was *sumati*.[3] Yes, said the peasant, and immediately quoted a famous line of Tulsi Das *jahān sumati tahān samptti nānā* – where there is goodwill and cooperation, there is an abundance and variety of wealth.

I regretted nothing so much in Muttra as my ignorance of Braj-Bhasha. I felt how cut off I was from the life of the people and the roots of their culture, and how much I had missed because of this. And straightaway I resolved that when I have to put up with my next period of enforced retirement I shall devote myself to the study of Hindi and Urdu literature. After all, it is the language that is the closest bond between people and is the mirror where one sees their minds and hearts.

The other day Dhanno (Lady Rama Rau) came to see us with her daughter Premi. Premi had grown up into a fine tall girl but India to her was a foreign land. Her younger sister was even more alien in India. Dhanno could not take her to various places as the sanitary arrangements were not according to European standards!

It is somewhat expensive to send the *N.H.* cuttings by air but it is worth it in order to keep you in touch with events here. I offered to pay the *Herald* people the postage but very magnanimously they said that they would not charge me as I was their most frequent unpaid contributor! Very generous of them – only the ultimate burden of the *N.H.* comes back to me! But if you like and if it amuses you, you can yourself pay for this by sending good cuttings from newspapers for reproduction in the *Herald*. Or sometimes, when you are much stronger and better, you can write a brief essay on conditions in Switzerland in wartime or anything else – the more informal

1. Tulsi Das: Hindi poet of medieval India who wrote the epic *Ramacharitmanas*.
2. A variant of the name of Lord Krishna.
3. Goodwill.

the better, just like a personal letter. You write good letters. But you must only do this for the fun of it, if you like doing it. It is amusing to write once you get into the hang of it.

Thank you for the cuttings about Byrd's expedition. This kind of thing is good and should be appreciated. My foreign papers have started coming again but they come most irregularly and in batches. Some numbers do not reach us at all. I have been getting both *Time* and *Life* – both are gifts from friends in America. It is difficult to read all this stuff, especially when a month's mail comes all in a bunch. And then it is so out of date. *Time* has been interesting. After glancing through *Time* & *Life* I have been sending them to Chand at Mussoorie. She loves these American weeklies. She and Tara & Rita will be coming here soon for their winter holidays.

Yesterday, on my return to Allahabad, I took things easy as is my custom after a tour. I revive by slackening for a few hours, pecking at my accumulated mail and generally lounging about. I sat down at the radio – it is a very neglected radio – and started listening in to all manner of stations. I must have listened to at least half a dozen languages. Curiously, India was mentioned in almost every broadcast and sometimes very pertinent things were said and sometimes they were rather ridiculous. It is quite extraordinary how even petty happenings in India are immediately reported in some foreign broadcasts. Soon the news and the comments began to bore me and I switched on to music. I had quite a feast of music, and apart from European music, I listened to Chinese and Balinese. I like Chinese songs, or some of them, but I like especially Balinese music. It is rather plaintive, as most oriental music is, but nevertheless it is pleasant and soothing. And so I spent two and a half hours at the radio at a stretch!

I understand that Sir Stafford Cripps is arriving here on 8th Dec. Krishna has casually mentioned the date and I am rather put out at this late information which upsets my programme. I expected Cripps or Krishna to be more businesslike and send me a cable in good time.

We are having a Working Committee meeting at Wardha on 18th Dec. That means my absence then for about a week – probably I shall go to Bombay afterwards.

Love,

> Your loving,
> Papu

319.   Les Frênes,
                                         Leysin,
                                Switzerland,
                     21st December, 1939

Darling Papu,

I have not the vaguest idea what the arrangements for airmail to India are in this country. Probably the letters go by rail to Rome.

I have been wanting to write to you ever since I arrived here in Leysin on the 16th. But the journey tired me out and I felt too exhausted to sit up straight and write anything coherent.

As you know, we came by plane to Paris. That was perhaps the most tiring phase of the journey. We had booked seats on the eleven o'clock plane – there are two services only these days. On the eve of our departure, at about six p.m. on the 14th, our travelling agency rang us up to say that our plane had been commandeered by the military authorities, but that we could go by the earlier one. This meant being at Airways House (nobody is allowed to go to the airport on their own) at seven thirty a.m. It is a good hour's drive to Victoria from Brentford and at that hour of the morning it is pitch dark and there is the early morning mist – into the bargain, it rained. So I had to get up at five thirty a.m. & leave hospital at six fifteen. Driving in the blackout is no fun at any time and the driver of my car was not exactly pleased. 'Where d'ye want to go?' – 'Airways House' – 'Don't know where it is! When d'ye have to be there?' – 'seven thirty' – 'Can't possibly make it!' But make it we did, only to have to wait there until eight thirty. Then we jogged along to Heston, where I was deprived of my identity card & ration book and was sternly reproved for having left my gas mask behind! At the passport examination we were each handed an important looking paper. Agatha very carefully put ours away in her bag for safety. Later I wondered what it was & she reluctantly brought it out again. This is what it said:

GOSSIP

You will not help Britain while abroad if you –
(1) run down the British war effort;
(2) allege that British government organisations are bad, muddled, and inept;
(3) give the impression that Britain is defenceless or in danger;
(4) talk thoughtlessly of military, aerial, or naval matters, even if, in your opinion, what you say is harmless.

As a British citizen you have the right to 'grouse' in your own country; but idle grumbles voiced abroad are a help to the enemy.

We wandered round at Heston until ten thirty when an official came and announced that he would let us know definitely at twelve noon, whether or not we should leave that day! We took off at eleven o'clock.

At the Paris office of Air France we found Nanu waiting. We took a room in a hotel opposite the station & I was promptly put to bed until we left by the eight o'clock Simplon Express. I had a good night – these train sleepers are comfortable. From what we had heard of the experiences of other people, we were not looking forward to Vallorbe – the French frontier. But everything went fine & customs & other officials did not even remind us of the war. When we thought we had finished all the formalities, there came yet another knock on the door, which was then opened by one of the quaintest persons I have ever seen. He might have been any age from fifty to 200 – his face was so wrinkled & yet not at all old and it was capped by a most peculiar furry affair. But all this I noticed later – the first thing that struck me was his smile: 'it was as long as a summer's afternoon with no teeth to stop its coming through'! Agatha & I lost all power of speech and stared most rudely – not that a little thing like that could disconcert the apparition. He bowed low and salaamed in the regular Lucknow manner. Then he spoke: 'I am the medical officer. Have you any infectious disease?' Another bow and salaam – exit.

Switzerland at last. It seemed so strange to see the lights along the railway track. We were met at 'Leysin-village' by Dr Sheth. By the way, Dr Sheth left Leysin yesterday – he is going to India from Venice. In Bombay he will meet Dr Mehta, who knows him, and tell him about Leysin & me.

This is not a bad place at all – very neat and comfortable rooms, very good food. I have rather an expensive room at the moment but I hope to change soon. I have a balcony & a magnificent view of the Dents du Midi. This view is reflected in my mirror inside the room, so actually I have the Dents du Midi on both sides of me!

You would like Dr Rollier, I am sure. I do. And Agatha was most impressed. I think she is writing to you at great length about all that he told her & showed her, so I shan't repeat it here. He wants me to stay here for about three months, at the end of which time I shall be transformed into a Diana! He said to me: 'You are like a perfectly good motor car whose engine & wheels and everything is quite in order but there is no petrol so it cannot run; sometimes you can push it a little way but not far. There is nothing wrong with you but you have no muscular development & no strength to make your organs run as smoothly as they can run. I do not want you fat as a goose, that is only good for Christmas!!'

Bijju Chacha would approve of him, for he believes in exercises, breathing and otherwise. Dr Rollier says my left lung is much smaller than the right & nothing can be done until its size is increased by breathing exercises. So would Shridhar Chacha approve of him: for he believes in the sun. He told me to eat mostly those things which grew in the sun.

But meanwhile I have to stay in bed for perhaps a month more. Agatha got me a lovely pot of cyclamens, which I love, and Mademoiselle Rollier (one of the Dr's daughters who is at least 6 ft tall) brought me a pot of maidenhair ferns. And I have a radio. So things are not quite as tedious as they might have been. So far, the acid voice of the German announcer from Bremen & Hamburg – they call him 'Lord Haw-Haw' in England – and the B.B.C. news are my only connection with the world outside. Listening to these two news services bent on contradicting and making fun of each other – how very ridiculous this wretched war seems!

22nd December

I couldn't write any more yesterday for my bed was taken out on the balcony and my fingers grew too cold to hold and direct a pen.

This morning brought me letters from Bertram Pickard of the 'Palais Wilson' and Gertrud Baer, who also sent me a pamphlet on Czechoslovakia, which she wants me to forward on to you. They both send you their greetings. Mr Pickard is going to send on some of the periodicals he gets – so I shan't be altogether cut off from the world, after all! Mlle Hemmerlin has sent me a whole heap of books & a little box of delicious home-made biscuits – they are packed rather nicely in a silvery box and every time Dr Rollier comes in, he says: 'Don't eat too many chocolates!'

Dr Rollier comes in every other day on a 'friendly' visit & once a week – Friday – officially. His daughter spent some years in England training in Margaret Morrison's exercises. She teaches them here now. She will start on me soon – with music. The doctor, or Monsieur le Professeur, as he is called here, is a great believer in handwork as a potent help towards better health, so it's a good thing I learnt knitting before I arrived here; else I should have had to do so here. Not far from here is Rollier's 'Factory clinic'. Here the patients make slippers, jigsaw puzzles, knitted articles, rugs and many other things, which the government helps to sell – thus these patients are not only enabled to pay something for their board & lodging & treatment but can also support their families to some extent, in spite of being ill.

This year is coming to an end – what does 1940 hold for us? It doesn't look as if it is going to be very cheerful. I do not know when this letter will reach you, but it brings with it my very best wishes for 1940.

Lots of love, darling,

Indu

APPENDICES

APPENDIX A: Letters from *Glimpses of World History*

The letters in this Appendix consist of extracts from a series which Jawaharlal Nehru wrote to Indira Nehru from various prisons between October 1930 and August 1933. These letters have been described by their author as a 'rambling account of history for young people'. They were later published as a book entitled: *Glimpses of World History* (Allahabad, 2 volumes, 1934).

While the letters in *Glimpses* seek to present an outline of world history, this Appendix reproduces extracts from some letters which are of a personal nature and throw light on Jawaharlal Nehru's thoughts and feelings. It may be emphasised that only a few of these letters were posted when they were written. Instead, Jawaharlal Nehru handed them over to Indira in a bunch after he had finished the last letter.

Footnotes in this section do not feature in *Glimpses of World History*.

1.
Central Prison, Naini
*October 26, 1930**

For Indira Priyadarshini**
on her Thirteenth birthday
On your birthday you have been in the habit of receiving presents and good wishes. Good wishes you will still have in full measure, but what present can I give you from Naini Prison? My presents cannot be very material or solid. They can only be of the air and of the mind and spirit, such as a good fairy might have bestowed on you – something that even the high walls of prison cannot stop.

You know, sweetheart, how I dislike sermonising and doling out good advice . . .

I must not therefore sermonise. But what am I to do then? A letter can hardly take the place of a talk; at best it is a one-sided affair. So, if I say anything that sounds like good advice do not take it as if it was a bad pill to swallow. Imagine that I have made a suggestion to you for you to think over, as if we really were having a talk.

In your history books you read of great periods in the life of nations. We read of great men & women and great deeds performed, and sometimes in our dreams and reveries we imagine ourselves back in those times and doing brave deeds like the heroes and heroines of old. Do you remember how fascinated you were when you first read the story of Jeanne d'Arc and how your ambition was to do something like her? Ordinary men and women are not usually heroic. They think

---

* In 1930, according to the Samvat era, Indira Nehru's birthday fell on 26th October.
** Priyadarshini: Indira's second name which can be translated as 'dear to the sight,' and also 'one who reveals the good'.

FREEDOM'S DAUGHTER

of their daily bread and butter, of their children, of their household worries and the like. But a time comes when a whole people become full of faith for a great cause, and then even simple, ordinary men and women becomes heroes, and history becomes stirring and epoch-making. Great leaders have something in them which inspires a whole people and makes them do great deeds.

The year you were born in – 1917 – was one of the great years of history when a great leader, with a heart full of love and sympathy for the poor and suffering, made his people write a noble and never-to-be-forgotten chapter of history. In the very month you were born, Lenin started his great Revolution which has changed the face of Russia and Siberia. And today in India another great leader, also full of love for all who suffer and passionately eager to help them, has inspired our people to great endeavour and noble sacrifice, so that they may again be free and the starving and the poor and the oppressed may have their burdens removed from them. Bapuji lies in prison; but the magic of his message steals into the hearts of India's millions, and men and women and even little children, come out of their little shells and become India's soldiers of freedom. In India today we are making history, and you and I are fortunate to see this happen before our eyes and to take some part ourselves in this great drama.

How shall we bear ourselves in this great movement? What part shall we play in it? I cannot say what part will fall to our lot; but whatever it may be, let us remember that we can do nothing which may bring discredit to our cause or dishonour to our people. If we are to be India's soldiers we have India's honour in our keeping, and that honour is a sacred trust. Often we may be in doubt as to what to do. It is no easy matter to decide what is right and what is not. One little test I shall ask you to apply whenever you are in doubt. It may help you. Never do anything in secret or anything that you would wish to hide. For the desire to hide anything means that you are afraid, and fear is a bad thing and unworthy of you. Be brave, and all the rest follows. If you are brave, you will not fear and will not do anything of which you are ashamed. You know that in our great Freedom Movement, under Bapuji's leadership, there is no room for secrecy or hiding – we have nothing to hide. We are not afraid of what we do and what we say. We work in the sun and in the light. Even so in our private lives let us make friends with the sun and work in the light and do nothing secretly or furtively. Privacy, of course, we may have and should have, but that is a very different thing from secrecy. And if you do so, my dear, you will grow up a child of the light, unafraid and serene and unruffled, whatever may happen.

I have written to you a very long letter. And yet there is so much I would like to tell you – how can a letter contain it?

You are fortunate, I have said, in being a witness to this great struggle for freedom that is going on in our country. You are also very fortunate in having a very brave and wonderful little woman for your Mummie and if you are ever in doubt or in trouble you cannot have a better friend.

Good-bye, little one, and may you grow up into a brave soldier in India's service.

With all my love and good wishes.

[Papu]

2.
[Naini Central Prison]
January 7, 1931

PRIYADARSHINI – dear to the sight, but dearer still when sight is denied! As I sat here today to write to you, faint cries, like distant thunder, reached me. I could not make out at first what they were, but they had a familiar ring and they seemed to find an answering echo in my heart. Gradually they seemed to approach and grow in volume, and there was no doubt as to what they were. *"Inqilab zindabad!"* *"Inqilab zindabad!"** The prison resounded with the spirited challenge, and our hearts were glad to hear it. I do not know who they were who shouted our war-cry so near us outside the Jail – whether they were men and women from the city or peasants from the villages. Nor do I know the occasion for it today. But whoever they were, they cheered us up, and we sent a silent answer to their greeting and all our good wishes went with it.

Why should we shout *"Inqilab zindabad"*? Why should we want revolution and change? India of course wants a big change today. But even after the big change we all want has come and India is independent, we cannot rest quiescent. Nothing in the world that is alive remains unchanging. All nature changes from day to day and minute to minute, only the dead stop growing and are quiescent. Fresh water runs on, and if you stop it, it becomes stagnant. So also the life of man and the life of a nation. Whether we want to or not, we grow old. Babies become little girls, and little girls big girls and grown-up women and old women. We have to put up with these changes. But many refuse to admit that the world changes. They keep their minds closed and locked up and will not permit any new ideas to come into them. Nothing frightens them so much as the idea of thinking! What is the result? The world moves on in spite of them, and because they and people like them do not adapt themselves to the changing conditions, there are big burst-ups from time to time. Big revolutions take place, like the great French Revolution of a hundred and forty years ago, or the Russian Revolution thirteen years ago. Even so in our own country, we are today in the middle of a revolution. We want independence of course. But we want something more. We want to clean out all the stagnant pools and let in clean fresh water everywhere. We must sweep away the dirt and the poverty and misery from our country. We must also clean up, as far as we can, the cobwebs from the minds of many people which prevent them from thinking and cooperating in the great work before us. It is a great work, and it may be that all this will require time. Let us, at least, give it a good push on – *"Inqilab zindabad!"*

We are on the threshold of our revolution. What the future will bring we cannot say. But even the present has brought us rich returns for our labours. See the women of India, how proudly they march ahead of all in the struggle! Gentle and yet brave and indomitable, see how they set the pace for others? And the *Purdah*, which hid our brave and beautiful women, and was a curse to them and to their country, where is it now? Is it not rapidly slinking away to take its rightful place in the shelves of museums, where we keep the relics of a bygone age?

See also the children – the boys and girls – the Vānar Sēnās and the Bāl and

---

* *Inqilab zindabad* means 'long live revolution.'

Bālikā Sabhās.* The parents of many of these children may have behaved as cowards or slaves in the past. But who dare doubt that the children of our generation will tolerate no slavery or cowardice?

And so the wheel of change moves on, and those who were down go up and those who were up go down. It was time it moved in our country. But we have given it such a push this time that no one can stop it.

Inqilab zindabad!

[Papu]

---

3.   [Naini Central Prison]
                                                             January 9, 1931

[Darling Indu]
I read yesterday in the *Bharat*, the Hindi newspaper which brings us some news of the outside world twice a week, that Mummie was not being properly treated in the Malacca Jail. Also that she is going to be sent to Lucknow Jail. I was put out a little and I worried. Perhaps there was no truth in the rumour given in the *Bharat*. But even a doubt about it is not good to have. It is easy enough to put up with discomfort and suffering. It does everyone good. Otherwise we might grow too soft. But it is not very easy or comforting to think of the suffering of others who are dear to us, especially if we can do nothing for them. And so the doubt that the *Bharat* raised in my mind made me worry about Mummie. She is brave and has the heart of a lioness, but she is weak in body, and I would not like her body to become weaker. What can we do, however stout-hearted we may be, if our bodies fail us? If we want to do any work well, we must have health and strength and perfect bodies.

Perhaps it is as well that Mummie is going to be sent to Lucknow. She may be more comfortable and happier there. There will be some companions in the Lucknow Jail. Probably she is alone in Malacca. Still, it was pleasant to think that she was not far, just four or five miles away from our prison. But this is a foolish fancy. Five miles or 150 miles are much the same when the high walls of two prisons intervene.

I was so glad to learn today that Dadu had come back to Allahabad and that he was better. I was also very pleased to learn that he had gone to see Mummie in Malacca Jail. Perhaps, with luck, I may see all of you tomorrow. For tomorrow is my interview day, and in Jail the *mulāqāt kā din*** is a great day. I have not seen Dadu for nearly two months. I shall see him, I hope, and satisfy myself that he is really better. And I shall see you after a long, long fortnight, and you will bring me news of yourself and of Mummie . . .

[Papu]

---

* The three terms – *Vānar Sēnās* and the *Bāl* and *Bālikā Sabhās* – refer to associations of young children formed during the civil disobedience movement to fight against imperialism.
** Day of meeting.

4.   [Naini Central Prison]
                                                    January 13, 1931

[Darling Indu]

It was good to see you all yesterday. But I had a shock to see Dadu. He was looking
so weak and ill. Look after him well and make him fit and strong again. I could
hardly speak to you yesterday. What can one do in a short interview? I try to make
up for all the interviews and talks we have not had by writing these letters. But
they are poor substitutes, and the make-believe does not last long! Still it is good
sometimes to play make-believe . . .

                                    [Papu]

5.   S.S. *Cracovia*
                                                          April 21, 1931

[Darling Indu]

It is long since I wrote to you. Nearly three months have gone by, three months of
sorrow and difficulty and strain. Three months of change in India, and change
above all in our family circle. India has stopped for a while the campaign of
Satyagraha, or Civil Disobedience, but the problems that face us are not easier of
solution; and our family has lost its dearly-loved head,* who gave us strength and
inspiration, and under whose sheltering care we grew up and learnt to do our bit
for India, our common mother.

How well I remember that day in Naini Prison. It was the 26th of January and I
sat down, as was my usual practice, to write to you about the days that have gone
by . . . That day was a great day for us, for a year ago that very day we had
celebrated all over India, in city and in village, as Independence Day, *Pūrna
Swarāj* day, and all of us in our millions had taken the pledge of Independence.
Since then a year had passed by, a year of struggle and suffering and triumph, and
again India was going to celebrate that great day. And as I sat in Barrack No. 6 of
Naini Prison, I thought of the meetings and processions and the *lāthi* charges and
arrests that would take place that day all over the country. I thought of this with
pride and joy and anguish, when suddenly my musing was cut short. A message
was brought to me from the outside world that Dadu was very ill and I was to be
released immediately to go to him. Full of anxiety, I forgot my musings, and put
away the letter to you I had just begun, and left Naini Prison for Anand Bhawan.

Ten days I was with Dadu before he left us. Ten days and nights we watched
his suffering and agony and his brave fight with the Angel of Death. Many a fight
had he fought during his life, and many a victory won. He did not know how to
surrender, and even face to face with Death, he would not give in. As I watched
this last struggle of his, full of anguish at my inability to help him whom I loved so
much, I thought of some lines which I had read long ago in a tale of Edgar Allan
Poe: "Man doth not yield himself to the angels, nor even unto death utterly, save
by the weakness of his feeble will."

  * Jawaharlal Nehru's father, Motilal Nehru died on 6th February, 1931. See letter
No. 24.

It was on the 6th of February, in the early morning, that he left us. We brought his body wrapped in the Flag he loved so well, from Lucknow to Anand Bhawan. Within a few hours it was reduced to a handful of ashes and the Ganga carried away this precious burden to the sea.

Millions have sorrowed for him, but what of us, children of his, flesh of his flesh and bone of his bone! And what of the new Anand Bhawan, child of his also, even as we are, fashioned by him so lovingly and carefully. It is lonely and deserted and its spirit seems to have gone; and we walk along its verandahs with light steps, lest we disturb, thinking ever of him who made it.

We sorrow for him and miss him at every step. And as the days go by the sorrow does not seem to grow less or his absence more tolerable. But, then, I think that he would not have us so. He would not like us to give in to grief, but to face it, as he faced his troubles, and conquer it. He would like us to go on with the work he left unfinished. How can we rest or give in to futile grief when work beckons and the cause of India's freedom demands our service? For that cause he died. For that cause we will live and strive and, if necessary, die. After all, we are his children and have something of his fire and strength and determination in us.

The deep blue Arabian Sea stretches out before me as I write; and on the other side, in the far distance, is the coast of India, passing by. I think of this vast and almost immeasurable expanse and compare it to the little barrack with its high walls in Naini Prison, from where I wrote to you my previous letters. The sharp outline of the horizon stands out before me, where the sea seems to meet the sky; but in jail, a prisoner's horizon is the top of the wall surrounding him. Many of us who were in prison are out of it today and can breathe the freer air outside. But many of our colleagues remain still in their narrow cells deprived of the sight of the sea and the land and the horizon. And India herself is still in prison and her freedom is yet to come. What is our freedom worth if India is not free?

[Papu]

6.

[Dehra Dun Jail]
September 15, 1932

[Darling Indu]
I am shaken up completely and I know not what to do. News has come, terrible news, that Bapu has determined to starve himself to death.* My little world, in which he has occupied such a big place, shakes and totters, and there seems to be darkness and emptiness everywhere. His picture comes before my eyes again and again – it was the last time I saw him, just over a year ago – standing on the deck of the ship that was taking him away from India to the West. Shall I not see him again? And who shall I go to when I am in doubt and require wise counsel, or am

---

* Mahatma Gandhi decided to 'fast unto death' in Yeravda Prison from 20th September, 1932 in disapproval of the British decision to create separate electoral constituencies for the untouchable classes within Hindu society. Indira Gandhi was in school in Poona (the city in which Mahatma Gandhi was imprisoned) and described the fast to her father in her letter dated 27th September, 1932. See letter No. 43.

afflicted and in sorrow and need loving comfort? What shall we all do when our beloved chief who inspired us and led us has gone? Oh, India is a horrid country to allow her great men to die so; and the people of India are slaves and have the minds of slaves to bicker and quarrel about trivial nothings and forget freedom itself.

I have been in no mood to write and I have thought even of ending this series of letters. But that would be a foolish thing. What can I do in this cell of mine, but read and write and think? And what can comfort me more when I am weary and distraught than thought of you and writing to you? Sorrow and tears are poor companions in this world. "More tears have been shed than the waters that are in the great ocean" said the Buddha, and many more tears will be shed before this unhappy world is put right. Our task still lies ahead of us, the great work still beckons, and there can be no rest for us and for those who follow us till that work is completed. So I have decided to carry on with my usual routine, and I shall write to you as before . . .

[Papu]

———————————◄ ►——————————

7.
[Dehra Dun Jail]
New Year's Day, 1933

[Darling Indu]
It is New Year's Day to-day. The earth has completed another cycle round the sun. It recognises no special days or holidays, as it rushes ceaselessly through space, caring not at all what happens on its surface to the innumerable midgets that crawl on it, and quarrel with each other, and imagine themselves – men and women – in their foolish vanity, the salt of the earth and the hub of the universe. The earth ignores her children, but we can hardly ignore ourselves, and on New Year's Day many of us are apt to rest awhile in our life's journey and look back and grow reminiscent, and then look forward and try to gather hope. So I am reminiscent to-day. It is my third consecutive New Year's Day in prison, though in between I was out in the wider world for many months. Going further back, I remember that during the last eleven years I have spent five New Year's Days in prison. And I begin to wonder how many more such days and other days I shall see in prison!

But I am a "habitual" now, in the language of the prison, and that many times over, and I am used to gaol life. It is a strange contrast to my life outside, of work and activity and large gatherings and public speaking and a rushing about from place to place. Here all is different; everything is quiet, and there is little movement and I sit for long intervals on a chair, and for long hours I am silent. The days and the weeks and the months pass by, one after the other, merging into each other, and there is little to distinguish one from the other. And the past looks like a blurred picture with nothing standing out. Yesterday takes one back to the day of one's arrest for in between is almost a blank with little to impress the mind. It is the life of a vegetable rooted to one place, growing there without comment or argument, silent, motionless. And sometimes the activities of the outside world appear strange and a little bewildering to one in prison; they seem distant and unreal – a phantom show. So we develop two natures, the active and the passive, two ways of living, two personalities, like Dr Jekyll and Mr Hyde. Have you read this story of Robert Louis Stevenson's? . . .

This letter has become much too dismal and for a New Year Day letter that is highly unbecoming. Indeed, I am not dismal, and why should we be dismal? We have the joy of working and struggling for a great cause; we have a great leader, a beloved friend and a trusty guide, whose sight gives strength and whose touch inspires; and we have the surety that success awaits us, and sooner or later we shall achieve it. Life would be dull and colourless but for the obstacles that we have to overcome and the fights that we have to win . . .

And you, my darling one, on the threshold of life, must have no dealings with the dismal and the dreary. You will face life and all that it brings with a joyful and serene countenance, and welcome such difficulties as may come your way for the pleasure of surmounting them.

And so, *au revoir, bien aimée*, and may this be not too long in coming!

[Papu]

Appendix B: Indira's Reading

I The parcel of books contained the following titles: 1) *Brave New World* by Aldous Huxley; 2) *Common Sense about Poetry* by L. A. G. Strong; 3) *The Soviets and the Next War* by R. D. Charques; 4) *An Egyptian Childhood* by Taha Hussein; 5) *A Last Chance in Kenya* by Norman Leys; 6) *The Unseen Assassins* by Sir Norman Angell; 7) *The Emergence of Man* by Gerald Heard; 8) *What Dare I Think?* by Julian Huxley; 9) *The Prisoner's Soul and Our Own* by Livend Berggrar; 10) *The Oxford Book of German Verse* by Fiedler; 11) *Which World: Which Way?* by Ernst Toller; 12) *The Life of the Butterfly* by Friedrich Schnack; 13) *The Work, Wealth, and Happiness of Mankind* by Wells; 14) *Far Away and Long Ago* by W. H. Hudson; 15) *A Grammar of the Arts* by Sir Charles Holmes; 16) *And no Birds Sing – The Autobiography of Pauline Leader;* 17) *Chaka* by Thomas Mofolo; 18) *Plato and his Dialogues* by G. Lowes Dickinson; 19) *Mal D'amour* par Jean Fayard; 20) *Swallows and Amazons* by Arthur Ransome; 21) *Swallowdale* by Arthur Ransome.

II The list comprised the following titles: 1) *La Suisse I* par Paul Guiton; 2) *La Suisse II* par Paul Guiton; 3) *Romain Rolland* par Stefan Zweig; 4) *Jean-Christophe* par Romain Rolland; 5) *Le jeu de l'amour et de la mort* par Romain Rolland; 6) *Vie de Michel-Ange* par Romain Rolland; 7) *La vie de Vivekananda I* par Romain Rolland; 8) *La vie de Vivekananda II* par Romain Rolland; 9) *La vie de Ramakrishna* par Romain Rolland; 10) *Quatrevingt-treize* par Victor Hugo; 11) *La Légende des Siècles I* par Victor Hugo; 12) *La Légende des Siècles II* par Victor Hugo; 13) *Le Prisonnier qui chantait* par John Bojer; 14) *Le Livre de mon ami* par Anatole France; 15) *Le Roman d'un enfant* par Pierre Loti; 16) *La petite Fadette* par George Sand; 17) *Colomba* par Prosper Mérimée; 18) *Le petit chose* par Alphonse Daudet; 19) *Le Rêve* par Emile Zola; 20) *Let petit Roi* par André Lichtenberger; 21) *Mon petit Trott* par Andrê Lichtenberger; 22) *La petite fille de Jérusalem* par Myriam Harry; 23) *Graine au vent* par Lucie Delarue Mardrus; 24) *Atala* par Châteaubriand; 25) *A tatons* par Benjamin Dallatton; 26) *Paroles d'un croyant* par Lamennais; 27) *Graziella Raphael* par Lamartine; 28) *Théâtre* par Alfred de Vigny; 29) *Histoires du Bon Dieu* par Rainer Maria Rilke; 30) *Le grand Meaulnes* par Alain-Fournier; 31) *Princesse de Lune* par Noelle Roger; 32) *La Princesse Lointaine* par Edmond Rostand; 33) *Cyrano de Bergerac* par Edmond Rostand; 34) *L'Aiglon* par Edmond Rostand; 35) *La Colonie* par Charles Vildrac; 36) *L'île Rose* par Charles Vildrac; 37) *Goethe – 5 I* par Emil Ludwig; 38) *Goethe – 11 III* par Emil Ludwig; 39) *Maroussia* par P. J. Stahl; 40) *Fables* (la Fontaine) par R. Radonant.

Appendix C: Translation of French Poems

The Leaf

I   Fallen off from your branch
Little dried-up leaf
Where are you going? – I do not know
The storm broke the oak-tree
which was my sole support
Since then, driven by the wilful breath
Of the West Wind and by the cold wind of the North
Ceaselessly I have wandered
From the forest to the plains
From the mountain to the vales
I go wherever the wind takes me
I neither oppose nor cry
I go where go all things
The rose as well as the laurel leaf.
(See letter No. 35, p. 59).

II   Oh! the gentle patter of the rain
On the ground and on the roof!

For a tired heart,
Oh! the song of the rain!
(See letter No. 63, p. 100).

III   Which God, which reaper
of eternal summers,
had casually cast off
this Scythe of gold in
the firmament of stars
(See letter No. 185, p. 291).

INDEX

NOTE: The figures in **bold** type refer to the brief biographical entries at the beginning of the book.